CONSTRUCTION OF MAYA SPACE

CONSTRUCTION OF MAYA SPACE

Causeways, Walls, and Open Areas
from Ancient to Modern Times

EDITED BY
THOMAS H. GUDERJAN AND **JENNIFER P. MATHEWS**

THE UNIVERSITY OF
ARIZONA PRESS
TUCSON

The University of Arizona Press
www.uapress.arizona.edu

We respectfully acknowledge the University of Arizona is on the land and territories of Indigenous peoples. Today, Arizona is home to twenty-two federally recognized tribes, with Tucson being home to the O'odham and the Yaqui. Committed to diversity and inclusion, the University strives to build sustainable relationships with sovereign Native Nations and Indigenous communities through education offerings, partnerships, and community service.

© 2023 by The Arizona Board of Regents
All rights reserved. Published 2023

ISBN-13: 978-0-8165-5187-3 (hardcover)
ISBN-13: 978-0-8165-5188-0 (ebook)

Cover design by Leigh McDonald
Cover photo by Macduff Everton
Typeset by Sara Thaxton in 10/14 Warnock Pro with Aria Text G2 and Electra LT Std

We thank Academic Affairs at Trinity University in San Antonio, Texas, for providing funding to support the publication of this book.

Library of Congress Cataloging-in-Publication Data
Names: Guderjan, Thomas H., editor. | Mathews, Jennifer P., 1969– editor.
Title: Construction of Maya space : causeways, walls, and open areas from ancient to modern times / edited by Thomas H. Guderjan and Jennifer P. Mathews.
Description: Tucson : University of Arizona Press, 2023. | Includes bibliographical references and index.
Identifiers: LCCN 2022061273 (print) | LCCN 2022061274 (ebook) | ISBN 9780816551873 (hardcover) | ISBN 9780816551880 (ebook)
Subjects: LCSH: Maya architecture—Central America. | Maya architecture—Mexico. | Landscape archaeology—Central America. | Landscape archaeology—Mexico. | Mayas—Antiquities.
Classification: LCC F1435.3.A6 C66 2023 (print) | LCC F1435.3.A6 (ebook) | DDC 720.89/9742—dc23/eng/20230216
LC record available at https://lccn.loc.gov/2022061273
LC ebook record available at https://lccn.loc.gov/2022061274

Printed in the United States of America
♾ This paper meets the requirements of ANSI/NISO Z39.48-1992 (Permanence of Paper).

CONTENTS

Acknowledgments   vii

Introduction: Thinking About Barriers and Connectivity in Maya Archaeological Landscapes   3
THOMAS H. GUDERJAN AND JENNIFER P. MATHEWS

1. Causeways and Geopolitical Connections in the Ucí-Cansahcab Region, Yucatán   17
   DANIEL VALLEJO-CÁLIZ AND SCOTT R. HUTSON

2. The Axis Connecting Classic Maya Economy and Ritual at Xunantunich, Belize   49
   BERNADETTE CAP, M. KATHRYN BROWN, AND WHITNEY LYTLE

3. Roads, Temples, and the Community Boundaries of Cobá, Quintana Roo   71
   TRAVIS W. STANTON, TRACI ARDREN, NICOLAS C. BARTH, JUAN FERNANDEZ DIAZ, STEPHANIE J. MILLER, KARL A. TAUBE, PATRICK ROHRER, ELIZABETH BECKNER, AND ALINE MAGNONI

4. Taming the Jungle: Decauville Railroads in Nineteenth- and Early Twentieth-Century Yucatán   99
   JENNIFER P. MATHEWS

5. The Chichén Itzá and Ek Balam Borderlands   119
   J. GREGORY SMITH AND ALEJANDRA ALONSO OLVERA

6. Crossing the Last Maya Boundary: The Central Line of the Military Campaign, 1899–1904 165
ALEJANDRA BADILLO SÁNCHEZ

7. All in All, It's (Not) Just Another Brick in the Wall: Examining the Diverse Functions of Wall Architecture in Western Belize 187
JAIME J. AWE AND SHAWN G. MORTON

8. Two Tales of a City: The *Sakbe'ob* at Yo'okop from the Viewpoints of Elites and Commoners 217
JUSTINE M. SHAW AND ALBERTO G. FLORES COLIN

9. Changing Perspectives on Ancient Maya Neighborhoods and Houselots at Xnoha in Northwest Belize 249
THOMAS H. GUDERJAN, C. COLLEEN HANRATTY, AND JOSHUA J. KWOKA

10. Prehistoric *Albarradas* at the Site of Buena Vista, Cozumel 273
ADOLFO IVÁN BATÚN-ALPUCHE

11. An Ethnoecological View of the Evolution of *Solares*: A Yucatán Maya Houselot Case Study 289
GRACE LLOYD BASCOPÉ AND ELIAS ALCOCER PUERTO

12. The Identity That Binds and the *Albarradas* That Divide: Residential Space and Ethnoarchaeology in Yaxunah, Yucatán 317
HÉCTOR HERNÁNDEZ ÁLVAREZ

13. Constructing a World Beneath Quintana Roo 337
CARMEN ROJAS SANDOVAL, MIGUEL COVARRUBIAS REYNA, AND DOMINIQUE RISSOLO

14. Not Seeing Is Believing: The Production of Space in Ancient Maya Cave Sites 373
HOLLEY MOYES

Contributors 417
Index 429

ACKNOWLEDGMENTS

When our previous effort, *The Value of Things: Prehistoric to Contemporary Maya Commodities*, was published in 2017, Tom Guderjan and Jennifer Mathews stepped across the street from the annual meeting of the Society for American Archaeology in Vancouver for a celebratory drink with Allyson Carter, our wonderful editor at the University of Arizona Press. Before the drinks arrived, Allyson asked if we would be interested in taking up another topic for another book. Instantly, we both agreed. Within a few months, the concept took shape, and we invited presenters and potential chapter authors to an organized symposium at the 2018 annual meeting of the SAA in Washington, D.C. The presenters gave lively in-person talks and we soon invited them to submit chapters for this volume while inviting a few other authors to join the effort. All things were proceeding handily.

Then came COVID, and despite the pandemic giving us free time from archaeological fieldwork for the first time in decades, it also created challenges that we never could have imagined. Many of our collaborators were also hit with hurricanes, floods, and extended power outages, and some of us lost loved ones and faced financial challenges and burnout. Five years later, in what seems like the longest five years of our careers, this volume finally comes to fruition. To our colleagues, co-authors, and chapter authors, we extend our deep gratitude for your patience and thank you all for staying with this project. Not one person ever voiced concern that this book would not see completion.

We also owe our gratitude to the thirty-three contributors to this volume for their intellectual visions. They have opened new doors to us and, we hope, to the readers of this book. As editors, we began this project with expectations of how it would proceed. The other contributors took us to places we had not anticipated. The strength of this volume is based on their insights.

In addition to her early suggestion, we are also grateful to Allyson Carter for her constant support and for ushering this volume to its publication. Lastly, we thank our spouses, Colleen Hanratty and Marco Martinez, for understanding that we needed to do this, COVID or not, and for their support in helping us get it there.

CONSTRUCTION OF MAYA SPACE

Introduction

Thinking About Barriers and Connectivity in Maya Archaeological Landscapes

THOMAS H. GUDERJAN AND JENNIFER P. MATHEWS

The purpose of this volume is to examine the construction of spatial features by ancient, historic, and contemporary Maya people of Mesoamerica. Like all humans, when Maya people encountered spaces like tropical landscapes, they modified them to meet their social and economic needs. They built towering pyramids around public plazas and constructed vast networks of ditched fields to produce food and other agricultural products. However, much of the focus of this volume goes beyond these spaces. Instead, we consider how and why Maya people of the ancient past and more recent present connected and divided the spaces they used daily in their homes, in their public centers, in their sacred places, and across their regions. How do the walls, roads, rails, and boundary markers that they left on today's archaeological landscape inform us about the mental constructs they used to create their lives and cultures of the past?

This theoretical approach is essentially a Taylorian view—one that believes that we can understand the behaviors that caused and created the archaeological data and, by extension, inform us about their defining mental constructs (Taylor 1948). Walter Taylor called for an ethnographic approach that brought together meaning from diverse data sets (Maca 2010, 5). Like Taylor himself, we may never fully reach that final goal. A major criticism of Taylor's approach was that he did not present a replicable method (Watson, 1991, 266). However, we challenged ourselves and our colleagues to reexamine how and why walls, roads, and other features can both connect and divide space. At first blush, the idea that "walls divide" or "roads connect" sounds simplistic. However, as the chapters in this volume demonstrate, the answers to our questions are complex and nuanced. To arrive at where we wanted this study to end involves deconstructing archaeological data, both temporally and in terms of the behavior that created those data. We believe we have made strides in our own understanding and hope to share them in this volume by thinking about how our notion of Maya landscapes, place-making, and memory work has evolved.

Re-examining Maya Landscapes

Due to their archaeological visibility in a challenging tropical environment, early explorations of the Maya region in the nineteenth and early twentieth centuries emphasized major site centers, monumental architecture, and stone monuments with texts and images (Chase et al. 2014, 210). As Wendy Ashmore (2015) aptly noted, for these Euro-American archaeologists, Maya landscapes were represented as romantic, untainted, and untamed. This intertwined with the ethnocentric notion during that time that societies ranged from savage to civilized and Maya landscapes were wild in comparison to the West. In this period, archaeologists also failed to emphasize that they were viewing ruins taken over by the encroaching vegetation rather than envisioning their original appearance and that Maya peoples lived in diverse environments (Ashmore 2015, 307) in a sustainable fashion.

As Jennifer P. Mathews discusses in chapter 4, this view of the Maya even shaped nineteenth-century infrastructure for the commodity industries. The henequen, chicle, hardwood, and sugarcane industries used railroads in the Yucatán Peninsula to "tame" the jungle and speed up labor production. Railroads also symbolized a "responsible" western management of the extraction of forest resources, as opposed to the view that Indigenous practices mismanaged natural resources. On these private commercial lands, railroads were a tool used to exploit labor in a brutal process of forest and agricultural extraction for global commodity consumption. She further argues that there is a continuing colonial legacy in the twenty-first century of this imposition of "modernizing" infrastructure upon Maya peoples through the case studies of trains in Yucatán and Guatemala that are designed to connect Maya centers for tourism. In both cases, these are designed and implemented largely for the economic benefit of outsiders and recent tourism-related arrivals with little thought regarding the nature of the impacts on Maya residents.

While American archaeology of the 1940s outwardly aligned itself with cultural anthropology, Taylor (1948) noted that in reality the discipline was practicing the "reconstruction of history" through the lens of the present and often falling short (Maca 2010, 22). By the 1950s and 1960s, geographers and archaeologists recognized that Maya landscapes were not pristine and that they needed to understand how they were changing over time (Ashmore 2015, 308), including in residential areas. Settlement archaeology concerned itself with how to identify a site and how regions were defined, although the ability to map these was limited by the heavily forested landscape. Further, "the frameworks for understanding the ancient occupation of Maya sites were in constant flux, rotating between more complex frameworks focused on a multi-class society and simpler polar models of priests and peasants. With the lack of detailed archaeological data, these interpretive frameworks became grounded in the ethnographic study of contemporary Maya peoples, leading to the notion of 'empty' urban centers that were surrounded by 'folk' residential areas" (Chase et al. 2014, 210).

In the 1960s and 1970s, the school of New Archaeology focused on adaptation models, using regional landscapes to interpret ancient Maya food production and the exploitation of natural resources. Dennis Puleston (1983) conducted extensive surveys on the cardinal directions radiating out from the site core of Tikal in Guatemala that demonstrated that residential architecture was dispersed throughout the site, dramatically increasing population estimates. Soon, the idea that "vacant" centers were actually densely populated urban communities developed (Haviland 1969, 430). These endeavors ultimately led to the notion of "cosmovision," or Maya ways of understanding landscape as organized and bounded versus disorganized and dangerous (Ashmore 2015, 318–19). In the decades following, projects began combining site core and settlement documentation (including new projects at Dzibilchaltun and Cobá, and updates to earlier projects at Calakmul and Chichén Itzá, which demonstrated significantly higher population densities). However, "despite some valiant attempts, regional archaeology has been dependent on limited samples of excavation data that have been tied into an even less understood landscape. . . . Until recently, full-coverage mapping of broad areas has been too expensive and laborious to be a possibility" (Chase et al. 2014, 212).

Despite these challenges, J. Gregory Smith and Alejandra Alonso Olvera (chapter 5) convincingly argue for identifying regional boundaries and the temporal dynamism in the Chichén Itzá and Ek Balam borderlands in

Yucatán. They note that the cities were contemporaneous for at least one hundred years but probably independent of each other. Using informant-aided surveys, they sought to identify sites between polity capitals and to characterize the borderlands by using these sites as a lens. They outline population increases, the proliferation of small polities, the growth of long-distance exchange networks and a greater diversity of trade goods, the commercialization of the economy, new forms of writing and iconography, and new patterns of stylistic interaction to understand processual trends during the Epiclassic period.

Another archaeological feature type that allows us to understand larger boundaries within the challenging forested environment of the Maya world is inter- and intrasite *sakbe'ob* (alternatively spelled *sacbe'ob or sakbe'job*), or roads. Sakbe'ob literally connect the daily life of commoners to the ceremonial life of the elite as well as these powerful lineages to other powerful lineages. James E. Snead, Clark L. Erickson, and J. Andrew Darling (2009, 1) argue that roads bring disparate populations and goods together and "represent *landscapes of movement*, a context for 'getting there.'" Similarly, they note that Charles D. Trombold (1991) makes the case that "some authors sought ways to bring trails, paths, and roads into larger explanatory structures of archaeological theory" (Snead, Erickson, and Darling 2009, 2).

While road networks are a major theme of this volume, our authors examine these features in new and different ways. For example, in chapter 1, Daniel Vallejo-Cáliz and Scott R. Hutson examine how causeways at the site of Ucí in Yucatán integrate multiple communities into a single polity. The authors explore the organizational principles for the construction of the sakbe'ob and the possible sociopolitical, economic, and ideological changes that these communities experienced because of integration. They note that the people of Ucí, the largest site in the vicinity, would have experienced these phenomena in different ways than those at smaller centers connected by this regional road. In chapter 2, Bernadette Cap, M. Kathryn Brown, and Whitney Lytle emphasize that at the site of Xunantunich in Belize, roads served as formal avenues of movement between and within ancient Maya ceremonial centers for the transportation of people, goods, and information. They further examine the integrative role that sakbe'ob construction projects played in the interplay between politics, ritual, and economy.

In contrast, Justine M. Shaw and Alberto G. Flores Colin (chapter 8) argue from the perspective of commoners that the roads of Yo'okop in Quintana

Roo could in fact be divisive. They emphasize that the vast majority of the inhabitants of Yo'okop were not the elites who planned the roadways and, potentially, most benefited from their existence. Neither were they archaeologists who can observe the clear and obvious ties created through inter- and intrasite causeways through maps and aerial images. Instead, on a day-to-day level, their experience of living around monumental roads as nonelite residents may have been a negative one as they served as features that segregated them from segments of their own cities and landscapes.

Maya Placemaking and Memory Work

The traditional archaeological concept of landscape derives from principles that British and European archaeologists first developed (Aston and Rowley 1974; David and Thomas 2008). This western view of the landscape is longitudinal and compares how the natural landscape first appeared upon human contact and the ways in which those humans continuously modified these spaces into evolving anthro-landscapes. This notion is closely tied with the study of cultural ecology (Rathje 1971), or how humans interact with their environment to fulfill their biological and other needs. However, we must now also recognize the role that archaeology plays in further modifying this landscape and changing how a viewer experiences the space. For example, when visiting the "restored" Maya site of Lamanai in Belize, the visitor views the towering High Temple or the Jaguar Temple in a way never seen by the people who constructed or lived around these buildings. Instead, occupation periods are compressed and the visitor sees parts of multiple construction phases, so they can perceive the multiplicity of events that led to the building as we see it today (David Pendergast, personal communication, 2000).

In fact, the archaeological landscape as we see it today through tools such Light Detection and Radar (LiDAR) shares many of these same attributes, as no ancestral Maya person saw the landscape from such a perspective. Instead, they carried a ground-based model in their mind. Further, through the LiDAR lens, we see a view of a terrain that has resulted from fifty or more generations of human endeavors. In other words, human landscapes are dynamic and reflect the changing social attitudes and principles of their creators and their viewers. We acknowledge that the way our field presents the archeological landscape today has been shaped by available technologies, the social attitudes, and the principles of past generations of scholars, and we try to disentangle these views. Nonetheless, we cannot overstate how the advent of LiDAR has helped overcome the major impediment to Maya archaeologists' ability to "see" the ancient and historical landscape in the dense jungle. This technological development is allowing scholars to better understand not only the modifications Maya peoples made to the landscape over time but to do so on a regional scale (Chase et al. 2014, 208–9).

In chapter 3, Travis W. Stanton et al. use LiDAR as a tool to examine the question of site boundaries from both quantitative and qualitative approaches. This approach tests hypotheses about the emic ideals of the spatial organization of communities and ancient urban boundaries. They employ LiDAR data from the Classic period city of Cobá, Quintana Roo, to show that sakbe'ob connect portions of the city to the center. They argue that using Mesoamerican ideals of community structure, in conjunction with high-quality spatial data, can help archaeologists understand how people in the past created places that we, in the present, can equate with the concept of archaeological sites.

While the landscape is the contextualizing theme for this volume, we find that it is important to note that there are other scholarly concepts that also add to our understanding. We give specific attention to two of these: the geographical concept of *placemaking* (Courage and McKowan 2008) and the archaeological concept of *memory work* (Mills and Walker 2008). Placemaking is "the set of social, political, and material processes by which people iteratively create and recreate the experienced geographies in which they live" (Pierce, Martin, and Murphy 2011, 55). The distinction between the archaeological concept of landscape and the geographical concept of placemaking hinges on intent and agency.

Archaeologists have long claimed to study "patterned" behavior. For example, they have argued that South African hunter-gatherers have learned about the resources available within their geographic ranges through the repetitive teachings from previous generations and annual cycles of moving camps to new catchment areas (Lee and DeVore 1968). However, the archaeological concept of landscape is not inherently built on intentionality or what social scientists refer to as *human agency*. Further, contemporary urban planners, often grounded in the study of urban geography, refer to placemaking as the intentional, creative process in which they engage in bettering the lives of those in our contemporary cities (Strydom, Puren, and Drewes 2018).

In a sense, then, the archaeological landscape is a result and consequence of contemporary placemakers (in this case, archaeological scholars) that apply their social attitudes and principles to understand the barriers and connectors that the original placemakers (in this case, ancient, historic, and contemporary Maya people) formed upon a past landscape. Archaeologists are attempting to interpret an evolving landscape in which the modifications of the original placemakers may have patterned the behavior of later generations on the landscape, even if they did not fully understand the original attitudes and principles of the original placemakers. Interpreting or translating this landscape, particularly for features like walls that can be easily modified, can be tricky.

David Webster (1980, 835) argues that perimeter walls around central precincts are emic representations of the organization of space by previous inhabitants. These walls at Maya sites can obviously play a defensive role to protect them from the outside world and can provide insight into warfare and political organization (Kurjack and Andrews 1976). However, they can serve dynamic functions over time. For example, while a wall at the site of Chichén Itzá that surrounded part of the sacred precinct may have been added to protect the site center later in the city's history, it appears to have been built originally as a symbolic structure (Hahn 2010; Hahn and Braswell 2012). As Bruce Dahlin (2000, 294) notes at sites like Uxmal and Ek Balam, these walls may have served as "symbolic markers" that denoted inner sanctums. Further, boundary features within site centers could direct pedestrian traffic and commerce (Hahn 2010; Hahn and Braswell 2012) or delineate domestic zones from social and sacred spaces by restricting access to elite and administrative zones (Hahn 2010; Hahn and Braswell 2012; Rice and Rice 1981, 272).

In this volume, several authors deal with walls (*albarradas*) and linear stone boundary markers (LSBMs) for houselots in both prehistoric and contemporary settings (see chapters by Jaime J. Awe and Shawn G. Morton; Grace Lloyd Bascopé and Elias Alcocer Puerto; Adolfo Iván Batún-Alpuche; Thomas H. Guderjan, C. Colleen Hanratty, and Joshua J. Kwoka; and Héctor Hernández-Álvarez). In each case, these features delineate houselots and have often been approached as synchronic, static, and fully evolved settlement features. However, it is quite unlikely that these features were built in a single phase of construction by an organized workforce that was executing a fully developed plan. In reality, the features were probably built and modified by members of the households as human and stone resources became available. Bascopé and Alcocer Puerto (chapter 11) inform us that the albarrada construction in the contemporary Maya village of Yaxunah continues on a piecemeal basis today.[1] Further, we have yet to broach questions regarding the dynamics of the construction of albarradas and LSBMs. Who built the first ones in these cases? What was their motivation? What were the social processes, attitudes, and principles that made these features become constructed on a community-wide scale? Unfortunately, as Guderjan, Hanratty, and Kwoka (chapter 9) point out, we do not even have data that enable us to answer the most simplistic archaeological question, "When were these walls first built?"

Instead, the initial emphasis of the chapters that focus on wall features is on how they *divide* space. Whether the features are in contemporary Yaxunah, ancient Cozumel, or northwest Belize, their fundamental purpose is or was to delineate houselots and to indicate what was/is "mine" and what was/is not. We are beginning to understand the temporal and spatial range of these features, and thanks to Bascopé and Alcocer Puerto (chapter 11) and Hernández Álvarez (chapter 12) are coming to understand what activities occurred/occur within and outside them. The space controlled by village households is marked by albarradas, and the exterior space within albarradas is referred to as *solares*. In chapter 11, Hernández Álvarez reiterates that solares are the locations of most household activities. He also informs us that albarradas, solares, houses, and other physical features are the manifestations of social identity. Equally, importantly, he reminds us that the contemporary village landscape, like archaeological landscapes, is the result of a history of changes. As he notes, Yaxunah is in a state of "constant change."

In ancient Xnoha in Belize, who built the LSBMs is less clear. Drawing on LiDAR data and terrestrial field work, Guderjan, Hanratty, and Kwoka (chapter 9) report that the LSBMs that bound houselots define space much like albarradas of prehistoric and historic northern Yucatán. Further, the space outside buildings but inside the LSBMs functions much like contemporary solares of northern Yucatán and Quintana Roo and enables archaeologists to more clearly discern household and neighborhood units. However, the

---

1. A note about spelling: The archaeological site is conventionally spelled "Yaxuná" but the villagers spell their village as "Yaxunah." We adhere to this distinction.

scale of these features at Xnoha would indicate that, unlike contemporary villages, the movement of such large amounts of small stones might require larger work teams than are available to a single family.

The chapters on wall features also show us that walls go beyond simple divisions of space and can guide behaviors. Wall features combine with roads and pathways to define ritual processual activities and demarcate land ownership or, at least, control. In some cases, prehistoric walls were built for defense and demarcated royal from nonroyal spaces such as at Becán, Tulum, and Ixpaatun in Quintana Roo. In chapter 7, Awe and Morton examine wall-like structures in the Belize Valley and show that structurally similar, linear features can both integrate and divide people depending on which ritual, political, and socioeconomic purposes the builders were serving. While recognizing the role of defensive or militaristic use of walls elsewhere, they focus on the evidence for ritual, political, and socioeconomic purposes that can bind and divide social groups.

In chapter 10, Batún-Alpuche reports on the prehistoric albarradas at Buena Vista, Cozumel. Like Xnoha, Buena Vista exhibits more complexity than previously known. While only a small central precinct exists at Buena Vista, households bounded by albarradas surround the central precinct for at least 2 km in each direction. To understand how these bounded spaces were used, he considers the importance of cultural and environmental factors in agricultural practices and settlement decisions. Looking at construction techniques, dimensions of walled features, associated features, and artifacts reveals that stone walls accomplished different functions in different environmental areas.

Although the processes of placemaking help us understand how archaeological landscapes became what we see today, the notion of *memory work* (Mills and Walker 2008; see also Hendon 2010) reminds us that elements of human cultural geography, that is, landscapes, are not visible to archaeologists employing traditional documentation approaches or even LiDAR. However, we find many examples in which the removal of things from the surface landscapes has been placed out of sight but not out of mind. Examples might include ancestral burials below residential buildings or the construction of royal tombs. A particularly striking case is the "jade shaft" of Structure 4 at Blue Creek, Belize (Guderjan 1998). At approximately AD 300–350, the people of Blue Creek excavated a large portion of Structure 4. They then rebuilt it with a 3 m deep, stone-lined shaft that dropped vertically from the upper step of the staircase. At approximately AD 500, they reopened the shaft and filled it with nearly one thousand jade artifacts, a set of *incensario* bases, and human phalanges. They then removed a stela from the base of Structure 4 and placed it horizontally over the shaft opening and buried it. This likely occurred at the same time as the construction of an addition to Structure 1 directly across the plaza to accommodate the tomb of a ruler. These events likely marked the termination of a royal lineage when the ruler died. After these events, significant changes were seen throughout the public architecture of the city. In this case, both objects and people were removed from the surface landscape, but surely no member of the community would not have known the importance of the places. Consequently, we acknowledge that the meaning of places to the people we study may be intentionally hidden from us and in some cases may forever be lost in the absence of a persistent oral tradition.

Alejandra Badillo Sánchez, in chapter 6, speaks of an Indigenous Maya landscape that is altered to become a Mexican military landscape. In this case, archaeology looks at the remnants of forts, camps, and barracks as a way of understanding how the Maya lost their lands, their homes, and their "places of memory" during this siege period. The Maya of Chan Santa Cruz dominated the central region of the Yucatán Peninsula and had been autonomous for more than fifty years prior to the Caste War (1847–1901). However, when the government of Mexico realized that Maya peoples were living off income from land rental and supplies to English colonists, it planned to retake control of Maya lands. To do this, it organized a military campaign that interrupted the Maya boundary, destabilized the inhabitants of the area, changed land use and appropriation, and transformed the landscape of the Yucatán Peninsula into a "Theater of War."

Carmen Rojas Sandoval, Miguel Covarrubias Reyna, and Dominique Rissolo (chapter 13) and Holley Moyes (chapter 14) examine hidden spaces and landscapes inside caves and explore how underground space is used and manipulated. Not only are physical and metaphysical boundaries defined, but they become the backdrops for ritual performances. Ancient Maya people transformed the natural environment of caves by creating pathways as well as structures that functionally divide space within caves. Rojas Sandoval, Covarrubias Reyna, and Rissolo survey east coast caves in the Quintana Roo and remind us that caves are, in effect, sacred geography connected to the role of the underworld in Maya belief systems. The authors expand on how the placement of miniature temple shrines in caves delimited metaphysical and physical boundaries and connected them to the surface world. Caves have a range of functions and walls are used to delineate space along with other features such as corridors and traps. Embedded into the sacred geography of caves are temples, altars, and *oratarios* that function similarly to their terrestrial analogs.

In the final chapter, Moyes looks at how social space is encoded in caves, arguing that the artificial constructions of space within caves are based on a complex cosmovision. Modifications of the cave send nonverbal signals that can guide behavior, influence communication, and create meaning for rituals in these sacred spaces. Moyes views space in caves to have been socially produced by the communities associated with them. She then elaborates on how architecture in caves expresses hierarchies and power differentials between human and nonhuman actors. Social space in the cave at Las Cuevas, one of the most architecturally elaborate caves in the Maya Mountains of Belize, was modified to define processual space and became a venue for establishing and maintaining stability in the Maya community of Las Cuevas.

Conclusion

This volume tackles two themes: "The Ties That Bind" and "The Walls That Divide." However, the thirty-three authors of the following fourteen chapters have clearly shown that such a simple dichotomy does not exist. Instead, we find highly nuanced variability. Roads or sakbe'ob certainly are ties that bind, but they bind many things. Sakbe'ob directed royal processionals; they integrated cities and connected cities to each other. They functioned to integrate multigenerational lineages, economically, politically, and in many other ways. Similarly, historical railroads connected functional units economically, often to the detriment of the local residents impacted by rail construction and operation. And we learn that one person's road can be another person's wall. Not only do walls divide, but they can also often guide. Walls define residential houselots, defend city centers, and construct processional space. Walls and similar features, when combined with pathways, define ritual processional space in caves and central precincts.

Throughout this volume, the authors show us that architecturally defined space was anything but a simple dichotomy of connectivity and barriers. All along, it was extremely unlikely that our efforts would have resulted in a set of simple principles that would move us to understand Maya "culture" as Taylor (1948) would have liked. Instead, we have found that there is a rich and nuanced variability around our concepts of connecting space and creating spatial barriers. Certainly, there is not any reason to think that we have found the limits of the variability that Maya and other people in the Maya world, in the past and today, have embedded into their construction of the "archaeological" landscape.

Works Cited

Ashmore, Wendy. 2015. "What Were Ancient Maya Landscapes Really Like?" *Journal of Anthropological Research* 71 (3): 305–26.

Aston, Michael, and Trevor Rowley. 1974. *Landscape Archaeology: An Introduction to Fieldwork Techniques on Post-Roman Landscapes*. Newton Abbot: David and Charles.

David, Bruno, and Julian Thomas, eds. 2008. *Handbook of Landscape Archaeology*. Walnut Creek, Calif.: Left Coast Press.

Chase, Arlen F., Diane Z. Chase, Jaime J. Awe, John F. Weishampel, Gyles Iannone, Holley Moyes, Jason Yaeger, and M. Kathryn Brown. 2014. "The Use of LiDAR in Understanding the Ancient Maya Landscape: Caracol and Western Belize." *Advances in Archaeological Practice* 2 (3): 208–21.

Courage, Cara, and Anita McKeown. 2008. *Creative Placemaking: Research, Theory, and Practice*. Routledge Studies in Human Geography. London: Routledge.

Dahlin, Bruce. 2000. "The Barricade and Abandonment of Chunchucmil: Implications for Northern Maya Warfare." *Latin American Antiquity* 11 (3): 283–98.

Guderjan, Thomas H. 1998. "The Blue Creek Jade Cache: Early Classic Maya Ritual and Architecture." In *The Sowing and the Dawning: Dedication and Termination Ritual Events in the Archaeology and Ethnology of Mesoamerica*, edited by Shirley Mock, 101–12. Albuquerque: University of New Mexico Press.

Hahn, Lauren D. 2010. "La Muralla de Chichén: Excavations of a Maya Site Perimeter Wall." PhD diss., University of California, San Diego.

Hahn, Lauren D., and Geoffrey E. Braswell. 2012. "Divide and Rule: Interpreting Site Perimeter Walls in the Northern Maya Lowlands and Beyond." In *The Ancient Maya of Mexico: Reinterpreting the Past of the Northern Maya Lowlands*, edited by Geoffrey E. Braswell, 278–96. London: Routledge.

Haviland, William A. 1969. "A New Population Estimate for Tikal, Guatemala." *American Antiquity* 34 (4): 429–33.

Hendon, Julia A. 2010. *Houses in a Landscape: Memory and Everyday Life in Mesoamerica*. Durham, N.C.: Duke University Press.

Kurjack, Edward B., and E. Wyllys Andrews IV. 1976. "Early Boundary Maintenance in Northwest Yucatan." *American Antiquity* 41 (3): 317–25.

Lee, Richard B., and Irven DeVore, eds. 1968. *Man the Hunter*. Chicago: Aldine.

Maca, Allan L. 2010. "Then and Now: W. W. Taylor and American Archeology." In *Pariah and Prophet: Walter W. Taylor and Dissention within American Archaeology*, edited by Allan L. Maca, Jonathan Reyman, and William Folan, 3–57. Boulder: University of Colorado Press.

Mills, Barbara J., and William H. Walker, eds. 2008. *Memory Work: Archaeologies of Material Practices*. Santa Fe, N.Mex.: School for Advanced Research Press.

Pierce, Joseph, Debra G. Martin, and James T. Murphy. 2011 "Relational Place-Making: The Networked Politics of Place." *Transactions of the Institute of British Geographers* 36 (1): 54–70.

Puleston, Dennis E. 1983. *The Settlement Survey of Tikal*. Vol. 48. Philadelphia: University of Pennsylvania Press.

Rathje, William L. 1971. "The Origin and Development of Lowland Classic Maya Civilization." *American Antiquity* 36 (3): 275–85.

Rice, Don S., and Prudence Rice. 1981. "Muralla de Leon: A Lowland Maya Fortification." *Journal of Field Archaeology* 8 (3): 271–88.

Snead, James E., Clark L. Erickson, and J. Andrew Darling. 2009. "Making Human Space: The Archaeology of Trails, Paths, and Roads." In *Landscapes of Movement: Trails, Paths, and Roads in Anthropological Perspective*, edited by James E. Snead et al., 1–19. Philadelphia: University of Pennsylvania Press.

Strydom, Wessel, Karen Puren, and Ernst Drewes. 2018. "Exploring Theoretical Trends in Placemaking: Towards New Perspectives in Spatial Planning." *Journal of Place Management and Development* 11 (2): 165–80.

Taylor, Walter W. 1948. *A Study of Archeology*. Menasha, Wis.: American Anthropological Association.

Trombold, Charles D., ed. 1991. *Ancient Road Networks and Settlement Hierarchies in the New World*. Cambridge: Cambridge University Press.

Watson, Patty Jo. 1991. "A Parochial Primer: The New Dissonance as Seen from the Midcontinental United States." In *Processual and Postprocessual Archaeologies: Multiple Ways of Knowing the Past*, edited by Robert W. Preucel, 265–74. Carbondale: Center of Archaeological Investigations, Southern Illinois University.

Webster, David. 1980. "Spatial Bounding and Settlement History at Three Walled Northern Maya Centers." *American Antiquity* 45 (4): 834–44.

CHAPTER 1

Causeways and Geopolitical Connections in the Ucí-Cansahcab Region, Yucatán

DANIEL VALLEJO-CÁLIZ AND SCOTT R. HUTSON

Although the phrase "ties that bind" serves as a title for several publications on the Maya (Canuto and Bell 2008; Houk 2003; Kintz 2004; Masson 2020; Mathews 1998; Restall 1998), our chapter takes after a publication on the Aztecs. In his essay "Roads, Routes, and Ties That Bind," Ross Hassig (1991) focuses predominantly on ancient roads, an archaeological feature that is secondary, if present at all, in the "ties that bind" publications from the Maya world. In 2008, the Ucí-Cansahcab Regional Integration Project (UCRIP; in Spanish, PASUC, Proyecto Arqueológico Sacbé Uci-Cansahcab) began investigating four sites with large architecture (Ucí, Kancab, Ucanha, and Cansahcab) and their hinterlands in Yucatán, linked in the Late Formative period by a string of stone causeways (figure 1.1). Contemporary speakers of Yucatec Maya use the term *sakbe*, plural *sakbe'ob*, to refer to these causeways. Causeways manifest a durable linkage that entailed potential economic, sociopolitical, and ideological connections. UCRIP's main goal is to understand the causes and consequences of these connections, and the causeways are important actors.

To the extent that the causeways incorporate these sites into a single polity, perhaps a voluntary confederation, these causeways and their builders reconfigured the geopolitical landscape. Undertaking such an ambitious project of political incorporation required the collective organization of many communities. Previously published research (Hutson and Welch 2014; Hutson et al. 2016) shows that Ucí was by far the largest site in the vicinity of the causeway and likely the major, but not the only, player in this collective

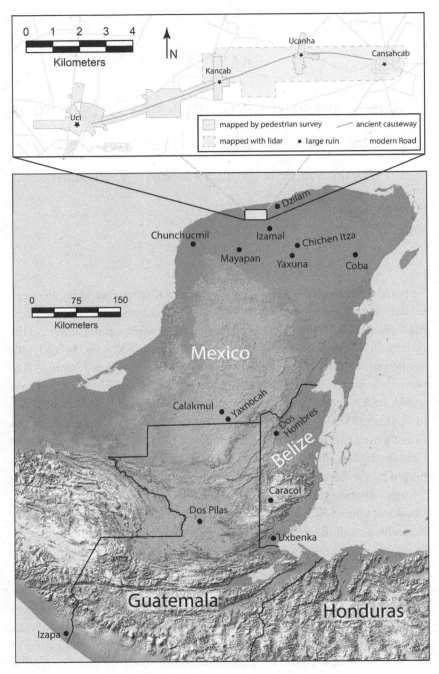

FIGURE 1.1 Broad map of the region (image created by Daniel Vallejo-Cáliz and Scott R. Hutson).

organization. The effects of the process on these communities are manifold and each sector of the population experienced the process in different ways.

To focus on each of these sectors and go beyond a top-down or elite-centered perspective, we apply a multiscalar approach that uses data from Ucí, other centers on the intersite causeways, and rural settlement between Ucí and Kancab. This will help us explore the organizational principles for the construction of the sakbe'ob and the possible sociopolitical, economic, and ideological changes that these communities experienced as a result of integration. Given that the construction of intrasite causeways at Ucí may serve as a potential analogy for the processes underlying intersite causeways, we present data from Ucí before moving to other scales, like the regional, intersite causeway network. Regarding the intersite causeways, we will explore their potential as political statements and assess their limited effect on the rural settlement. The process did not bring about major economic benefits or hindrances for the populations involved. Nevertheless, people's interaction with the sakbe'ob did have a series of social repercussions that transformed the social fabric of the various communities involved. The use of integration as a means of reducing structural conflict and factionalism during the Formative has a precedent in the El Mirador basin (Hansen 1998). The process would be used in later time periods in the context of socioeconomic integration (Chase and Chase 2014).

Regional integration as an encompassing process can transform political, economic, and social institutions in all the participant communities, in a multidirectional way. In this chapter, we examine integration processes both within the site of Ucí, Yucatán, Mexico, and a wider regional process with neighboring sites up to 18 km away. Incorporation in this case was materialized by the construction of a causeway network. Perceiving this process through dichotomies such as center-periphery or paramount-subordinate clouds the agency of the multiple stakeholders involved. Active manipulation of social systems by intermediate leaders and the rest of the population seems to have had a great influence on the general process of integration. During the complex negotiations between the various sectors involved, it seems likely that the activities carried out through the sakbe'ob (e.g., processions, exchange of products) would have greatly mitigated the frictions that would have been created in the preceding times. Studies at the communities connected by the Ucí-Cansahcab sakbe'ob are geared toward exploring these negotiations by considering multiple social sectors. Looking more closely at Ucí as the proposed center along the sakbe system during the Formative period, we can assess the benefits and hindrances of regional integration.

Theory—Intrasite Integration, Intersite Integration

Regional integration involves the active manipulation of the landscape to help formalize the process. For the northern Maya lowlands during the Late Formative, this would have required a substantial, organized, and collective labor force. In the absence of mechanisms like physical coercion, an individual's participation in labor pools would have had to be largely voluntary, likely embedded within the ideological fabric of the communities involved. Therefore, a shared sense of responsibility and mutual monitoring was probably present in the socio-ideological institutions of the time. Such institutions can be more successful when individual needs and wants are equated to those of the community as a whole. This kind of organization has been observed in communal labor schemes such as *tequio* in central Mexico, *mita* in South America, and *fagina* in Yucatán (Shaw 2008; see also Shaw and Flores Colin, this volume). Participation in collective work was seen as necessary to maintain personal social contracts, fulfill community obligations, and even perpetuate supernatural congress and protection.

For communal labor projects to be properly deployed in a broader, ambitious project like that of regional integration, they would have needed to prove effective in a previous context. In this regard, building projects might have been first employed within the site of Ucí and later for the region. Aspects of structural conflict such as factionalism and the need to create a sense of *communitas* are shared both within Ucí and at the regional level. Therefore, the application of an incorporation process at both levels would seem fruitful. In order to make this assertion, we must first create an assessment of the social processes involved in both intrasite and intersite incorporation.

Preliminary results from excavations of Structure E1N1-14 at Ucí show that in the Middle Formative, the Ucí community joined to build a nonresidential, finely stuccoed platform that measured 34 m long and at least 3.5 m high. We believe the platform had ceremonial functions that benefited the settlement at large, perhaps allowing the community to satisfy covenants with other-than-human entities. This building, which underwent several modifications in the Middle Formative, Late Formative, and Late Classic, could have then been appropriated by rising local, civic-religious leaders and manipulated to fulfill their own agenda. Rising elites could have then operated as cultural and ideological brokers, restricting access to knowledge, inserting themselves into the collective imagination of the population, and finally naturalizing the differences between themselves and the rest of the community (Brown et al. 2018; Robles Castellanos and Ceballos Gallareta 2018). This kind of appropriation could have occurred through focalized redistribution practices around specific households. In middle-range societies (e.g., prestate, complex stateless, intermediate), like those theorized for the Middle-Late Formative in the northern lowlands (Stanton and Ardren 2005), this was most likely achieved through ritualized displays of generosity. These would eventually allow for the empowerment of particular households, but at the same time such displays would lead to factionalism at the community level. The structural conflict created by factions vying for power would have to be managed to prevent exodus (Bandy 2004; Clark 2000; Clark and Blake 1994).

One way to reduce factionalism would be to create periodic shifts in power. In this situation, a structure of rotating positions would allow prominent and aspiring members of the community to cycle in and out of power (Coe 1965). Given that such positions are still under the tutelage of already established leaders, the efficacy of this strategy of delegating responsibilities is two-fold. First, it diminishes factionalism by providing an outlet for empowering figures to cement a position within the community. Second, it re-emphasizes a social hierarchy where the leaders and, by recursive association, the central polity itself are the central focus of the population (Ringle 1999). Linkages made between buildings connected by causeways would represent a fixed ceremonial circuit, with periodic shifts shared between agents previously vying for power. These intermediate figures would enjoy special benefits given their status but at the same time would have to act as social brokers to fill demands imposed by the governing body (Elson and Covey 2006; Pauketat 2004).

Sakbe'ob could be seen as a medium for reducing conflict between factions; they could also be seen as a way of enhancing extant cooperation. Either way, it is important to discuss how they might have been used. The principal means of operationalizing sakbe'ob would be through processions. Processions (Coleman 2002; Eade and Sallnow 1991; Kong 2005; Stoddard 1997) offer a mechanism that helps reduce conflict between factions through the creation of a site-wide identity. At the same time, the act of procession creates an arena in which social agents can discuss and resolve disagreements and reaffirm or transform their place within the community. A procession enables the creation of a recursive relation where agents and places become enmeshed through social memory (Arnold et al. 2013). This relation would ideally be helpful in propelling a desired collective imaginary and thus result in a process of subjectification.

Regardless, processions should not be seen as arenas free of conflict. Meanings communicated in ritual performances involve a degree of ambiguity and can therefore be understood in a variety of ways (Bell 1997). Some people may openly or covertly resist certain meanings and respond in ways not intended by those who organize the performance (Hutson 2002; Inomata 2006, 808). Therefore, a procession carries the risk of backfiring, fomenting dissent as opposed to unity. Unfortunately, many responses to processions, some comprising a hidden transcript (Scott 1990), would leave little material evidence for us to ponder. This would be obscured further by the fact that the causeways were most likely used for utilitarian purposes (i.e., transportation, traffic), besides the ideological or ritual ones. In sum, processions not only promote a sense of community but may also highlight fractures within the social fabric.

The creation of a sole sociopolitical identity during the Middle and Late Formative could not have been easy. Therefore, we must consider that the sakbe'ob networks are not simply representations of a final product, an established status quo, but also illustrative of a medium where negotiations could take place constantly and periodically accordingly to the needs of the community (Hutson, Magnoni, and Stanton 2012). This active manipulation is not only done by certain, specialized performers or privileged actors. The sakbe itself becomes a facility for the community, and at the same time it provides a very specific social environment that can serve as a platform for extranormal interactions. Within these interactions, social actors from all backgrounds are able to insert their opinions and agency to meet their own needs during a transformative period, like that of the Middle-Late Formative.

Intrasite Causeways at Ucí

Ucí has five intrasite causeways (figure 1.2), named Sakbe'ob 2, 3, 4, 5, and 6 (Sakbe 1 is the intersite causeway that links Ucí with Kancab). Sakbe 5 begins about 600 m south of the site core and continues southward (it might be an intersite causeway), but is not well preserved and does not appear to

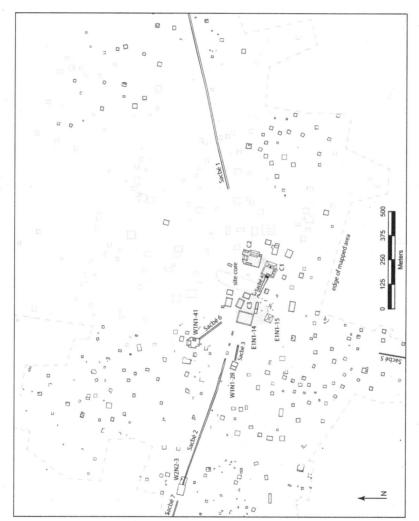

FIGURE 1.2 Map of Ucí site core showing causeways, structures, and compounds named in the text (image created by Daniel Vallejo-Cáliz and Scott R. Hutson).

TABLE 1.1 Dimensions of main architectural compounds at Ucí

Name	Surface area (m²)	Height (m)	Volume (m³)
Compound 1	4,597	13.0	27,293
Compound 2	6,777	10.0	21,644
Compound 3	13,586	4.5	32,381
E1N1-15	1,330	12.0	9,600
W2N2-3	3,005	1.5	2,844
W1N1-41	2,904	6.0	5,780
W1N1-28	1,319	4.0	3,520

link to any particular structures. We, therefore, cannot say more about it. Sakbe'ob 2, 3, and 6 are similar in that they link the site's largest architectural compound—Compound 3, which contains structure E1N1-14—with three substantially smaller compounds, W2N2-3, W1N1-28, and W1N1-41, which are nevertheless much larger than average residences at Ucí (table 1.1). Compound 3 contains a 5,300 m² paved plaza that likely served as Ucí's main space for public ceremonial gatherings. The plaza contains at least seven preserved plaster floors, and excavations of Structure E1N1-14, on the west side of the plaza, revealed major construction in the Middle Formative, Late Formative, and Late Classic. Excavations of the other structures in Compound 3 are limited to a trench in Str. E1N1-18 on the south side, which revealed Late Formative and Late Classic construction.

Like Causeways 2, 3, and 6, Causeway 4 also connects to Compound 3, but its other terminus, Compound 1, located 120 m east of Compound 3 (figure 1.2), is the second-largest compound at Ucí and is much larger than W2N2-3, W1N1-28, and W1N1-41. Ucí's third-largest compound—Compound 2—is immediately north of Compound 1. Given the stark differences in construction volume between Compounds 1, 2, and 3 on the one hand and W2N2-3, W1N1-28, and W1N1-41 on the other (see table 1.1), we believe Compounds 1, 2, and 3, as well as structure E1N1-15, housed Ucí's rulers, ruling institutions, and its main public plaza, whereas W2N2-3, W1N1-28, and W1N1-41 housed secondary leaders. Thus, Causeways 2, 3, and 6 connect secondary leaders with Ucí's primary rulers and performance spaces. As such, they are comparable to sakbe'ob 1 and 3 at Yo'okop (see Shaw and Flores Colin, this volume). Given that we have partially excavated all four buildings linked by Causeways 2, 3, and 6 but lack excavations in Compound 1, Compound 2, and structure E1N1-15, we focus on what Causeways 2, 3, and 6 and structures W2N2-3, W1N1-28, and W1N1-41 tell us about Ucí's secondary leaders and their linkages with the rulers.

Causeways 2, 3, and 6 range between 5 m and 7 m wide, with heights between 30 cm and 60 cm. They all lead to Compound 3, but none connect directly to it. As Justine M. Shaw and Alberto G. Flores Colin note in their chapter, some of the causeways within Y'okop also fall short of their final destinations. The missed connections at Ucí might be due to stone robbing in the Late Classic when Str. E1N1-14 was enlarged. Sakbe 2 begins on the east side of W2N2-3 and runs 816 m before stopping 50 m short of the northwest corner of Compound 3's largest structure, E1N1-14. In the last 100 m before it stops, Sakbe 2 fragments into three small pieces. Thus, the eastern end of the sakbe is disturbed, lending support to the idea that Sakbe'ob 2, 3, and 6 originally reached Compound 3. To the west of W2N2-3, Sakbe 7, an unfinished intersite road, continues westward with the same alignment as Sakbe 2 and stops after 460 m (see Shaw and Flores Colin, this volume, for an unfinished intrasite causeway at Yo'okop; and Hutson, Magnoni, and Stanton 2012 for an unfinished intersite causeway near Yaxunah). Sakbe 3 begins 5 m east of the eastern edge of W1N1-28 and extends 82 m to the east, stopping 108 m short of the west side of E1N1-14. Sakbe 6 begins at the southeast corner of W1N1-41 and continues 140 m to the southeast, stopping about 100 m short of the northwest corner of Compound 3.

Unlike some of the causeways at Yo'okop (see Shaw and Flores Colin, this volume), which in some cases rise up to 4 m high, none of Ucí's causeways are tall enough to create barriers. People could have climbed across them easily. Causeways 3, 4, and 6 were probably not meant to be used in everyday transit across the site because they do not span high-traffic pedestrian routes and they are all short and localized to the site core. Sakbe 2 is longer and, combined with Sakbe 7, may have brought people from the west edge of the site and beyond to the site core. Yet the fact that it runs parallel to and only 40 m away from Sakbe 3 at its eastern end suggests a form of symbolic communication.

Intrasite Causeway Termini

Before exploring the architectural compounds linked by the intrasite causeways, we provide an overview of settlement chronology at Ucí. The earliest evidence of occupation at Ucí comes in the form of Middle Formative ceramics from the Early Nabanché ceramic sphere. In most sites along the Ucí/Cansahcab causeways, surface collections recover minimal diagnostic potsherds, so most of our chronological reconstructions come from excavations (Hutson et al. 2016; Vallejo-Cáliz, Hutson, and Parker 2019). At Ucí, thirty-one of the thirty-five compounds that we have test-pitted yielded viable ceramic samples, and of these thirty-one, nine (28 percent) had significant amounts of Middle Formative pottery. Given the total number of architectural compounds at Ucí (about nine hundred), we estimate that Ucí had about 250 Middle Formative households. Ucí and the region as a whole saw a sharp rise in settlement during the Late Formative, when Ucí was by far the largest site in the micro-region (sites connected by the intersite sakbe'ob or found within about 10 km of them). Given that twenty-nine of our sample of thirty-one compounds at Ucí had significant amounts of Late Formative pottery, we estimate that 93 percent of its nine hundred architectural compounds were occupied during this time. This is more than three times the amount of the next largest settlement (Ucanha) during the Late Formative, leading us to believe that Ucí was instrumental in the construction of the intersite sakbe'ob network.

During the Early Classic, there seems to have been a sharp population decline. Two different scenarios might explain this. First, people left Ucí for rural areas in the micro-region or larger sites like Izamal, located 43 km to the southeast, which thrived in the Early Classic (Quiñones-Cetina 2006). Alternatively, we have not been able to properly identify Early Classic diagnostics in the region, and the "depopulation" is a mirage (Glover and Stanton 2010). Some platforms at Ucí (including W2N2-3) had substantial occupation at the end of the Early Classic, evidenced by Oxkintok Regional pottery. Oxkintok Regional pottery was also common at Chunhuayum, a small site located 4 km to the northeast of Ucí (Lamb 2022). In the Late Classic, there is clear ceramic evidence for a substantial (re)population at Ucí, though density was 25 percent lower than in the Formative. Excavations show a reduced but continued occupation in Postclassic and Colonial times.

The compounds linked by Causeways 2, 3, and 6 were all inhabited for most of the Prehispanic period sequence, though we will focus on the Formative since this was the initial era of regional integration. Our data on W2N2-3, W1N1-28, and W1N1-41 indicate that they housed highly ranked families that rose to power during the Formative. They would have gained ample political support in their communities, most likely through their ability as supernatural mediators (Kertzer 1988). Later, their status as social brokers would have made them important players in the integration process. Information recovered through excavations allows us to suggest ties that members of these three households had with the paramount leaders and local constituents, and possibly members of the rural communities east of the center. By the Late Formative period, the construction volume of each of these compounds exceeded 2,000 m³. Therefore, building the platforms would have required a collective, organized labor force. Given the common assumption that social differences in the Formative would not have been totally naturalized, this power to draw labor is a feat in and of itself. The artifacts found in these structures allow us to interpret how the individual groups could have achieved such a place in the community.

Of the three compounds connected to intrasite causeways, the best data on the processes of rising social hierarchy and intrasite integration during the Middle-Late Formative come from W1N1-41. This compound (figure 1.3) consists of a 2,904 m², 1.4 m high basal platform (W1N1-41) supporting two small foundation braces, a 4.5 m high pyramid (W1N1-41a) on the north side measuring 26 × 21 m, and a 1 m high platform (W1N1-41b) on the east side measuring 15 × 15 m. W1N1-b supports its foundation brace on the east side. In 2016, we excavated four test pits and twenty-three 50 × 50 cm shovel tests along the perimeter of W1N1-41 and returned in 2017 for 56 m² of broader excavations.

W1N1-41 has some of the best evidence for Middle Formative architecture at the site, consisting of a buried substructure, W1N1-41 Sub-1. We located a portion of a retaining wall for this structure underneath the southwest edge of the pyramid (W1N1-41a) on the north side of the basal platform. The wall continued beyond our excavations. This substructure is associated with Middle Formative ceramic types, such as Kin Naranja incised and early versions of both Sabán Chancenote striated and Dzudzuquil cream-to-buff (Andrews 1989). The W1N1-41 Sub-1 wall has a different style than most later platform retaining walls at Ucí. The wall consists of a series of cut stones averaging about 40 cm long. Late Formative platform retaining walls contain Megalithic-style stones (Mathews and Maldonado Cárdenas 2006), ranging from 60 cm to 1 m long, often with rounded corners.

We believe that the inhabitants of this structure represent what Christina M. Elson and Alan Covey (2006) call intermediate elites or also faction or interest-group leaders. This is reflected in the size of the structures and

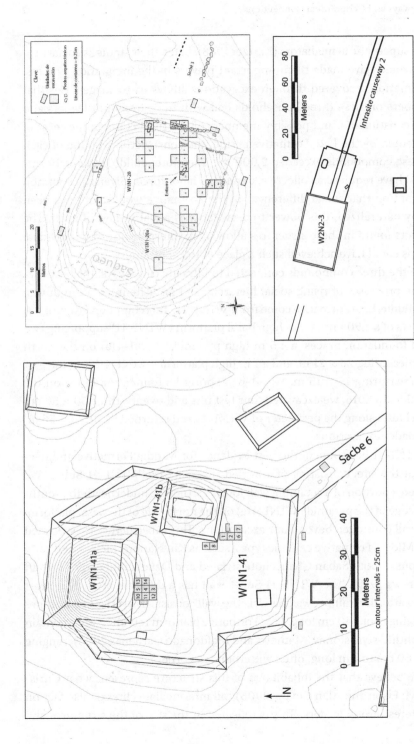

FIGURE 1.3 Maps of Ucí intrasite sakbe termini groups (image created by Daniel Vallejo-Cáliz and Scott R. Hutson).

their relation to labor investments. For example, the volume for W1N1-41, W1N1-41a, and W1N1-41b is 7,110 m³. So, using Elliot M. Abrams's (1994, 50) estimate solely for nuclear, construction fill of 4.8 m³/person-day, we come to a total of 1,481 person-day. This estimate is just of fill and does not consider masonry walls, cutting and transporting Megalithic stones, or constructing plaster floors. This is a significant effort considering that a population estimate for the Late Formative is about 5,800 people. Differential access to multiple labor pools would denote a differential status of the leaders represented through these structures.

We see them as neighborhood leaders during the Late Formative, but how were they able to establish themselves as such? We believe that they began to build the foundations of their Late Formative power in the Middle Formative through redistribution practices, such as displays of generosity, perhaps without foreseeing the consequences of their actions (Clark and Blake 1994). At W1N1-41, we have evidence for the creation of unequal power relations during the Middle Formative, most likely based on ritual leadership. This evidence includes a cache of several pots from the Early Nabanché ceramic sphere that seemed to have been smashed in place all at once. This is similar to what has been described as end-of-period dumps (Voorhies and Arvey 2016), which is related to the rituals described by Diego de Landa for the Maya (Tozzer 1941, 151).

The voluntary destruction of the vessels signals two processes that could have solidified the structure as a place of importance for their followers and their community at large. First, it demonstrates that this was a place where food was presented in ceramics not readily available to the rest of the population. Survey and test-pitting at the site demonstrate that ceramics during the Middle-Late Formative at Ucí and surrounding occupation were not widely available (Hutson et al. 2016). The presentation of foodstuffs in special vessels to their commensals would have created a special occasion directly associated with the structure and its hosts. Pottery vessels were scarce during these times in most households. The interaction with vessels would have created a unique experience along with other ritual expressions. Second, it could demonstrate that these vessels were part of a broader ritual that ladened them with a specific force that deemed them to be destroyed and buried. Both of these events, the presentation of food and the destruction of the vessels, would have denoted the structure as a place for special rituals and occasions.

In certain Maya rituals (Coe 1965), wealthier members of society were chosen from the general populace to fulfill managerial, ritual positions periodically. This could have been the case for the people occupying W1N1-41, W1N1-28, and W2N2-3. The human factions occupying these structures could have competed with one another but still had to answer to a paramount elite. The allotting of this temporary office would have provided them with further status and prestige within their community.

Structures like W1N1-41 Sub-1 during the Middle Formative were probably used as centers of worship dedicated to specific gods (Cheetham 2004) but may also have been residences. The people living there most likely served as supernatural mediators for the populace, allowing them to gain social support and augment their position within the community (Kertzer 1988). Aside from serving and processing vessels that serve as evidence to suggest daily habitation, we also found a miniature vessel that could have been used in ritual activities at the structure. Vessels of this form have been misidentified as "poison" bottles. Chemical analyses of Classic period flasks from the Ucí region and elsewhere in the Maya area show that they held tobacco (Loughmiller-Cardinal and Zagorevski 2016; Zimmermann et al. 2021). Examples of such flasks with texts on them state that they held tobacco, while iconographic evidence suggests the use of tobacco juice in enemas (Houston, Stuart, and Taube 2006, 114). The presence of this vessel reinforces the magico-ritual component of activities performed at W1N1-41 Sub1.

Sometime during the Late Formative, W1N1-41 went through a transformation. The earlier component, W1N1-41 Sub-1, was completely buried by the basal platform we see today, and structures W1N1-41a and W1N1-41b were built over it. Structure W1N1-41a, the 4.5 m high pyramid on the north end of the basal platform, suggests civic-ceremonial activities, while W1N1-41b is more reminiscent of a residential structure. Excavations at W1N1-41b recovered a large suite of domestic pottery, and what we interpret as a dedicatory burial in units 8 and 9 (figure 1.3). The burial is quite peculiar given that it was neither laid in a cist nor accompanied by offerings, while all seven other UCRIP burials that were located in narrow stone cists had offerings. Instead, it was set into nuclear construction fill, in an inverted (i.e., upside-down), possibly flexed position. We found the human remains directly adjacent to the stone W1N1-41b platform retaining wall at a depth of approximately 1.30 m below the surface. Though the bones consisted only of a femur, part of the pelvis, and what is perhaps part of the tibia and fibula, their articulation allows us to propose a primary context. We have not been able to determine sex or age. This internment is most likely a dedicatory offering to the structure. The offering could also solidify relationships between hosts and followers (Olsen et al. 2014) through the fulfillment of mutual obligations, where it would be the hosts' responsibility to procure such an offering and thus maintain the status of the compound. The importance of the W1N1-41 compound within the community would be further highlighted by its direct connection to the Ucí site core, which we now describe.

In the Late Formative, W1N1-41 was materially linked to the center of the site by means of Sakbe 6, which begins at the southeast corner of W1N1-41 and extends for 140 m at a bearing of 147°. An excavation unit placed on top of Sakbe 6 detected an earlier version of the road bed with three superimposed plaster floors. Thus, the sakbe was constructed, its surface was replastered twice, and then its surface was elevated once more. As previously noted, the sakbe stops about 100 m short of Compound 3, the largest at Ucí, but this premature stoppage might be due to later disturbance. If Sakbe 6 did reach all the way to Compound 3, it would thread the needle between structures E1N1-14 and E1N1-13, entering Compound 3's plaza, Ucí's largest, covering about 5,300 m². Sakbe'ob 2 and 3, linked to W1N1-28 and W2N2-3, respectively, would also connect to Compound 3 if these sakbe'ob were extended eastward. Yet rather than entering the Compound 3 plaza, they would connect to the back/west side of E1N1-14, Ucí's putative palace.

Compound W1N1-28 is located south of W1N1-41 and to the west of E1N1-14 (see figure 1.2). The compound consists of a basal platform (W1N1-28) with a badly damaged superstructural platform (W1N1-28a) atop its west end (see figure 1.3). The basal platform measures 44 × 32 × 2.5 m. We estimate that W1N1-28a measured 26 × 20 × 1.5 m. We excavated four test pits and nine shovel tests around the perimeter of W1N1-28 in 2016 and then 124 m² of broader exposures in 2017. Exposure of the east retaining wall of W1N1-28 revealed fine Late Formative Megalithic–style construction. As opposed to W1N1-41, we did not find a buried Middle Formative structure.

Structure W2N2-3 is located 860 m to the west of Compound 3. Apart from the link with Compound 3, W2N2-3 shares other similarities with W1N1-41 and W1N1-28, such as large size. W2N2-3 measures 54 × 35 × 1.2 m with a 40 × 29 × 0.4 m extension (W2N2-3a) to the east on the north and south sides of Sakbe 2 (see figure 1.3). The extension supports two apsidal foundation braces and appears to have been built after Sakbe 2. W2N2-

3's platform retaining walls were built in the Megalithic style. We excavated three 2 × 1 m test pits off the north side of the platform and performed seven shovel tests off its other sides. Though most of the pottery from our excavation dates to the Classic period, we also recovered Late Formative pottery.

It is worth noting the differences and similarities between the three architectural groups. In terms of layout, W2N2-3 is quite different from W1N1-41 and W1N1-28. Despite sharing the same orientation (103°) as W1N1-28, W2N2-3 lacks a prominent superstructural mound and instead features a long, low extension that has no parallel at the other two compounds. Though W1N1-41 and W1N1-28 both have a large superstructural mound, W1N1-41 has a second major superstructure and the two compounds have different orientations. At the same time, all three have causeways leading to Compound 3. This combination of similarity and difference suggests negotiations between different social groups and classes. The mutual connections to Compound 3 exemplify a community-wide project that integrates powerful households at these outlying compounds, while the architectural differences show the agency of each of the groups and their ambition to distinguish themselves from their competitors.

These three compounds must be placed in the context of the social fabric of Ucí at this time. The Late Formative represents the biggest occupation at the site and is consistent with a demographic rise in other parts of the peninsula (Stanton 2012). Therefore, a population increase at the site would have represented a perfect opportunity for local leaders to acquire more support. Given the diversity of competing local leaders as represented by the three compounds discussed here, a sense of factionalism could have arisen and sharpened the mechanisms of social inequality already present since the Middle Formative. To mitigate factionalism and maintain a somewhat collective sense of community, the rulers that we believe inhabited and operated out of Compound 3 could have agreed to an exchange of rights and responsibilities with the social groups occupying the large compounds (W1N1-41, W1N1-28, W2N2-3, Compound 1, Compound 2) surrounding Compound 3. We believe that the rulers, housed in Compound 3, had the deepest connection to the site given that we have encountered substructures at Compound 3 with pre-Nabanché materials, from the early Middle Formative. This is different from the outlying structures (W1N1-28, W1N1-41, and W2N2-3), where processes of differentiation start at the beginning of the late Middle Formative or Late Formative.

Each one of the structures (W1N1-28, W1N1-41, and W2N2-3) is individually linked to the center of the site, which could potentially allow the inhabitants of the different structures to emulate the actions and roles of rulers. We believe that the individual connections to the civic-ceremonial center of the site mean that the paramount elite was allowing the occupants of these structures to participate in community-wide rituals (Coe 1965). This individual signaling could also mean that the inhabitants of the structures were key participants in these rituals. Dubbed *principales* by Landa (Tozzer 1941) and Michael D. Coe (1965), Batabs would be the name in Yucatec Maya of these intermediate beings who would be able to pose as elites during ceremonies like processions. This type of emulation, in a sense performing the duties the paramount elite was obligated to do, would have permitted them some of the same benefits allotted to the ruling class (Skoglund et al. 2006).

The distribution of the intrasite causeway terminus compounds also allows us to consider the particular trajectory that processions along the causeways could have taken and what that could have meant for the various social groups involved. Processional circuits could include from two to five architectural groups (Compound 3, Compound 1, W1N1-41, W1N1-28, W2N2-3), but any leg of the circuit must include Compound 3. The end goal of this kind of movement is then two-fold. It reifies each terminus as a civic-ceremonial locus, while at the same time it creates a vision of a collective community centered at Compound 3 (Ringle 1999).

The rulers must have authorized the linkage of the intrasite causeways with Compound 3 and perhaps organized part of the construction of these causeways. The leaders at W1N1-41, W1N1-28, and W2N2-3 likely took some part in the planning of these causeways and the organization of their construction (W1N1-28 and W2N2-3 are approximately aligned with their respective causeways). Lastly, client households of more modest status supplied labor. In order not to base all our interpretations on evidence from Ucí as a possible central polity, we need to look at other communities involved in the process of integration. In the next section, we discuss the intersite causeways between Ucí and Cansahcab.

Intersite Causeways

Three separate causeways connected Ucí, Kancab, Ucanha, and Cansahcab, the four major sites shown in figure 1.1. In other publications, we have presented details on these causeways and discussed the role they played in the creation of political alliances (Hutson and Davies 2015; Hutson and Welch 2021; Hutson et al. 2016). In this section, we review these conclusions while adding new details on chronology and on how the causeways connect to the sites.

Understanding the nature of political alliances requires the chronology of construction as well as settlement chronologies of the sites linked by intersite causeways. As described in the previous section, Ucí already had a sizable population and a degree of political centralization (as seen in E1N1-14) during the Middle Formative and reached its apogee in the Late Formative. Unfortunately, we have no chronological data for Cansahcab, which is largely destroyed by the modern municipal center of the same name. Test-pitting and other types of excavation provide settlement chronologies for Kancab and Ucanha. At Kancab, 8 of 19 excavated compounds (42 percent) with viable ceramic samples had significant amounts of Middle Formative pottery. One of these contexts is the main plaza, where our excavations into plaza fill located a complete Kin Naranja vessel dating to the early Middle Formative. Given the total number of architectural compounds (143) at Kancab, we estimate that Kancab had about sixty Middle Formative households. We estimate that 89 percent of its 143 compounds had Late Formative occupation. We have chronological data from 33 architectural compounds at Ucanha, 6 of which (18 percent) include evidence of Middle Formative occupation (see also Kidder et al. 2019). Given an estimated total of 416 architectural compounds at the site, Ucanha's Middle Formative occupation would have amounted to perhaps seventy-five households. Of the 33 contexts with chronological data, about two-thirds have Late Formative occupation.

Thus, Kancab and Ucanha were communities of respectable size (a few hundred people each) during the Middle Formative. Though both sites were less than half the size of Ucí in the Middle Formative, we emphasize the fact that Kancab and Ucanha were much more than tiny villages during this period and already had important growth trajectories before the construction of the causeways in the Late Formative. Like Ucí, both Ucanha and Kancab grew substantially in the Late Formative, but Ucanha came to be about twice the size of Kancab. This detail relates to our understanding of the political processes behind causeway construction, which builds from a proposal first made by Rubén Maldonado Cárdenas (1995).

Specifically, Maldonado Cárdenas (1995) proposed that the Ucí–Kancab and the Ucanha–Cansahcab causeways were built before the causeway connecting Kancab and Ucanha. This proposal implies that there were two small polities—Ucí/Kancab and Ucanha/Cansahcab—that were eventually joined into a single polity once the Kancab–Ucanha causeway was built. Our data help flesh this out. First, our documentation of rapid growth at Ucanha in the Late Preclassic (e.g., doubling the size of Kancab) and excavations revealing powerful leaders at Ucanha during the Late Formative (Hutson et al. 2020) support the notion that Ucanha was a polity capital in the Late Formative. Likewise, our finding that Ucí reached its apogee in the Late Formative, with a complex political structure, indicates that Ucí headed the other small polity. Light Detection and Radar (LiDAR) and pedestrian survey methods in the rural areas between the large sites also support the suggestion of two distinct micropolities (Hutson et al. 2016). Settlement density along the Ucí–Kancab and Ucanha–Cansahcab causeways is six times higher than that between the Kancab and Ucanha. The low settlement density between Kancab and Ucanha is precisely what we would expect if this were a sparsely occupied buffer zone between the two polities.

Our excavations (n = 7) of the causeways themselves neither support nor contradict the idea that the Kancab/Ucanha causeway was the last of the three to be built. All seven excavations showed that the intersite causeways had a single construction phase. Unfortunately, the surface of the causeway has been disturbed by a variety of processes, so the causeway fill does not represent a sealed context. We dug two trenches across the Ucí–Kancab causeway, both in the vicinity of farmsteads located 4 km to the west of Ucí. We purposefully placed one of these trenches where the causeway comes closest to the residential compound of Structure 39n1, hoping that debris from the structure, which was extensively excavated, would help us date the construction of the causeway. We also dug a portion of the causeway as part of excavations at Structure 66n1, a residential platform connected to the causeway and located on the western edge of Kancab, 600 m west of Kancab's main plaza. Ceramics in the fill of the causeway at Structure 66n1 and near Structure 39n1 were dominated by Late Formative pottery. Structure 66n1 itself crosses above the causeway and dates to the Classic and Postclassic periods. This supports the notion that the causeway was built before the Classic period and was no longer in use by the Classic when 66n1 was built. The three trenches we dug across the Kancab–Ucanha causeway (two within Kancab and one within Ucanha) recovered a small amount of pottery (twenty-two chronologically diagnostic sherds) from both the Late Formative and Late Classic. The single trench we dug across the Ucanha/Cansahcab causeway yielded only two diagnostic sherds, both Late Formative.

Though our excavations of the intersite causeways do not help us determine whether they were built at the same or different times, details on how they articulate (or do not articulate) with the sites they extend from shed some light. We have a decent view of five of the six causeway termini (the Cansahcab endpoint of the Ucanha–Cansahcab causeway is destroyed). As we have emphasized elsewhere (Hutson and Welch 2021), both termini of the Ucí–Kancab causeway do not connect directly with important architecture or plazas. This is also the case with the Ucanha endpoint of the Ucanha–Cansahcab causeway. We believe that these two causeways (Ucí–Kancab and Ucanha–Cansahcab) served as routes for pilgrimages and processions between the sites but also reflected political alliances and spoke to the power of the authorities who sponsored their construction (Kurjack and Andrews 1976).

In contrast, the Kancab–Ucanha causeway, though it does not link with the Main Plazas of Kancab and Ucanha, connects directly with ceremonial architecture: Structure 30 at Kancab and Structure 120 at Ucanha (figure 1.4; Hutson and Davies 2015; Hutson and Welch 2014). Structure 30 may have been built at the same time as the causeway. The causeway seamlessly articulates with the Structure 30 basal platform, rising upward, ramp-like, to the level of the platform. The platform is rather open, and though it is only about a meter high, it is built on a 0.7 m high natural rise and supports a small, 1.3 m high structure on its north side. Thus, people on the platform or superstructure are easily visible thanks to their elevation and lack of visual impediments.

Structure 120, which is much larger than Structure 30, predates the causeway and is similar to W1N1-41 and W1N1-28 at Ucí since it has its short intrasite causeway leading to the Ucanha site core and was likely the headquarters of the neighborhood-level leaders. Structure 120 is a basal platform measuring 50 × 38 × 1.2 m. On its west side, it supports Structure 120a, an east-facing temple that rises 2.7 m above the basal platform and has a Megalithic-style staircase on its east side. Masonry structures line the north and south sides of the basal platform, creating a 550 m^2 patio that is mostly private given that people standing outside Structure 120 to the north, south, and west could not see activities on the patio. The causeway connects to the southwest corner of the basal platform where there is a gap between

Causeways and Geopolitical Connections

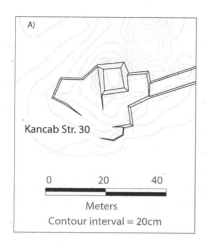
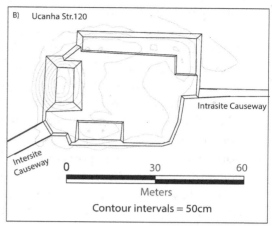

FIGURE 1.4 Maps of Kancab Str. 30 and Ucanha Str. 120, at the same scale (image created by Daniel Vallejo-Cáliz and Scott R. Hutson).

the west pyramid and the south structure. The causeway and Structure 120 do not have the same orientation.

In sum, the Kancab–Ucanha causeway connects to a small but prominent public structure at Kancab and a larger, more private, residential/ceremonial patio at Ucanha. These two endpoints were formally planned to articulate important built landmarks at Kancab and Ucanha, unlike the three known endpoints of the other two intersite causeways. Our tentative impression is that the other two causeways connect sites without much fanfare, whereas the construction of the Kancab/Ucanha causeway represented something more noteworthy and potentially controversial: the conjoining of what we believe were two previously independent and competing polities. We speculate that the leaders of this enlarged polity understood the charged circumstances surrounding the construction of the causeway and therefore explicitly anchored it with a purpose-built terminus at Kancab (Str. 30) and an already established outpost of leadership at Ucanha (Str. 120).

Rural Integration Along the Ucí–Kancab Causeway

To better understand the function of the intersite causeways and their link to regional politics, we focus more closely on the Ucí–Kancab causeway and settlement in its vicinity. Yaxché refers to a 3.93 km^2 mapped polygon located halfway between Ucí and Kancab. The causeway bisects the polygon. We have test-pitted twenty-four platforms in the survey block and conducted broad-scale excavations at five of these. Céline Lamb (2022) has conducted additional excavations at the site of Chunhuayum, at the northwest corner of Yaxché, though these excavations are not discussed here. Excavations at Yaxché demonstrate that people in both locations had reduced access to basic, utilitarian goods such as pottery and lithics. Though some of the platforms tested were probably not occupied year-round, extensively excavated platforms with low amounts of pottery had evidence of long-term occupation, such as *metates* (stone tools for processing corn and other foods) and several phases of construction. Whereas in Ucí we have a ceramic density of 266 sherds per m³ of excavation, at Yaxché we find 40 sherds per m³. We have argued elsewhere that these disparities show that hinterland farmsteads were relatively impoverished and that integration with Ucí via the causeway did not bring many benefits (Hutson and Davies 2015).

How else might the causeways have changed people's actions? The Tzacauil causeway, constructed in the Late Formative near Yaxunah (Hutson, Magnoni, and Stanton 2012), had a pull on the people living near it, who oriented their houses to align with the causeway, especially in later periods (Fisher 2020). The Ucí–Cansahcab causeways did not seem to have this pull. Between Ucí and Kancab, where pedestrian survey enabled accurate measurements of building orientation, only 6 of the 272 buildings with orientation data located within 250 m of the causeway have an orientation within 5° of the orientation of the causeway. All of these are small (between 18 m² and 54 m²), with average elevations between 0 and 0.3 m. Furthermore, LiDAR mapping shows that residential compounds in between the major centers do not cluster near the causeway (Hutson et al. 2016, 277). Finally, as previously noted, Structure 66n1 at Kancab was constructed on top of the Ucí–Kancab causeway. Does this suggest a lack of reverence for the causeway and the earlier people associated with it?

Is there evidence that leaders at Ucí reached out to rural households in some form? One possibility is Structure 21N2, also called Hubichen, which is linked to the causeway by its own 40 m long causeway (figure 1.5). Located 3 km east of Ucí's monumental core, Hubichen consists of a basal platform that measures 25 × 23 × 2 m and supports a south-facing superstructure measuring 14 × 9 × 1 m. In terms of height and architectural volume, Structure 21N2 is the largest Late Formative architectural compound in the 17 km²

FIGURE 1.5 The Yaxche survey block, located between Ucí and Kancab, with the rural settlements of Hubichen and Chunhuayum (image created by Daniel Vallejo-Cáliz and Scott R. Hutson).

of the survey in the rural areas between Ucí and Cansahcab. Hubichen's large size (more than 1,000 m^3) indicates substantial labor investment, yet since there are no residential structures within a 300 m radius, we do not see a local labor base that could have helped build it. Hubichen may have been the home of a wealthy household, but all other large platforms like this in our study area are situated among clusters of residential settlements. The fact that Hubichen is disembedded from local rural settlement yet directly linked to Ucí's intersite causeway suggests to us a close affiliation with Ucí and that leaders at Ucí may have organized the investment of labor and materials. Substantial excavations of Hubichen, conducted by Jacob Welch, revealed high proportions of sherds from fancy Late Formative and Early Classic serving wares: Shangurro bichromes and Timucuy polychromes. We have considered the possibility that Hubichen was an outpost of Ucí where its officials served food to local people to maintain the support and compliance of rural farmers. This parallels Jason Yaeger's (2000) argument for Structure SL-13 near Xunantunich: an attempt by Xunantunich's leaders to co-opt the local community of San Lorenzo. Yet the fact that Hubichen is located at least 500 m from the nearest concentration of rural settlement suggests that it was not built as part of a strategy to administer the rural settlement.

We believe instead that Hubichen functioned primarily as a waystation for pilgrims heading to Ucí (Hutson and Welch 2021). Feeding pilgrims on the causeway would solidify the bonds between the participants and the hosts. As David Carballo (2013, 13) mentions, "symbols of affiliation and cooperative intent are likely to converge within built environments involving public ritual and mutual monitoring. An excellent example of such convergence is pilgrimage networks, which involve honest and transparent signals of participation and affiliation." Displays of generosity in the structure not only fulfilled mutual obligations within a single ideological system but were most likely used as empowering mechanisms that would ultimately benefit the hosts (Dietler 2001). The process of traversing the causeway between the sites would also ideally create a wider sense of communitas between the various communities. Furthermore, if we take for granted that Ucí guided Hubichen's construction and operation, then we must consider that the polity had to source labor and materials from Ucí, Kancab, or rural settlements such as Yaxché. The purpose for the construction must have been presented in a way that would surpass people's association with particular places with deeper cultural and temporal ties (i.e., W1N1-41). The construction and operation of Hubichen would also require intermediate, managerial positions (Elson and Covey 2006, 12).

If, in the end, the Ucí–Kancab causeway had few direct effects on the rural areas through which it passed, we nevertheless believe there were some unintended effects. Causeways regionalize (Giddens 1984, 118; Hutson, Magnoni, and Stanton 2012, 308). They transform a less differentiated space into a more differentiated space by creating three zones: the causeway itself, the space on one side, and the space on the other side. Causeways also direct attention to the destinations at either end. More than just directing attention, this kind of regionalization likely helped define new boundaries and may have influenced land tenure. Formal demarcations of land boundaries in colonial El Salvador solidified what may have been fluid forms of access, affecting what Kathryn E. Sampeck (2014, 201) calls symbolic violence. Parts of the 100 km causeway between Yaxunah and Cobá, built in the seventh or eighth century AD, became a boundary line in later periods (Villa Rojas 1934, 205). For those who lived in rural areas near the path of a causeway, the appearance of the causeway probably added new points of reference. All of a sudden, one's home is now on a particular side of the track. Would they have lost access to resources on the other side? The low height of the Ucí intersite causeways (normally about 50 to 60 cm) would not have prevented people from crossing them, unlike some causeways at Yo'okop (Shaw and Flores Colin, this volume).

Conclusion

In this chapter, we discussed the process of integration at three scales: within Ucí, among Ucí and other centers connected by an intersite causeway, and in the rural area between Ucí and Kancab. Within Ucí, integration was not a homogenous, synchronic process. The earliest occupation is during the Middle Formative. Social distinction at this time seems to be centered around unequal power relations concerning access to ritual information. People living at Structure W1N1-41 acted as supernatural brokers and civic-religious leaders and consolidated their power during the Late Formative. The occupants of the structure would ultimately become enmeshed in community-wide politics and the gears of a rising social hierarchy. The same ability to call on labor assured them a special place within the community but also created ripples that would crash against the authority of the rulers. People living at

Structures W1N1-28 and W2N2-3 seemed to follow a similar trajectory. This factionalism would have directly acted against the authority of the rulers and may have challenged the notion of a unified Ucí community.

The governing body at the site may have met this challenge by supporting the creation of the Late Formative intrasite causeway system that connected W1N1-41, W1N1-28, and W2N2-3 with Compound 3 and therefore integrated these factions with centralized leaders. Though this process may have had the purpose of diminishing political tension, it may also have impacted tensions between factional leaders and followers by enhancing and naturalizing the legitimacy of the factional leaders as intermediate elites. Following authors who observe intrasite causeways at other sites in the Yucatán Peninsula (Ringle 1999; Shaw 2008; Stanton and Freidel 2005), we argue that these intrasite causeways were used for processions from the site core outward. Such processions from the town center to the periphery were documented at the time of conquest and interpreted by Coe (1965) as part of a political system in which the governing body periodically and cyclically appointed officials to bear the responsibilities of community-wide rites. Within these, processions become an important mechanism for integration. They allow for social actors and the built environment to become entangled in a recursive relationship that could emphasize a specific communal identity. At the same time, the act also highlights structural fractures within society.

Once these differences are established, households like the one at Structure W1N1-41 would not solely rest on their ability to draw labor but would be naturalized through their relationship with the governing body and their homologs. Though they seem to have been in a condition for reaping the benefits of elite emulation, their tutelage under the same group likely did not allow them the totality of the same benefits. In this sense, they might be able to constitute a different group, that of an intermediate elite (Elson and Covey 2006). They may also represent faction or interest-group leaders, where the structures can be seen as a locus for congregating.

In the Late Formative, people in the UCRIP region built three intersite causeways, stretching 18 km from Ucí to Cansahcab. This was a substantial construction effort that symbolized the sociopolitical transformations occurring in the region. Our research provides minor support for the idea that the region witnessed the creation of two smaller polities, headed by Ucí and Ucanha, which later joined into a single polity with the construction of the third and final intersite causeway. The will and ability to concretize these alliances through the construction of causeways attests to clearly coordinated action. Given Ucí's large size, it is tempting to say that Ucí functioned as a capital for the micro-region, but it is clear that the other polities maintained a high level of autonomy in their own communities. We, therefore, see the resulting configuration as reminiscent of the decentralized polities of the Classic period (Runggaldier and Hammond 2016).

The effects of these alliances on rural populations living near the causeways were minimal. Households near the Ucí–Kancab causeway did not receive economic benefits visible in the archaeological record. Furthermore, households did not begin to cluster near the intersite causeways, nor did they orient their buildings in line with the causeways. Finally, the construction of Hubichen, which may have been merely the compound of a wealthy household but which we have argued was an Ucí outpost along the causeway, probably played a greater role in pilgrimages as opposed to rural administration. We venture to say that integration for the Ucí-Cansahcab micro-region was more symbolic and sociopolitical than economic. The goal was to redefine existing social and geographical boundaries and create new ties between the entities within them.

Works Cited

Abrams, Elliot M. 1994. *How the Maya Built Their World: Energetics and Ancient Architecture*. Austin: University of Texas Press.

Andrews, E. Wyllys, V. 1989. "Ceramics of Komchen, Yucatán Mexico." Unedited manuscript on file. Middle American Research Institute, Tulane University.

Arnold, Dean, Hayley Schumacher Wynne, and Josiah Ostoich. 2013. "The Materiality of Social Memory: The Potter's Gremio in Ticul, Yucatán, México." *Ethnoarchaeology* 5 (2): 81–99.

Bandy, Matt. 2004. "Fissioning, Scalar Stress, and Social Evolution in Early Village Societies." *American Anthropologist* 106 (2): 322–33.

Bell, Catherine. 1997. *Ritual: Perspectives and Dimensions*. New York: Oxford University Press.

Brown, M. Kathryn, Jaime J. Awe, and James F. Garber. 2018. "The Role of Ideology, Religion, and Ritual in the Foundation of Social Complexity in the Belize River Valley." In *Pathways to Complexity: A View from the Maya Lowlands*, edited by M. Kathryn Brown and George J. Bey, 87–117. Gainesville: University Press of Florida.

Canuto, Marcello A., and Ellen E. Bell. 2008. "The Ties That Bind: Administrative Strategies in the El Paraíso Valley, Department of Copan, Honduras." *Mexicon* 30 (1): 10–20.

Carballo, David. 2013. "Cultural and Evolutionary Dynamics of Cooperation in Archaeological Perspective." In *Cooperation and Collective Action: Archaeological Perspectives*, edited by David Carballo, 3–33. Boulder: University Press of Colorado.

Chase, Diane Z., and Arlen F. Chase. 2014. "Ancient Maya Markets and the Economic Integration of Caracol, Belize." *Ancient Mesoamerica* 25 (1): 239–50.

Cheetham, David. 2004. "The Role of 'Terminus Groups' in Lowland Maya Site Planning: An Example from Cahal Pech." In *The Ancient Maya of the Belize Valley: Half a Century of Archaeological Research*, edited by J. F. Garber, 125–49. Gainesville: University Press of Florida.

Clark, John E. 2000. "Towards a Better Explanation of Hereditary Inequality: A Critical Assessment of Natural and Historic Human Agents." In *Agency in Archaeology*, edited by Marcia-Anne Dobres and John Robb, 92–112. London: Routledge.

Clark, John E., and Michael Blake. 1994. "The Power of Prestige: Competitive Generosity and the Emergence of Rank Societies in Lowland Mesoamerica." In *Faction Competition in the New World*, edited by Elizabeth M. Brumfiel and John W. Fox, 17–30. Cambridge: Cambridge University Press.

Coe, Michael D. 1965. "A Model of Ancient Community Structure in the Maya Lowlands." *Southwestern Journal of Anthropology* 21 (2): 87–115.

Coleman, Simon. 2002. "Do You Believe in Pilgrimage? Communitas, Contestation and Beyond." *Anthropological Theory* 2 (3): 355–68.

Dietler, Michael. 2001. "Theorizing the Feast: Rituals of Consumption, Commensal Politics, and Power in African Contexts." In *Feasts: Archaeological and Ethnographic Perspectives on Food, Politics, and Power*, edited by Michael Dietler and Bryan Hayden, 65–114. Washington, D.C.: Smithsonian Institution Press.

Eade, John, and Michael J. Sallnow. 1991. *Contesting the Sacred: The Anthropology of Pilgrimage*. Urbana: University of Illinois Press.

Elson, Christina M., and Alan Covey, eds. 2006. *Intermediate Elites in Pre-Columbian States and Empires*. Tucson: University of Arizona Press.

Fisher, Chelsea. 2020. "Walking Rural in Tzacauil, Yucatan, Mexico." *Ancient Mesoamerica* 33 (1): 148–61.

Giddens, Anthony. 1984. *The Constitution of Society*. Berkeley: University of California Press.

Glover, Jeffrey B., and Travis W. Stanton. 2010. "Assessing the Role of Preclassic Traditions in the Formation of Early Classic Yucatec Cultures, México." *Journal of Field Archaeology* 35 (1): 58–77.

Hansen, Richard. 1998. "Continuity and Disjunction: The Pre-Classic Antecedents of Classic Maya Architecture." In *Function and Meaning in Classic Maya Architecture*, edited by Stephen D. Houston, 49–112. Washington, D.C.: Dumbarton Oaks Research Library and Collection.

Hassig, Ross. 1991. "Roads, Routes and Ties That Bind." In *Ancient Road Networks and Settlement Hierarchies in the New World*, edited by Charles D. Trombold, 17–27. Cambridge: Cambridge University Press.

Houk, Brett A. 2003. "The Ties That Bind: Planning in the Three Rivers Region." In *Heterarchy, Political Economy, and the Ancient Maya*, edited by Vernon L. Scarborough, Fred Valdez Jr., and Nicholas Dunning, 52–63. Tucson: University of Arizona Press.

Houston, Stephen D., David Stuart, and Karl Taube. 2006. *The Memory of Bones: Body, Being, and Experience Among the Classic Maya*. Austin: University of Texas Press.

Hutson, Scott R. 2002. "Built Space and Bad Subjects: Domination and Resistance at Monte Albán, Oaxaca, Mexico." *Journal of Social Archaeology* 2 (1): 53–80.

Hutson, Scott R., and Gavin Davies. 2015. "How Material Culture Acted on the Ancient Maya of Yucatan, Mexico." *Archaeological Papers of the American Anthropological Association* 26 (1): 10–26.

Hutson, Scott, Barry Kidder, Céline Lamb, Daniel Vallejo-Cáliz, and Jacob Welch. 2016. "Small Buildings and Small Budgets: Making LiDAR Work in Northern Yucatan, Mexico." *Advances in Archaeological Practice* 4 (3): 268–83.

Hutson, Scott R., Aline Magnoni, and Travis Stanton. 2012. "'All That Is Solid . . .': Sacbes, Settlement and Semiotics at Tzacauil, Yucatan." *Ancient Mesoamerica* 23 (2): 297–311.

Hutson, Scott R., and Jacob A. Welch. 2014. "Sacred Landscapes and Building Practices at Uci, Kancab, and Ucanha, Yucatan, Mexico." *Ancient Mesoamerica* 25 (2): 421–39.

Hutson, Scott R., and Jacob A. Welch. 2021. "Roadwork: Long Distance Causeways at Uci, Yucatan, Mexico." *Latin American Antiquity* 32 (2): 310–30.

Hutson, Scott R., Jacob Welch, Shannon E. Plank, and Barry Kidder. 2020. "Buried Alive: Buildings, Authority, and Gradients of Being in Northern Yucatan, Mexico." In *Sacred Matter: Animacy and Authority in the Americas*, edited by Steven Kosiba, John W. Janusek, and Thomas B. F. Cummins, 299–326. Washington, D.C.: Dumbarton Oaks Research Library and Collection.

Inomata, Takeshi. 2006. "Plazas, Performers, and Spectators." *Current Anthropology* 47 (5): 805–42.

Kertzer, David. 1988. *Ritual, Politics, and Power*. New Haven, Conn.: Yale University Press.

Kidder, Barry, Scott R. Hutson, Shannon E. Plank, and Jacob Welch. 2019. "Building Quality of Life and Social Cohesion at Ucanha During the Terminal Formative." *The Mayanist* 1 (1): 37–58.

Kintz, Ellen R. 2004. "Considering the Ties That Bind: Kinship, Marriage, Household, and Territory Among the Maya." *Ancient Mesoamerica* 15 (1): 149–58.

Kong, Lily. 2005. "Religious Processions: Urban Politics and Poetics." *Temenos* 41 (2): 298–319.

Kurjack, Edward B., and E. Wyllys Andrews V. 1976. "Early Boundary Maintenance in Northwest Yucatan, Mexico." *American Antiquity* 41 (3): 318–25.

Lamb, Céline. 2022. "Rural Social Differentiation in Early Classic Chunhuayum, Yucatan, Mexico." *Ancient Mesoamerica* 33 (1): 162–85.

Loughmiller-Cardinal, Jennifer, and Dmitri Zagorevski. 2016. "Maya Flasks: The Home of Tobacco and Other Godly Substances." *Ancient Mesoamerica* 27 (1): 1–11.

Maldonado Cárdenas, Rubén. 1995. "Los sistemas de caminos del Norte de Yucatan." In *Seis ensayos sobre antiguos patrones de asentamiento en el área Maya*, edited by Ernesto Vargas Pacheco, 68–92. Mexico City: Instituto de Investigaciones Antropológicas, Universidad Nacional Autónoma de México.

Masson, Marilyn A. 2020. "Conclusion: The Ties That Bind." In *The Real Business of Ancient Maya Economics: From Farmers' Fields to Rulers' Realms*, edited by Marilyn A. Masson, David A. Freidel, and Arthur A. Demarest, 464–87. Gainesville: University Press of Florida.

Mathews, Jennifer P. 1998. "The Ties That Bind: The Ancient Maya Interaction Spheres of the Late Preclassic and Early Classic Periods in the Northern Yucatan Peninsula." PhD diss., University of California, Riverside.

Mathews, Jennifer P., and Ruben Maldonado Cárdenas. 2006. "Late Formative and Early Classic Interaction Spheres Reflected in the Megalithic Style." In *Lifeways in the Northern Lowlands: New Approaches to Maya Archaeology*, edited by Jennifer P. Mathews and Bethany A. Morrison, 95–118. Tucson: University of Arizona Press.

Olsen, Karyn C., Stephanie A. Cleland, Christine White, and Fred John Longstaf. 2014. "Human Dedicatory Burials from Altun Ha, Belize: Exploring Residential History Through Enamel Microwear and Tissue Isotopic Compositions." In *The Bioarchaeology of Space and Place: Ideology, Power, and Meaning in Maya Mortuary Contexts*, edited by Gabriel D. Wrobel, 169–92. New York: Springer.

Pauketat, Timothy R. 2004. "The Economy of the Moment: Cultural Practices and Mississippian Chiefdoms." In *Archaeological Perspectives on Political Economies*, edited by Gary M. Feinman and Linda M. Nichols, 25–39. Salt Lake City: University of Utah Press.

Quiñones-Cetina, Lucia. 2006. "Del preclásico medio al clásico temprano: Una propuesta de fechamiento para el área nuclear de Izamal, Yucatán." *Estudios de Cultura Maya* 28:51–65.

Restall, Matthew. 1998. "The Ties That Bind: Social Cohesion and the Yucatec Maya Family." *Journal of Family History* 23 (4): 355–81.

Ringle, William M. 1999. "Pre-Classic Cityscapes: Ritual Politics Among the Early Lowland Maya." In *Social Patterns in Pre-Classic Mesoamerica*, edited by David C. Grove and Rosemary A. Gross, 183–223. Washington, D.C.: Dumbarton Oaks Research Library and Collection.

Robles Castellanos, Fernando, and Teresa Ceballos Gallareta. 2018. "The Genesis of Maya Complexity in the Northwestern Region of the Yucatan Peninsula." In *Pathways to Complexity: A View from the Maya Lowlands*, edited by M. Kathryn Brown and George J. Bey, 223–52. Gainesville: University Press of Florida.

Runggaldier, Astrid, and Norman Hammond. 2016. "Maya States: The Theoretical Background in Historical Overview." In *The Origin of Maya States*, edited by Loa P. Traxler and Robert J. Sharer, 33–57. Philadelphia: University of Pennsylvania Press.

Sampeck, Kathryn E. 2014. "From Ancient Altepetl to Modern Municipios: Surveying as Power in Colonial Guatemala." *International Journal of Historical Archaeology* 18 (1): 175–203.

Scott, James C. 1990. *Domination and the Arts of Resistance.* New Haven, Conn.: Yale University Press.

Shaw, Justine M. 2008. *White Roads of the Yucatán: Changing Social Landscapes of the Yucatec Maya.* Tucson: University of Arizona Press.

Skoglund, Thanet, Barbara L. Stark, Hector Neff, and Michael Glascock. 2006. "Compositional and Stylistic Analysis of Aztec-Era Ceramics: Provincial Strategies at the Edge of Empire, South-Central Veracruz, Mexico." *Latin American Antiquity* 17 (4): 542–59.

Stanton, Travis W. 2012. "The Rise of Formative-Period Complex Societies in the Northern Maya Lowlands." In *The Oxford Handbook of Mesoamerican Archaeology*, edited by Deborah L. Nichols, 268–82. New York: Oxford University Press.

Stanton, Travis W., and Traci Ardren. 2005. "The Middle Formative of Yucatan in Context: The View from Yaxuna." *Ancient Mesoamerica* 16 (2): 213–28.

Stanton, Travis W., and David A. Freidel. 2005. "Placing the Centre, Centring the Place: The Influence of Formative Sacbeob in Classic Site Design at Yaxuna, Yucatan." *Cambridge Archaeological Journal* 16 (2): 225–49.

Stoddard, Robert. 1997. "Defining and Classifying Pilgrimages." *Geography Faculty Publications* 2:41–60.

Vallejo-Cáliz, Daniel, Scott R. Hutson, and Megan D. Parker. 2019. "Excavaciones en Ucí 2017." In *Proyecto Arqueológico Sacbé de Ucí/Cansahcab: Octava temporada de campo*, edited by Scott R. Hutson, 254–351. Informe técnico presentado al Instituto Nacional de Antropología e Historia, Mexico City.

Villa Rojas, Alfonso. 1934. "The Yaxuna-Cobá Causeway." *Contributions to American Archaeology* 2 (9): 187–208.

Voorhies, Barbara, and Margaret Arvey. 2016. "Classic-Period Ritual Ceramics from the Coast of Chiapas, Mexico." *Ancient Mesoamerica* 27 (1): 91–108.

Yaeger, Jason. 2000. "The Social Construction of Communities in the Classic Maya Countryside: Strategies of Affiliation in Western Belize." In *The Archaeology of Communities: A New World Perspective*, edited by Marcello A. Canuto and Jason Yaeger, 123–43. London: Routledge.

Zimmermann, Mario, Korey J. Brownstein, Luis R. Pantoja Díaz, Iliana Ancona Aragón, Scott R. Hutson, Barry Kidder, Shannon Tushingham, and David R. Gang. 2021. "Metabolomics Based Analysis of Miniature Flask Contents Identifies Tobacco Mixture Use Among the Ancient Maya." *Scientific Reports* 11:1590.

CHAPTER 2

The Axis Connecting Classic Maya Economy and Ritual at Xunantunich, Belize

BERNADETTE CAP, M. KATHRYN BROWN,
AND WHITNEY LYTLE

Avenues of movement between and within ancient Maya ceremonial centers were often formalized through the construction of *sakbe'ob* (causeways). These features, although not found at all ancient Maya sites, facilitated both intrasite and intersite connections, built for the transportation of people, goods, and information. The fact that extensive labor and resources were necessary to build and maintain sakbe'ob suggests that they were an important aspect of the built environment and likely served political, economic, and ideological functions.

In this chapter, we examine the role of sakbe'ob in the Classic period Maya polity of Xunantunich, Belize (figure 2.1), which presents an ideal setting to examine the integration of politics, ritual, and economy through activities conducted on and at the ends of the site's sakbe'ob. We focus on two of the three sakbe'ob at the site (Sakbe I and Sakbe II), which were part of the intentionally planned construction of Xunantunich to symbolically replicate aspects of the ancient Maya cosmos (Ashmore 1989; Fields 2004; Keller 2006). Sakbe I and Sakbe II connect the site's marketplace in the west to a ritual hilltop shrine group located in the east. At the center of these two features lies the political focus of the site, El Castillo, a 39 m tall acropolis. We suggest that the Xunantunich sakbe'ob served as an axis that connected economic and ritual activities. Furthermore, we argue that these built features functioned as processual routes associated with economic and ritual activities while reinforcing hierarchical relationships within the political landscape of the society.

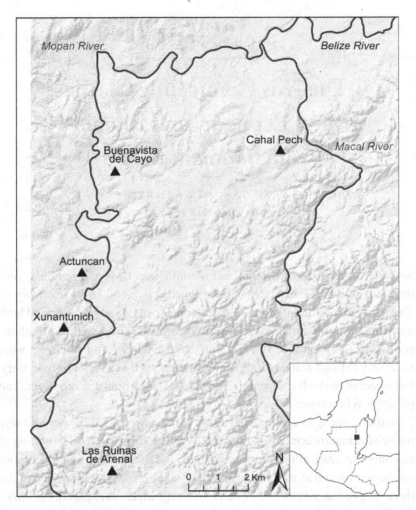

FIGURE 2.1 Location of Xunantunich within the Mopan River valley, Belize (created by the Mopan Valley Preclassic Project).

Maya Sakbe'ob, Ritual Processions, and Cosmological Aspects to Site Planning

Justine M. Shaw suggests that sakbe'ob serve several functions in ancient Maya society, including those "related to transport, boundary maintenance, water management, and religion" (Shaw 2001, 261; see also Shaw and Flores Colin, this volume). There is variability in the width, height, and length of sakbe'ob across the Maya lowlands, but Shaw (2001) has grouped them into two broad types based on the physical links they make: (1) intrasite sakbe'ob that connect major architectural groups within a site, and (2) intersite sakbe'ob that connect sites to each other. There has been much scholarly research on sakbe'ob focusing on the important connections that these roads made between significant architectural features as well as the connection between communities and even polities. Undoubtedly, the sakbe'ob destinations were important to the ancient Maya, as were the connections between these destinations (both intrasite and intersite). Since many of the chapters in this volume provide excellent summaries of the different functions of sakbe'ob (see, e.g., Shaw and Flores Colin, Stanton et al., and Vallejo-Cáliz and Hutson), we briefly highlight the economic and ceremonial aspects of these important built features as a backdrop for the case study we present in this chapter.

Sakbe'ob are recognized as having economic functions (Chase and Chase 1996), but interpretations have been generalized around their efficiency in moving goods and people across a landscape. This bias is due in part to categorizing the function of Maya urban centers primarily as ritual, royal, and administrative places. The recent influx in the identification of Classic period marketplace facilities (e.g., Cap 2015, Dahlin et al. 2010; Jones 1996, 2015; Shaw and King 2015; Wurtzburg 1991) has expanded our understanding of the Maya urban center and allows for a more targeted discussion of the economic functions of sakbe'ob. For example, a sakbe would have provided smoother physical transport to the marketplace and, in some cases, served as a guide to its location within the site.

Many scholars have focused on the role of sakbe'ob as ceremonial routes that start/end at important religious and political locations (Freidel and Sabloff 1984; Inomata 2006; Keller 2010). Additionally, places such as open plazas, ballcourts, and/or marketplaces would have been ideal beginning points and endpoints of intrasite sakbe'ob, thus providing formal access to economic and ceremonial hubs within ancient cities. Ritual processions to significant ceremonial buildings and features would have been an important aspect of religious ceremonies, and sakbe'ob would have served as key corridors for these ceremonies. These elevated roads were focal points for observation of ritual pageantry along processual pathways as the ceremonial destination, or sakbe endpoints likely would have been restricted to more privileged members of the society. The case study from Xunantunich illustrates this point nicely.

Ethnohistorical and ethnographic accounts from Mesoamerica are valuable resources that have been particularly helpful in shedding light on possible characteristics of ancient processions (e.g., Freidel and Sabloff 1984; Landa 1941; Lizana 1633; Villa Rojas 1934, 207–8). Focusing on the processional route, in a description of the religious pilgrimage center of Izamal in the early seventeenth century, Bernardo de Lizana (1633, chap. 3; see also Villa Rojas 1934, 189) wrote, "There they offered great alms and made pilgrimages from all parts, for which reason there have been made four roads or causeways to the four cardinal points. . . . So great was the concourse of People who assisted at these oracles of Itzamut-tul and Tiab-ul that they had made these roads." Lizana's comments illustrate the importance of site planning relative to the cardinal directions and the concept of centering on the landscape. These basic concepts are deeply rooted in Maya ideology and cosmology beginning as early as the Formative period as seen in the layout of early public architecture. In the case of Izamal, the sakbe'ob functioned as a means to center the site both physically and symbolically on the landscape.

Also key to understanding the significance of sakbe'ob is that the ancient Maya perceived the world as divided into four sectors based on the cardinal directions and linked in the center by the world tree. The world tree in turn connects the three vertical realms of the cosmos perceived by the Maya—the earthly realm, the sky realm, and the watery underworld (Schele and Freidel 1990). Each of the cardinal directions has a religious and symbolic meaning. For example, the east–west axis is tied to the sun's natural daily cycle of (re)birth and death. The north–south axis is also a complementary dualism with an association of the upperworld and the ancestors who reside there to the north and the underworld realm to the south (Ashmore 1991). Wendy Ashmore (1989, 1991) has noted there is a tendency for particular features to be associated with specific directions and therefore materials, patterns from which to create interpretations about Maya urban planning.

Xunantunich

The site of Xunantunich is composed of two ceremonial centers physically separated and distinct from each other (figure 2.2). One was a Late Classic ceremonial center and the second was thriving in the Formative period and is referred to as Early Xunantunich (Brown, Awe, and Garber 2018; Brown et al. 2017). We focus here on the Classic period of Xunantunich, which was a

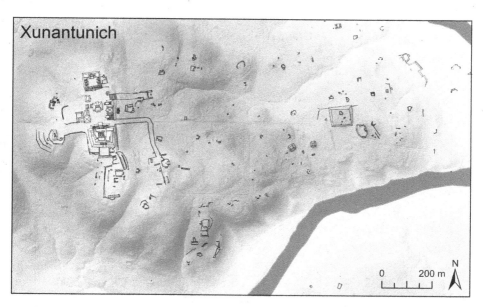

FIGURE 2.2 Map showing spatial relationship between Early and Classic period Xunantunich (created by the Mopan Valley Preclassic Project).

political capital for the Mopan River valley during the Late to Terminal Classic (AD 600 to 850; LeCount and Yaeger 2010; LeCount et al. 2002). While there is some evidence of Formative occupation buried under the Classic period architecture at Xunantunich, most of the ceremonial center was built over two hundred years due to a rapid coalescence of power (LeCount and Yaeger 2010; LeCount et al. 2002). Because it is rare for ancient Maya centers to have been this short-lived and not have a significant earlier occupation that guided later arrangement of architecture, Xunantunich presents a rare opportunity to examine the integration of sakbe'ob within the initial iteration and intentional design of an urban center.

The Sakbe'ob of Xunantunich

The Xunantunich center consists of four named architectural groups (Groups A to D) (figure 2.3). Within, between, and extending from the groups are three sakbe'ob—the Northwest Causeway, Sakbe I, and Sakbe II. Jason Yaeger (2000, fig. 3.2) documented a section of a sakbe running north–south between the architectural centers of Xunantunich and Actuncan, but further

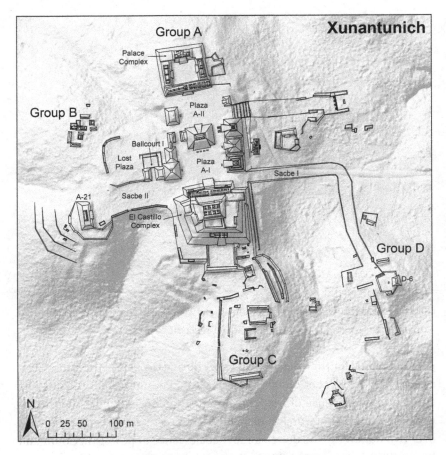

FIGURE 2.3 Site core of Classic period Xunantunich (created by the Mopan Valley Preclassic Project).

investigation is required to determine its extent and connection point to either site center. The Northwest Causeway is a core-outlier intrasite causeway that is a short 150 m in length and extends east from the northern portion of the site center into the near hinterlands. Sakbe I and II are classified as local intrasite causeways because they link architectural groups within Xunantunich. In this chapter, we limit our discussion to Sakbe I and II as these two features illustrate the integration processes that took place within the site center of Xunantunich.

Sakbe I and II were initially investigated by Angela Keller and Wendy Ashmore of the Xunantunich Archaeological Project. Keller's (2006) excavations revealed that both sakbe'ob were constructed using similar methods and materials. Stone parapets lined portions of their edges, which we take as an indication of a desire to clearly delineate their size and direction. Sakbe I and II were both constructed in the latter part of the Late Classic period, during the greatest period of construction in the Xunantunich center, suggesting that they were intentional and integral features of the urban plan.

The arrangement of the sakbe'ob and the other site center architecture created a cruciform pattern that Ashmore (1991) and Keller (2006, 2010) suggest is intentional and built to replicate Maya ideas of the cosmos and directionality. At the physical center of the site is the 39 m tall acropolis, El Castillo, which includes ritual architecture, *audiencias*, a palace, courtyards, and storage areas (Leventhal 2010; McCurdy 2016). Recent investigations on the eastern side of the complex have also identified what was likely a series of rooms used for the instruction of scribes/sages (Brown, McCurdy, and Yaeger, forthcoming; McCurdy, Brown, and Dixon 2018). Stucco-molded friezes on the uppermost east and west tiers of El Castillo would have added grandeur to its already impressive height. The imagery on both friezes, which is only partially preserved, references the sky realm and the rising of the sun (Fields 2004; Schele 1998, 491). On the western frieze are images associated with the underworld that may make connections to the setting sun (Fields 2004; Keller 2006).

Extending from the base of El Castillo are Sakbe I (to the east) and Sakbe II (to the west). Although constructed in similar ways, they differ in their physical configurations and dimensions. Therefore, we suggest that this would have affected the experience of observers and participants in the activities conducted along the sakbe'ob in different ways. Our examination of them takes into consideration the physicality of the sakbe'ob themselves and their relation to the features they connect in the urban center. From this, we infer the significance of them to be linked to the sociopolitical and economic organization of the site. The basis of this work is recent research conducted by the Mopan Valley Preclassic Project (MVPP), which has expanded our previous understanding of Sakbe I and II through the investigation of key places associated with these features (Cap 2019; Lytle 2020; Lytle et al. 2019).

Sakbe I

The entrance to Sakbe I is marked by an uncarved stela (Stela 5) between the El Castillo complex and Structure A-4 (a pyramidal structure used for ritual activities). The placement of a stela at an entryway is not uncommon and may have been a planned feature of cruciform architectural layouts (Christie 2005; Taube 1988). Around 20 m east of the stela and along the south parapet, Keller (2006, 308–9) discovered a concentration of obsidian blades that were larger in dimension than those found elsewhere in the site center. Within the same excavation area, she also recovered several ceramic drum fragments, pyrite mirror fragments, and one broken, crescent-shaped chert eccentric. These ritual objects are suggestive of ceremonial activity and some may have been offerings. They present a contrast to the sheet midden composed of ceramic sherds and lithic debris resting on the terrace surface along the west side of Str. A-4 where it abuts the Sakbe I north parapet. Thus, we believe that their placement near the threshold of Sakbe I was intentional and had symbolic meaning. Keller (2006) suggests that these special items may have been used in rituals and processions associated with the sakbe. For example, obsidian blades are well known in the Maya region to have been used in auto-sacrifice rituals. The inclusion of a chert eccentric is especially interesting in light of the predominance of this type of ritual implement seen at the end of Sakbe I at Group D.

Sakbe I is approximately 19 m wide along its full extent, which is half the width of Sakbe II. This narrow width may have been intentional and would have restricted access to the activities that took place along the causeway. Sakbe I extends 140 m to the east and then turns 90° to the south for another 145 m. It follows the natural topography of the landscape, which includes a 20 m dip in elevation toward the bend in both directions. The decision to not create a raised, level causeway also seems to have been intentional. Perhaps it was for the sake of efficiency; however, we consider the possibility that the slope of the road contributed to the symbolic meaning of activities that took place there. The interior portion of Sakbe I's bend abuts a large *aguada* (water storage feature). Pools of water, such as aguadas, had symbolic meaning for the Maya and represented portals to the watery underworld (Freidel, Schele, and Parker 1993; Scarborough 1998). The elevation difference on Sakbe I may have symbolized the ritual act of entering the underworld and returning to the earthly realm. In other words, movement along Sakbe I may reflect a transformational process (Keller 2006; see also Gillespie 1991; Ringle 1999). Keller (2006, 309) discovered a granite *mano* and *metate* (the handheld and base stones used for grinding maize) along the bend and lowest elevation point on Sakbe I, which is intriguing, as Andrea Stone (1995, 41) has noted that the Maya often placed grinding implements in caves (also considered an entryway into the underworld [see also Rojas Sandoval, Covarrubias Reyna, and Rissolo, this volume; and Moyes, this volume]). Because manos and metates were commonly used to grind corn, Keller (2006) suggests they might be linked to agricultural fertility rituals in this location. Thus, the bend in Sakbe I may have been a location for rituals, possibly associated with fertility and the underworld.

Sakbe I terminates at Group D, a natural hilltop on which was built an elevated platform complex with an eastern pyramidal shrine (Str. D-6). At the entrance to this group is an uncarved stela fragment (Stela 12) (Braswell 1998) that mirrors Stela 5 at the opposite end of Sakbe I. Initial investigations of Group D were conducted by Jennifer Braswell in the 1990s as part of the Xunantunich Archaeology Project. More recently, Whitney Lytle (Mopan Valley Preclassic Project) conducted extensive excavations of the central platform (Str. D-8) and the eastern shrine (Str. D-6) of Group D that reshapes the interpretation of the group and use of Sakbe I (Lytle 2020; Lytle et al. 2019).

Buried within the Group D central platform (Str. D-8), Lytle (2020) found a small Formative platform or altar-like feature with two phases (Str. D-8-sub-a and Str. D-8-sub-b). This is the earliest architectural feature found thus far on the hilltop. The small platform/altar feature was associated with thousands of Formative ceramic sherds that have been interpreted as the remains of cyclical ritual activities (Lytle 2020; Lytle et al. 2019). This hilltop location was part of a larger sacred landscape centered on the Formative E Group at Early Xunantunich (Brown and Yaeger 2020). This hilltop location and the small, altar-like platform appear to have been a ritual destination during the Formative period. By the end of the Late Formative, however, the location was no longer in use, likely corresponding to the abandonment of Early Xunantunich.

During the Late Classic period, this hilltop location was again used as a ritual destination. The small altar/platform was covered over by a large, raised platform (Str. D-8). Str. D-6, a 6 m tall eastern pyramidal structure, was built atop the elevated platform. Several other structures were also built nearby. Jennifer B. Braswell (1998) originally suggested Group D was an elite residential group; however, MVPP's recent investigations have expanded our understanding of the primary function of the group. Lytle (2020) argues that the group was used for specialized ritual practices centering on the veneration of important ancestors buried in Str. D-6. The excavations of Str. D-6

FIGURE 2.4 Carved marine shell pendant found in a burial in Str. D-6 (created by the Mopan Valley Preclassic Project).

demonstrate that the final phase of the pyramid had three (possibly four) rooms, set one behind the other on the central axis. Several elaborate burials and caches were placed within the structure. We highlight just two of the internments here because they provide intriguing evidence to suggest that those laid to rest in Str. D-6 may have been ritual specialists.

Within a crypt resting directly on bedrock at the base of, and below, the Str. D-6 central staircase were two individuals—an adult male placed in an extended position with his head to the south (a common burial pattern for the Belize River valley) and a bundle-burial of a child in the corner of the crypt (Lytle 2020). The adult male was interred with a single, long obsidian blade at his pelvis area and two carved marine shell disks located near his shoulders (figure 2.4). The marine shell disks had drilled suspension holes and were likely worn as a headdress or ear ornaments. These intricately carved objects had identical carved iconography in reverse that depicts a seated deer-headed individual in ritual transformation with both eyes popped out from the eye socket and dangling from the optic nerve (Lytle 2020). The individual holds one eye in their hand while the other arches over their head and peers at a feathered serpent, likely the vision serpent, that is curved around the individual's back.

David Stuart and Stephen Houston (Houston and Stuart 1989; Stuart 2005) have discussed similarly depicted creatures in Maya art as representing a *way*—a spirit animal-like creature with shamanic power or manifestations of spells or curses sorcerers use to influence others. Similar creatures to those depicted in Group D, Str. D-6, shell ornaments that have been termed the "eye great deer" way (Helmke and Nielsen 2009; Stuart 2005) are a separate entity from that of other deer iconographic representations. The "eye deer" is frequently depicted with a coiled serpent, which Christophe Helmke and Jesper Nielsen (2009, 73) propose may "represent cramps and spasms affecting the orbits and the organs of sight." Noting that the word for deer in several Maya dialects is used in reference to types of cramping ailments, Matthew Looper (2019, 178) suggests that variations in the illustration of deer way may reflect differing types of cramps. For example, the way named "Mok" or "Chij" is often depicted with a serpent and occasionally with vines extruding from empty eye sockets (Looper 2019, 175), whereas the "eye-deer," "Hutis Chij," is most often shown with dangling eyeballs but no snake imagery (Grube and Nahm 1994, 692; Looper 2019, 175).

These carved marine shell ornaments, paired with the intact obsidian bloodletting implement, may provide clues to the role served in life by the individual interred within this crypt (Lytle et al. 2019), just as objects interred with Maya kings and queens reflect their status. It seems plausible that these items associate the individual with ritual practices involving ways, perhaps even the specific "eye-deer" way. Indeed, he may have possessed shamanic or curative abilities and served as a shaman or sage within the community of Xunantunich.

Excavations also revealed a crypt burial capped with large stones beneath the floor of the central room of Str. D-6. It held the comingled remains of three individuals, with one that appears to be the primary internment (Lytle 2020). Grave goods within the crypt included marine shell ornaments (some of which had colored shell and stone inlays), animal tooth pendants (likely dog), obsidian and chert eccentrics, obsidian blades, and jade objects (Lytle 2020). Although all these objects are typically associated with elite individuals, it is interesting to note the lack of ceramic vessels within this burial as well as the one described previously. Lytle (2020) has suggested that the lack of ceramic objects typically found with high-status individuals may signal that the persons buried within Str. D-6 had a special role within the community.

Resting atop the crypt's southernmost capstone was a layered offering that contained more than twenty eccentrics, animal bones (bird and caiman), coral fragments, and marine shells (three spondylus and one large bivalve acting as a lid to a spondylus shell). Fourteen of the clustered eccentrics are chert with the identifiable forms of centipedes and scorpions, notched flakes, and a possible crocodile and bundled form. Six of the eccentrics are obsidian and include identifiable forms such as a crescent and several centipedes and/or scorpions. In the upper layer of the offering were bird bones, while caiman bones were in the lowest layers. This layered cache symbolically represents the Maya cosmos, including the sky realm (bird remains), the three-stone place (represented by the marine shells), and the watery underworld (caiman, marine shells, and coral) (Lytle 2020). Furthermore, the eccentrics also likely represent other important symbolic aspects of the cosmos. This important cache appears to be dedicated to the interred person and/or persons.

Several other bundled caches of eccentrics were found at the base and near the summit of Str. D-6, which further emphasizes the sacred nature of this burial shrine within the Xunantunich community (Lytle 2020). This, coupled with the fact that this small eastern shrine was situated on a hilltop to the east of the Classic period ceremonial core and attached to the core by a rather narrow sakbe (Sakbe I), has strong implications for its ritual significance and likely more restricted access. It is interesting to juxtapose Sakbe I and Group D with the more public nature of Sakbe II and its associated spaces.

Sakbe II

Sakbe II extends in a straight path west of the El Castillo complex for 136 m (figure 2.5). It is double the width of Sakbe I, measuring 40 m across. Given these dimensions, Sakbe II has a slightly larger footprint and was a space more conducive to accommodating larger crowds. At the terminus of Sakbe II is Str. A-21, a double-tiered platform. A possible displaced stela fragment was found near the eastern face of Str. A-21, but none were present at the entrance to Sakbe II.

Str. A-21 was constructed in a single phase and did not exhibit evidence of a superstructure (Keller 2006, 375–88). Additionally, it has a central staircase with nine steps on the lower tier and four on the upper tier, for a total of thirteen stairs. The numbers nine and thirteen have significance among the Maya because they represent layers of the underworld (nine) and sky realm (thirteen). Thus, Str. A-21 also provides symbolic connections to the cosmos, albeit more subtly than symbolism present within the highly visible stucco frieze iconographic programs on El Castillo and the symbolically charged offerings within Str. D-6.

The Axis Connecting Classic Maya Economy and Ritual   61

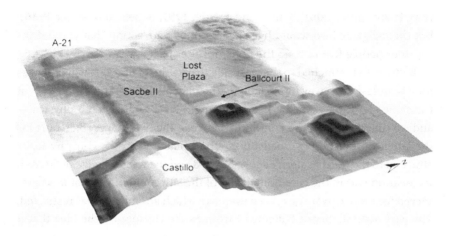

FIGURE 2.5 3D view of Sakbe II's layout in relation to other features (created by the Mopan Valley Preclassic Project).

Keller (2006) recovered a jade bead and ceramic sherds from *incensarios* (ceramic vessels for burning incense) within the collapse of Str. A-21 and a nearby midden. She interpreted these finds as evidence of ritual activities that could include performances atop the Str. A-21 platform and processions conducted along Sakbe II. Based on these items, one can imagine rituals filled with music, smoke, and fire, as well as elaborately adorned elites.

The width of Sakbe II was limited by a steep slope to the south and a nearly 1 m rise in the bedrock to the north. The southern edge is made up of a formally constructed parapet that clearly delimits it. On the sakbe's northern edge are a ballcourt (Ballcourt I) and marketplace (referred to as the Lost Plaza). A short staircase was built between Sakbe II and the marketplace, thus extending the amount of activity space available (see figure 2.5). Examples of spatial proximity of ballcourts and marketplaces with sakbe'ob have been found at other sites such as Tikal (Jones 1996, 2015), Chunchucmil (Dahlin et al. 2010), and Blue Creek (Thomas Guderjan, personal communication, 2020). Their co-occurrence is suggestive of the importance of making physical links to economic and public ritual spaces.

Scholars (e.g., Ashmore 1989; Schele and Miller 1986; Tedlock 1996) have noted that the ballgame was an important part of Maya mythology as symbolic entrances to the underworld. The ballgame ritual was likely performed by elite individuals who were playing out a role to maintain cosmic order

(Fox 1996; Miller 2001; Schele and Freidel 1991; Schele and Miller 1986), but the ballgame also would have been a public attraction that could draw together people from across the polity for the spectacle.

Ballcourt I is attached to the west side (backside) of Str. A-7, which makes for a seamless entryway into Sakbe II. The playing floor of the ballcourt is at the same elevation as Sakbe II, which would have established a physical—and we suggest symbolic—continuity between the two spaces. Ballcourt I is the larger of the site's two ballcourts. The smaller Ballcourt II is physically attached to the northeastern edge of Str. A-8 and the western edge of Str. A-1. Its location within the ceremonial core of the site could mean that it was reserved for more private or special events in which attendance was restricted. The easy accessibility of Ballcourt I from Sakbe II supports the idea that it likely served a wider audience and played a more public role within the city.

Adjacent to both Ballcourt I and Sakbe II is the Lost Plaza, the location of a marketplace (Cap 2019; Keller 2006). Low, limestone, cobble platforms found in several areas of the plaza are interpreted as the remains of vendor stall foundations. Each is associated with one type of raw material used to make items, such as chert and obsidian. Two areas are dominated by chert end-stage biface production debris and flakes resulting from the resharpening of tools. Obsidian debris is concentrated in a different area of the marketplace. Only a few whole or large obsidian blade fragments and broken chert bifaces were recovered. This is to be expected in a marketplace where finished goods were purchased and used elsewhere (Cap 2015; Hirth 2009). The predominance of production debris indicates that stone tools were bought directly from their makers. Given that most of this debris was from the final stages of production, it appears that vendor-producers maximized the limited space within the marketplace.

In addition to the evidence for stone-cutting tools, Bernadette Cap (2019) discovered a cluster of limestone spindle whorls near the obsidian production area. Whether the whorls or the thread made by the whorls (or both) were the saleable items is not clear, but they are evidence for the inclusion of textile production within the network of marketplace exchange.

Cap's (2019) excavations also revealed clusters of broken ceramics and chemical signatures indicative of organics, which points to the possibility of the exchange of food products as well. The recent discovery of the murals depicting vibrant scenes of exchange at the Calakmul marketplace, which includes ceramics and food goods, reinforces the interpretation of the Lost

Plaza as a marketplace. The murals also demonstrate the public aspect of these important economic features within ancient Maya sites (Martin 2012).

With only a few studies of Classic Maya marketplace facilities across the lowlands (e.g., Cap 2015; Dahlin et al. 2010; King 2015; Roche Recinos 2021), we currently do not have the data to suggest widespread directional patterning of market placement within different sites; however, in the known cases, marketplaces are found within public zones, often near civic/ceremonial buildings, suggesting that market and public ritual events may have occasionally coincided. This is certainly the case at the Classic site core of Xunantunich, where it seems that the placement of the marketplace on the west side of the ceremonial precinct connected by a sakbe may have facilitated the integration of economic and ritual activities.

Further connecting economy to ritual is the ancient Maya merchant deity—God L—who in Maya ideology resides in the underworld (Schele and Friedel 1990). The placement of the Xunantunich marketplace on the western side of the site core may have symbolically linked it to the underworld through activities associated with God L. Often depicted as an old man, God L typically is dressed in the trappings of an elite personage, such as a jaguar pelt and feline-shaped ears (Taube 1992). However, he is sometimes shown as subordinate to upperworld deities, and a few Classic period vessels have images of God L stripped of his clothing and kicked by deities of the upperworld (Miller and Martin 2004). Although God L appears to have been powerful and wealthy, these visual clues reinforce the superordinate position of upperworld deities. By extension, these implicit iconographic messages may have been a reminder to wealthy marketplace vendors of their subordinate position to more prominent Maya elites and the ruling family. For example, a panel from Palenque's Temple of the Sun shows God L and another deity from the underworld slumped at the feet of Pakal and his son. The two deities are symbolically holding the burden of warfare and sacrifice on their shoulders (Schele and Freidel 1990, 243, fig. 6.13). This panel places the position of God L beneath that of King Pakal and links him to underworld themes of sacrifice.

Therefore, we believe that at Xunantunich, the placement of the marketplace on the west side of the ceremonial core may have been an intentional decision to connect broad ideological concepts of travel, trade, and the underworld with the exchange hub of the city. Whether this arrangement indicates some level of elite control in market exchange is up for debate.

Public attractions, such as the marketplace and ballcourt, would have presented opportunities for the elite to demonstrate their power and authority, thus reinforcing and legitimizing their elevated role in society. The strategic placement of the marketplace within the site core would have made it possible for political elites to monitor marketplace activities and the accumulation of wealth by traders. This again would have been important for maintaining economic control to some degree but more broadly to maintain the implicit hierarchy of prominent elites over the marketplace vendors regardless of the accumulation of wealth.

Conclusion

Xunantunich provides an excellent case study for understanding intentional site-planning efforts by Maya rulers since the Classic period site core was built over a relatively short time frame during the Late Classic period. As the likely master planners of the site core, Xunantunich rulers appear to have designed a city to hold activities that would draw a wide audience, including market exchange, public events, and religious celebrations. Such activities would have had dual functions. As they worked to build an inclusive community among hinterland populations, they also would have included aspects of exclusion to reinforce the powerful role of the ruling elite. The design of Sakbe I and Sakbe II epitomizes this duality as they connected key places and spaces related to public and private activities.

Royal rulership among the Maya was in part based on creating links to important ancestors and deities. Thus, embedding important ideological concepts within the built features of the site's center would have reinforced the social order and legitimized the authority of the ruling elites. Given the short timeframe in which Classic period Xunantunich expanded in the Late Classic, rulers may have required more overt, physical expressions of their power. The configuration of Sakbe I as a narrower walkway implies a restricted number of participants and exclusive activities along its surface. The symbolism of traveling from the earthly realm, skirting the edge of a large watery place (aguada), and re-emergence in the earthly realm along Sakbe I may have been a sacred path that not all community members could traverse. Sakbe I terminated at a historic place (Formative Group D), which seems unlikely to be coincidental. Classic period activities at Group D, in particular Str. D-6, reanimated the group as a sacred place. Therefore, we interpret

Sakbe I as a restricted ritual avenue where the primary performers and participants in rituals and processions along it were elite members of society and ritual practitioners. As such, the restricted ritual activities occurring on Sakbe I and in Group D would have reaffirmed hierarchical order at the site.

In contrast, we view Sakbe II as a public space for activities that facilitated interactions and integration in part due to its wider width. From Sakbe II, one would also have open access to Ballcourt I and the marketplace located in the Lost Plaza. Sakbe II terminates at Str. A-21, a two-tiered building without an obvious superstructure, which may have been a platform for performance and hosting public events. It is likely that elites also would have sponsored public events to legitimize their authority. The placement of Ballcourt I in the west symbolically references the underworld. Also linked to the underworld is the marketplace, through ties to God L, the merchant deity that resides in the underworld. God L has a lower status relative to other deities, which may have been mirrored in the status and perception of Maya merchants. The ability to gain wealth through trade could have posed a threat to royal elites. These elites likely would have had a great interest in monitoring the accumulation of wealth by merchants. One way to do so would be to incorporate a center of trade into the site core on which they could keep a watchful eye. They could also control the movement of people in and out of the marketplace through the construction of Sakbe II. Most of the goods recovered in the marketplace would be those used in the household, indicating that it served an important role in integrating household economies and social networks. Thus, the social order of the society as a whole could be reinforced when everyday people participating in the marketplace could witness the important political and sacred rituals that were conducted in the site core and overseen by the ruling elite.

Although the restricted access of Sakbe I and the open nature of Sakbe II present a contrast, we view them as complementary. We envision processions starting or ending at either of the sakbe'ob. Those that took place on Sakbe II included crowds of people that could participate in the ritual celebration. The procession would then pass through the site core in front of the awe-inspiring El Castillo acropolis. When the ritual procession entered the restricted accessway of Sakbe I, a smaller segment of society would have had visual access to the ritual event. The shifts between public and private would have both legitimized and reinforced the hierarchical social system of the community. The intentional cruciform design of Classic period Xunantunich may have been a strategic way for rulers to connect ritual and economy, thus consolidating their power through private and public activities at the end of their roads.

Works Cited

Ashmore, Wendy. 1989. "Construction and Cosmology: Politics and Ideology in Lowland Maya Settlement Patterns." In *Word and Image in Maya Culture: Explorations in Language, Writing, and Representation*, edited by William F. Hanks and Don S. Rice, 272–86. Salt Lake City: University of Utah Press.

Ashmore, Wendy. 1991. "Site-Planning Principles and Concepts of Directionality Among the Ancient Maya." *Latin American Antiquity* 2 (3): 199–226.

Braswell, Jennifer B. 1998. "Archaeological Investigations at Group D, Xunantunich, Belize." PhD diss., Tulane University.

Brown, M. Kathryn, Jaime Awe, and James F. Garber. 2018. "The Role of Ritual in the Foundation of Social Complexity in the Belize River Valley." In *Pathways to Complexity: A View from the Maya Lowlands*, edited by M. Kathryn Brown and George Bey III, 87–116. Gainesville: University Press of Florida.

Brown, M. Kathryn, Whitney Lytle, Zoe Rawski, Victoria Ingalls, and Alessandra Villareal. 2017. "Understanding the Preclassic Ritual Landscape in the Mopan River Valley: A View from Early Xunantunich." *Research Reports in Belizean Archaeology* 14:53–64.

Brown, M. Kathryn, Leah McCurdy, and Jason Yaeger. Forthcoming. "Chamber of Secrets at Xunantunich." In *Maya Materialization of Time: History and Prophecy in Long-Term Perspective*, edited by David Freidel, Arlen Chase, Diane Chase, and Anne Dowd. Gainesville: University Press of Florida.

Brown, M. Kathryn, and Jason Yaeger. 2020. "Monumental Landscapes, Changing Ideologies, and Political Histories in the Mopan Valley." In *Approaches to Monumental Landscapes of the Ancient Maya*, edited by Brett A. Houk, Barbara Arroyo, and Terry G. Powis, 290–312. Gainesville: University Press of Florida.

Cap, Bernadette. 2015. "Classic Maya Economies: Identification of a Marketplace at Buenavista del Cayo." PhD diss., University of Wisconsin–Madison.

Cap, Bernadette. 2019. "A Classic Maya Marketplace at Xunantunich, Belize." *Research Reports in Belizean Archaeology* 16:111–22.

Chase, Arlen F., and Diane Z. Chase. 1996. "More than Kin and King: Centralized Political Organization Among the Ancient Maya." *Current Anthropology* 37 (5): 803–10.

Christie, Jessica J. 2005. "The Stela as a Cultural Symbol in Classic and Contemporary Maya Societies." *Ancient Mesoamerica* 16 (2): 277–89.

Dahlin, Bruce H., Daniel A. Bair, Timothy Beach, Matthew Moriarty, and Richard E. Terry. 2010. "The Dirt on Food: Ancient Feasts and Markets Among the Lowland Maya." In *Precolumbian Foodways: Interdisciplinary Approaches to Food, Culture, and Markets to Ancient Mesoamerica*, edited by John E. Staller and Michael Carrasco, 191–232. New York: Springer.

Fields, Virginia M. 2004. "The Royal Charter at Xunantunich." In *The Ancient Maya of the Belize Valley: Half a Century of Archaeological Research*, edited by James F. Garber, 180–90. Gainesville: University Press of Florida.

Fox, John G. 1996. "Playing with Power: Ballcourts and Political Ritual in Southern Mesoamerica." *Current Anthropology* 37 (3): 483–509.

Freidel, David A., and Jeremy Sabloff. 1984. *Cozumel: Late Maya Settlement Patterns*. New York: Academic Press.

Freidel, David A., Linda Schele, and Joy Parker. 1993. *Maya Cosmos: Three Thousand Years on the Shaman's Path*. New York: William Morrow.

Gillespie, Susan. 1991. "Ballgames and Boundaries." In *Mesoamerican Ballgame*, edited by Vernon L. Scarborough and David R. Wilcox, 317–45. Tucson: University of Arizona Press.

Grube, Nicholai, and Werner Nahm. 1994. "A Census of Xibalba: A Complete Inventory of 'Way' Characters on Maya Ceramics." In *The Maya Vase Book: A Corpus of Rollout Photography of Maya Vases*, vol. 4, edited by Barbara Kerr and Justin Kerr, 686–715. New York: Kerr Associates.

Helmke, Christophe, and Jesper Neilsen. 2009. "Hidden Identity and Power in Ancient Mesoamerica: Supernatural Alter Egos as Personified Diseases." *Acta Americana* 17 (2): 49–98.

Hirth, Kenneth G. 2009. "Craft Production, Household Diversification, and Domestic Economy in Prehispanic Mesoamerica." In *Housework: Craft Production and Domestic Economy in Ancient Mesoamerica*, edited by Kenneth G. Hirth, 13–32. Archaeological Papers of the American Anthropological Association 19. Hoboken, N.J.: Wiley.

Houston, Stephen, and David Stuart. 1989. "The *Way* Glyph: Evidence for 'Co-essences' Among the Classic Maya." *Research Reports on Ancient Maya Writing* 30:1–16.

Inomata, Takeshi. 2006. "Plazas, Performers, and Spectators: Political Theaters of the Classic Maya." *Current Anthropology* 47 (5): 805–42.

Jones, Christopher. 1996. *Excavations on the East Plaza of Tikal*. Tikal Report no. 16. Vol. 1. Philadelphia: University Museum, University of Pennsylvania.

Jones, Christopher. 2015. "The Marketplace at Tikal." In *The Ancient Maya Marketplace: The Archaeology of Transient Space*, edited by Eleanor M. King, 67–90. Tucson: University of Arizona Press.

Keller, Angela. 2006. "Roads to the Center: The Design, Use, and Meaning of the Roads of Xunantunich, Belize." PhD diss., University of Pennsylvania.

Keller, Angela. 2010. "The Social Construction of Roads at Xunantunich, from Design to Abandonment." In *Classic Maya Provincial Politics: Xunantunich and Its Hinterlands*, edited by Lisa J. LeCount and Jason Yaeger, 187–208. Tucson: University of Arizona Press.

King, Eleanor, ed. 2015. *The Ancient Maya Marketplace: The Archaeology of Transient Space*. Tucson: University of Arizona Press.

LeCount, Lisa J., and Jason Yaeger, eds. 2010. *Classic Maya Provincial Politics: Xunantunich and Its Hinterlands*. Tucson: University of Arizona Press.

LeCount, Lisa J., Jason Yaeger, Richard M. Leventhal, and Wendy Ashmore. 2002. "Dating the Rise and Fall of Xunantunich, Belize: A Late and Terminal Classic Lowland Maya Regional Center." *Ancient Mesoamerica* 13 (1): 41–63.

Leventhal, Richard. 2010. "Changing Places: The Castillo and the Structure of Power at Xunantunich." In *Classic Maya Provincial Politics: Xunantunich and Its Hinterlands*, edited by Lisa J. LeCount and Jason Yaeger, 79–96. Tucson: University of Arizona Press.

Lizana, Bernado de. 1633. *Historia de Yucatán*. Mexico City: Museo Nacional de México.

Looper, Matthew. 2019. *The Beast Between: Deer in Maya Art and Culture*. Austin: University of Texas Press.

Lytle, Whitney. 2020. "A Diachronic Approach to the Sociopolitical Role of Ancestor Veneration at Xunantunich Group D, Belize." PhD diss., University of Texas at San Antonio.

Lytle, Whitney, M. Kathryn Brown, Rachel Horowitz, and Carolyn Freiwald. 2019. "Late Classic Burials and Eccentric Caches from Structure D-6 at Xunantunich." *Research Reports in Belizean Archaeology* 16:123–31.

Martin, Simon. 2012. "Hieroglyphs from the Painted Pyramid: The Epigraphy of Chiik Nahb Structure Sub 1-4, Calakmul, Mexico." In *Maya Archaeology 2*, edited by Charles Golden, Stephen Houston, and Joel Skidmore, 60–81. San Francisco: Precolumbia Mesoweb Press.

McCurdy, Leah. 2016. "Building Xunantunich: Public Building in an Ancient Maya Community." PhD diss., University of Texas at San Antonio.

McCurdy, Leah, M. Kathryn Brown, and Neil Dixon. 2018. "Tagged Walls: The Discovery of Ancient Maya Graffiti at El Castillo, Xunantunich." *Research Reports in Belizean Archaeology* 15:181–94.

Miller, Mary. 2001. "The Maya Ballgame: Rebirth in the Court of Life and Death." In *The Sport of Life and Death: The Mesoamerican Ballgame*, edited by E. Michael Whittington, 79–87. Charlotte, N.C.: Mint Museum of Art.

Miller, Mary, and Simon Martin. 2004. "The Divine Models of Courtly Culture." In *Courtly Art of the Ancient Maya*, edited by Mary Miller and Simon Martin, 51–65. New York: Thames and Hudson.

Ringle, William M. 1999. "Pre-Classic Cityscapes: Ritual Politics Among the Early Lowland Maya." In *Social Patterns in Pre-Classic Mesoamerica*, edited by David C. Grove and Rosemary M. Joyce, 183–224. Washington, D.C.: Dumbarton Oaks Research Library and Collection.

Roche Recinos, Alejandra. 2021. "Regional Production and Exchange of Stone Tools in the Maya Polity of Piedras Negras, Guatemala." PhD diss., Brown University.

Scarborough, Vernon L. 1998. "Ecology and Ritual: Water Management and the Maya." *Latin American Antiquity* 9 (2): 135–59.

Schele, Linda. 1998. "The Iconography of Maya Architectural Facades During the Late Classic Period." In *Function and Meaning in Classic Maya Architecture*, edited by Stephen D. Houston, 479–518. Washington, D.C.: Dumbarton Oaks Research Library and Collection.

Schele, Linda, and David Freidel. 1990. *A Forest of Kings: The Untold Story of the Ancient Maya*. New York: William Morrow.

Schele, Linda, and David Freidel. 1991. "The Courts of Creation: Ballcourts, Ballgames, and Portals to the Maya Otherworld." In *The Mesoamerican Ballgame*, edited by Vernon L. Scarborough and David R. Wilcox, 289–316. Tucson: University of Arizona Press.

Schele, Linda, and Mary E. Miller. 1986. *The Blood of Kings: Dynasty and Ritual in Maya Art*. Fort Worth: Kimbell Art Museum.

Shaw, Justine M. 2001. "Maya *Sacbeob*: Form and Function." *Ancient Mesoamerica* 12 (2): 261–72.

Shaw, Leslie C., and Eleanor M. King. 2015. "The Maya Marketplace at Maax Na, Belize." In *The Ancient Maya Marketplace: The Archaeology of Transient Space*, edited by Eleanor M. King and Leslie C. Shaw, 168–94. Tucson: University of Arizona Press.

Stone, Andrea. 1995. *Images from the Underworld: Naj Tunich and the Tradition of Maya Cave Painting*. Austin: University of Texas Press.

Stuart, David. 2005. *Glyphs on Pots: Decoding Classic Maya Ceramics*. Sourcebook for the 2005 Maya Meetings at Texas, Department of Art and Art History. Austin: University of Texas at Austin.

Taube, Karl A. 1988. "The Ancient Yucatec New Year Festival: The Liminal Period in Maya Ritual and Cosmology." PhD diss., Yale University.

Taube, Karl A. 1992. *The Major Gods of Ancient Yucatan*. Washington, D.C.: Dumbarton Oaks Research Library and Collection.

Tedlock, Dennis. 1996. *Popul Vuh: The Definitive Edition of the Mayan Book of the Dawn of Life and the Glories of God and Kings*. New York: Simon and Schuster.

Tozzer, Alfred M., trans. 1941. *Landa's Relación de las cosas de Yucatán*. Peabody Museum of Archaeology and Ethnology 18. Cambridge, Mass.: Harvard University.

Villa Rojas, Alfonso. 1934. *The Yaxuna-Coba Causeway*. Publication 436. Washington, D.C.: Carnegie Institution of Washington.

Wurtzburg, Susan J. 1991. "Sayil: Investigations of Urbanism and Economic Organization at an Ancient Maya City." PhD diss., State University of New York.

Yaeger, Jason. 2000. "Changing Patterns of Social Organization: The Late and Terminal Classic Communities at San Lorenzo, Cayo District, Belize." PhD diss., University of Pennsylvania.

CHAPTER 3

Roads, Temples, and the Community Boundaries of Cobá, Quintana Roo

TRAVIS W. STANTON, TRACI ARDREN, NICOLAS C. BARTH,
JUAN FERNANDEZ DIAZ, STEPHANIE J. MILLER, KARL A.
TAUBE, PATRICK ROHRER, ELIZABETH BECKNER, AND
ALINE MAGNONI

Defining the boundaries of sites has always been challenging for archaeologists (e.g., Willey and Phillips 1958, 18). These challenges have to do with the arbitrariness of separating the distribution of material culture on a landscape into meaningful categories, but they also have to do with the different treatments of the term *site* itself. In Robert C. Dunnell's (1992, 21) words, the term *site* "usually provides the framework for recording artifact provenience; it usually serves as a sampling frame at some level in most fieldwork (e.g., Binford 1964; McManamon 1981; Redman 1973); and, largely by default, it, or some partitioning of it (e.g., Dewar 1986), serves as a unit of artifact association." Yet, as Dunnell further notes, the term has been associated with the notion of place, in particular locations on the landscape where clusters of "things" such as architecture or artifacts are found: "spatial aggregates of archaeological significance" (1992, 36) or a "discreet and potentially interpretable locus of cultural materials" (Plog, Plog, and Wait 1978, 389). Frank Hole and Robert F. Heizer (1973, 86–87, quoted in Dunnell 1992, 23) even go as far as to include single artifact finds in their definition of sites, effectively conflating the term *site* with that of provenience: "A site is any place, large or small, where there are to be found traces of ancient occupation or activity. The usual clue is the presence of artifacts. . . . Some [sites] . . . are as large as a city, others as small as the spot where an arrowhead lies." Other definitions of sites emphasize aspects such as the continuity of the distributions of material culture (Willey and Phillips 1958, 18) and their spatial relationships (Binford 1964, 431; 1992; see also Dunnell 1992, 24).

As archaeologists are well aware, regardless of the definition of *site* employed, the distribution of material culture is often not as spatially discrete as we might want (see McCoy 2020). Sites, places, or units, whether they are characterized by lithic scatters or housemounds, are rarely neat and tidy, leading some to discuss the utility of "siteless" archaeology, where artifacts and features are simply located in three-dimensional space (see Dunnell 1992; Dunnell and Dancy 1983; Foley 1981; Sullivan, Mink, and Uphus 2007; D. Thomas 1975). Even in cases where features such as city walls exist, the spatial distribution of material culture often presents ambiguities, thus allowing more room for variability in how archaeologists choose to partition and define site boundaries. Maybe there are house foundations, terraces, or field walls outside those city walls, and while they may not occur with great frequency, surveys show that they consistently occur over the landscape until the next city with well-defined walls appears; where to draw lines between sites (creating useful units of archaeological analysis) in such cases is not cut and dry. Further complicating matters, change in the spatial distributions of clusters of "things" can occur over time. A small city usually increases in size, engulfing the once spatially and socially discrete communities that surrounded it. Or, deflation of the ground surface (or other formation processes; see Foley 1981, 10–14) can create giant contiguous spatial palimpsests of what were once numerous small camps across a landscape occupied for hundreds of thousands of years. Ultimately, as with all archaeological data, sites are modern phenomena, although we hope that they reflect archaeologically recoverable meanings that past peoples ascribed to the landscape. As this volume illustrates, the meanings we recover, especially in relation to the boundary or border of ancient sites, can and will be interpreted in many ways.

Faced with these challenges, archaeologists have either tended to treat the concept of sites as wholly heuristic devices, etic analytical categories created by archaeologists in the present to systematically treat a wide range of material phenomena across landscapes, or as real phenomena that meaningfully represent past behavior and organization, in some cases going as far as to suggest they are emic categories that can be gleaned from the data. While all those that use the site concept share a common initial goal of identifying discrete empirical units in the archaeological landscape that are comparable (Willey and Phillips 1958, 18), archaeologists differ in their willingness to assert that these material groupings reflect culturally meaningful social entities of the past (see Ingold 1986; Wilson 1988, 50). Emic approaches have been applied in particular contexts where historical data are found bearing on these kinds of questions, where spatial data tend to be very discreet, or where some sort of material data have been interpreted as an emic boundary (e.g., Kemp 2012; see also Bradley 1994, 100).

In the Maya lowlands, there has been an overwhelming tendency to use the concept of site as a unit of archaeological analysis that can tell us something about how the Maya of the past organized themselves. Sites tend to be phenomena like cities, towns, workshops, or pilgrimage destinations such as caves (see Rojas Sandoval, Covarrubias Reyna, and Rissolo, this volume; and Moyes, this volume), or places we believe had intrinsic meaning for the people that inhabited and used them. More recently there has been an increased emphasis on landscape archaeology (see Ardren and Lowry 2011; Brady and Ashmore 1999; Stanton and Magnoni 2008), in some ways moving further away from the idea that the focus of analysis should be on drawing solid boundaries around sites and more toward a focus on the meanings of places (that we often still call sites). This work has stressed the cultural importance of place among the lowland Maya and further fostered the perspective that archaeologists *can* approach sites as emic cultural constructions and meaningful places. Perhaps the popularity of this perspective is due, in part, to vast evidence for monument construction linked to polity names or Maya names used by modern or historic local communities (some of which also match readings of emblem glyphs from the Classic period [e.g., Grube 2004]). Regardless of the reason, the landscape perspective may have in some ways drawn attention away from the quantitative approaches to defining sites in recent years, quantitative approaches that historically were slow to gain traction given the difficulties in identifying material remains on the surface of the low-visibility Maya tropical environment (Sharer and Ashmore 1979, 72; but see Smith and Alonso Olvera, this volume). In the age of Light Detection and Radar (LiDAR) (Canuto et al. 2018; Chase, Chase, and Weishampel 2010, 2013; Chase et al. 2011, 2012, 2014; Inomata et al. 2018; Stanton, Ardren, et al. 2020), however, the problem of visibility, at least for architectural remains, has become less of an impediment to the identification and analysis of the material culture needed to test hypotheses regarding site boundaries from a more quantitative perspective.

In this chapter, we approach the question of site boundaries from both quantitative and qualitative approaches, specifically by viewing LiDAR data through the lens of the archaeology of place. We believe this hybrid approach facilitates our ability to test hypotheses about the emic ideals of the spatial organization of communities and ancient urban boundaries. We employ LiDAR data from the Classic period city of Cobá, Quintana Roo, to argue that using Mesoamerican ideals of community structure, in conjunction with high-quality spatial data, can help archaeologists understand how people in the past attempted to create places that we, in the present, can equate with the concept of archaeological sites. Using data from our recent investigations at Cobá as an example, we suggest that at least some Maya communities were organized with formally defined community boundaries that divided spaces of human habitation (what we term domesticated spaces; see Stanton and Taube, forthcoming; Stanton, Taube, and Collins, in press) from wild spaces (Dine, Ardren, and Fisher, forthcoming; Taube 2003). Ritual processions and targeted constructions created and maintained this differentiation of space, but it is also visible in a sudden decline in the settlement near targeted constructions (see also Ardren 2015; Vallejo-Cáliz and Hutson, this volume, for a discussion of causeways and processions). At Cobá, procession routes appear to have influenced the distribution of domestic settlement, which relates to Indigenous conceptions of place during the Classic period.

Domesticated and Wild Spaces in Mesoamerica

Mesoamerican peoples have long been known to have used structuring principles in the creation and maintenance of communities. Archaeologists have explored many avenues of research along these lines, including Indigenous principles of geometry and measurement (Clark 2004; Sugiyama 2010), astronomical alignments (Aveni 1980; Aveni, Milbrath, and Peraza Lope 2004; Bricker and Bricker 1999; Ruppert 1940), geomancy (Ashmore 1989, 1991; Stanton and Freidel 2005), and more general studies of settlement patterns such as concentric zonation models (Arnold and Ford 1980; Folan, Fletcher, and Kintz 1979; Kurjack 1974). In an early seminal article on this topic, Michael D. Coe (1965) discussed the quadripartite organization of communities, citing the four entrances to towns (one at each of the cardinal directions) mentioned by the sixteenth-century Spanish bishop Diego de Landa in the context of *wayeb* rituals (Tozzer 1941, 135–50).

Then the nobles and priests chose a *principal* (an official whose role will be discussed in length below) in whose house the festival was to be celebrated, and who was in charge of the ceremony. A second image of another god was then fashioned and placed in the house of the *principal*. Following this, the nobles, priest(s), and townsmen assembled at this house, and formed a procession over a specially prepared road, which had been cleaned and adorned with arches and greenery. The road led directly to the appropriate entrance and to the image of the *Uayeb* god for the coming year. (Coe 1965, 100)

Associated rituals included the sacrifice of turkeys and the erection of "standards" representing the world trees (color-coded by their place in the directional model). These activities are paralleled by scenes in the Madrid (pages 34–37) and Dresden (pages 25–28) codices (Coe 1965, 100) and are similar to representations of cosmological foundation events such as those portrayed in the San Bartolo murals (Taube et al. 2010), indicating that the "ideal" structure of communities was understood as a microcosm of the quadripartite universe (the quincunx, four horizontal directions converging on a fifth vertical axis). Of note, Landa mentions the act of procession within the community cosmogram, an activity visually represented in the well-known cosmogram of the Madrid Codex (Tozzer 1941). Coe (1965, 111) suggests that causeways at Classic Maya sites "could have been the analogues of the ceremonial roads of the Uayeb Rites."

Much has been said of the quadripartite cosmogram over the years (e.g., Freidel et al. 1993; Reilly 1994; Stanton and Freidel 2005; Taube 1996, 2000), including the idea that Mesoamerican communities could be laid out in a quadripartite form (Stanton and Collins 2021, 116), shaping the landscape into a model of the cosmos (e.g., Fedick et al. 2012; Stanton and Freidel 2005; Stanton, Taube, and Collins, in press; Stanton et al., in press; Taube et al. 2020). Fundamentally, this cosmogram unites various essential conceptions held by Mesoamerican peoples into one single cognitive structure replicated at multiple scales, from as small as the human body or an individual milpa (Mathews and Garber 2004; Taube 2000, 301–2; 2004, 13) to as large as the very cosmos itself. In the context of site planning, Travis W. Stanton, Karl A. Taube, and Ryan H. Collins (in press) have explored the use of the quadripartite cosmogram as a structuring principle for explaining the distribution of monumental architecture and causeways at the site of Yaxuná. Building on earlier work at the site (Freidel, Schele, and Parker 1993; Stanton and Freidel 2005), they argue that the center of the site shifted several times but that it served as a central quadripartite focus for processions along causeways. In particular, they draw on Angel J. García-Zambrano's (1994) study of early colonial rituals of foundation. In this work, he establishes a pattern of a community organization that forms the quincunx: a central mountain (which could be natural or artificial), which is associated with a cave, and a water source surrounded by four smaller mountains located in the cardinal directions. In the words of Stanton, Taube, and Collins (in press):

> While rituals of foundation were complex, they centered on practices that established a quadripartite time-space frame, variably using existing natural features and built space, which extended outwards from the central mountain. Spatially, the four directions emanating out from the central mountain were marked by smaller mountains. Prior to the selection (or creation) of the central mountain, music, including the playing of drums and flutes and the blowing of conch trumpets, accompanied the establishment of the center and served as a prelude to the "shouting" in all directions to gather kinship groups. The central mountain/cave/water hole was then selected/created and processional groups set out in the four directions to measure and delimit the territory, an activity reminiscent of Hanks's (1990, 299; see also Freidel, Schele, and Parker 1993, 130) description of modern Yucatec shamans "opening the path" when laying out the cardinal directions of an altar. The limits of the territory are described as the *rinconada* by García-Zambrano (1994, 218), often depicted in a horseshoe valley shape in toponyms from Western Mesoamerica. The *rinconada*, or what we will refer to as the community limits in this paper, separated the ordered, human world of structured time from the wild, timeless, and chaotic world of the *monte*. In a sense, we see the practices associated with the foundational rituals as a way to "domesticate" space-time from its wild origins and make it a singularly human phenomenon that would remain so as long as moral behavior was maintained, especially by the ruler and the four directional wardens of a center.

Drawing on Taube's (2003; see also Stanton and Taube, forthcoming) influential work on conceptions of wild spaces, Stanton, Taube, and Collins argue that the careful preparation in measuring and placing the architectural elements and boundaries of the community is a way to create a human, or domesticated, space out of the wilderness. Importantly, the act of procession is critical not only in establishing these boundaries but in maintaining them as well (García-Zambrano 1994). Yaxuná presents an interesting case for testing the quadripartite cosmogram model, as it has a fairly obvious quadripartite organization to its monumental architecture and causeway system as well as a large body of stratigraphic data from across the site to test how the site plan transformed over time.

While there are some other sites, such as Xunantunich (Keller 2006; see also Cap, Brown, and Lytle, this volume), that have clear quadripartite arrangements in their final surface form, most Maya sites do not show such an arrangement even when they have visible causeways. How then do we explain this discrepancy? Interestingly, the map of San Mateo Ixtlahuaca (Estado de México) used by García-Zambrano to support his model of rituals of foundation also depicts processions to the riconada in noncardinal directions. These data suggest that while the quadripartite form may have been an ideal, held as a mythological or cosmological template, other factors may have structured the arrangement of procession ways as well. Such factors include alignments to important geographic features such as mountains and caves, alignments to other important and socially meaningful places, features of historical construction, and factional competition (Stanton and Freidel 2005).

Thus, instead of focusing on finding the quadripartite form where it may not exist, we suggest that a more appropriate way to explore the kinds of community boundaries that may have intentionally defined domestic places (as separate from the wild) is to correlate settlement density with the two features of the built environment that García-Zambrano (1994) singles out in his research: procession ways and peripheral temples (the smaller "mountains"). It is this last point that brings us back to Cobá, a site characterized by a series of substantial causeways that could have functioned as procession routes to temple (mountain) complexes located at their termini. Does the residential settlement exhibit patterning in regard to the distribution of causeways and terminal monumental groups? If it does, can we link any such correlation to the creation and maintenance of a bounded, domesticated space as discussed previously? Given the presence of a shared monumental causeway, are there any connections in the Cobá data to the pattern documented at Yaxuná we discussed earlier? To answer these questions, we turn to the LiDAR data.

Sakbe'ob and Settlement at Cobá

Cobá is a large Maya city that dates primarily to the sixth to eighth centuries AD (Folan, Kintz, and Fletcher 1983; Robles Castellanos 1990). Mapping at the site has revealed a series of monumental groups connected by causeways (*sakbe'ob*) as well as an extensive domestic settlement characterized by a high frequency of houselot walls (*albarradas*) (figure 3.1; Benavides Castillo 1976, 1981; Cortés de Brasdefer 1984a, 1984b, 1984c; Folan and Stuart 1974, 1977; Folan, Kintz, and Fletcher 1983; Folan et al. 2009; Gallareta 1981, 1984; Garduño Argueta 1979; Navarette, Uribe, and Martínez Muriel 1979; Thompson, Pollock, and Charlot 1932). While the extensive and detailed maps of the domestic zones of the ancient city are well known (figure 3.2), groundbreaking work in the 1970s and 1980s had to contend with the arduous task of ground survey and transit mapping in a tropical forest environment, mitigating the amount of area that could be covered. Through LiDAR surveys, we have been able to expand our knowledge of settlement patterns at Cobá to cover what we believe to be most, if not all, of the emic boundaries of the site.

Considering one of the striking features of the settlement pattern at Cobá is the distance between monumental groups (e.g., 10.4 km between Kucicán and San Pedro) and the length of the internal causeways (e.g., 6.1 km between Kucicán and Group D), we felt that Cobá would be an interesting place to test hypotheses concerning processions and community boundaries, with Caracol, Belize, being perhaps the best comparison in terms of the extension and complexity of the causeways system (Chase and Chase 2001). Previous work indicates that Cobá has an early occupation beginning at least during the Late Formative period (Añejo Complex, 100 BC/AD 100–AD 300/350; Robles Castellanos 1990), but that settlement is generally restricted to the central part of the site around the Cobá Group through the beginning of the Blanco Complex (AD 300/350–550/600; Robles Castellanos 1990), when the site is known to have had a dynastic line (María José Con Uribe, personal communication, 2016; Esparza 2016). During the Palmas Complex (ca. AD 550/600–700/730; Robles Castellanos 1990), the site experienced a demographic explosion. The apogee was first clearly articulated in Fernando Robles Castellanos's (1990) study of the ceramics of the site and has been corroborated by our work performed over three field seasons (2015, 2016, and 2018) in residential zones across the site.

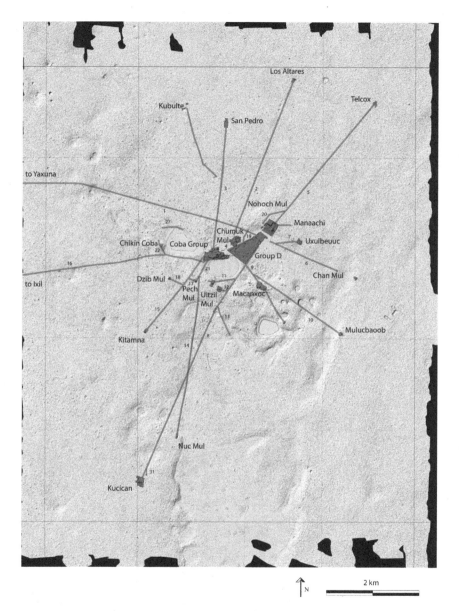

FIGURE 3.1 Hillshade of Cobá marking the monumental groups and causeways (image created by Travis Stanton).

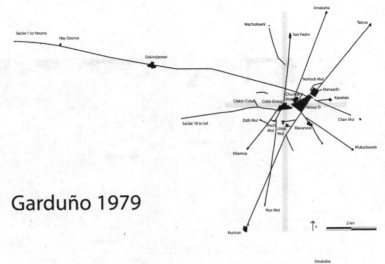

Garduño 1979

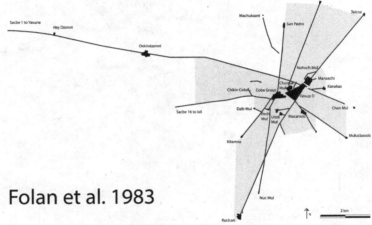

Folan et al. 1983

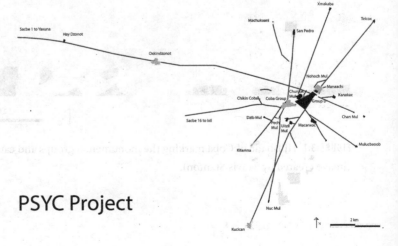

PSYC Project

FIGURE 3.2 Plan of Cobá showing the approximate areas mapped by Garduño Argueta (1979) and Folan, Kintz, and Fletcher (1983), as well as the areas ground-validated by our project (image created by Travis Stanton).

Through a program of off-mound test-pitting, we have slowly been collecting chronological data from across the site (see figure 3.2). To date, all fifty-three residential groups (not including our excavations in public plazas) we have tested have evidence of Palmas Complex occupations. We have found Formative, Early Classic, Terminal Classic materials (Oro Complex, AD 700/730–1100/1200) and Postclassic (AD 1100/1200–1500/1550) in far smaller frequency, with Postclassic materials being the most prevalent of these. Ceramic evidence from Instituto Nacional de Antropología e Historia (INAH) excavations at large groups located at the termini of the causeways demonstrates relatively small amounts of Blanco materials (Robles Castellanos 1990, 46–49). The presence of these early materials suggests that these groups, and potentially the causeways leading to them, may have been established at some point during the Early Classic period (Oro Complex) when the royal dynasty was established. However, there is substantial material data dated to the Palmas Complex compared to the Blanco Complex at the terminus groups (Robles Castellanos 1990, 46–49). Of note, Sakbe 1, the great causeway to Yaxunah, has been dated to the Palmas Complex through work at that western site (Ardren 2003; Johnstone 2001; Loya González 2008; Loya González and Stanton 2013, 2014; Shaw and Johnstone 2001; Stanton et al. 2010; Stanton, Magnoni, et al. 2020; Tiesler et al. 2017, 36–40) and could be later than some of the internal causeways at Cobá. Thus, the internal causeways and terminus groups may have been constructed during the Oro Complex, but it is more likely that like much of the architectural construction at Cobá, they date to the initial years of the Palmas Complex. Further work on this question is needed to better clarify the timing and is critical for understanding the processes of urbanization at Cobá. The difference between whether the terminus groups were built as separate communities that were subsequently linked by the causeways during the process of urbanization at Cobá or if they were planned to define a huge urban area at the beginning of the process during the early portion of the Palmas Complex has important implications for understanding the long-term development of Cobá as a city.

Methods

The LiDAR survey was performed by the National Center for Airborne Laser Mapping (NCALM) in May 2017 as part of a broader effort to survey areas of the central and eastern areas of the northern Maya lowlands that began in 2014 (Magnoni et al. 2016). Data for Cobá were collected using a Teledyne-Optech Titan MW (Fernandez Diaz et al. 2016). Details for the LiDAR data collection and processing can be found in Stanton, Ardren, et al. (2020). For the analysis presented in this work, approximately 122 km^2 of LiDAR has been considered. This includes a block centered on Cobá with additional 1 km wide and 7 km long transects along the length of Sakbe 1 (Rohrer and Stanton 2019) leading back to Yaxunah and Ixil to the west as well as to Xelhá (5 km long) on the Caribbean coast to the east. These transects are longer, but the areas sampled for this study are limited to the areas closest to Cobá.

Analysis of the LiDAR data is still ongoing and includes several phases (Stanton, Ardren, et al. 2020; see also Hutson et al. 2021). First, a program to ground-validate the data has been implemented by teams of mappers using LiDAR on globally positioned tablets. Detailed maps of architectural and other features (small *aguadas*, *metates*, etc.) visible on the surface are drawn on top of printed images of LiDAR at 1:40 scale; these are then digitized and georeferenced in the laboratory (see figure 3.2 for the areas that have been ground-validated by the project to date). Some of this ground-validating overlaps with previously mapped areas of the settlement. Maps created by earlier projects, in particular those published by Jaime Garduño Argueta (1979) and William J. Folan, Ellen R. Kintz, and Laraine A. Fletcher (1983), are in the process of being redrawn over the LiDAR, an interpretive process that has methodological issues. In areas where we have not had the opportunity to ground-validate, these maps give us important spatial data based on the observations of researchers who documented spatial features on the ground, representing an important historical record that may document buildings and other features that have been disturbed since the time they were first recorded. The combination of conventional maps with LiDAR data gives us a greater sense of how many architectural features may be present in areas where no ground survey has been performed.

Finally, we have completed the preliminary identification of architectural features visible in the LiDAR data in areas that have yet to be surveyed on the ground. Guided by our previous work identifying structures in the LiDAR of central Yucatán (Magnoni et al. 2016), we have drawn polygon shapefiles around the edges of features that show more tell-tale indicators of architectural construction, such as sharp corners that may indicate platforms (12,542 separate polygons over a ~122 km^2 area). We did not include structures that were not recorded through earlier mapping and are not visible in the LiDAR data, as we are still in the process of digitizing earlier maps. Plazas enclosed by visible structures on at least three sides are included within the area of the shapefiles, but not those with only two sides enclosed unless the plaza is on a clearly raised platform. Other features such as causeways and visible albarradas have also been digitized as polylines along their centers (there is a total length of 73.3 km of causeways within the ~122 km^2 area). Due to the resolution of the imagery from Cobá, we have been able to explore the presence of exposed bedrock within two domestic groups as a test of the usefulness of this technology in visualizing houselot terrain (Dine, Ardren, and Fisher, forthcoming). Facilitating this work is the fact that the terrain of Cobá is characterized by fewer limestone hummocks, which presents issues when identifying features at Yaxuná. The change to a Titan MW LiDAR machine as well as the extremely dry conditions at the time of the flight also increased the potential to more accurately identify features in comparison to the data collected in central Yucatán in 2014.

In terms of the geographic information system (GIS) analysis of the data, we focused on two primary variables: volume and area of construction. Since the beginning of settlement pattern archaeology, many projects have made calculations based on the density of structures. We have struggled with applying this approach to the LiDAR data we have in our area of study (Stanton, Ardren, et al. 2020). First and foremost, there is currently no clear method for defining what constitutes a structure for the kind of analysis we perform here. This is particularly problematic in the northern lowlands where structures are often found on basal platforms. In fact, structural remains are often too small to be detected in LiDAR imagery. Therefore, following methods recently published, we have decided to analyze the data in terms of the sheer area and volume of construction, both of which may have very different implications for understanding settlement patterns but can be easily calculated from polygons drawn around external extents of contiguous architectural features (Stanton, Ardren, et al. 2020).

All analysis was done using ArcGIS 10 Desktop software. The area of structures was calculated for the polygons using standard ArcGIS tools for determining area. The structures have a total area of 3,104,481 m^2 with a mean area of 248 m^2. The minimum area of a structure was 4.1 m^2 and the maximum was 11,011 m^2 for a monumental group. A multistep process using our inventory of structures as polygons and the LiDAR bare-earth DEM was necessary

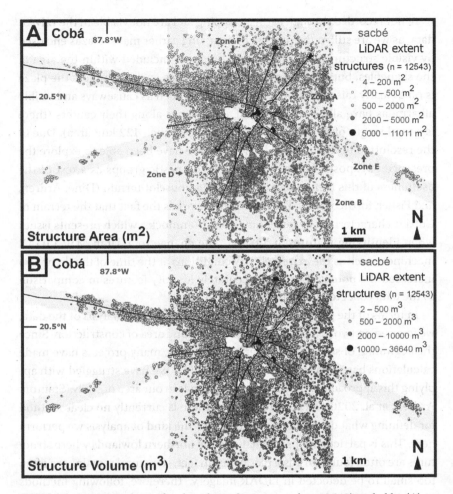

FIGURE 3.3 Spatial analysis of archaeological structures (n = 12543) scaled by (A) structure area (m²) and (B) structure volume (m²). Overlaid are mapped causeways (sacbés) and the LiDAR extent. Low-density areas near the site center are underwater (white) or disturbed by modern settlement (image created by Nicolas Barth).

to determine volumes of structures, which is fully described in Stanton, Ardren, et al. (2020). The structures have a total volume of 5,271,821 m³ (equivalent to approximately 2,100 Olympic swimming pools) with a mean volume of 420 m³. The minimum volume of one contiguous construction enclosed by a polygon was 2.2 m³ and the maximum was 36,640 m³. For ease of further spatial analyses, the structure polygons were converted to points (one point per structure averaged on the polygon's center with area and volume data imprinted) (figure 3.3). We also determined the distance of every mapped structure's midpoint to the nearest causeway using the Near tool. We found that the mean distance of a structure from its nearest causeway was 920 m and the median was 606 m. About 10 percent of all structures are within 100 m of a causeway, 45 percent within 500 m, 68 percent within 1,000 m, and 88 percent within 2,000 m.

We note a strong correlation between the causeway termini and the sheer area of visible construction in the LiDAR (figure 3.3). As might be expected, there are high values for area density at many of the termini where extensive monumental groups (e.g., Kucicán and San Pedro) are located; this pattern is accentuated by viewing the volume density. Beyond these high values for area and volume around the causeway termini, both variables drop off sharply in most areas beyond these termini, usually within just a few hundred meters. There is considerable value in examining both structure density area and volume; overall trends are similar but there are considerable differences in the details. Structure area provides a smoother measure of land use patterns (since several small basal platforms can add up to a larger monument in terms of area). Structure volume emphasizes larger projects, such as monuments, likely requiring community organization, and so produces a more point-centric spatial trend. The area around the Kubulte Group (Zone F) is a good example of structure density dropping off beyond a causeway terminus (figure 3.4). This pattern contrasts with the higher structure density on the interior side of the terminus groups and the even higher densities closer to the central zone around the lakes.

There are some areas that do not fit the pattern exactly. For instance, Zone D appears as an island of high values for both area and volume. This "hot spot" is not much farther from the central core of the site (e.g., the Cobá Group) than the Telcox Group, but it is some distance from a causeway terminus. The high values to the east of the visible end of Sakbe 6, where it appears to terminate at the Chan Mul Group, seem to be another example of the settlement extending some distance from the end of the causeway (Zone C; see figure 3.4). A close examination of the Zone C area, however, reveals another monumental group in this location that is in line with Sakbe 6. The area between the Zone C spike in values and the area around the Chan Mul Group is a low-lying *bajo*, a zone that may have filled with sediment, thus obscuring a possible continuation of Sakbe 6.

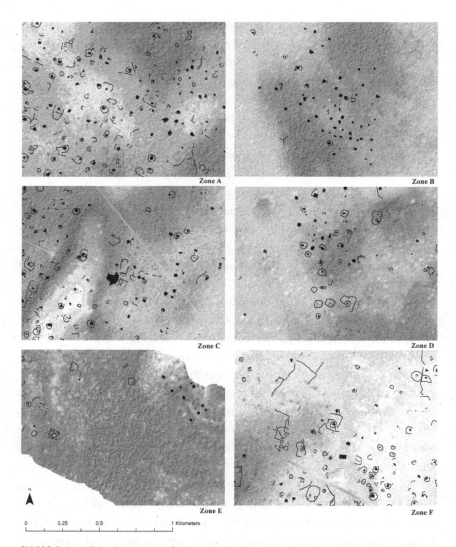

FIGURE 3.4 Hillshade images of Zones A, B, C, D, E, and F (image created by Travis Stanton).

A further exception is Zone B, an area that is much further outside the pattern than either Zones C or D. Zone B is truly an island of high values surrounded by low values, although in fairness it is about the same distance from the central Cobá Group as the Telcox Group. One factor to consider is that Zone B is in line with Sakbe 10, which leaves the Macanxoc Group around its southeast corner, ending in a smaller civic group next to the most southeasterly of the lakes around Cobá. Zone B may represent construction that anticipated the extension of this causeway that was not realized due to the abandonment of the site. However, we also think it could be quite likely that this area may not date to the Oro and Palmas Complex occupations of the site. As with other Maya landscapes, this area of Quintana Roo likely has a very complex history of changing settlement, and we expect that quite a few of the surface features visible in the landscape might date to periods like the Middle Formative or Late Postclassic when Cobá was not an urban environment. Since we do not have chronological data from Zone B, it is impossible to address this question at this time. Interestingly, Zone A is comparable to Zone B in that it represents another spike in construction area and volume in line with a causeway, in this case one that terminates at the Kitamná Group. There is no evidence that the causeway continues after the Kitamná Group, but Zone A is also around the same distance from the Cobá Group as the Telcox Group.

Other "islands" of high area and volume density appear to be spatial aggregations that we might call other sites. Zone E is a good example (see figure 3.3) where there are some of the lowest values of both area and volume. In these areas there are structures, but they are quite small. To further illustrate this point, on the extreme western part of the transect to Yaxuná (see figure 3.3), there are nine small structures or clusters of structures (the largest of which, by far, is a domestic patio group measuring 40 × 22 m with a maximum height of its tallest structure of less than 2 m). Returning to Zone E, there are more than a kilometer of low area and volume density between it and the higher values closer to Cobá. The visible settlement between Cobá and Zone E is very light, possibly indicating that Zone E might be a separate settlement. Further east of Zone E in the direction of Xelhá, there is a substantial gap. This area, more than a kilometer in length, had absolutely no features visible in the LiDAR before another spike in settlement occurs, a spike we interpret as another separate site. Such gaps are also visible along the other transects on the western side of Cobá. We believe that these data not only indicate a substantial drop-off in settlement after the terminus groups at Cobá but that the smaller communities around Early and Late Classic Cobá (unless some of the spatial clusters date to other periods) maintained a fair degree of spatial separation from their neighbors.

One final pattern that we would like to draw attention to is the relationship of settlement to intersite causeways. Using GPS points gathered in previous field seasons as well as imagery from Google Earth, we attempted to plot the LiDAR transects along the paths of Sakbe 1 to Yaxunah and Sakbe 16 to Ixil. To our surprise, the causeways varied in direction much more than anticipated, and we were unsuccessful in mapping either causeway in its entirety (Rohrer and Stanton 2019; Stanton, Ardren, et al. 2020). This fact is visible in figure 3.3, where Sakbe 16 veers off the path of the LiDAR transect quite dramatically. However, it is clear that settlement is quite substantial along Sakbe 16 in terms of area and volume, until it leaves our survey area. More obvious is the pattern of settlement along Sakbe 1, where both area and volume densities are high through Oxkindzonot (6.7 km west along Sakbe 1 from the Nohoch Mul Group) to Hay Dzonot (10.7 km west along Sakbe 1 from the Nohoch Mul Group), with a small area of lesser values between these two civic groups. In their cursory explorations of these places, Alfonso Villa Rojas (1934) and J. Eric S. Thompson, H. E. D. Pollock, and Jean Charlot (1932) believed Oxkindzonot and Hay Dzonot to be separate sites. Yet, looking at the LiDAR data, there is substantial contiguous settlement past the Oxkindzonot civic complex and to the Hay Dzonot monumental group, appearing just after the group's domestic settlement drops off precipitously. It is along this causeway that contiguous settlement from Cobá reaches its furthest limit from the Cobá Group, indicating that, much like modern roads between towns, settlement can be drawn out away from community centers by routes of transportation and communication. It is important to note, however, that although the settlement along Sakbe 1 extends for a greater distance from the Cobá Group, it is concentrated along the causeway itself and drops off precisely where a monumental group is located, fitting the model of processions and community boundaries we outlined earlier in the chapter, perhaps suggesting that this settlement was, through the practice of procession, part of the emic place we call Cobá today.

Conclusion

In this chapter, we have considered the LiDAR data from Cobá in light of their relationship to causeways and monumental groups found at the termini of causeways. We suggested at the beginning of this chapter that causeways represent, in part, procession routes that were used in practices of defining and maintaining community boundaries, separating the "domestic space" of humans from the "wild space" of the forest. In general terms, we believe

Cobá settlements correlate well with the ends of the causeways and their peripheral "mountain-temples." With a few exceptions that might be explained by historical processes related to the site's urban decline at the end of the Palmas Complex, or even by potential dating of these settlement spikes to periods other than the Oro and Palmas Complexes, both the volume and area of construction decline quite markedly within several hundred meters of the causeway termini, a pattern noted elsewhere in the Maya lowlands (see Garber 2003; Thomas 1981). Likewise, the residential settlement closest to these peripheral temples is contemporaneous with the primary period of construction at Cobá, the Palmas Complex (Late Classic). To us, this suggests the causeway system, with its peripheral temples and associated dense settlement, was a deliberate effort by ancient Cobanecos to create and maintain a bounded domestic space. Are there connections to the pattern established at Yaxuná? Yes and no. The causeway system of Cobá does not rely on the cruciform pattern like the one at Yaxuná, and it appears to be much later in date than the main internal causeways at Yaxuná. But both sites used the combination of causeways and associated settlements to structure a sense of place. In both ancient centers, causeways and their associated activities, including processions, structured a manipulation of the landscape to express ideas about a culturally appropriate settlement. Does this mean that the model we proposed at the beginning of this chapter is valid? We suggest that this model of community boundaries as an emic phenomenon visible in landscape modification and settlement density has merit, although there is much more work to be done to continue to test this model at Cobá and at other sites with internal causeway systems.

Besides speculating that the settlement outside the area bounded by the causeway termini might date to other periods, what can we make of these structures, however small and dispersed they might be? One idea to explore is the possibility that some of them might represent field houses, which we have occasionally noted for modern-day peoples living in the town of Yaxcabá, Yucatán. A city the size of Cobá had to produce and/or import substantial quantities of food, and some fields might have been a sizable distance from where people lived. Another possibility is that some people, perhaps those who were marginalized within the hierarchical social system that existed during the Classic period, chose to live outside the preferred domesticated space or were disenfranchised in some way. Without systematic excavations in these areas, we will not be able to adequately address these questions but leave these ideas here as working hypotheses as we move forward with our research.

We have argued that a hybrid model that combines both quantitative data from new technologies like LiDAR and qualitative data from ethnohistoric and ethnographic sources can be combined to generate convincing explanations for the site design of Yaxuná and Cobá. While exciting, LiDAR data alone do not adequately address the human component of borders and boundaries, although this class of data greatly enhances our understanding of ancient landscape modifications like causeways and associated settlement. We do not argue that the quadripartite model applies to all Maya sites. Indeed, it does not seem to apply particularly well at Cobá, but we suggest that internal causeways be considered as integrative features created by the ancient Maya to mark and define "human space" in opposition to "wild space." Even when evidence supports the presence of an ideal community structure, spatial communities like cities are messy and boundaries are often disputed. In fact, in our minds, it would be surprising to find an absolute correlation with the model we employ. The correlation of settlement to our model is high, but the social contexts of past urban environments were most likely as complex as they are for modern societies today.

Acknowledgments

We thank the Consejo de Arqueología of the Instituto Nacional de Antropología e Historia for granting the permits to conduct this research; all data are the cultural patrimony of Mexico. This research was generously supported by the National Science Foundation (#1623603), Fundación Roberto Hernández, and Selz Foundation. We also appreciate the support and guidance of María José Con Uribe, José Manuel Ochoa Rodríguez, Adriana Velázquez, and Fernando Robles Castellanos in our efforts to work at Cobá. Finally, we thank the communities of Cobá, Nuevo Xcan, San Juan, and San Pedro for allowing us to conduct research in their ejidos and imparting their knowledge of the local landscape.

Works Cited

Ardren, Traci. 2003. "Memoria y la historia arquitectónica en la Estructura 6E-13 de Yaxuná." *Temas Antropológicos* 25 (1–2): 129–46.

Ardren, Traci. 2015. "Procesiones y *sacbeob* de las Tierras Bajas del norte en el Clásico Maya." *Arqueología Mexicana* 2015 (2): 22–27.

Ardren, Traci, and Justin P. Lowry. 2011. "The Travels of Maya Merchants in the Ninth–Tenth Centuries: Investigations at Xuenkal and the Greater Cupul Province, Yucatan, Mexico." *World Archaeology* 43 (3): 428–43.

Arnold, Jeanne E., and Anabel Ford. 1980. "A Statistical Examination of Settlement Patterns at Tikal, Guatemala." *American Antiquity* 45 (4): 713–26.

Ashmore, Wendy. 1989. "Construction and Cosmology: Politics and Ideology in Lowland Maya Settlement Patterns." In *Word and Image in Maya Culture: Explorations in Language, Writing, and Representation*, edited by William F. Hanks and Don S. Rice, 272–86. Salt Lake City: University of Utah Press.

Ashmore, Wendy. 1991. "Site-Planning Principles and Concepts of Directionality Among the Ancient Maya." *Latin American Antiquity* 2 (3): 199–225.

Aveni, Anthony F. 1980. *Skywatchers of Ancient Mexico*. Austin: University of Texas Press.

Aveni, Anthony F., Susan Milbrath, and Carlos Peraza Lope. 2004. "Chichen Itza's Legacy in the Astronomically Oriented Architecture of Mayapán." *RES*, no. 45 (Spring): 123–43.

Benavides Castillo, Antonio. 1976. "El sistema prehispánico de comunicaciones terrestres en la región de Cobá, Quintana Roo, y sus implicaciones sociales." Master's thesis, Universidad Nacional Autónoma de México, Mexico City.

Benavides Castillo, Antonio. 1981. *Los caminos de Cobá y sus implicaciones sociales (Proyecto Cobá)*. Mexico City: Instituto Nacional de Antropología e Historia.

Binford, Lewis R. 1964. "A Consideration of Archaeological Research Design." *American Antiquity* 29 (4): 425–41.

Binford, Lewis R. 1992. "Seeing the Present and Interpreting the Past—and Keeping Things Straight." In *Space, Time, and Archaeological Landscapes*, edited by Jacqueline Rossignol and LuAnn Wandsnider, 43–64. New York: Plenum Press.

Bradley, Richard. 1994. "Symbols and Signposts: Understanding the Prehistoric Petroglyphs of the British Isles." In *The Ancient Mind: Elements of Cognitive Archaeology*, edited by Colin Renfrew and Ezra B. W. Zubrow, 95–106. Cambridge: Cambridge University Press.

Brady, James E., and Wendy Ashmore. 1999. "Mountains, Caves, Water: Ideational Landscapes of the Ancient Maya." In *Archaeologies of Landscapes: Contemporary Perspectives*, edited by Wendy Ashmore and A. Bernard Knapp, 124–45. Oxford: Blackwell.

Bricker, Harvey M., and Victoria R. Bricker. 1999. "Astronomical Orientation of the Skyband Bench at Copán." *Journal of Field Archaeology* 26 (4): 435–42.

Canuto, Marcello A., Francisco Estrada-Belli, Thomas G. Garrison, Stephen D. Houston, Mary Jane Acuña, Milan Kováč, Damien Marken, et al. 2018. "Ancient Lowland Maya Complexity as Revealed by Airborne Laser Scanning of Northern Guatemala." *Science* 28 (361). https://doi.org/10.1126/science.aau0137.

Chase, Arlen F., and Diane Z. Chase. 2001. "Ancient Maya Causeways and Site Organization at Caracol, Belize." *Ancient Mesoamerica* 12 (2): 273–81.

Chase, Arlen F., Diane Z. Chase, Jaime J. Awe, John F. Weishampel, Gyles Iannone, Holley Moyes, Jason Yaeger, and M. Kathryn Brown. 2014. "The Use of LiDAR in

Understanding the Ancient Maya Landscape: Caracol and Western Belize." *Advances in Archaeological Practice* 2 (3): 147–60.
Chase, Arlen F., Diane Z. Chase, Christopher T. Fisher, Stephen J. Leisz, and John F. Weishampel. 2012. "Geospatial Revolution and Remote Sensing LiDAR in Mesoamerican Archaeology." *Proceedings of the National Academy of Sciences of the United States of America* 109 (32): 12916–21.
Chase, Arlen F., Diane Z. Chase, and John F. Weishampel. 2010. "Lasers in the Jungle: Airborne Sensors Reveal a Vast Maya Landscape." *Archaeology* 63 (4): 27–29.
Chase, Arlen F., Diane Z. Chase, and John F. Weishampel. 2013. "The Use of LiDAR at the Maya Site of Caracol, Belize." In *Mapping Archaeological Landscapes from Space: In Observance of the 40th Anniversary of the World Heritage Convention*, edited by Douglas C. Comer and Michael J. Harrower, 179–89. New York: Springer.
Chase, Arlen F., Diane Z. Chase, John F. Weishampel, Jason B. Drake, Ramesh L. Shrestha, K. Clint Slatton, Jaime J. Awe, and William E. Carter. 2011. "Airborne LiDAR, Archaeology, and the Ancient Maya Landscape at Caracol, Belize." *Journal of Archaeological Science* 38 (2): 387–98.
Clark, John E. 2004. "Surrounding the Sacred: Geometry and Design of Early Mound Groups as Meaning and Function." In *Signs of Power: The Rise of Cultural Complexity in the Southeast*, edited by Jon L. Gibson and Philip J. Carr, 162–213. Tuscaloosa: University of Alabama Press.
Coe, Michael D. 1965. "A Model of Ancient Community Structure in the Maya Lowlands." *Southwestern Journal of Anthropology* 21 (2): 97–114.
Cortés de Brasdefer, Fernando. 1984a. "La extensión de Cobá: Una contribución al patrón de asentamiento." *Boletín de la Escuela de Ciencias Antropológicas de la Universidad de Yucatán*, no. 64: 3–13.
Cortés de Brasdefer, Fernando. 1984b. "La extensión de Cobá: Una contribución al patrón de asentamiento." In *Investigaciones recientes en el área Maya: XVII Mesa Redonda, Sociedad Mexicana de Antropología, Sn. Cristóbal de Las Casas, Chiapas, 21–27 Junio 1981, Tomo II*, 63–74. Chiapas: Sociedad Mexicana de Antropología.
Cortés de Brasdefer, Fernando. 1984c. "La zona habitacional de Cobá, Quintana Roo." In *Investigaciones recientes en el área Maya: XVII Mesa Redonda, Sociedad Mexicana de Antropología, Sn. Cristóbal de Las Casas, Chiapas, 21–27 Junio 1981, Tomo II*, 129–41. Chiapas: Sociedad Mexicana de Antropología.
Dewar, Robert E. 1986 "Discovering Settlement Systems of the Past in New England Site Distributions." *Man in the Northeast* 31:77–88.
Dine, Harper, Traci Ardren, and Chelsea Fisher. Forthcoming. "Vegetative Agency and Social Memory in Houselots of the Ancient Maya." In *The Power of Nature: Agency and the Archaeology of Human-Environmental Dynamics*, edited by Monica L. Smith. Bolder: University Press of Colorado.
Dunnell, Robert C. 1992. "The Notion Site." In *Space, Time, and Archaeological Landscapes*, edited by Jacqueline Rossignol and LuAnn Wandsnider, 21–41. New York: Plenum Press.

Dunnell, Robert C., and William S. Dancy. 1983. "The Siteless Survey: A Regional Scale Data Collection Strategy." *Advances in Archaeological Method and Theory* 6: 267–87.

Esparza Olguín, Octavio Q. 2016. "Estudio de los monumentos esculpidos de Cobá, Quintana Roo, y su contexto arqueológico." PhD diss., Universidad Nacional Autónoma de México, Mexico City.

Fedick, Scott L., Jennifer P. Mathews, and Kathryn Sorensen. 2012. "Cenotes as Conceptual Boundary Markers at the Ancient Maya Site of T'isil, Quintana Roo, Mexico." *Mexicon* 34 (5): 118–23.

Fernandez-Diaz, Juan Carlos, William E. Carter, Craig Glennie, Ramesh L. Shrestha, Zhigang Pan, Nima Ekhtari, Abhinav Singhania, Darren Hauser, and Michael Sartori. 2016. "Capability Assessment and Performance Metrics for the Titan Multispectral Mapping LiDAR." *Remote Sensing* 8 (11): 936. https://doi.org/10.3390/rs8110936.

Folan, William J., Armando Anaya Hernández, Ellen R. Kintz, Laraine A. Fletcher, Raymundo González Heredia, Jacinto May Hau, and Nicolas Caamal Canché. 2009. "Coba, Quintana Roo, Mexico: A Recent Analysis of the Social, Economic, and Political Organization of a Major Maya Urban Center." *Ancient Mesoamerica* 20 (1): 59–70.

Folan, William J., Laraine A. Fletcher, and Ellen R. Kintz. 1979. "Fruit, Fiber, Bark, and Resin: Social Organization of a Maya Urban Center." *Science* 204 (4394): 697–701.

Folan, William J., Ellen R. Kintz, and Laraine A. Fletcher, eds. 1983. *Coba: A Classic Maya Metropolis.* New York: Academic Press.

Folan, William J., and George E. Stuart. 1974. "Coba Archaeological Mapping Project, Quintana Roo, Mexico." *Boletín de la Escuela de Ciencias Antropológicas de la Universidad de Yucatán* 22:20–29.

Folan, William J., and George E. Stuart. 1977. "El Proyecto Cartográfico Arqueológico Cobá, Q. Roo: Informes interinos números 1, 2, y 3." *Boletín de la Escuela de Ciencias Antropológicas de la Universidad de Yucatán* 22:30–79.

Foley, Robert A. 1981. *Off-Site Archaeology and Human Adaptation in Eastern Africa.* British Archaeological Reports, International Series 97. Oxford: BAR.

Freidel, David A., Linda Schele, and Joy Parker. 1993. *Maya Cosmos: Three Thousand Years on the Shaman's Path.* New York: William Morrow.

Garber, James F., ed. 2003. *The Ancient Maya of the Belize Valley: Half a Century of Archaeological Research.* Gainesville: University Press of Florida.

García-Zambrano, Angel J. 1994. "Early Colonial Evidence of Pre-Columbian Rituals of Foundation." In *Seventh Palenque Round Table, 1989*, edited by Merle Greene Robertson and Virginia G. Fields, 217–27. San Francisco: Pre-Columbian Art Research Institute.

Garduño Argueta, Jaime. 1979. "Introducción al patrón de asentamiento del sitio de Cobá, Quintana Roo." Master's thesis, Escuela Nacional de Antropología e Historia, Mexico City.

Grube, Nikolai. 2004. "Akan: The God of Drinking, Disease and Death." In *Continuity and Change: Maya Religious Practices in Temporal Perspectives*, edited by Daniel

Graña-Behrens, Nikolai Grube, Christian M. Prager, Frauke Sachse, Stephanie Teufel, and Elisabeth Wagner, 59–76. Acta Mesoamericana 14. Markt Schwaben, Germany: Verlag Anton Saurwein.

Hanks, William. 1990. *Referential Practice: Language and Lived Space Among the Maya.* Chicago: University of Chicago Press.

Hole, Frank, and Robert F. Heizer. 1973. *An Introduction to Prehistoric Archaeology.* 3rd ed. New York: Holt, Rinehart and Winston.

Hutson, Scott R., Timothy S. Hare, Travis W. Stanton, Marilyn Masson, Nicolas C. Barth, Traci Ardren, and Aline Magnoni. 2021. "A Space of One's Own: Houselot Size Among the Ancient Maya." *Journal of Anthropological Archaeology* 64 (December): 1–15. https://doi.org/10.1016/j.jaa.2021.101362.

Ingold, Tim. 1986. *The Appropriation of Nature.* Manchester: Manchester University Press.

Inomata, Takeshi, Daniela Triadan, Flory Pinzón, Melissa Burham, José Luis Ranchos, Kazuo Aoyama, and Tsuyoshi Haraguchi. 2018. "Archaeological Application of Airborne LiDAR to Examine Social Changes in the Ceibal Region of the Maya Lowlands." *PLoS ONE* 13 (2): e0191619. https://doi.org/10.1371/journal.pone.0191619.

Johnstone, Dave. 2001. "The Ceramics of Yaxuna." PhD diss., Southern Methodist University, Dallas.

Keller, Angela H. 2006. "Roads to the Center: The Design, Use, and Meaning of the Roads of Xunantunich, Belize." PhD diss., University of Pennsylvania, Philadelphia.

Kemp, Barry. 2012. *The City of Akhenaten and Nefertiti: Amarna and Its People.* London: Thames and Hudson.

Kurjack, Edward B. 1974. *Prehistoric Lowland Maya Community Social Organization: A Case Study at Dzibilchaltun, Yucatan, Mexico.* Middle American Research Institute 38. New Orleans: Tulane University.

Loya González, Tatiana. 2008. "La relación entre Yaxuná, Yucatán y Cobá, Quintana Roo durante el Clásico Tardío (600–700/750 D.C.)." Master's thesis, Universidad de las Américas, Puebla, Cholula.

Loya González, Tatiana, and Travis W. Stanton. 2013. "The Impact of Politics on Material Culture: Evaluating the Yaxuná-Cobá Sacbé." *Ancient Mesoamerica* 24:25–42.

Loya González, Tatiana, and Travis W. Stanton. 2014. "Petrographic Analysis of Arena Red Ceramics at Yaxuná, Yucatán." In *The Archaeology of Yucatán: New Directions and Data,* edited by Travis W. Stanton, 337–62. BAR International Series. Oxford: Archaeopress.

Magnoni, Aline, Travis W. Stanton, Nicolas Barth, Juan Carlos Fernandez Diaz, José Francisco Osorio León, Francisco Pérez Ruíz, and Jessica A. Wheeler. 2016. "Assessing Detection Thresholds of Archaeological Features in Airborne LiDAR Data from Central Yucatán." *Advances in Archaeological Practice* 4 (3): 232–48.

Mathews, Jennifer P., and James F. Garber. 2004. "Models of Cosmic Order: Physical Expression of Sacred Space among the Ancient Maya." *Ancient Mesoamerica* 15 (1): 49–59.

McCoy, Mark D. 2020. "The Site Problem: A Critical Review of the Site Concept in Archaeology in the Digital Age." *Journal of Field Archaeology* 45, Sup. 1: S18–S26.

McManamon, Francis P. 1981. "Parameter Estimation and Site Discovery in the Northeast." *Contract Abstracts and CRM Archaeology* 1:43–48.

Navarette, Carlos, María José Con Uribe, and Alejandro Martínez Muriel. 1979. *Observaciones arqueológicas en Cobá, Quintana Roo*. Mexico City: Universidad Nacional Autónoma de México.

Plog, Stephen, Fred Plog, and Walter Wait. 1978. "Decision Making in Modern Surveys." *Advances in Archaeological Method and Theory* 1:383–421.

Redman, Charles L. 1973. "Multistage Fieldwork and Analytical Techniques." *American Antiquity* 38 (1): 61–79.

Reilly, F. Kent, III. 1994. "Visions to Another World: Art, Shamanism, and Political Power in Middle Formative Mesoamerica." PhD diss., University of Texas at Austin.

Robles Castellanos, Fernando. 1990. *La secuencia cerámica de la región de Cobá, Quintana Roo*. Mexico City: Instituto Nacional de Antropología e Historia.

Rohrer, Patrick, and Travis W. Stanton. 2019. "Imaging and Imagining Ancient Maya Causeways: When Sacbes Turn." In *Chacmool at 50: The Past, Present, and Future of Archaeology*, edited by Kelsey Pennanen and Susanne Goosney, 25–36. Calgary: University of Calgary.

Ruppert, Karl. 1940. "A Special Assemblage of Maya Structures." In *The Maya and Their Neighbors: Essays on Middle American Anthropology and Archaeology*, edited by Clarence L. Hay, Ralph L. Linton, Samuel K. Lothrop, Harry L. Shapiro, and George C. Valliant, 222–31. New York: D. Appleton-Century Company.

Sharer, Robert J., and Wendy Ashmore. 1979. *Fundamentals of Archaeology*. Menlo Park, Calif.: Benjamin/Cummings.

Shaw, Justine M., and Dave Johnstone. 2001. "The Late Classic of Yaxuna, Yucatan, Mexico." *Mexicon* 23:10–14.

Stanton, Travis W., Traci Ardren, Nicolas C. Barth, Juan Fernandez-Diaz, Patrick Rohrer, Dominique Meyer, Stephanie J. Miller, Aline Magnoni, and Manuel Pérez. 2020. "'Structure' Density, Area, and Volume as Complementary Tools to Understand Maya Settlement: An Analysis of LiDAR Data Along the Great Road between Cobá and Yaxuná." *Journal of Archaeological Science: Reports* 29 (February): 1–10. https://doi.org/10.1016/j.jasrep.2019.102178.

Stanton, Travis W., and Ryan H. Collins. 2021. "The Role of Middle Preclassic Placemaking in the Creation of Late Preclassic Yucatecan Cities: The Foundations of Yaxuná." In *Early Mesoamerican Cities: New Perspectives on Urbanism and Urbanization in the Formative Period*, edited by Michael Love and Julia Guernsey, 99–120. Cambridge: Cambridge University Press.

Stanton, Travis W., and David A. Freidel. 2005. "Placing the Centre, Centring the Place: The Influence of Formative Sacbeob in Classic Site Design at Yaxuná, Yucatán." *Cambridge Archaeological Journal* 15 (2): 225–49.

Stanton, Travis W., David A. Freidel, Charles K. Suhler, Traci Ardren, James N. Ambrosino, Justine M. Shaw, and Sharon Bennett. 2010. *Excavations at Yaxuná,*

1986–1996: Results of the Selz Foundation Yaxuná Project. BAR International Series 2056. Oxford: Archaeopress.

Stanton, Travis W., and Aline Magnoni. 2008. "Places of Remembrance: The Use and Perception of Abandoned Structures in the Maya Lowlands." In *Ruins of the Past: The Use and Perception of Abandoned Structures in the Maya Lowlands*, edited by Travis W. Stanton and Aline Magnoni, 1–24. Boulder: University Press of Colorado.

Stanton, Travis W., Aline Magnoni, Stanley P. Guenter, José Osorio León, Francisco Pérez Ruíz, and María Rocio González de la Mata. 2020. "Borderland Politics: A Reconsideration of the Role of Yaxuná in Regional Maya Politics in the Latter Part of the Classic." In *A Forest of History: The Maya after the Emergence of Divine Kingship*, edited by Travis W. Stanton and M. Kathryn Brown, 135–53. Boulder: University Press of Colorado.

Stanton, Travis W., and Karl A. Taube. Forthcoming. "Concepts of Wild and Centered Among the Ancient Maya: Reconfiguring the Notion of Natural Landscapes in Mesoamerica." In *The Coming of Kings: A Reflection on the Early Periods in the Maya Area*, edited by M. Kathryn Brown and Travis W. Stanton. Manuscript submitted for review.

Stanton, Travis W., Karl A. Taube, and Ryan H. Collins. In press. "Domesticating Time: Quadripartite Symbolism and Rituals of Foundation at Yaxuná." In *Telling Time: Myth, History, and Everyday Life in the Ancient Maya World*, edited by David A. Freidel, Arlen F. Chase, Ann S. Dowd, and Jerry Murdock. Manuscript submitted for review.

Stanton, Travis W., Karl A. Taube, José Francisco Osorio León, Francisco Pérez Ruíz, María Rocio González de la Mata, Nelda I. Marengo Camacho, and Jeremy D. Coltman. n.d. "Urbanizing Paradise: The Implications of Pervasive Images of Flower World Across Chichen Itza." In *The Flexible Maya City: Attraction, Contraction, and Planning in Lowland Urban Dynamics*, edited by Damien B. Marken and M. Charlotte Arnauld. In press.

Sugiyama, Saburo. 2010. "Teotihuacan City Layout as a Cosmogram: Preliminary Results of the 2007 Measurement Unit Study." In *The Archaeology of Measurement: Comprehending Heaven, Earth and Time in Ancient Societies*, edited by Iain Morley and Colin Renfrew, 130–49. Cambridge: Cambridge University Press.

Sullivan, Alan P., Philip B. Mink, and Patrick M. Uphus. 2007. "Archaeological Survey Design, Units of Observation, and Characterization of Regional Variability." *American Antiquity* 72 (2): 322–33.

Taube, Karl A. 1996. "The Olmec Maize God: The Face of Corn in Formative Mesoamerica." *RES*, no. 29/30 (Spring–Autumn): 39–81.

Taube, Karl A. 2000. "Lightning Celts and Corn Fetishes: The Formative Olmec and the Development of Maize Symbolism in Mesoamerica and the American Southwest." In *Olmec Art and Archaeology in Mesoamerica*, edited by John E. Clark and Mary E. Pye, 297–337. Studies in the History of Art 58. Washington, D.C.: National Gallery of Art.

Taube, Karl A. 2003. "Ancient and Contemporary Maya Conceptions about Field and Forest." In *The Lowland Maya Area: Three Millennia at the Human-Wildland Interface*, edited by Arturo Gómez-Pompa, Michael F. Allen, Scott L. Fedick, and Juan J. Jiménez-Osornio, 461–92. New York: Food Products Press.

Taube, Karl A. 2004. *Olmec Art at Dumbarton Oaks*. Pre-Columbian Art at Dumbarton Oaks, no. 2. Washington, D.C.: Dumbarton Oaks Research Library and Collection.

Taube, Karl A., Travis W. Stanton, José Francisco Osorio León, Francisco Pérez Ruíz, María Rocio González de la Mata, and Jeremy D. Coltman. 2020. *The Initial Series Group at Chichen Itza, Yucatan: Archaeological Investigations and Iconographic Interpretations*. San Francisco: Precolumbia Mesoweb Press.

Taube, Karl A., David Stuart, William A. Saturno, and Heather Hurst. 2010. *The Murals of San Bartolo, El Petén, Guatemala. Part 2, The West Wall*. Ancient America 10. Barnardsville, N.C.: Center for Ancient American Studies.

Thomas, David H. 1975. "Nonsite Sampling in Archaeology: Up the Creek Without a Site?" In *Sampling in Archaeology*, edited by James W. Mueller, 61–81. Tucson: University of Arizona Press.

Thomas, Prentice M., Jr. 1981. *Prehistoric Maya Settlement Patterns at Becan, Campeche, Mexico*. Middle American Research Institute 45. New Orleans: Tulane University.

Thompson, J. Eric S., H. E. D. Pollock, and Jean Charlot. 1932. *A Preliminary Study of the Ruins of Coba, Quintana Roo, Mexico*. Carnegie Institution of Washington, Pub. 424. Washington, D.C.: Carnegie Institution of Washington.

Tiesler, Vera, Andrea Cucina, Travis W. Stanton, and David A. Freidel. 2017. *Before Kukulkán: Maya Life, Death, and Identity at Classic Period Yaxuná*. Tucson: University of Arizona Press.

Tozzer, Alfred M. 1941. *Landa's Relación de las cosas de Yucatán*. Peabody Museum of Archaeology and Ethnology 18. Cambridge, Mass.: Harvard University.

Villa Rojas, Alfonso. 1934. *The Yaxuna-Coba Causeway*. Contributions to American Archaeology, no. 9, Carnegie Institution of Washington, Pub. 436. Washington, D.C.: Carnegie Institution of Washington.

Willey, Gordon R., and Philip Phillips. 1958. *Method and Theory in American Archaeology*. Chicago: University of Chicago Press.

Wilson, Peter J. 1988. *The Domestication of the Human Species*. New Haven, Conn.: Yale University Press.

CHAPTER 4

Taming the Jungle

Decauville Railroads in Nineteenth- and Early Twentieth-Century Yucatán

JENNIFER P. MATHEWS

In the Yucatán Peninsula during the nineteenth century, commodity industries such as henequen, chicle, hardwoods, and sugarcane required the installation of narrow-gauge Decauville railroads.[1] Mules, horses, or people pulled simple low and flat, four-wheeled wooden carts (figure 4.1) along these rails. These small-scale rail networks often created the boundaries around the hacienda grounds and connected workers' camps and agricultural fields to the processing areas and ultimately to the large-scale rail networks that led to the cities and coastal ports. For the elites who ran commodity industries, Decauville rails were part of the larger modernizing infrastructure used to "tame" the jungle and speed up labor production. This tied into the national view that Mexican railroads were an economic and socializing force for good. Railroads also symbolized a "responsible" Western management of the extraction of forest resources, as opposed to the view that Indigenous practices mismanaged natural resources.

However, for the Indigenous workers, the rails were laid atop stone roads built by their ancient ancestors, along jungle paths that their families had walked centuries (Mathews and Lizama 2006, 117–18) or through agricultural fields on lands that had been taken from them. Since the Spanish arrival

---

1. Decauville railroads are named for their inventor, Paul Decauville, who created narrow-gauge track that could be easily moved and reassembled and was used around the world in the nineteenth and twentieth centuries during military campaigns, as tourist trains, for transporting materials from quarries and harvesting agricultural products such as chicle and henequen (Shaw 1958).

FIGURE 4.1 Workers hauling hardwood logs out of the forest on a horse-pulled Decauville railway near Puerto Morelos, Quintana Roo (photo courtesy of Jorge Sánchez).

in the sixteenth century, the Maya populations in the Yucatán Peninsula that had not been decimated by disease faced a continuous loss of autonomy and access to lands. Populations were forced into pueblos with gridded streets surrounding a central church and plaza to facilitate religious conversion and control (Eiss 2010, 21). During the seventeenth century, although Mexican legislation limited Spaniards from acquiring Indigenous lands, ranches and haciendas still expanded into communal lands (Eiss 2010, 23). Although nineteenth-century Reform Laws divested church ownership of former Indigenous lands, this only further facilitated private land ownership (Alston, Mattiace, and Nonnenmacher 2009, 107). On these private commercial lands, railroads were a tool used to exploit labor in a brutal process of forest and agricultural extraction for global commodity consumption. They were also a symbol of Indigenous peoples' loss of property rights, resources, and the ability to feed their own families. And yet, in some cases, the rails that traversed from the haciendas and into the forest allowed Maya workers to be away from the watchful eye of managers, hidden away in the untamable forest. Thus, this chapter examines the contradictory roles that railroads played as symbolic boundaries during the nineteenth century for both the elites who ran the commodity industries and for Maya peoples who provided the back-breaking labor. It also looks at the continuing legacy of this imposition of "modernizing" infrastructure upon Maya peoples in the twenty-first century through two proposed examples of train tourism development projects in Mexico and Guatemala.

Railroads as Modernizing Forces

In the nineteenth and early twentieth centuries, the goal of modernist development was to conquer and control nature in a process known as "the urbanization of nature." On the one hand, the objective was to remove natural resources that could be turned into profitable commodities, and on the other hand, it was to transform nature to form an urban environment (Kaika 2006, 276, 295). During this time, postindependence nations like Greece and Mexico were attempting to shake off a colonialist past while trying to enter into the political and economic arena as modern states. Infrastructure in both nations had fallen into ruin during long periods of warfare, and these countries were better known for their "glorious" archaeological past than their contemporary splendor. As Shannon Lee Dawdy (2010, 762) states, the ruins of modernity "remind us that modernity is always incomplete, always moving on, and always full of hubris. . . . There is a growing consensus that modernity is best understood not as a hodgepodge of ideas and practices but more basically as a form of temporal ideology that valorizes newness, rupture, and linear plot lines." Thus, government officials around the world wanted to demonstrate their renewed strength through the control of nature via the engineering of innovative infrastructure that broke dramatically from the natural landscape. For the central states in Greece and Mexico, modernizing also involved bringing in foreign architects to design public buildings and infrastructure in the capitals as a way of signaling their transformation to the rest of the world (for Greece, see Kaika 2006; for Mexico, see Oles 2013; Wakild 2007). In Greece, a clear example of this was the construction of the Marathon Dam, which through marvels of modern engineering would dramatically increase the water supply in Athens (Kaika 2006).

In Mexico, as President Porfirio Díaz came to power in 1876, he measured modernization through metrics such as the proportion of land that was dedicated to export crops such as chicle and henequen, and the number of miles of railroads and trams that had been installed across the country

(Alston, Mattiace, and Nonnenmacher 2009). The railroad network was a symbol of Mexico's economic growth and commemorated its status in the modern world (Matthews 2014, 24). Díaz and his advisers believed these goals would work hand in hand and that the Mexican economy would improve as the country was able to move these forest commodities as well as agricultural products, minerals, and laborers. They further believed that the railroad was an agent of social change that would integrate and "civilize" isolated regions. This was in part because the government could mobilize the military to more easily control uprisings, but it was also a cultural project that promoted national unity by bringing Indigenous peoples "into the national fold." This was based on the underlying notion that the "shortcoming" of Native peoples could be improved through racial integration and result in social uplift (Matthews 2014, 2–4, 24). One Díaz supporter argued that Indigenous people actually wanted to assimilate, using the example of Texcoco peoples who were willingly working on the Morelos railroad project. He believed their participation in the national railroad project would help lift their towns toward a prosperous future that matched their glorious past prior to the conquest. Among some intellectual elites in Mexico, there was pride in the Aztec and Chichimeca empires, and they believed that the railway would bring out the noble and hardworking characteristics of the "fallen Indian" (Matthews 2014, 124–25).

Many non-Indigenous urbanites across Mexico believed that in addition to railroads, modern conveniences such as electric streetlights, parks, and underground sewers were markers of civilization and differentiated them from "backward" rural residents (Wakild 2007, 103). A fictional account published in a Mexico City newspaper made note that rural visitors were often stunned by electric lights, comparing them to the glow of the moon. Elites ridiculed these comparisons, implying that provincial residents could not appreciate or understand these amenities, as they only understood the world through the lens of nature (Matthews 2014, 73).

This also reflected the broader Western notion of the human need to "dominate" nature through science, technology, and engineering that worked as cures for ignorance and superstition (Matthews 2014, 25) and drove major development projects such as the Panama Canal (Frenkel 1996, 321). This era was dominated by rationalist ideology that prioritized scientific knowledge and modernized infrastructure over "primitive" knowledge. The Indigenous relationship with the natural world separated them from Westerners and was a central component in constructing Western development theory. In constructing hierarchies of industrial development, this "oneness" with nature was a negative quality. The West aimed to dominate, exploit, and even destroy nature, which required a certain distance from nature, while they viewed an underdeveloped closeness to nature as backward and unscientific (Steet 2000, 136–37).

For example, in the 1930s when Mexican officials surveyed the forests of southern Chihuahua, they viewed the Rarámuri of Chihuahua as a great threat due to what they viewed as the indiscriminate practice of clearing the best trees and the foolish idea that clearing trees brought the rains. Instead of recognizing that the Rarámuri were engaged in small-scale and sustainable forestry management, Mexican officials believed the forest would be better cared for by timber companies. By the 1960s, commercial lumber companies were ignoring extraction limits, cutting lumber on designated Indigenous lands and filling the forest with caravans of trucks loaded down with lumber (Boyer 2015, 1–2). From the Rarámuri perspective, the forest shaped their settlements, was the foundation of their survival as a source of cooking fuel and food, and provided the topography for their collective community memory (Boyer 2015, 3, 7).

Similarly, in the mid-nineteenth century, Maya farmers in British Honduras (now Belize) objected to the British loggers' use of oxen to drag felled timber to rivers for transport, as they often passed through their milpas, causing major damage (Cal 1983, 249–50; Houk, Bonorden, and Kilgore 2022, 152). This became an even bigger issue in the 1920s when gas-powered tractors were introduced, as they could reach mahogany sources that were previously off-limits to cattle teams (Camille 2000, 108). Among Lacandon Maya of Chiapas, conflicts arose when woodcutters or chicle gatherers stole food products from their agricultural fields, raped women, or attempted to capture the men as slaves or laborers. They reacted by hiding their fields or houses deep in the forest, insisting on being compensated for lost resources, or exacting revenge through threats, violence, or killing (Palka 2005, 234–35).

British loggers in Belize argued that Maya slash-and-burn agriculture was wasteful because the clear-cutting of the forest destroyed prized mahogany trees (Church, Yaeger, and Dornan 2011, 180; Ng 2007, 68; Thompson 1939, 4; see also Houk, Bonorden, and Kilgore, 2022, 152). Further, they complained that when Maya laborers who worked for the logging companies could grow their own food, it meant that they didn't have to purchase food at inflated prices from the company stores (Church, Yaeger, and Dornan 2011, 180). Even when Maya *chicleros* had a vested interest in maintaining the chicozapote trees for collecting latex, the British protested that they lacked oversight and were destructive to the trees (Houk, Bonorden, and Kilgore, forthcoming). Similarly, in a "Monographic Album" on the territory of Quintana Roo from 1936, a member of the Department of Forestry discussed how the responsible exploitation of the forest required scientific knowledge to successfully conserve the forest: "However, the wonderful location of these forests requires that their exploitation uses scientific systems that allow their reforestation and conservation" (Menéndez 1936, 130, translation mine). The implication was that traditional Maya agricultural practices were destructive and that tree species such as cedar, chicozapote, and mahogany should be preserved (Menéndez 1936, 130).

In this same monograph, there is also an article on a railroad abandoned during the Mexican Revolution of 1912 under the Maya uprising based out of Chan Santa Cruz: "After 1915, when Santa Cruz was handed over to the Maya, this locomotive, already unusable, was macheted *by the enemies of civilization*" (Menéndez 1936, 34, emphasis mine). He further derided them for blowing up the public cistern with dynamite, setting the railroad cars on fire, and derailing the locomotives, and "in their eagerness to isolate themselves from the Peninsula and the Republic, they undid all of the existing telephone and telegraph lines" (Menéndez 1936, 136). However, the writer celebrated that another train that the Maya allowed to be engulfed by the forest was eventually put back into service (Menéndez 1936, 38). From an elite Mexican perspective, any Indigenous act of resistance toward Western development would be an affront to the modernization movement, which meant being less Indigenous and more European (Matthews 2014, 70). This resulted in attempts to control Indigenous peoples and their actions through various policies and practices, including land ownership.

The Loss of Indigenous Property Rights

In 1856, Mexican legislation known as the "disentailment law" forced communities to divide up commonly held land and reclassify it as privately and individually held lands, which meant that tracks could be sold to corporations (Boyer 2015, 7). And although the 1857 Constitution of Mexico forbade the corporate ownership of lands, during the Porfiriato these laws were regularly violated with the encouragement of foreign investment and the distribution of significant land grants to private corporations (Alston, Mattiace, and Nonnenmacher 2009, 107–8). Díaz divided these subvention (government-granted) lands in Yucatán into large lots (between 7,000 and 23,000 hectares), but they were interspersed with public and private properties that included sharecroppers, tenants, and squatters (Van Hoy 2008, 37). This furthered the demand for forest resources during this time, and foreign capital-funded railroads and corporations scaled up production (Boyer 2015, 8). The government passed new laws that did away with ejidos and most other group ownership of land. In some cases, villagers lost their lands on a technicality, such as when they had failed to file petitions to protest land grants being given to developers within the given time limits (Wells 1982, 247). The Mexican government hired professional foresters to manage the removal of natural resources and generally gave preference to the corporations over the Indigenous populations that lived there. They characterized local populations as backward and ignored their land ownership claims (Boyer 2015, 9). Communal villages were further isolated when the government also allowed for the privatization of vital resources such as water and game (Alston, Mattiace, and Nonnenmacher 2009, 110; Sweitz 2012, 241). In some cases, Indigenous peoples harvested forest resources illegally and derided the notion that professional foresters understood the landscape better than they did. In some cases, they bribed or even killed wardens and threatened to rebel against local authorities (Boyer 2015, 9). Since coming to Mexico, upper-class white settlers focused efforts on isolating lower-class people and keeping them disengaged from politics, as they feared these kinds of uprisings (Anderson 2006, 48). Further, many farmers had accumulated significant debt due to the loss of crops as a result of drought or locusts. Thus, in the nineteenth century, a significant number of Maya people attached themselves to privately owned haciendas out of economic necessity (Alston, Mattiace, and Nonnenmacher 2009, 110–11).

In response to the development of haciendas and commodity industries like henequen, engineers in Yucatán began a massive project of building a railroad that ran between Mérida and Progreso in 1874. The construction process faced obstacles of funding shortages and engineering challenges aiming to connect the primary port of the region with the state capital (Wells 1982, 235). By 1881, there were only ten miles of the railway complete, although by 1890 they had constructed four railways of more than 450 miles almost entirely by Native labor. The work was slow because most of the rock quarrying was done by hand, as it was difficult to maintain quarrying machinery. However, one advantage of the region was that there were no rivers or streams to traverse (Yucatán's water comes primarily from an underground aquifer), and thus they did not need to construct any bridges. Each worker was given a section to construct a dry rock bed that would be made of varying heights depending on the terrain, which was then generally topped with a layer of *sascab* (fine limestone plaster) upon which the rails and ties were laid. Much of the rail materials were imported from the United States, including pine ties from Louisiana, which in the more arid climate of western Yucatán tended to last up to six years (Engineering News 1890, 217).

The completion of the Mérida–Progresso line allowed Mérida to be connected to worldwide trade markets and dramatically reduced the costs of shipping (Wells 1982, 235). For the haciendas, having direct access to these railroads could make all the difference in their success. The United Railway Company of Yucatán (Unidos de Yucatán) was able to curry favor to those growers who relied on the larger *casas exportadas* (middlemen who imported agricultural machinery and provided mortgages, loans, and lines of credit) by ensuring that railroad cars were dispatched to them first. As henequen prices changed daily, those who had to wait for transport service were at a distinct disadvantage (Wells 1982, 241). In the case of the powerful Peón family of Mérida, they simply built their own local railway, recognizing that the investment would provide them easier access to the port and ensure a slight advantage in a market that had razor-thin margins (Wells 1982, 249).

Within the haciendas during the 1890s, there were between 200 and 300 miles of portable railways that had been imported from France and installed on the grounds (Engineering News 1890, 217). By 1907, this had grown to more than 1,300 miles (Geographical Section of the Naval Intelligence Division n.d., 502). The track was comparably lightweight (weighing around 20 pounds per meter and generally 12 to 19.5 inches in width) and used animal labor for moving the flatbed cars (Engineering News 1890, 217). Although the Decauville narrow-gauge railways were considerably smaller in size and scale than the national railway network put in place during the Porfiriato (see, e.g., Goldfrank 1976; Van Hoy 2008), they seemingly were still a symbol of progress and an attempt to modernize the region. The railroad network also promoted social and cultural communication in the region, for better or for worse, as foreign ideologies were imposed on Indigenous populations (Goldfrank 1976, 3).

As Brian Larkin (2013, 330) notes, infrastructures often start as "independent technologies with widely varying technical standards... [that] converge into a network." Thus, although the carts were small and run with human or animal labor, the narrow railways were laid within haciendas to bring commodities like henequen and sugarcane from the fields to the processing areas. They also brought the finished products to the full-scale railroad depots or ports for export, linking the two systems (Hansen and Bastarrachea 1983, 65; Wells 1982, 248). Outside the haciendas, there were some dispersed Decauville railways constructed as distant sites that were primarily focused on extracting lumber (Hansen and Bastarrachea 1983, 65) or chicle (Mathews and Schultz 2009). Thus, the Decauville and full-scale railways formed a broader infrastructure network that created a literal and symbolic set of boundaries. Those haciendas with the most capital and power could exploit these to their advantage, while for smaller haciendas, access to these boundaries limited their ability to grow. Those communities located at the terminus of a rail line could benefit from being connected to larger cities; however, it made it easier to overexploit their resources such as lumber or usurp their communal lands, sometimes leading to social conflict (Goldfrank 1976, 4). It also meant that remote Indigenous communities that could previously fly under the radar of government authorities could be repressed by troops arriving in a short time if they showed signs of rebellion (Goldfrank 1976, 17).

Supporters of the Porfirian regime emphasized that the railroad was one of the major achievements of Díaz's presidency, as they believed it had so much potential to remake Mexican society into a nation of order and progress (Matthews 2014, 4). In Yucatán, the *ayuntamientos* (counties) of Mérida, Temax, and Motul all commended the president's legacy of the railroads for bringing prosperity to the region and giving energy and movement across the country (Matthews 2014, 4, 52). Through the addition of this railroad infrastructure, local leaders believed they could even transform traditional villages into modernized pueblos. This view was commemorated by a poet who stated at the inauguration of the railroad from the Maya village of Umán into Mérida: "'Today the West / covers itself in splendor / The spirit of progress / visits its mansion.' Soon the railroad would 'bring glory to the country, and fortune to el pueblo, allowing 'radiant Yucatán / to glimpse its future'" (Eiss 2010, 55).

Railroads from the Indigenous Perspective

While we often analyze the advantages that infrastructures like railroads provide through the lens of development and improved access, scholars are also advocating for examining these networks through other perspectives. For example, Doreen Massey (1993, 61) argues for the "power-geometry" of infrastructure, stating that "different social groups and different individuals are placed in very distinct ways in relation to these flows and interconnections. This point concerns not merely the issue of who moves and who doesn't . . . it is also about power in relation to the flows and the movement . . . some are more in charge of it than others; some initiate flows and movement, others don't; some are more on the receiving end of it than others; some are effectively imprisoned by it."

For Maya workers, the hacienda rails that bound their world were a constant reminder of their loss of autonomy. The expansion of rail lines facilitated land grabbing, and thus the narrow-gauge tracks traversed through lands they once owned (Goldfrank 1976, 17). The rails were sometimes laid atop *sakbe'ob* (roads) or constructed by their ancient ancestors, or followed along jungle paths that their families had walked freely for centuries (Mathews and Lizama 2006, 117–18). The rail trucks also moved large amounts of product such as harvested sugarcane quickly to be processed. Rather than making laborers' jobs easier, they upped their workload since more could be processed in a single day.

And yet there were some benefits of these train networks to the laborers. The railbeds were kept relatively clear from the impeding forest (see figure 4.1), making it easier for them to avoid snakes and other dangers of the jungle. They also provided an elevated path for pedestrians to be able to pass through seasonally flooded areas like mangroves or savannas. Additionally, in the case of full-scale railroads, it was the railroad companies that paid for the cost of maintenance, replacing the traditional practice of corvée labor and taxation that had been previously placed on community members. The railroad companies further provided other infrastructure benefits such as stations that could be used for shelter, rentable storage space, and potable water (Van Hoy 2008, 158–60).

Within henequen and sugar haciendas, Decauville railroads were generally within the hacienda grounds. Laborers were constricted within the boundaries of the railways and fairly restricted in their movements. They were closely supervised while weeding, harvesting, transporting, and processing the raw product. However, those who were attached to chicle haciendas generally had more freedom of movement as their commodity came from the chicozapote trees that wouldn't grow in orchards. Instead, they were scattered throughout the jungle, often located long distances from the big house. *Plataformeros*, the drivers of the narrow-gauge railways, often spent their days in the forest, away from the watchful eyes of managers. They would meet up with chicleros at their remote camps to collect mahogany logs or blocks of chicle to transport back. And although the chicleros worked in dangerous conditions in the forest, they usually only rode the rails back to the hacienda or into town at the end of the collecting season (Mathews and Schultz 2009, 92).

Additionally, belief systems across the Maya world distinguish between the forest and the community, seeing a sharp difference between the dangers and wildness of the natural world and the social-constructed space that makes up villages and milpas. Maya peoples often believe the forest contains danger because there are evil spirits or demons, wild animals, and threatening plants. These wild spaces are characterized by darkness and shadows, whereas cultivated fields and domestic plots are filled with light (Taube 2003, 466–67). Forest lands are also identified with ancient peoples, and they must be treated with awe and apprehension, and often served as a place of defiance against religious conversion and Spanish conquest (Taube 2003, 468). Additionally, features such as sakbe'ob or boundaries cut around corn fields or towns are straight lines that intentionally provide order, balance, and harmony. The Yucatec Mayan word *toh* means "straight" as well as "good," "truth," and "social correctness," while in colonial Tzotzil Mayan, the term *togh* means "straight" and to be "socially correct." Karl A. Taube (2003, 465) explains, "Implicit in the concept of *toh* is that making milpa, houses, art, and other efforts of construction are inherently good and ethically correct human acts. On their straight paths defining the town and milpa, the Yucatec *b'alamob'ob'* defend the physical and spiritual well-being of humans and their efforts." Thus, in some ways the Maya views of the control of the forest were parallel to those of the West, and some Maya workers may have wanted to associate with this "modernization" effort, as exemplified by a photograph of a family on a Decauville rail truck (figure 4.2).

FIGURE 4.2 Family gathered on top of a Decauville rail truck in Puerto Morelos, Quintana Roo (photo courtesy of Jorge Sánchez).

Contemporary Maya Train Development Projects

If we are to understand contemporary inequalities, such as those faced by Maya peoples today, we must recognize that these were set in motion during the colonial period (Manuel-Navarrete and Redclift 2012). Through studying Maya history and drawing connections to present-day social concerns, we may emphasize that these social systems have subjugated Maya people for centuries (Liebmann and Rizvi 2008). Currently, there are two proposed development projects that would build train networks to support Maya tourism. Arguably, developers believe that they are designed to benefit Indigenous populations by providing them with access to technology that could help advance their circumstances. However, they fail to recognize that there is a legacy of leaving Indigenous people out of the loop, which they seem to be doing once again.

El Tren Maya, Yucatán Peninsula

The first project under development is in southern Mexico. Soon after his election in 2018, Mexican president Andrés Manuel López Obrador (AMLO) proposed the construction of "The Maya Train / El Tren Maya," a 1,500 km (950 miles) high-speed railroad that would encourage Mexican tourism by

Taming the Jungle   111

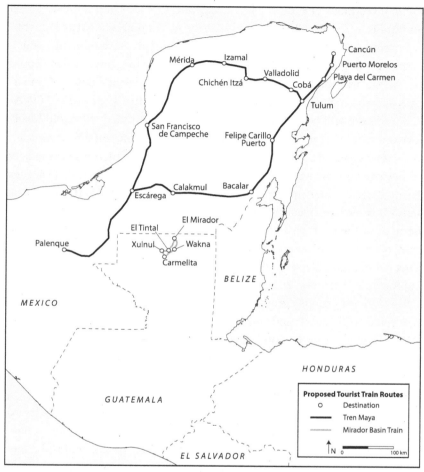

FIGURE 4.3 Map showing the proposed locations of the Tren Maya in Yucatán and the tourist train in the Petén region of Guatemala (image created by Tina Ross).

connecting well-known archaeological sites in the states of Chiapas, Tabasco, Campeche, Yucatán, and Quintana Roo (figure 4.3). At an estimated cost of $6.5 billion, it has seventeen proposed stops, including Palenque in Chiapas; Tenosique in Tabasco; Escárcega, Campeche City, and Campeche in Campeche; Maxcanú, Mérida, Yucatán, Izamal, Chichén Itzá, and Valladolid in Yucatán; Cancún, Puerto Morelos, Playa del Carmen, Tulum, Felipe Carrillo Puerto, and Bacalar in Quintana Roo; and wrapping up at Xpujil and Calakmul in Campeche. AMLO's argument is that the project represents a public investment in rural Mexico that will create jobs and improve social conditions in Yucatán. The project is run by the Fondo Nacional de Fomento al Turismo (FONATUR, National Fund for Tourism Development), which anticipates that as many as 8,000 passengers a day (3 million a year) could use the rail system, with tourists potentially visiting lesser-known Maya villages and colonial cities in the region (Pskowski 2019). The head of FONATUR argues it will be an eco-friendly tourism project that will avoid "overdevelopment." He further argues that Mexico's environmental problems are social issues caused by a "failure to integrate certain populations into society so they can co-exist with the rainforest" (Whelan 2020, C3). AMLO argues that this project attempts to level the unequal playing field, stating, "This is an act of justice, because this region has been the most abandoned. The moment of the southeast has arrived, and it's just in time. That's why [the train] is a very important public works project." He believes that the train will bring about regional jobs, reducing the need for Maya people to migrate for employment (Pskowski 2019).

Some Maya groups agree with this assessment, as it would allow them to develop ATV rentals and small hotels rather than having to rely on clearcutting timber or honey. But conservationists are raising concerns about the environmental impacts of the proposed train and related development, including damage to forests, air and water pollution, invasive species, and disrupted animal routes (Whelan 2020, C3). There is a concern that Maya people will not benefit from this and that their voices are not being heard during this process. Developers have highlighted that the remote archaeological site of Calakmul would become the "jewel" of the peninsula, and yet Indigenous peoples have been petitioning the government to help with climate change–driven drought, as there is no water for the community of more than twenty-eight thousand Indigenous people. Despite the promise of developing a new aqueduct in the area, some Maya people are arguing that this will only bring devastation, as deforestation leads to further drought: "The problem is that it's creating divisions among the very Mayan [sic] communities it aims to serve, igniting a fierce debate over who gets to speak for Indigenous people, who have historically been silenced and sidelined" (Beatley and Edwards 2020). Members of the Zapatistas (who, in 1994, led an armed uprising against the federal government) have vowed to "defend the land with their lives" and believe that this will simply repeat the mistakes of the past, bringing corruption, overdevelopment, and cartel violence to their region. Others are putting together petitions and have requested an injunction to halt the train's construction, with concerns focusing on the "development centers" that would come with the train, further stressing natural resources (Beatley and Edwards 2020).

In an open letter to AMLO, members of Indigenous communities in the Yucatán Peninsula are protesting that outsiders did not have the right to decide what would or would not be done in their territories. They are arguing that they are being left out as stakeholders because they already have a budget and a plan that would impact their lands, and the only information they received about the project was through the media or leaks. They warn that the Tren Maya project could become another Cancún or Riviera Maya that has no benefit to the Maya population (Ramos 2018): "It's a tourism project that will only benefit the wealthy and foreigners. We, who are the owners of the land, will only see it pass by" (Pskowski 2019).

Mexico has ratified Convention 169 of the International Labour Organization, which states that when there are development projects that will impact Indigenous lands, they must be consulted. A developer is required to lay out the risks, explain long-term impacts for the community, and allow a vote. Although a vote was held in December 2019 with tremendous support for the project, the UN Commission on Human Rights has proclaimed that it did not meet these requirements. Voter turnout was below 3 percent, women were sorely underrepresented, and the consultation process focused almost exclusively on benefits, promising medical care and access to water with a "yes" vote. Additionally, Mexico is the fourth-highest nation in killing environmental activists, which intimidates people into silence (Beatley and Edwards 2020). Thus, it appears that despite the stated intentions, the Mexican government is attempting to impose infrastructure upon Maya peoples "for their benefit," but they are not being made part of the planning process, nor are they consulted in a representative fashion about the plan and its potential outcomes.

Maya Disneyland, Petén, Guatemala

For the past two decades, Maya archaeologist Richard Hansen and his colleagues have championed a second train tourism development project in the Petén region of Guatemala (Devine 2018; Rahder 2015). They are proposing to change the way in which land is managed through concessions in the

Maya Biosphere Reserve of El Mirador Basin (a kind of "green land grab"; see Devine 2018). Since 1995, this has been run by Guatemala's Consejo Nacional de Áreas Protegidas (CONAP, National Council of Protected Areas) and allows Maya farmers to practice agroforestry while living within the reserve. In 2020, Vice News reported that Hansen needs to change the Guatemalan law to reclassify the land from a National Park to a wilderness area, which would then allow for a ban on logging and the ability to develop private tourism. The bill, "The Mirador-Calakmul Basin Act, Maya Security, and Conservation Partnership," would use U.S. taxpayer money to fund the project (Vice News 2020). Hansen has hired a lobbying firm to garner support in the U.S. Congress. Supporters of the bill include Senator Jim Inhofe (R-Oklahoma). Inhofe is an ardent climate change denier, who supports the bill because he sees it as a way to stem immigration to the United States (Vice News 2020).

Hansen proposes to first build a US$13 million tourist train that would lead to what he calls "Maya Disney." "We have a real live Disneyland here," Hansen says. "We don't have to invent anything. It's all here. Animals, crocodiles, tapirs, jaguars, ruins, jungle, macaws, parrots, toucans, it's all here" (Maya Biosphere 2019). Hansen argues that the wilderness area will have no airstrips or roads, which he feels will keep narco-traffickers at bay. He says this will also limit the money laundering that he claims criminals are currently conducting through the development of cattle pastures. The narrow-gauge, propane-driven train would leave from the Maya village of Carmelita every morning, which he asserts will bring money to that community, and would connect nine archaeological sites, including El Mirador, Nakbe, Wakna, Tintal, and Xulnal (see figure 4.3). The new president of Guatemala and the current congress are showing support for Hansen's plan, so the project might be moving forward (Vice News 2020).

There are several issues with Hansen's proposed model. First, he cannot demonstrate that narco-trafficking is the cause of increased cattle ranching, nor that the region is under environmental threat. In fact, the current community-run forestry concessions are responsible for safeguarding the forest from loggers and drug traffickers, and it has been working so well that the rate of deforestation has decreased. They have been so effective at these efforts that they have won awards and the support of USAID, Guatemalan governmental agencies, and various environmental groups (García 2020). Second, local people would lose income and autonomy because the plan would allow private management firms to take over local businesses, would remove local logging concessions, and would replace existing Maya tourism businesses that offer site tours via horseback (Vice News 2020). Hansen, who has had control over the research project at El Mirador for more than thirty years, is recruiting foreign investors to develop a private hotel in the heart of a Maya biosphere, exploiting Maya culture for profit (Montejo 2022, 270–71). This falls into the same pattern that we've seen in other Maya tourism projects, in which locals are forced into low-wage jobs managed by foreigners or other outsiders with no opportunities for advancement. In a 2020 interview, local resident Lindoro Hernandez (a carpentry manager in the village of Carmelita, where the train would commence its journey) states that Hansen wants to shut the communities out and hire them as employees, essentially removing them as main actors in their own livelihood and forcing them to move to the cities. When Hansen is asked about the long-term stake for Maya campesinos, he argues that tourism will bring more money to the area than logging does. However, when pressed about how this benefits the locals, Hansen says, "Okay, you're an entrepreneur and you want to build a $5 million hotel and turn it over to the local campesino? That doesn't work in the real world" (Vice News 2020).

A third issue is that Indigenous and Guatemala communities are not being properly consulted (Montejo 2022, 271) and Hansen is proposing that the U.S. government should provide funding to help advance the project. Although Hansen has ardent supporters, there is also growing opposition to his plan among environmentalists and archaeologists. The president of the Society for American Archaeology sent a letter to Senator Inohe indicating the professional organization's opposition to the bill (Montejo 2022, 271; Watkins 2020). Further, Guatemalan archaeologist Francisco Estrada-Belli states, "It concerns me that those outside the academic community who currently support Hansen's project genuinely believe he is working to benefit Guatemala, while the plan appears to be more about him having control of a large portion of the country than about benefitting Guatemala or science" (Maya Biosphere 2019). Guatemalan archaeologist Tomas Barrientos says that his concern about this bill is that Hansen does not have genuine involvement of the Guatemalan people in the decision-making of the future of El Mirador, and he hopes that Hansen will improve this participation (Vice News 2020). Thus, in these two modern railroad development projects we see the continued pattern of Maya peoples being pushed to the sidelines of the process while the wealthy, connected, and powerful advance developments for their own benefit. Although both projects will surely bring increased tourism to these regions, it appears it will be at a cost to the environment and the local people, a colonialist legacy that has carried over the past five hundred years. Until the developers of new rail lines truly include and respect the input of the Indigenous populations whose lives they traverse, the growing infrastructure will continue to impose on local lives instead of helping to enrich them.

Works Cited

Alston, Lee J., Shannan Mattiace, and Tomas Nonnenmacher. 2009. "Coercion, Culture and Contracts: Labor and Debt on Henequen Haciendas in Yucatán, Mexico, 1870–1915." *Journal of Economic History* 69 (1): 104–37.

Anderson, Benedict. 2006. *Imagined Communities: Reflections on the Origin and Spread of Nationalism.* Rev. ed. London: Verso.

Beatley, Meaghan, and Sam Edwards. 2020. "Is Mexico's 'Mayan Train' a Boondoggle?" *The Nation,* May 22. https://www.thenation.com/article/world/is-mexicos-mayan-train-a-boondoggle/.

Boyer, Christopher R. 2015. *Political Landscapes: Forests, Conservation, and Community in Mexico.* Durham, N.C.: Duke University Press.

Cal, Angel Eduardo. 1983. "Anglo Maya Contact in Northern Belize: A Study of British Policy Toward the Maya During the Caste War of Yucatán, 1847–1872." Master's thesis, University of Calgary.

Camille, Michael. 2000. "The Effects of Timber Haulage Improvements on Mahogany Extraction in Belize: An Historical Geography." *Yearbook (Conference of Latin Americanist Geographers)* 26:103–15.

Church, Minette C., Jason Yaeger, and Jennifer L. Dornan. 2011. "The San Pedro Maya and the British Colonial Enterprise in British Honduras." In *Enduring Conquests: Rethinking the Archaeology of Resistance to Spanish Colonialism in the Americas,* edited by Matthew Liebmann and Melissa S. Murphy, 173–97. Santa Fe, N.Mex.: School for Advanced Research Press.

Dawdy, Shannon Lee. 2010. "Clockpunk Anthropology and the Ruins of Modernity." *Current Anthropology* 51 (6): 761–93.

Devine, Jennifer A. 2018. "Community Forest Concessionaires: Resisting Green Grabs and Producing Political Subjects in Guatemala." *Journal of Peasant Studies* 45 (3): 565–84.

Eiss, Paul. 2010. *In the Name of the Pueblo: Place, Community, and the Politics of History in the Yucatán.* Durham, N.C.: Duke University Press.

Engineering News. 1890. "Railroading in Yucatán." *Engineering News* 24 (36): 217.

Frenkel, Stephen. 1996. "Jungle Stories: North American Representations of Tropical Panama." *Geographical Review* 86 (3): 317–33.

García, Beatriz. 2020. "The Suspicious Initiative of an Archaeologist to 'Save' an Ancient Mayan City." *Al Día*, June 18. https://aldianews.com/articles/culture/social/suspicious-initiative-archaeologist-save-ancient-mayan-city/58920.

Geographical Section of the Naval Intelligence Division. n.d. *A Handbook of Mexico*. London: His Majesty's Stationary Office.

Goldfrank, Walter L. 1976. "The Ambiguity of Infrastructure: Railroads in Prerevolutionary Mexico." *Studies in Comparative International Development* 11 (3): 3–24.

Hansen, Asael T., and Juan R. Bastarrachea M. 1983. *Mérida: Su transformación de capital colonial a naciente metrópoli en 1935*. Mexico City: Instituto Nacional de Antropología e Historia.

Houk, Brett A., Brooke Bonorden, and Gertrude Kilgore. Forthcoming. "Living on the Edge: Kaxil Uinic Village and the San Pedro Maya in British Honduras." In *Coloniality in the Maya Lowlands: Archaeological Perspectives*, edited by Kasey Diserens Morgan and Tiffany C. Fryer, 147–70. Boulder: University Press of Colorado.

Kaika, Maria. 2006. "Dams as Symbols of Modernization: The Urbanization of Nature Between Geographical Imagination and Materiality." *Annals of the Association of American Geographers* 96 (2): 276–301.

Larkin, Brian. 2013. "The Politics and Poetics of Infrastructure." *Annual Review of Anthropology* 42:327–43.

Liebmann, Matthew, and Uzma Z. Rizvi. 2008. *Archaeology and the Postcolonial Critique*. New York: Alta Mira Press.

Manuel-Navarrete, David, and Michael Redclift. 2012. "Spaces of Consumerism and the Consumption of Space: Tourism and Social Exclusion in the 'Mayan Riviera.'" In *Consumer Culture in Latin America*, 177–93. New York: Macmillan.

Massey, Doreen. 1993. "Power-Geometry and a Progressive Sense of Place." In *Mapping the Futures: Local Cultures, Global Change*, edited by Jon Bird, Barry Curtis, Tim Putnam, George Robertson, and Lisa Tickner, 59–89. New York: Routledge.

Mathews, Jennifer P., and Lilia Lizama. 2006. "Jungle Rails: A Historic Narrow-Gauge Railway." In *Quintana Roo Archaeology*, edited by Justine Shaw and Jennifer P. Mathews, 112–24. Tucson: University of Arizona Press.

Mathews, Jennifer P., and Gillian P. Schultz. 2009. *Chicle: Chewing Gum of the Americas, from the Ancient Maya to William Wrigley*. Tucson: University of Arizona Press.

Matthews, Michael. 2014. *The Civilizing Machine: A Cultural History of Mexican Railroads, 1876–1910*. Lincoln: University of Nebraska Press.

Maya Biosphere. 2019. "Maya Biosphere Watch Opposes Proposal for Jungle Train and Disney-like Theme Park." https://www.prnewswire.com/news-releases/maya-biosphere-watch-opposes-proposal-for-jungle-train-and-disney-like-theme-park-300945952.html.

Menéndez, Gabriel Antonio, ed. 1936. *Quintana Roo: Álbum monográfico*. Mexico City: Baldera.

Montejo, Victor. 2022. "Indigenous Threated Heritage in Guatemala." In *Cultural Heritage and Mass Atrocities*, edited by James Cuno and Thomas G. Weiss, 264–77. Los Angeles: Getty Publications.

Ng, Olivia. 2007. "View from the Periphery: A Hermeneutic Approach to the Archaeology of Holotunich (1865–1930), British Honduras." PhD diss., University of Pennsylvania, Philadelphia.

Oles, James. 2013. *Art and Architecture in Mexico*. New York: Thames and Hudson.

Palka, Joel. 2005. *Unconquered Lacandon Maya: Ethnohistory and Archaeology of Indigenous Culture Change*. Gainesville: University Press of Florida.

Pskowski, Martha. 2019. "Mexico's 'Mayan Train' Is Set for Controversy." *Bloomberg News*, February 22. https://www.bloomberg.com/news/articles/2019-02-22/mexico-s-Yucatán-train-brings-promise-of-a-tourism-boom.

Rahder, Micha. 2015. "But Is It a Basin? Science, Controversy, and Conspiracy in the Fight for Mirador, Guatemala." *Science as Culture* 24 (3): 299–324.

Ramos, Claudia. 2018. "Nadie nos ha consultado nada: Comunidades indígenas rechazan construcción del Tren Maya." *Animal Politico*, November 16. https://www.animalpolitico.com/2018/11/comunidades-indigenas-rechazan-tren-maya/.

Shaw, Frederic J. 1958. *Little Railways of the World*. Berkeley, Calif.: Howell-North.

Steet, Linda. 2000. *Veils and Daggers: A Century of National Geographic's Representation of the Arab World*. Philadelphia: Temple University Press.

Sweitz, Sam R. 2012. "Total History: The Meaning of Hacienda Tabi." In *On the Periphery of the Periphery*, 239–51. New York: Springer.

Taube, Karl A. 2003. "Ancient and Contemporary Maya Conceptions About Field and Forest." In *The Lowland Maya Area: Three Millennia at the Human-Wildland Interface*, edited by Arturo Gómez-Pompa, Michael F. Allen, Scott L. Fedick, Juan J. Jiménez-Osornio, 461–92. New York: Food Products Press.

Thompson, J. Eric S. 1939. *Excavations at San José, British Honduras*. Publication 506. Washington, D.C.: Carnegie Institution of Washington.

Van Hoy, Teresa. 2008. *A Social History of Mexico's Railroads: Peons, Prisoners and Priests*. Lanham, M.d.: Rowman and Littlefield.

Vice News. 2020. "Mayan Ruins in Guatemala Could Become a U.S.-Funded Tourist Attraction." YouTube video, June 20. https://www.youtube.com/watch?v=uiZZQhnGveE.

Wakild, Emily. 2007. "Naturalizing Modernity: Urban Parks, Public Gardens and Drainage Projects in Porfirian Mexico City." *Mexican Studies / Estudios Mexicanos* 23 (1): 101–23.

Watkins, Joe E. 2020. Letter to the Honorable James M. Inhofe. July 13. https://documents.saa.org/container/docs/default-source/doc-governmentaffairs/s3131_statement_final.pdf?sfvrsn=dffe78a6_2.

Wells, Allen. 1982. "Family Elites in a Boom-and-Bust Economy: The Molinas and Peóns of Porfirian Yucatán." *Hispanic American Historical Review* 62 (2): 224–53.

Whelan, Robbie. 2020. "Rainforest and Ruins: The Battle Over a Maya Tourist Train." *Wall Street Journal*, June 13–14, C3.

CHAPTER 5

The Chichén Itzá and Ek Balam Borderlands

J. GREGORY SMITH AND ALEJANDRA ALONSO OLVERA

As the chapters in this volume demonstrate, studying the use of space at various scales and from various theoretical perspectives provides many opportunities for a better understanding of the Maya past and present. For our contribution, we zoom out for a macroscale point of view at the area between the two Maya cities of Chichén Itzá and Ek Balam in Yucatán during the Epiclassic period of roughly AD 700–1050 (figure 5.1).[1] For at least a hundred years, Chichén Itzá and Ek Balam were contemporaneous and probably politically independent of each other. Accordingly, the area between them was, for a time, a boundary zone. This study contributes to the handful of projects whose focus has been the investigation of boundaries between two adjacent ancient Maya polities. In pre-LiDAR (Light Detection and Radar) days, interpolity projects were daunting undertakings that were carried out in several different ways. Some investigators spent years conducting pedestrian surveys in those areas where surface visibility made it possible (de Montmollin 1989, 1995; Kepecs 1999). Others have hacked a narrow survey line through the rainforest that connected capitals and investigated the settlement patterns in between (Ford 1986; Puleston 1974, 1983). Still others have worked at a single small site between two polity capitals and used that

---

1. Because so much of our discussion in this chapter involves Chichén Itzá and settlements in the vicinity, we follow Ringle, Gallareta Negrón, and Bey (1998) and use the term *Epiclassic* because it underscores Chichén Itzá's connections to greater Mesoamerica, where the term is commonly used. We also find the terms *Late-Terminal Classic* and/or *Early Postclassic* rather clumsy and riddled with baggage involving invading Toltecs.

as a proxy for boundary dynamics (Dunham 1990; Iannone 2010) or employed an informant-aided survey to look for as many sites between polity capitals as possible (A. Andrews, Gallareta Negrón, and Cobas Palma 1989; Dunning 1992; Golden et al. 2008; J. Smith 2000; Vlcek and Fash 1986). We obtained the data for this chapter using this last strategy. LiDAR, of course, has added a revolutionary new tool to aid in studying the area between polity capitals. In the southern Maya lowlands, LiDAR work in Belize (Chase et al. 2014) and Guatemala (Canuto et al. 2018) has had a profound effect on our understanding of Maya settlement systems. Closer to the geographical focus of this chapter in northern Yucatán, several projects have used LiDAR to interpret the areas between Cobá, Yaxunah, and Chichén Itzá (Stanton et al. 2020; Stanton et al., this volume), between Ucí and Cansahcab (Hutson 2015; Vallejo-Cáliz and Hutson, this volume), and multiple settlements in a block of the Puuc area (Ringle et al. 2021).

Terminology and Interpretive Framework

We wish to contribute both to our understanding of a particular case of boundary dynamics in the Maya area and to the wider body of social science literature (including history, geography, sociology, and political sciences, among others) concerning boundaries. Because of the explicitly interdisciplinary approach and considerable effort to provide a standardized set of terminology to facilitate this approach, this chapter closely follows the framework provided by Bradley J. Parker (2006).

We use the term *borderlands* to refer to the region between two political/cultural entities: in this case, Chichén Itzá and Ek Balam. For most of our discussion, when referring to the borderlands, we generally mean all the known settlements within a 20 km wide swath that connects Chichén Itzá and Ek Balam (see figure 5.1). By *territory*, we mean a geographic area over which control is often exerted or sought. As we will see, there are good reasons to suspect that Maya rulers cared less about controlling a specific territory than they did about controlling the rulers in other cities and towns and the legacy they could provide. By *boundary*, we mean the entity that separates different territories. There are many kinds of boundaries, each ranging from static to fluid, and they rarely coincide. We consider several boundary types in our chapter, with the primary goal of coming to a better understanding of the borderlands between Ek Balam and Chichén Itzá. We also trace the pro-

FIGURE 5.1 The Chichén Itzá–Ek Balam borderlands showing sites mentioned in the text (map created by J. Gregory Smith).

cesses we see at work in these borderlands diachronically from the Classic period into the Postclassic period. With some of the terminological waters and goals of the chapter charted out, we now paint a brief portrait of both poles of borderlands: Ek Balam and Chichén Itzá.

An Overview of Ek Balam and Chichén Itzá

Ek Balam

Rising 30 m above the limestone bedrock it was built on, the Acropolis (also known as La Torre or, more prosaically, GT-1) is easily the largest building at Ek Balam (figure 5.2a). Measuring 165 m east–west by 65 m north–south at its base, the Acropolis and other monumental architecture at Ek Balam first caught the attention of M. Désiré Charnay in 1886 (Charnay 1888). For the next century, it received only sporadic visits from archaeologists (Garza Tarazona de González and Kurjack 1980; Morley 1928). Finally, between 1986 and 1995, William M. Ringle and George J. Bey III conducted the first sustained archaeological research at Ek Balam (Ringle and Bey 2008; Ringle et al. 2003). Ringle mapped the site center and the urban residential zone, while Bey concentrated his attention on excavating the Sacrificios Group just outside the site center and a Middle Classic *popol na* within it (Bey, Hanson, and Ringle 1997; Ringle et al. 2003). Mapping revealed a double wall encircling the monumental architectural core of the site and four *sakbe'ob* (causeway roads) that radiate out from the center in the cardinal directions. A short fifth *sakbe* extends to a large architectural complex to the southwest. Urban settlement mapping crews never encountered a decrease in structure density and so only a minimum size of Ek Balam can be determined: 12–15 km^2 (Ringle et al. 2004, 488).

More recent research by Instituto Nacional de Antropología e Historia (INAH) archaeologists Leticia Vargas de la Peña and Victor R. Castillo Borges (2014) has focused on the monumental core of Ek Balam. By far, their most spectacular discovery was associated with Room 35 on the west side of the Acropolis. There, Vargas de la Peña and Castillo Borges discovered a Chenes-style stucco monster mask in an excellent state of preservation. They encountered the royal tomb of Ukit Kan Lek, the most famous Ek Balam king, within the gaping maw of the mask. Ek Balam Stela 1 (figure 5.3a) shows how later kings would depict Ukit Kan Lek as a deified ancestor. Texts from Ek Balam (Lacadena García-Gallo 2004; Voss and Eberl 1999), most of

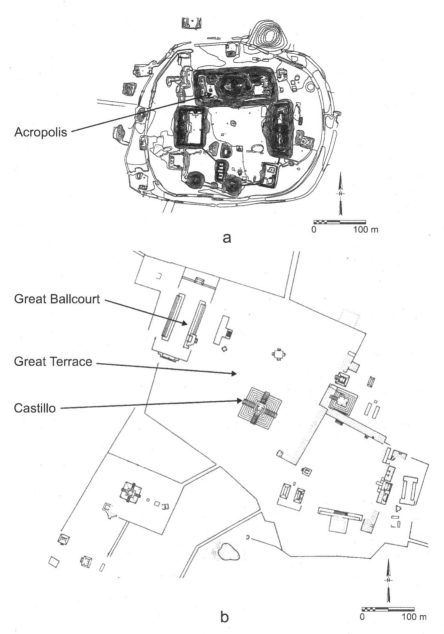

FIGURE 5.2 Maps of Monumental Architectural Cores at the same scale: (a) Ek Balam (created by J. Gregory Smith modified from J. Smith 2000, fig. 1.5), (b) Chichén Itzá (created by J. Gregory Smith modified from L. Schele and Freidel 1990, fig. 9.4).

which have been discovered by the INAH project, feature an emblem glyph (figure 5.3b) and record rule by *kaloomte'*, a supreme title of rulership that originated in the southern lowlands (Martin and Grube 2008, 17). As many authors have commented (Grube and Krochock 2011; Lundy 2016; Ringle et al. 2004), Ek Balam appears to have been a Maya kingdom rooted in the traditions of the Classic period southern lowlands.

Chichén Itzá

Only a little over 50 km to the southwest of Ek Balam is one of the most visited archaeological sites in the world and a UNESCO World Heritage Site: Chichén Itzá (see figure 5.1). Visitors today (and certainly those in the past) gravitate toward the architectural centerpiece of the site: an artificially leveled area known as the Great Terrace (see figure 5.2b). It is on the Great Terrace where most of the monumental architecture is located, including a four-sided pyramid known as the Castillo and the Great Ballcourt, the largest one known in Mesoamerica. It was Charnay (1888) who first noted the similarities in architecture and art between Chichén Itzá and the highland site of Tula, and Mesoamerican scholars have been arguing about what it means ever since. For a recent recap of the history of scholarly research and debates on Chichén Itzá, see the informative essay by Beniamino Volta, Nancy Peniche May, and Geoffrey E. Braswell (2018).[2]

One of the most significant advances in the study of Chichén Itzá in the past twenty years has been the development of an interpretive framework centered on the idea of the pan-Mesoamerican Quetzalcoatl Cult or Feathered Serpent Ideology (FSI). Beginning in 1998, Ringle, Tomás Gallareta Negrón, and Bey have argued that the similarities seen in major Epiclassic sites (Chichén Itzá, Tula, El Tajín, Cholula, Xochicalco, and others) were due to the spread of a political ideology associated with the man-god Quetzalcoatl (Bey and Ringle 2011; Ringle 2004, 2009, 2014; Ringle and Bey 2009; Ringle, Gallareta Negrón, and Bey 1998). They concentrated their analysis on

---

2. Chichén Itzá has been the focus of some exciting new research, including mapping outlying architectural groups and sakbe'ob, the excavation of new structures, new interpretations of "Toltec" and Maya art and architecture, and problem-oriented research aimed at addressing the thorny issue of Chichén Itzá's chronology (Cobos Palma 2003; Cobos Palma and Winemiller 2001; Hahn and Braswell 2012; Kowalski and Kristan-Graham 2011; Volta and Braswell 2014; Wren et al. 2018).

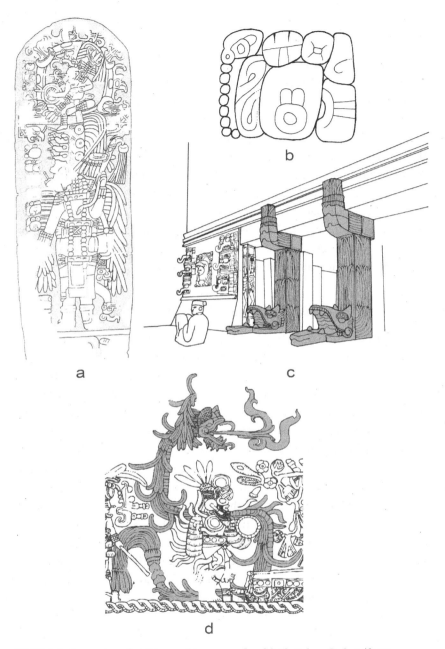

FIGURE 5.3 Examples of writing and iconography: (a) Ek Balam Stela 1 (from Lacadena García-Gallo 2004, fig. 2a); (b) emblem glyph of Ek Balam (drawing by Alexander Voss); (c) Feathered Serpent columns at Chichén Itzá (modified from D. Schele 2000, Schele no. 5007); (d) Feathered Serpent in Chichén Itzá relief carving (modified from D. Schele 2000, Schele no. 7676).

the major centers of Feathered Serpent Ideology, known as Tollans, across Mesoamerica, with much of their focus set on Chichén Itzá.

In contrast to Ek Balam, the Feathered Serpent iconography so common at Chichén Itzá (figure 5.3c, 5.3d) is absent at Ek Balam, as are I-shaped ballcourts, radial pyramids, gallery-patios, and colonnaded halls. To summarize the differences between these two great Maya cities, Ek Balam was probably well known to other local ruling dynasties within the Maya area, while Chichén Itzá was much more widely connected to greater Mesoamerica. In other words, Ek Balam was more culturally insular while Chichén Itzá was more internationally oriented. Perhaps the modern U.S. cities of Baltimore and Washington, D.C., are somewhat analogous: similarly sized neighbors but with very different levels of international significance.

Chronological Considerations

Some consideration must be paid to chronology since our claim that the area between Chichén Itzá and Ek Balam is a boundary zone hinges upon the argument that these two cities were at least partially coeval. At Ek Balam, a principal finding of the Ringle and Bey project was that although Ek Balam experienced a Late/Terminal Classic (AD 700–1050) zenith (Bey et al. 1998), it also had a robust Formative (Bond-Freeman 2007) and Colonial (Hanson 2008) occupation. Up until the 1970s, the archaeological consensus was that Chichén Itzá was primarily an Early Postclassic (AD 1000–1200) city that outlasted or conquered places such as Uxmal, Cobá, and, most pertinent to this study, Ek Balam. Thus, in the traditional chronology, there was not much of a boundary between Chichén Itzá and Ek Balam because the two cities reached their peak of power during two different time periods. In the Late/Terminal Classic, Ek Balam was at its zenith while Chichén Itzá awaited its future glory, and in the Early Postclassic, Chichén Itzá reigned supreme while Ek Balam was withering away to the east.

By the 1990s, numerous scholars were arguing for an earlier chronological placement and realigned its prime to the Terminal Classic (Cobos Palma 2004; Grube and Krochock 2011; Lincoln 1986; Ringle, Bey, and Peraza Lope 1991; Ringle, Gallareta Negrón, and Bey 1998; L. Schele and Mathews 1998). While this may seem like a minor chronological calibration, for Mayanists the difference between moving Chichén Itzá from the Early Postclassic to the Terminal Classic was profound (Chase and Chase 1982, 608–10). In the traditional chronology, an Early Postclassic Chichén Itzá would have been the only city of any size in the northern lowlands and therefore easy to peg as the capital of a large regional state or even empire. Moving Chichén Itzá back two hundred years made it contemporary with dozens of Terminal Classic polities like Ek Balam, Cobá, Uxmal, and Edzna.

Excavations at Chichén Itzá on the Great Terrace by Braswell and his team (Peniche May, Hahn, and Braswell 2009) and Eduardo Pérez de Heredia's ceramic analysis (2010) have reignited discussions about the chronology at Chichén Itzá. In 2014, Volta and Braswell (2014, 388), argued for a ninth-century peak for "Old Chichén," an eleventh-century florescence of "New Chichén," and a tenth-century (AD 897–998) decline or hiatus in between. In a thorough dissection of these chronological claims, Ringle (2017) contends that there is very little convincing evidence that Chichén Itzá was erecting new monumental architecture much past AD 1000.

To sum up our current thinking on chronology, we favor the placement of Chichén Itzá in the Terminal Classic (or Epiclassic) but with partial overlap with Ek Balam. Ceramically, the decline of Ek Balam was around AD 1000, but as the dynastic history of the site started to come into focus in the late 1990s, the series of Long Count dates ended in the ninth century. The last hieroglyphic date at Ek Balam is AD 844 (though it is mentioned at the small Chichén Itzá outlier site of Halakal at AD 870), and it appears that by AD 900, the city was on the decline. There is a robust occupation at Chichén Itzá in the Late Classic (Pérez de Heredia and Biró 2018), and it is clear that the two capitals coexisted in the 700s and 800s, with Ek Balam having the upper hand (Grube and Krochock 2011). At the beginning of the tenth century, just as Ek Balam was on the wane, Chichén Itzá entered its heyday. But it was not to last: monumental construction ceased at Chichén Itzá around AD 1000 and appears to have been in steep decline by AD 1100. Having established partial contemporaneity, we now enter the borderlands between these two great Maya cities.

Geographic Boundaries

Bradley J. Parker (2006, 83) defines geographic boundaries as naturally occurring features of the landscape between two polities. Geographic boundaries can include items such as mountain ranges, rivers, soil composition, and weather patterns.[3] However, because the physical geography between Chichén Itzá and Ek Balam is virtually uniform, it does not appear that geographic boundaries existed between these two polities. While stating that there are no mountain ranges or rivers separating Chichén Itzá and Ek Balam is pointing out the obvious, even more subtle geographic boundaries appear to be absent. For example, the availability of groundwater in the form of cenotes could be an important basis for boundary formation in the northern plains of the Yucatán Peninsula. Another feature that could be worth defending is a concentration of *rejolladas* (sinkholes that do not reach the water table but act as catchment basins for soil), which were used to grow valuable crops like cacao. Yet a careful examination of aerial photographs available on platforms such as Google Maps or GIS-based analysis (Aguilar et al. 2016) shows that these karstic features are essentially uniform in their distribution between Chichén Itzá and Ek Balam.

Economic Boundaries

Of economic boundaries, Parker (2006, 88) writes, "This category includes but is not limited to the extraction and export of natural resources in borderlands, the production of finished products in borderlands, the import of raw materials and manufactured goods into borderlands, and the transshipment of raw materials and manufactured goods across borderlands." To explore these kinds of boundaries in the Chichén Itzá–Ek Balam borderlands, we examine the presence of ceramics, obsidian, chert, and shell artifacts at the sites between the two major centers.[4]

---

3. In the Maya area, Olivier de Montmollin (1995, 84–85) discusses the various geographic boundaries among the polities he investigated during his pedestrian surveys in the southwestern Maya periphery. There, natural ridges or impassable swamps were argued to be the basis for some polity boundaries. On the southeastern periphery, the ridges between fertile river valleys created natural boundaries for the Copán polity (Fash 2001; Willey and Leventhal 1979). Along the Usumacinta River in the southern lowlands, Charles Golden et al. (2012) report that narrow valleys along the river formed choke points that the Yaxchilan and Piedras Negras polities used as a basis for boundary definition. In northern Yucatán, Nicholas P. Dunning's (1992) investigations in the Puuc area revealed that major centers were located in pockets of fertile soil perfect for agriculture and boundaries between them tended to be less productive rugged uplands.

4. Most Mayanists looking into the theme of economics are concerned about characterizing the kind of economy ancient Maya had (i.e., markets or no markets) or looking at the intrasite distribution of artifacts to better understand the organizing principles within single settlements.

Ceramics

It was not clear until the 1980s what kinds of ceramics were present at Ek Balam. After several field seasons of systematic surface collections and excavation, it became evident that Epiclassic Ek Balam was clearly a member of the greater Cehpech ceramic sphere and not the related and mostly coeval Sotuta sphere (Bey et al. 1998). Meanwhile, ceramic studies at Chichén Itzá conducted by George W. Brainerd (1958), Robert E. Smith (1971), Charles E. Lincoln (1991), and Pérez de Heredia (2010) make it certain that Chichén Itzá was the epicenter of Sotuta ceramic consumption. Outliers of both sites, for example Yula (Anderson 1998) and Popola de Yaxcaba (Johnson 2012, 2018) near Chichén Itzá and Yohdzadz and Xuilub (Houck 2004) near Ek Balam, tend to have ceramic assemblages that resemble their larger neighbor.[5] In the borderlands, we found light scatters of Sotuta ceramics at sites like Ichmul de Morley, Popola de Dzitas, and Santa Cruz. This situation is strikingly different from the pattern that T. Kam Manahan, Traci Ardren, and Alejandra Alonso Olvera (2012) discovered at Xuenkal, a large site located 45 km northeast of Chichén Itzá (see figure 5.1). There, researchers identified discrete Sotuta platforms that postdated most of the monumental site core associated with Cehpech ceramics.

The Sotuta ceramic sphere in the borderlands may have been more of a smaller, elite-level distribution network. At the two sites that had the most Sotuta pottery, Santa Cruz and Ichmul de Morley, we found a pattern where common Cehpech types like Muna Slate outnumbered their Sotuta counterpart Dzitas Slate. However, when looking at more ornate representatives

---

Thus, numerous studies look at ceramic manufacture and distribution (e.g., Foias and Bishop 1997), obsidian procurement (e.g., Braswell and Glascock 2002), and chert (e.g., Shafer and Hester 1991). Use of these data to look at boundaries between Maya polities is harder to come by. The relative abundance of obsidian at Tikal compared to its Classic period nemesis Calakmul has been argued to indicate that the well-documented political conflicts between these two "superstates" (Martin and Grube 2008) led to economic trade blocks (Masson and Freidel 2013, 221). Similarly, Kazuo Aoyama, Toshiharu Tashiro, and Michael D. Glascock (1999) looked at economic boundaries in western Honduras using the distribution of obsidian artifacts.

5. There are two sites near Chichén Itzá named Popola. To avoid confusion, we have added the municipio where they are located to differentiate them. Thus, Popola de Dzitas is where J. Gregory Smith (2000) mapped and excavated and is 16 km northeast of Chichén Itzá, and Popola de Yaxcaba is where Scott A. Johnson (2012, 2018) carried out research and is located about 13 km southwest of Chichén Itzá. See figure 5.1.

TABLE 5.1 Comparison of common and rare Sotuta and Cehpech ceramics

Site	Cehpech Muna	Cehpech Teabo	Sotuta Dzitas	Sotuta Dzibiac	Muna: Dzitas (more utilitarian)	Teabo: Dzibiac (more fancy)
Chichén Itzá Grupo Sakbe 61[a]	0	1	2,090	364	—	1:364
Ek Balam[b]	78,135	666	63	36	1,240:1	19:1
Santa Cruz[c]	4,996	49	300	373	17:1	1:8
Ichmul de Morley[d]	3,340	62	442	154	8:1	1:27

[a] Cobos Palma 2003.
[b] Bey et al. 1998.
[c] Alonso Olvera and Smith 2019.
[d] J. Smith 2000.

of the two spheres, there is an inversion: Sotuta Dzibiac sherds outnumber Cehpech Teabo sherds (table 5.1). As Scott A. Johnson (2018) has modeled, economic boundaries operated quite differently between elites and commoners. Local elites at Ichmul de Morley or Santa Cruz may have been the recipient of gift giving from elites at Chichén Itzá in the form of lavish Dzibiac Red vessels, while commoners had less access to this pottery.

Only a few rare Sotuta tradewares made their way into the borderland sites. Five sherds of Tohil Plumbate were found at Popola de Dzitas and five sherds of Silho Fine Orange were collected: one each at Cho, Ichmul de Morley, and Popola de Dzitas, while two were collected at Poxil (see figure 5.1). Ringle, Gallareta Negrón, and Bey (1998) argue that these tradewares are associated with the spread of the FSI, and this is a good example of how different kinds of boundaries (in this case, religious and economic) can be intertwined.

There is some evidence of local ceramic production in the borderlands. At Ichmul de Morley, we found "hybridized" ceramic forms that had attributes of both Cehpech and Sotuta wares. The most striking were bowls with a Cehpech Muna Slate slip and paste, yet with a *molcajete* (mortar) form that is virtually absent in the Cehpech sphere but present in the Sotuta sphere. We found this same pattern during our 2017 fieldwork at Santa Cruz, as most of the 147 molcajete sherds were typed as Muna Slate.[6] Since this kind

---

6. Johnson (2018, 128) reports this exact same pattern at Popola de Yaxcaba.

of Cehpech molcajete is not present at either Chichén Itzá or Ek Balam, we argue that these were probably manufactured locally.

Obsidian

There are two striking differences in the obsidian assemblages at Chichén Itzá and Ek Balam: the sheer amount traded in and its geological source. Taken together, they create perhaps one of the most obvious cases of a boundary that is present in the borderlands. To ascertain the quantity of obsidian that was traded into Chichén Itzá and Ek Balam, we wanted to go beyond raw obsidian counts and control for the different amounts of fieldwork conducted at both sites. To do this, we compared the amount of obsidian collected with a much more common artifact: fragments of pottery vessels. The results (table 5.2) confirm that Chichén Itzá was importing a tremendous amount of obsidian compared to Ek Balam. Only a trickle of obsidian flowed into Ek Balam and most of it is found in elite contexts. It is tempting to see the obsidian distribution network centered at Ek Balam as a prestige redistribution system where client elites outside the capital were rewarded with obsidian in exchange for fealty. Meanwhile, Braswell and Michael D. Glascock (2002) argue that the obsidian distribution at Chichén Itzá is consistent with a market in operation. They base this on their determination that obsidian is not tied to social class: all social strata had roughly equal access to obsidian.

In the borderlands, the result of comparing the amount of obsidian to potsherds indicates that there was a striking economic boundary in the form of obsidian exchange (see table 5.2). Places like Popola de Dzitas, Ichmul de Morley, and Santa Cruz were plugged into the obsidian market operation at Chichén Itzá, while communities associated with Ek Balam like Metkuche, Xuilub, and Yohdzadz were left out.[7]

In addition to the quantity of obsidian flowing into the borderlands, the sources of it were quite distinct as well. Braswell (Braswell 1997; Braswell and Glascock 2007; Braswell, Paap, and Glascock 2011) has sourced thousands

---

7. Was obsidian being distributed to borderland towns like Ichmul de Morley, Popola de Dzitas, and Santa Cruz by the traders moving from Isla Cerritos on their way to Chichén Itzá? Alternatively, was all the obsidian going first to Chichén Itzá and then redistributed to these centers? Were borderland people traveling to Chichén Itzá to acquire obsidian from the market there?

TABLE 5.2 Comparison of obsidian and ceramic artifacts

Site	Total sherds	Obsidian artifacts	Sherds: Obsidian
Chichén Itzá Group Sakbe 61[a]	10,359	71	146:1
Chichén Itzá Op. AB on Great Terrace[b]	8,393	19	442:1
Cho[d]	872	2	436:1
Ek Balam[c]	238,961	139	1,719:1
Metkuche[d]	1,184	1	1,184:1
Nohmozon[g]	1,477	2	739:1
Popola de Dzitas[d]	1,918	17	113:1
Popola de Yaxcaba[h]	32,378	31	1,044:1
Santa Cruz[f]	12,638	23	549:1
Xuilub[g]	15,172	3	5,057:1
Yaxkukul[d]	1,427	12	119:1
Yohdzadz[g]	658	0	N/A
Yula[e]	25,515	65	393:1
Ichmul de Morley[d]	24,594	38	647:1

[a] Cobos Palma 2003.
[b] Peniche May, Hahn, and Braswell 2009.
[c] Bey et al. 1998; Ringle et al. 2003.
[d] J. Smith 2000 (Yaxkukul sherd counts include 1998 surface collections and 1999 ballcourt excavations).
[e] Anderson 1998.
[f] Alonso Olvera and Smith 2019.
[g] Houck 2004.
[h] Johnson 2012.

of obsidian artifacts from the INAH project at both Chichén Itzá and Ek Balam (table 5.3). The vast majority (192 of 198, or 97 percent) of the obsidian artifacts from Ek Balam come from the Guatemalan source of El Chayal, while only 3 pieces (2 percent) are from the green Pachuca source. On the other hand, 788 out of 3,620 obsidian artifacts (22 percent) at Chichén Itzá are from Pachuca.

Using the percentage of green Pachuca obsidian as a proxy of connection with Chichén Itzá or Ek Balam, table 5.3 reveals that Ichmul de Morley and Santa Cruz had almost identical Pachuca percentages as Chichén Itzá, and Popola de Dzitas was even higher. Meanwhile, it appears that communities affiliated with Ek Balam had virtually no access to Pachuca obsidian. As Braswell has written (2003, 141), the stark differences in access to Central

TABLE 5.3 Pachuca percentages

Site	Total obsidian count	Pachuca count	Pachuca percentage
Chichén Itzá[a]	3,620	788	22%
Cho[b]	2	0	0
Chumul[b]	11	4	36%
Ek Balam[a]	198	3	2%
Metkuche[b]	2	0	0
Nohmozon[d]	2	0	0
Popola de Dzitas[b]	18	6	33%
Santa Cruz[c]	23	6	26%
Xuilub[b]	3	0	0
Yaxkukul[b]	12	0	0
Ichmul de Morley[b]	38	8	21%

[a] Braswell and Glascock 2007.
[b] J. Smith 2000.
[c] Alonso Olvera and Smith 2019.
[d] Houck 2004.

Mexican obsidian like Pachuca between Chichén Itzá and Ek Balam are also present in the borderlands that separate them.

Shell

Our 2017 investigations at the site of Santa Cruz yielded a surprising amount of marine shell artifacts (Alonso Olvera and Smith 2019). Alonso Olvera recently completed an analysis of this surface-collected material; the sample collected includes 228 fragments of recognizable tools or finished products, including plaques, discs, beads, pendants, chisels, drills, scrapers, and graters. Additionally, we collected 529 pieces of irregularly broken shell that probably represent production waste. The specialized production of shell objects at Santa Cruz is quite similar to the situation at Xuenkal, a large Rank 2 site 19 km north of Santa Cruz (Alonso Olvera 2013).[8]

Following Michael Smith's (2014) useful distinction between tax and tribute, we suggest that finished shell products were sent on the backs of porters

---

8. We discovered a similar pattern at Santa Cruz with chert artifacts (Alonso Olvera and Smith 2019). Of the total sample, 39 flakes, 9 cores, and 27 waste fragments were located, and more than 402 tools were classified as used flakes, projectile points, blades, scrapers, drills, beaks, celts, and bifaces.

as either tax (if there was a regular payment plan) or tribute (if there was an irregular or even single payment) to Chichén Itzá, where these shell objects were used and ultimately discarded. If this was the case, then it would be interesting to know how shell collection at Santa Cruz was administered. Did Chichén Itzá send collectors to places like Santa Cruz to make sure obligations were being fulfilled? How involved were the local political leaders at Santa Cruz? Considering that we do not know how some of these nuts-and-bolts aspects of collection operated in the Aztec Empire (M. Smith 1996, 180), it is even less understood in the Epiclassic Yucatán Peninsula.

Political Boundaries

Political boundaries refer to political, administrative, and military boundaries (Parker 2006, 83). Mayanists have employed a number of generic and homegrown models from the Maya area to better understand the nature of political boundaries.[9] One approach to Maya political boundaries takes an emic perspective and looks at how the Maya viewed them. One such approach entails tracing how ancient Maya sometimes literally connected large cities to smaller outlying settlements with sakbe'ob to cement political relationships and make boundary statements against rival kingdoms (Hutson 2014; Kurjack and Andrews 1976; Shaw 2008; Stanton et al., this volume). Unfortunately, however, there are no known regional sakbe'ob in the Chichén Itzá–Ek Balam borderlands.[10]

By far the most common epigraphic method for inferring boundaries stems from an examination of emblem glyphs (Biró 2016; Marcus 1976; Martin and Grube 2008; Mathews 1991; Tokovinine 2011). Epigraphers once thought that emblem glyphs simply referred to a specific city, but recent

---

9. Borrowing from the playbook of locational geography, the Thiessen model has been used for several decades now (Dunning and Kowalski 1994; Hammond 1974; Iaonne 2010; Mathews 1991). These authors concede that Thiessen lines, drawn at right angles exactly halfway between polity capitals, do not indicate the boundary but rather provide a starting point for the researcher to hypothesize the general vicinity of where a boundary may have been.

10. As we briefly mentioned in our overview of Ek Balam, there is an intrasite sakbe'ob system at Ek Balam: like wheel spokes, five causeways extend out from the hub of the central city (Bey et al. 1998, fig. 3). The three longest ones are about 1.5 km in length and are oriented in the cardinal directions of west, north, and east. Similarly, Rafael Cobos Palma and Terance L. Winemiller (2001, fig. 5) have documented numerous intrasite sakbe'ob radiating out from Chichén Itzá. The longest one that enters the borderlands is a little over 2 km in length and extends northeast from the center of Chichén Itzá to the outlying community or suburb of Poxil.

work has suggested that they are better thought of as a personal title of lords that ruled over a specific domain (Martin 2020, 28). While the identification of an emblem glyph remains elusive for Chichén Itzá, Ringle first identified one on Ek Balam Stela 1. Alexander W. Voss and Markus Eberl (1999) first published a drawing of it (see figure 5.3b) based on two examples found on serpent balustrades on either side of the main stairway on the Acropolis. Alfonso Lacadena García-Gallo (2004, 96) reports twelve appearances of this glyph in texts from Ek Balam.

There are only two sites in the borderlands that have any hieroglyphic inscriptions, and one of them is Ichmul de Morley, located almost halfway between Chichén Itzá and Ek Balam (see figure 5.1). Two ballplayer panels from the site were first photographed by Teobert Maler sometime at the turn of the twentieth century and later by Sylvanus Morley in 1918 (J. Smith 2019). Both are partially eroded, but Daniel Graña-Behrens (2006) has recently identified some glyphs on them (figure 5.4a, b). He argues that an emblem glyph is present on Panel 2 and is most likely an emblem glyph of Ichmul de Morley. Moreover, according to Graña-Behrens, the left figure on Ichmul de Morley Panel 1 is the most famous king of Ek Balam, Ukit Kan Lek. If so, this helps date Panel 1 more securely since this king took the throne in AD 770 and evidently died in AD 801. Thus, the limited epigraphic and iconographic evidence appears to indicate that local elites at Ichmul were tethered to Ek Balam during the eighth and ninth centuries AD.

The other site in the borderlands with any epigraphic data to draw from is Halakal, located about 4 km northeast of Chichén Itzá (see figure 5.1). The Halakal lintel (figure 5.5) depicts three lords, two of which are from Chichén Itzá, and one is probably K'inich Jun Pik To'ok of Ek Balam (Graña-Behrens 2006; Voss and Eberl 1999). The hieroglyphic band that frames the three figures features the Ek Balam emblem glyph at block G5-G6 (Lacadena García-Gallo 2004; Voss and Eberl 1999) but might also be an emblem glyph that represents Halakal itself (Graña Behrens 2006, 113).

The presence of their own emblem glyphs may have been a boast of political independence (Mathews 1991) for both Ichmul de Morley and Halakal. However, it also seems likely that rulers in both towns may have had the title of *sajal* (secondary lord) and were subservient to the holy divine lords at Ek Balam. If so, then the location of Halakal is revealing, as it appears that around AD 870 (the most likely date for the lintel [Grube, Lacadena, and Martin 2003, 43; Voss and Kremer 2000, 158]), we have a community politically connected to Ek Balam yet only 4 km away from the center of Chichén

FIGURE 5.4 Ichmul de Morley ballplayer panels: (a) Panel 1 (from Love 2019); (b) Panel 2 (from Love 2019).

The Chichén Itzá and Ek Balam Borderlands

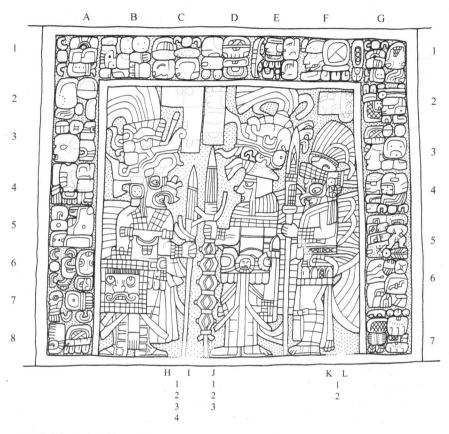

FIGURE 5.5 Halakal lintel (created by J. Gregory Smith from Voss and Kremer 2000, fig. 7).

Itzá. Epigraphically, the evidence suggests that Ek Balam dominated the area between it and Chichén Itzá, at least during the eighth and ninth centuries AD (Grube and Krochock 2011).

In addition to Classic period epigraphy, another emic source of Maya political boundaries derives from an analysis of early Colonial period documents (Okoshi Harada, Izquierdo, and Williams-Beck 2006; Quezada 1993, 1998, 2014; Restall 1997; Roys 1957). The work of Ralph L. Roys (1957) laid the foundation for what we call the ethnohistoric model, with his definition of three Maya polity types and the resulting map of northern Yucatán at the time of the Spanish arrival, which has made its way into dozens of discussions of Maya political geography. More recently, Tsubasa Okoshi Harada, Ana Luisa Izquierdo, and Lorraine Williams-Beck (2006) and Sergio Quezada (1993, 1998, 2014) have added to the ethnohistoric model by pointing out that Maya polities were much more unstable and less territorially contiguous than the Roys model suggests. In their view, some towns had leaders (*batabs*) that ascended to the title of *halach uinic* and had centralized power over several batabs in other towns. Critically, these subsidiary towns were not necessarily the ones geographically closest to the town of the halach uinic. In other words, a batab might live in a town near a halach uinic but would only be affiliated with a different halach uinic located much further away. The resulting map of political geography is thus a mess: a series of overlapping lines connecting halach uinic to their dependent batabs. Moreover, Quezada (1998, 2014) and Okoshi Harada, Izquierdo, and Williams-Beck (2006) point out that this configuration of elite connections constantly shifted. The ethnohistoric model, while providing some interpretive headaches for archaeologists, nevertheless paints a more accurate portrait of what Maya polities were actually like. Many archaeologists have incorporated this ruler-centric rather than territory-centric model into their interpretation of the Maya political landscape of earlier time periods (Kepecs and Masson 2003; J. Smith 2000; Voss and Eberl 1999; Williams-Beck 2001), and Michael Smith (2003, 36) suggests this might be a generic pattern for the greater Postclassic Mesoamerica.

There is some support for this spatially discontinuous pattern that Quezada (1993, 1998, 2014) and Okoshi Harada, Izquierdo, and Williams-Beck (2006) write about in the Chichén Itzá–Ek Balam borderlands. For example, the site of Metkuche is located some 18 km northeast of Chichén Itzá and 34 km west of Ek Balam (see figure 5.1). Yet the ceramic assemblage that resulted from a series of surface collections revealed some 717 Cehpech sherds and only 11 Sotuta sherds (J. Smith 2000). So Metkuche has closer ceramic affiliations with Cehpech-using Ek Balam despite being much closer to Sotuta-using Chichén Itzá. In addition to ceramic evidence, the civic architecture at Metkuche consists of a temple assemblage, an arrangement of a temple, a range structure, and an altar that Tatiana Proskouriakoff (1962) identified at Mayapán long ago. Temple assemblages are quite common at Ek Balam (Ringle and Bey 1992, 2001; Ringle et al. 2004) and less so at Chichén Itzá. If Metkuche had the same demographic trajectory as Ek Balam (a population peak in the ninth century followed by a tenth-century decline), it means that it overlapped in time with its close neighbor Chichén Itzá for at least a century yet ceramically and architecturally was similar to its more distant neighbor Ek Balam.

Another example of a situation that is more understandable when cast in the light of the ethnohistoric model is demonstrated at the site of Yaxkukul, some 17 km southwest of Ek Balam (see figure 5.1). Here, the presence of an I-shaped ballcourt that is a miniaturized version of the Great Ballcourt at Chichén Itzá makes it clear that this town must have had some kind of political and/or ideological ties to Chichén Itzá, even though Yaxkukul is much closer geographically to Ek Balam (figure 5.6). In the old chronological scheme of Robert Smith (1971), the Yaxkukul ballcourt, an obvious example of "Toltec" architecture, would be dated to the Early Postclassic, AD 1000–1200, and therefore not contemporary with Ek Balam at all. We discuss this anomalous ballcourt and its chronology in more detail later in this chapter, but we do think it dates to the Epiclassic and was probably built and used in the ninth or tenth century AD. If true, then, like Metkuche, it represents the kind of community that Okoshi Harada, Izquierdo, and Williams-Beck (2006) and Quezada (1993, 1998, 2014) documented in early colonial times: one physically close to a large city but socially tethered to a more distant one.

What were the political boundaries of the borderlands in the tenth century? With the decline of Ek Balam, we suggest that Ichmul de Morley ceased to function as a boundary center between Chichén Itzá and Ek Balam. The location of Ichmul northward toward Chichén Itzá's presumed port of Isla Cerritos and the Emal salt works is what made this site strategic (see figure 5.1). In a discussion of Chichén Itzá's relationship with Ichmul (J. Smith and Bond-Freeman 2018), we contend that the site may have acted as a waystation for traders and pilgrims coming and going to Chichén Itzá. At the time of Chichén Itzá's apogee, the political boundary between it and Ek Balam became somewhat irrelevant as Ek Balam faded. Chichén Itzá's political focus was much more concerned with other Epiclassic Tollans across Mesoamerica and not so much with local Maya polities of the Yucatán Peninsula.

Demographic Boundaries

Parker (2006, 85) defines demographic boundaries as encompassing things like population density, gender, and ethnicity.[11] Turning first to interpolity population studies, while far from a full-coverage survey, J. Gregory Smith's dissertation (2000) attempts to document as many sites as possible between

---

11. While population (Culbert and Rice 1990), gender (Ardren 2002), and ethnicity (Beyyette and LeCount 2017) have been the focus of numerous Mayanist studies over the years, few of them have employed the interpolity scale we use here.

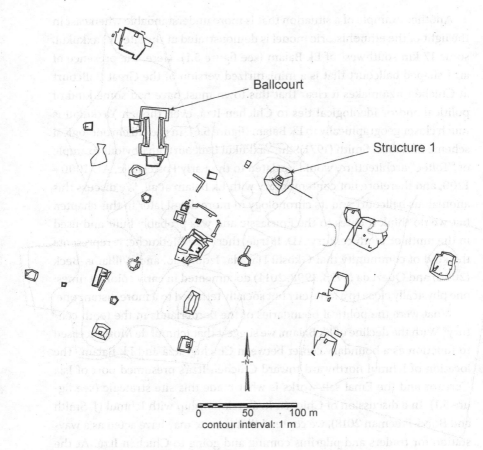

FIGURE 5.6 Map of Yaxkukul (created by J. Gregory Smith).

Chichén Itzá and Ek Balam.[12] We detected no clear drop in settlement, and more investigations in the area would inevitably find dozens more previously

---

12. Until the advent of LiDAR, these kinds of projects were rare. Dennis E. Puleston's transect between Tikal and Uaxactun (1974, 1983) and Anabel Ford's transect between Yaxha and Tikal (1986) were pioneering in their attempts to document population densities between polity capitals. The expectation is that there might be a noticeable drop in settlement between polities, creating a "no man's land" that marked a boundary. Both of these transect projects did document a slow decline in settlement density as they moved further away from polity capitals. However, demographic boundaries were difficult to delineate since there were no clear gaps encountered. Various LiDAR projects are currently dealing with the same problem but on a much wider scale: instead of a single trail hacked through the jungle, large interpolity swaths are revealing a tremendous amount of settlement and very ambiguous demographic boundaries between polities (Canuto et al. 2018; Golden et al. 2016).

unrecorded sites. Thus, there is no compelling reason to believe that there is a drop in settlement density somewhere between Chichén Itzá and Ek Balam that would indicate a demographic boundary.

Turning to ethnic boundaries, while sometimes not explicit, most discussions of Chichén Itzá deal with ethnicity at some level because of the infusion of so many non-Maya elements into the city.[13] The "Emulating Locals or Invading Foreigners" debate at Chichén Itzá is an old one and is ongoing (i.e., Cobos Palma 2006; Jordan 2016; Kowalski and Kristan-Graham 2011; Lincoln 1991; Pérez de Heredia and Biró 2018; Ringle 1990; Taube 1994; Wren et al. 2018). Most of these have focused on the styles of monumental architecture and iconographic representations of people with non-Maya attributes such as costume elements.

How might ethnic differences be detected in the iconographically impoverished Chichén Itzá–Ek Balam borderlands? In some of our previous work (J. Smith 2000; J. Smith and Bond-Freeman 2018; J. Smith, Ringle, and Bond-Freeman 2006), our central bridging argument was that ethnic identity can be tied to archaeologically visible items such as the layout of houses and cuisine preferences (see also Jones 1997). By looking at differences in domestic architecture and food preparation techniques, we may come to a better understanding of ethnicity in the borderlands.

While mapping residential settlement in 1997, we identified the remains of houses with a previously unknown (to us) floor plan at Ichmul de Morley that we called open-front houses (figure 5.7a). One hypothesis we have considered is that these novel house forms may have been an example of the formation of a new kind of ethnic identity (ethnogenesis). The floor plan (figure 5.7b) consists of three rooms that all share a back wall, but the central room lacks a front wall. The central room often has a bench along the back wall. The two end rooms have front walls that often include discernable doorways. We initially thought these structures had a nonresidential function that may have had a special use for storage, food preparation, or feasting.

---

13. Numerous studies have examined ethnic boundaries, with most of them focused on the edges of the Maya area and attempting to cast light on Maya versus non-Maya population and the utility of this dichotomy. The southwestern periphery of the Maya area is still within the Mesoamerican culture area and involves societies of roughly similar complexity encountering each other (de Montmollin 1995, 269–85; Marken, Guenter, and Freidel 2017). On the other hand, the southeastern periphery has ethnic Maya interacting in one form or another with ostensibly fewer complex forms of organization in the Intermediate culture area (E. Andrews 1976; Demarest 1988; Schortman, Urban, and Ausec 2001).

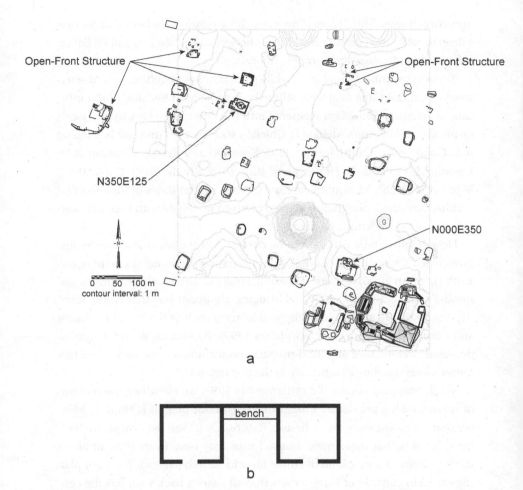

FIGURE 5.7 Ichmul de Morley: (a) map of civic center (*lower right*) and adjacent block of residential settlement; (b) schematic layout of the open-front house (created by J. Gregory Smith).

However, when we compared the ceramic assemblages between open-front houses and the more common laterally connected houses at Ichmul de Morley, we saw almost exactly the same proportions of serving and storage vessels (J. Smith and Bond-Freeman 2009). Because rooms in Ek Balam houses are connected laterally and each with its own door and the ones at Chichén Itzá tend to have a public front room and a private back room, we have suggested that the open-front houses at Ichmul de Morley might have been the result of ethnogenesis (J. Smith 1998, 2000).

Turning to cuisine preferences to explore ethnicity, we discuss a ceramic form known as a molcajete or mortar bowl. Because molcajetes are common at Chichén Itzá but are virtually absent at Cehpech-using polities like Ek Balam, this ceramic form is a useful indicator of foodways associated with Chichén Itzá. Our fieldwork in the borderlands revealed some twelve sites that had at least one grater bowl fragment, including 147 at Santa Cruz and 99 at Ichmul de Morley (see figure 5.1). Their presence suggests that at least some members of these communities had adopted the foreign cuisine associated with Chichén Itzá.

The last of Parker's demographic boundaries concerns gender. Before the ascendance of Chichén Itzá as a Mesoamerican powerhouse, there is no compelling reason to think that gender in the borderlands was significantly different from earlier time periods: upper-class men were political leaders, while lower-class men were farmers, with traders occupying an ambiguous class position. Upper-class women were often—but not always—behind the scenes in Maya royal courts. Besides references to Ukit Kan Le'k's mother, the epigraphic corpus at Ek Balam makes no mention of any other royal women (Lacadena García-Gallo 2004). Lower-class women dominated the domestic realm with childrearing, crafting, and food preparation.

In the tenth century, we see some changes in the borderlands that directly affected gender.[14] Because both pilgrims and merchants were usually men (Tokovinine and Beliaev 2013), there was an unprecedented influx of men from other areas of the Yucatán Peninsula and greater Mesoamerica. In addition to having a possible ethnic tie, the open-front houses at Ichmul de Morley could have been special rest houses for these traveling men. There is some support for the idea that long-distance traders had special housing. Kenneth G. Hirth (2016, 257) reports that Aztec pochteca had access to special houses known as *oztomecacalli* and, citing the work of Roys, reports that Maya in the Yucatán Peninsula had a tradition of merchant rest houses as well. If the open-front houses at Ichmul de Morley had this function, then they must be chronologically late, as they would have been used during Chichén Itzá's tenth-century heyday. In this scenario, we would expect them to have a significantly higher proportion of Sotuta ceramics compared to the rest of the residences at Ichmul de Morley.

---

14. Linnea Wren, Kaylee Spencer, and Travis Nygard (2018) have recently explored the changes in gender relations at Chichén Itzá itself as it embraced a more militaristic outlook focused on male warriors.

To evaluate this idea, we recently reanalyzed the ceramic distributions of each open-front house to see if they had significantly more Sotuta ceramics in them. If so, then perhaps they were occupied during the tenth century after we think the site center had been largely abandoned. This hypothesis would be analogous to the situation at Xuenkal, where Alonso Olvera and others (Alonso Olvera 2013; Manahan, Ardren, and Alonso Olvera 2012) documented several residential platforms that had almost pure Sotuta ceramic associations and postdated the monumental core. The open-front houses have a clumped distribution northwest of the site center (see figure 5.7a), which makes us suspicious that this could have been a locus of postmonumental activity at Ichmul de Morley. Somewhat surprisingly, we found that structures with open-front houses tend to have less Sotuta sherds than those structures without open-front houses (table 5.4). Thus, it does not appear that the open-front houses postdate the other residences at Ichmul de Morley, weakening the interpretation that the open-front houses functioned as merchant rest houses.

Regarding the role of women, we suggest that there were some important transformations taking place in the tenth century. The foreign cuisine we referred to was probably not being prepared by men but instead by local women. Evidence for intensified food production at Ichmul de Morley has been recently discussed elsewhere (J. Smith and Bond-Freeman 2018). As discussed earlier, our 2017 investigations at the previously unknown site of Santa Cruz documented evidence of intensive shell crafting. We hypothesize that this crafting activity fell largely on the shoulders of women (Ardren and

TABLE 5.4 Sotuta and Cehpech ceramic counts at Ichmul de Morley open-front structures

Open-front structure	Cehpech sherds	Sotuta sherds	Cehpech:Sotuta ratio
N300W150	107	8	13:1
N350E090	33	0	N/A
N350E125	540	72	8:1
N400E150	102	6	17:1
N400E350	371	25	15:1
N450E0030	426	8	53:1
All open-front structures	1,579	119	13:1
All other structures	10,456	1,316	8:1

Source: Sherd counts from J. Smith 2000.

Alonso Olvera 2013; Ardren, Alonso Olvera, and Manahan 2016; Ardren et al. 2010). We envision that the gendered labor at Santa Cruz was similar to the situation that Ardren and Alonso Olvera documented at Xuenkal.

Cultural Boundaries

Parker (2006, 87) uses the phrase "cultural boundaries" to refer primarily to linguistic, religious, and material culture boundaries. We decided to parcel out material culture boundaries into different boundary discussions (see especially the section on economic boundaries) and focus here on linguistic and religious boundaries between Chichén Itzá and Ek Balam.[15]

Based on epigraphic evidence, there probably were some linguistic differences between Chichén Itzá and Ek Balam. The language represented in the Ek Balam writing is probably Ch'olti' with an admixture of Yucatecan (Lacadena García-Gallo 2004; Ringle and Bey 2012, 388), and the hieroglyphs have many things in common with Classic Maya texts in the southern lowlands (Grube, Lacadena, and Martin 2003). Meanwhile, it appears that the linguistic situation at Chichén Itzá was more complicated. José Miguel García Campillo (2000) argues that Ch'olti' is present, Nikolai Grube and Ruth J. Krochock (2011) point out some phrases resembling Yucatec, and Eduardo Pérez de Heredia and Péter Biró (2018, 92) argue for some Nawa words in the inscriptions of Chichén Itzá. As Nawa languages originated in the highlands of Mesoamerica and spread from there (Kaufman 2001), we have some linguistic evidence of Mesoamerican integration during the Epiclassic. As Nawa loan words made their way into the existing Mayan languages, it presumably created a unique prestige language appropriate for the booming international character of Chichén Itzá. Where was the boundary of this Nawa-infused Mayan language? The only known inscriptions from the borderlands are those from the aforementioned Ichmul de Morley ballplayer panels, which are linguistically Mayan and almost certainly predate

---

15. Studies of Maya linguistic boundaries have targeted the southwestern (de Montmollin 1995) and southeastern (Schortman, Urban, and Ausec 2001) peripheries of Mayaland, where Maya speakers give way to non-Maya languages. While studies of ancient Maya religion are ubiquitous (Freidel, Schele, and Parker 1993; Houston 1999; Taube 1992; Thompson 1970; Vail 2000), there are fewer scholars working on religious boundaries within the Maya area, probably because Classic Maya religion is usually seen as a uniformly distributed, conservative, and durable institution.

the time when Nawa loan words had been incorporated into the inscriptions at Chichén Itzá.[16]

In examining religious boundaries in the borderlands, in principle one could look at the distribution of different censer ceramic forms (which have a ritual function in that they were used to burn incense) across the borderlands and see if there are any discernible patterns. This approach has been used at the intrasite scale by Kelli Carmean (1998), who looked at the distribution of a Cehpech censer type known as Oxkutzcab Applique at Sayil to examine the spatial location of rituals associated with ancestor veneration. Carmean used their diffusion across Sayil at palaces and humble house mounds alike to argue for religious decentralization. Curiously, only one sherd of Oxkutzcab Applique was identified in the borderlands, found at the central plaza of Santa Cruz. Only a few other Cehpech censer sherds were found in the borderlands, all of them at Ichmul de Morley.

To return to the Feathered Serpent Ideology outlined earlier in this chapter, looking at the distribution of what Ringle, Gallareta Negrón, and Bey (1998, 214–18) label the Incensario Complex in the borderlands might yield some interesting information on the boundary of rituals associated with the FSI. Censers that are part of Chichén Itzá's Sotuta ceramics sphere may indicate participation in the FSI. Alas, we identified only a few examples of putative Incensario Complex sherds in the borderlands. Tinum Red-on-cinnamon is a rare ladle censer present at Chichén Itzá (R. Smith and Gifford 1965, fig. 12d) and is almost identical to the kind that Ringle, Gallareta Negrón, and Bey (1998, fig. 29d) place in the FSI Incensario Complex. Sherds of this type were found on two elite platforms at Ichmul de Morley: nine on Structure N000E350, located just northwest of the site center; and two on N350E125, located some 430 m northwest of the site center (see figure 5.7a). Therefore, there is some ceramic evidence of rituals associated with the FSI at Ichmul de Morley. Our recent investigations at Santa Cruz yielded a surprising number of Sotuta censer sherds: forty. Four were typed as Espita Applique and the rest were Sisal Unslipped (Alonso Olvera and Smith 2019).

---

16. Though not exactly amenable to archaeological testing, it is nevertheless interesting to think about non-Maya speakers making their way through Yucatán from Isla Cerritos to arrive at Chichén Itzá (see also Ardren and Lowry 2011). For those that did not speak Yucatec, did they need to use a guide in the form of a multilingual trader, akin to an Aztec pochteca? Or was the path between Isla Cerritos and Chichén Itzá so well worn that knowledge of the local language wasn't needed?

In terms of architecture, the one surprisingly unambiguous example of FSI architecture is the aforementioned Yaxkukul ballcourt (see figure 5.6). Our surface collections and test excavations on the Yaxkukul ballcourt yielded 789 ceramic sherds mostly dating to the Late Yumcab (AD 700–1050/1100), and yet not one sherd was conclusively identified as belonging to the Sotuta sphere. Thus, we have concrete evidence that architecture in the direct style of Chichén Itzá completely overlapped with the Cehpech ceramic sphere encapsulated in this one structure.[17] The fact that a clear example of Chichén Itzá–inspired architecture is associated with Cehpech ceramics is extremely important in light of ongoing debates about the chronology of Chichén Itzá. If the Great Ballcourt dates to the early or middle eleventh century as Braswell and Peniche May (2012, 255) suggest, then the Yaxkukul ballcourt predates the Great Ballcourt or Cehpech ceramics were being used in the latter half of the eleventh century. Assuming that the Great Ballcourt inspired the one at Yaxkukul and not the other way around, it could be that Cehpech ceramics are that late. In our view, however, a more parsimonious explanation is that the Great Ballcourt dates instead to the tenth century, as this chronological placement allows for plenty of time for Cehpech-using residents at Yaxkukul to replicate it.

What is curious about the Yaxkukul ballcourt is that there is not much other archaeological evidence suggestive of a connection (religious or otherwise) with Chichén Itzá. Of the thirty-one structures we mapped, none of them besides the ballcourt looked remotely like the civic architecture that is present at Chichén Itzá (see figure 5.6), and only 12 Sotuta sherds were identified compared to 263 Cehpech sherds.[18] We also collected 12 pieces of obsidian, none of which were from Pachuca (see table 5.3); however, the *quantity* of obsidian is suggestive of a link to the Chichén Itzá distribution system.

Given all this, what does the Yaxkukul ballcourt mean in terms of religious boundaries between Chichén Itzá and Ek Balam? Since I-shaped ballcourts are central to the FSI (Ringle, Gallareta Negrón, and Bey 1998, 196), an attractive interpretation is that Chichén Itzá was making a provoc-

---

17. In fact, we were surprised at the number of early (i.e., Early Classic and Late Formative) sherds that were associated with the ballcourt. We found some evidence of a substructure in the west range building and therefore argue that the ballcourt was built on a razed earlier building.

18. While the main civic building at Yaxkukul was not a radial pyramid like the Castillo or Osario at Chichén Itzá, we did note that its location southeast of the ballcourt is suspiciously similar to the location of the Castillo relative to the Great Ballcourt.

ative boundary statement by either directly overseeing the construction of a small-scale replica of the Great Ballcourt or indirectly encouraging local Yaxkukul personnel to do so. Another related interpretation would be that local religious leaders at Yaxkukul commissioned the ballcourt as a way of unambiguously severing their Classic Maya religious ties present at Ek Balam and embracing the ideology of Ek Balam's rival. On the other hand, if the Yaxkukul ballcourt was the actual location of rituals associated with the FSI, then at least some sherds belonging to the Incensario Complex would be expected at the ballcourt or elsewhere at Yaxkukul. As we have seen, there is very little artifactual evidence for any ties with Chichén Itzá at the ballcourt; if ever there should be a structure found beyond the urban limits of Chichén Itzá associated with large quantities of Sotuta ceramics and Pachuca obsidian, it should be an I-shaped ballcourt. Yet the lack of this kind of evidence means that direct ties to Chichén Itzá are quite tenuous. It may be that the construction of the Yaxkukul ballcourt is best thought of as a boundary symbol, given that Susan D. Gillespie (1991) has made a case for the connection between ballcourts and boundaries in Mesoamerica. Another interpretation is based on the argument that ballcourts of similar form were used to play similar games. If so, it could be that the Yaxkukul ballcourt is an example of elite emulation, with local religious leaders attempting to gain legitimacy by replicating ballgames taking place at Chichén Itzá.

Conclusion

Using Parker's cross-disciplinary framework, we have attempted to characterize the Epiclassic borderlands between Chichén Itzá and Ek Balam. Yet Parker acknowledges that his strategy for characterizing borderlands is just that: a descriptive technique to better understand many kinds of boundaries. Turning to the processes that explain how these boundaries came about is a different matter entirely. In the conclusion of our chapter, we would like to touch on what processes we see in the Chichén Itzá–Ek Balam borderlands, and in so doing, enter a wider discussion of Maya civilization in particular and Mesoamerica in general.

Frances F. Berdan, Susan Kepecs, and Michael Smith (2003, 315–16) provide many interesting points about what they identify as seven processual trends in Mesoamerica from the Classic to the Postclassic periods: population growth, the proliferation of small polities, increased volume of long-distance exchange, greater diversity of trade goods, commercialization of the economy, new forms of writing and iconography, and new patterns of stylistic interaction. We examine these themes through the lens of the Chichén Itzá–Ek Balam borderlands.

Population Growth

Of all the trends, population growth seems to us to be the least applicable to our case. While certainly Chichén Itzá itself increased in population as the Epiclassic unfolded, Ek Balam probably reached its peak in the late ninth century and then declined during the tenth. In the borderlands, we see communities tethered to Chichén Itzá such as Popola de Dzitas, Ichmul de Morley, and Santa Cruz increasing in size; however, those connected to Ek Balam, such as Yohdzadz or Metkuche, actually lost population. However, by the end of the eleventh century, all the communities we discussed were in serious decline, during a collapse that appears to have afflicted the entire northern Maya lowlands (Andrews, Andrews, and Robles Castellanos 2003). In contrast with other areas of Mesoamerica, the overall Postclassic population of the northern Yucatán Peninsula declined compared to the Epiclassic.

The Proliferation of Small Polities

The proliferation of small polities is difficult to evaluate in our case since our scale of analysis is between two polity capitals. Certainly, this trend would not apply to the northern Maya lowlands in general from the Epiclassic into the Middle Postclassic since Mayapán (Masson and Peraza Lope 2014) becomes a dominant regional capital for a good portion of the northern lowlands at this time. One could argue that because Mayapán was a voluntary confederacy, smaller polities were never absorbed into one political unit before being dissolved. The political map on the eve of the Spanish conquest that was first made famous by Roys (1957) and later modified by Quezada (1993, 1998, 2014) and Okoshi Harada, Izquierdo, and Williams-Beck (2006) appears to have been quite similar to the political landscape in the Epiclassic. Therefore, it does not appear that there was a Postclassic proliferation of small polities in the Yucatán Peninsula, as Berdan, Kepecs, and Smith (2003) argue happened in other areas of Mesoamerica.

Increased Volume of Long-Distance Exchange

As our discussion of obsidian makes quite clear, we definitely detected an increased volume of long-distance exchange in our study. It is without a doubt that the amount of obsidian flowing into the Yucatán Peninsula increased during the course of the Epiclassic period. What were the underlying causes of this? While Ringle, Gallareta Negrón, and Bey (1998) suggest that increased trade was a by-product of the spread of the FSI, Kepecs (2011) maintains that political-economic processes—chiefly Chichén Itzá's control of Yucatecan salt beds—are what drove the obsidian trade.

Greater Diversity of Trade Goods

A greater diversity of trade goods is also present in the borderlands and can be measured in different ways. Ceramically, tradewares like Tohil Plumbate probably first started arriving in northern Yucatán in the tenth century (Cobos Palma 2003; Ringle, Gallareta Negrón, and Bey 1998). Obsidian sources diversify from an almost exclusive reliance on Guatemalan obsidian from El Chayal to incorporating several more sources, such as the distant highlands of Mexico like Pachuca, Ucareo, and Zaragoza. Additionally, other types of raw materials are present at Chichén Itzá, such as copper, gold, and turquoise (Lothrop 1952; Morris, Charlot, and Axtell Morris 1931), that are exceptionally rare or completely absent at Ek Balam.

Commercialization of the Economy

While we agree with Marilyn A. Masson and David A. Freidel (2013, 221) when they point out that Maya markets did not begin with Chichén Itzá, we also think there is stronger evidence of markets operating at the end of the Epiclassic rather than at the beginning. Though no research has been carried out to address commercialization of the economy, we suspect that there was a market at Ek Balam but not at the scale as was present at Chichén Itzá. We see this in the distribution of obsidian. At Ek Balam, hardly any obsidian made its way into commoner households and outlying communities like Nohmozon and Yohdzadz. Yet at Chichén Itzá–affiliated communities like Santa Cruz, we see obsidian associated not only with larger residential platforms near the site center but also with humbler residences on the outskirts of town. Santa Cruz also provides evidence of shell and chert workshops that have not been identified within the Ek Balam polity.

New Forms of Writing and Iconography

Our investigations in the borderlands have yet to reveal any new examples of writing and iconography, although the development of more international forms of writing and iconography at Chichén Itzá itself has been thoroughly covered elsewhere (Ringle, Gallareta Negrón, and Bey 1998; Taube 1994; see also chapters in Kowalski and Kristan-Graham 2011 and Wren et al. 2018). In contrast, with its emphasis on divine kingship, Ek Balam seems to be one of the last holdouts of old Classic Maya canons of writing and iconography, with ruler portraits on stelae (see figure 5.3a), leaning lords and gods, and ancestor cartouches.

New Patterns of Stylistic Interaction

Besides the Ichmul de Morley panels and the Halakal lintel, there is a lack of pictorial art in the borderlands. But there is a clear pattern of new art styles and symbols developing at Chichén Itzá during the Epiclassic while Ek Balam retained the styles that were present before and during the Classic period. Ek Balam artists represented individuals in a curvilinear style that is quickly recognizable as Classic Maya. While there are plenty of examples of Classic Maya artistic styles at Chichén Itzá, there are also examples of mural artwork with sweeping compositions depicting entire landscapes and numerous people interacting with them (Coggins 1984; Ringle 2004). Additionally, we get a set of symbols not previously seen in abundance in the Yucatán Peninsula, which Ringle, Gallareta Negrón, and Bey (1998, 208) call the Epiclassic Visual System, with symbols like the Reptile Eye and the ubiquitous Feathered Serpent (see figure 5.3c, 5.3d).

In a comparative analysis of Classic Tikal and Postclassic Mayapán, Masson and Freidel (2013, 202) argue that there are no profound differences in the political economy between the two sites and suggest that this was the case throughout the Maya area: "In short, we see no major political-economic disjunction between the Classic and Postclassic periods." In contrast, in this same edited volume, Patricia A. McAnany (2013) sees important differences in Maya political economy between the Late Classic and the ensuing Terminal Classic.

Our observations concerning the area between Chichén Itzá and Ek Balam during the Epiclassic lead us to the conclusion that there was an important transformation during this period. Thus, we agree with scholars who see profound differences between the Classic and Postclassic periods in the Maya area (Kepecs and Masson 2003; Manahan, Ardren, and Alonso Olvera 2012; McAnany 2013; Sabloff and Rathje 1975) and argue that this transformation occurred during the Epiclassic period in the Yucatán Peninsula. In a few generations, the economic, political, and religious landscape of the borderlands had changed dramatically between AD 850 and 950. The macroscale examination of boundaries we employ not only allows for a better understanding of the multifaceted ways in which they operated in the borderlands but also can be used to address issues more germane to scholars working on larger issues of processual change through time.

Works Cited

Aguilar, Yameli, Francisco Bautista, Manuel E. Mendoza, Oscar Frausto, and Thomas Ihl. 2016. "Density of Karst Depressions in Yucatán State, Mexico." *Journal of Cave and Karst Studies* 78 (2): 51–60.

Alonso Olvera, Alejandra. 2013. "Economic Strategies of Terminal Classic Households in the Northern Maya Lowlands: Multicrafting and Economic Diversification of a Mid-Elite Residential Compound at Xuenkal, Yucatán." PhD diss., Calgary University.

Alonso Olvera, Alejandra, and J. Gregory Smith, eds. 2019. "Informe técnico de las actividades de campo y laboratorio del Proyecto Arqueológico Ichmul de Morley: Temporada de trabajo 2017." Instituto Nacional de Antropología e Historia, Mexico City.

Anderson, Patricia K. 1998. "Yula, Yucatán, Mexico: Terminal Classic Maya Settlement and Political Organization in the Chichén Itzá Polity." PhD diss., University of Chicago.

Andrews, Anthony P., E. Wyllys Andrews V, and Fernando Robles Castellanos. 2003. "The Northern Maya Collapse and Its Aftermath." *Ancient Mesoamerica* 14 (1): 151–56.

Andrews, Anthony P., Tomás Gallareta Negrón, and Rafael Cobos Palma. 1989. "Preliminary Report of the Cupul Survey Project." *Mexicon* 11 (5): 91–95.

Andrews, E. Wyllys, V. 1976. *The Archaeology of Quelepa, El Salvador*, Middle American Research Institute 42. New Orleans: Tulane University.

Aoyama, Kazuo, Toshiharu Tashiro, and Michael D. Glascock. 1999. "A Pre-Columbian Obsidian Source in San Luis, Honduras: Implications for the Relationship between Late Classic Maya Political Boundaries and the Boundaries of Obsidian Exchange Networks." *Ancient Mesoamerica* 10 (2): 237–49.

Ardren, Traci, ed. 2002. *Ancient Maya Women*. Walnut Creek, Calif.: AltaMira Press.

Ardren, Traci, and Alejandra Alonso. 2013. "Multiproduccion domestica y espacio femenino: Buscando una perspectiva de género para la producción de artefactos de concha en el Clasico maya." In *Género y arqueología en Mesoamérica: Homenaje a Rosemary A. Joyce*, edited by Maria J. Rodriguez-Shadow and Susan Kellogg, 87–102. Mexico City: Centro de Estudios de Antropología de la Mujer.

Ardren, Traci, Alejandra Alonso Olvera, and T. Kam Manahan. 2016. "The Artisans of Terminal Classic Xuenkal, Yucatán, Mexico: Gender and Craft During a Time of Economic Change." In *Gendered Labor in Specialized Economies: Archaeological Perspectives on Female and Male Work*, edited by Sophia E. Kelly and Traci Ardren, 91–115. Boulder: University Press of Colorado.

Ardren, Traci, and Justin Lowry. 2011. "The Travels of Maya Merchants in the Ninth and Tenth Centuries AD: Investigations at Xuenkal and the Greater Cupul Province, Yucatán, Mexico." *World Archaeology* 43 (3): 428–43.

Ardren, Traci, T. Kam Manahan, Julie Kay Welp, and Alejandra Alonso. 2010. "Cloth Production and Economic Intensification in the Area Surrounding Chichén Itzá." *Latin American Antiquity* 21 (3): 274–89.

Berdan, Frances F., Susan Kepecs, and Michael E. Smith. 2003. "A Perspective on Late Postclassic Mesoamerica." In *The Postclassic Mesoamerican World*, edited by Michael E. Smith and Francis F. Berdan, 313–17. Salt Lake City: University of Utah Press.

Bey, George J., III, Tara M. Bond, William M. Ringle, Craig A. Hanson, Charles W. Houck, and Carlos Peraza Lope. 1998. "The Ceramic Chronology of Ek Balam, Yucatán, Mexico." *Ancient Mesoamerica* 9 (1): 101–20.

Bey, George J., III, Craig A. Hanson, and William M. Ringle. 1997. "Classic to Postclassic at Ek Balam, Yucatán: Architectural and Ceramic Evidence for Defining the Transition." *Latin American Antiquity* 8 (3): 237–54.

Bey, George J., III, and William M. Ringle. 2011. "From the Bottom Up: The Timing and Nature of the Tula-Chichén Itzá Exchange." In *Twin Tollans: Chichén Itzá, Tula, and the Epiclassic to Early Postclassic Mesoamerican World*, edited by Jeff Karl Kowalski and Cynthia Kristan-Graham, 299–340. Rev. ed. Washington, D.C.: Dumbarton Oaks Research Library and Collection.

Beyyette, Bethany J., and Lisa J. LeCount, eds. 2017. *"The Only True People": Linking Maya Identities Past and Present*. Boulder: University Press of Colorado.

Biró, Péter. 2016. "Emblem Glyphs in Classic Maya Inscriptions: From Single to Double Ones as a Means of Place of Origin, Memory and Diaspora." In *Places of Power and Memory in Mesoamerica's Past and Present: How Sites, Toponyms and Landscapes Shape History and Remembrance*, edited by Daniel Graña-Behrens, 123–58. Estudios Indiana 9. Ibero-Amerikasches Institut, Preubischer Kulturbesitz. Berlin: Mann Verlag.

Bond-Freeman, Tara M. 2007. "The Maya Preclassic Ceramic Sequence at the site of Ek Balam, Yucatán, Mexico." PhD diss., Southern Methodist University, Dallas.

Brainerd, George W. 1958. *The Archaeological Ceramics of Yucatán.* Anthropological Records 19. Berkeley: University of California Press.

Braswell, Geoffrey E. 1997. "El intercambio prehispánico en Yucatán, México." In *X Simpósio de Investigaciones Arqueológicos en Guatemala,* vol. 2, edited by Juan Pedro Laport and Héctor L. Escobedo, 595–606. Ciudad de Guatemala: Museo Nacional de Arqueología y Etnología.

Braswell, Geoffrey E. 2003. "Obsidian Exchange Spheres." In *The Postclassic Mesoamerican World,* edited by Michael E. Smith and Frances F. Berdan, 131–58. Salt Lake City: University of Utah Press.

Braswell, Geoffrey E., and Michael D. Glascock. 2002. "The Emergence of Market Economies in the Ancient Maya World: Obsidian Exchange in Terminal Classic Yucatán, Mexico." In *Geochemical Evidence for Long-Distance Exchange,* edited by Michael D. Glascock, 33–52. Westport, Conn.: Bergin and Garvey.

Braswell, Geoffrey E., and Michael D. Glascock. 2007. "El intercambio de la obsidiana y el desarrollo de las economías de tipo mercado en la región Maya." In *XX Simposio de Investigaciones Arqueológicas en Guatemala, 2006,* edited by Juan P. Laporte, Bárbara Arroyo, and Héctor Mejía, 15–28. Ciudad de Guatemala: Museo Nacional de Arqueología y Etnología.

Braswell, Geoffrey E., Iken Paap, and Michael D. Glascock. 2011. "The Obsidian and Ceramics of the Puuc Region: Chronology, Lithic Procurement, and Production at Xkipche, Yucatán, Mexico." *Ancient Mesoamerica* 22 (1): 135–54.

Braswell, Geoffrey E., and Nancy Peniche May. 2012. "In the Shadow of the Pyramid: Excavations of the Great Platform of Chichén Itzá." In *The Ancient Maya of Mexico: Reinterpreting the Past of the Northern Maya Lowlands,* edited by Geoffrey E. Braswell, 229–63. New York: Routledge.

Canuto, Marcello A., Francisco Estrada-Belli, Thomas G. Garrison, Stephen D. Houston, Mary Jane Acuña, Milan Kováč, Damien Marken, et al. 2018. "Ancient Lowland Maya Complexity as Revealed by Airborne Laser Scanning of Northern Guatemala." *Science* 361 (6409): 1–17.

Carmean, Kelli. 1998. "Leadership at Sayil: A Study of Political and Religious Decentralization." *Ancient Mesoamerica* 9 (2): 259–70.

Charnay, M. Désiré. 1888. *Viaje a Yucatán a Fines de 1886.* Mérida: Imp. de la Revista de Mérida.

Chase, Arlen F., Diane Z. Chase, Jaime J. Awe, John F. Weishampel, Gyles Iannone, Holley Moyes, Jason Yaeger, and M. Kathryn Brown. 2014. "The Use of LiDAR in Understanding the Ancient Maya Landscape: Caracol and Western Belize." *Advances in Archaeological Practice* 2 (3): 208–21.

Chase, Diane Z., and Arlen F. Chase. 1982. "Yucatec Influence in Terminal Classic Northern Belize." *American Antiquity* 47 (3): 596–614.

Cobos Palma, Rafael. 2003. "The Settlement Patterns of Chichén Itzá, Yucatán, Mexico." PhD diss., Tulane University, New Orleans.

Cobos Palma, Rafael. 2004. "Chichén Itzá: Settlement and Hegemony During the Terminal Classic Period." In *The Terminal Classic in the Maya Lowlands: Collapse,*

Transition & Transformation, edited by Arthur Demarest, Prudence Rice, and Don Rice, 517–44. Boulder: University Press of Colorado.

Cobos Palma, Rafael. 2006. "The Relationship Between Tula and Chichén Itzá: Influences or Interactions?" In *Lifeways in the Northern Maya Lowlands*, edited by Jennifer P. Mathews and Bethany A. Morrison, 173–83. Tucson: University of Arizona Press.

Cobos Palma, Rafael, and Terance L. Winemiller. 2001. "The Late and Terminal Classic-Period Causeway Systems of Chichen Itza, Yucatan, Mexico." *Ancient Mesoamerica* 12 (2): 283–91.

Coggins, Clemency Chase. 1984. "Murals in the Upper Temple of the Jaguars, Chichén Itzá." In *Cenote of Sacrifice: Maya Treasures from the Sacred Well at Chichén Itzá*, edited by Clemency Chase Coggins and Orrin Shane III, 157–65. Austin: University of Texas Press.

Culbert, T. Patrick, and Don S. Rice, eds. 1990. *Precolumbian Population History in the Maya Lowlands*. Albuquerque: University of New Mexico Press.

Demarest, Arthur A. 1988. "Political Evolution in the Maya Borderlands: The Salvadoran Frontier." In *The Southeast Classic Maya Zone*, edited by Elizabeth Hill Boone and Gordon R. Willey, 335–94. Washington, D.C.: Dumbarton Oaks Research Library and Collection.

de Montmollin, Olivier. 1989. *The Archaeology of Political Structure*. Cambridge: Cambridge University Press.

de Montmollin, Olivier. 1995. *Settlement and Politics in Three Late Classic Maya Polities*. Madison, Wis.: Prehistory Press.

Dunham, Peter S. 1990. "Coming Apart at the Seams: The Classic Development and Demise of Maya Civilization: A Segmentary View from Xnaheb, Belize." PhD diss., State University of New York, Albany.

Dunning, Nicholas P. 1992. *Lords of the Hills: Ancient Maya Settlement in the Puuc Region, Yucatán, Mexico*. Madison, Wis.: Prehistory Press.

Dunning, Nicholas P., and Jeff Karl Kowalski. 1994. "Lords of the Hills: Classic Maya Settlement Patterns and Political Iconography in the Puuc Region Mexico." *Ancient Mesoamerica* 5 (1): 63–95.

Fash, William L. 2001. *Scribes, Warriors, and Kings: The City of Copan and the Ancient Maya*. Rev. ed. New York: Thames and Hudson.

Foias, Antonia E., and Ronald L. Bishop. 1997. "Changing Ceramic Production and Exchange in the Petexbatun Region, Guatemala: Reconsidering the Classic Maya Collapse." *Ancient Mesoamerica* 8 (2): 275–91.

Ford, Anabel. 1986. *Population Growth and Social Complexity: An Examination of Settlement and Environment in the Central Maya Lowlands*. Anthropological Research Paper 35. Tempe: Arizona State University.

Freidel, David A., Linda Schele, and Joy Parker. 1993. *Maya Cosmos: Three Thousand Years Down the Shaman's Path*. New York: William Morrow.

García Campillo, José Miguel. 2000. *Estudio introductorio del léxico de las inscripciones de Chichén Itzá, Yucatán, México*. British Archaeological Reports, International Series 831. Oxford: BAR.

Garza Tarazona de González, Silvia, and Edward B. Kurjack. 1980. *Atlas arqueológico del Estado de Yucatán*. Mexico City: Instituto Nacional de Antropología e Historia.

Gillespie, Susan D. 1991. "Ballgames and Boundaries." In *The Mesoamerican Ballgame*, edited by Vernon L. Scarborough and David R. Wilcox, 317–45. Tucson: University of Arizona Press.

Golden, Charles, Timothy Murtha, Bruce Cook, Derek S. Shaffer, Whittaker Schroeder, Elijah J. Hermitt, Omar Alcover Firpi, and Andrew K. Scherer. 2016. "Reanalyzing Environmental Lidar Data for Archaeology: Mesoamerican Applications and Implications." *Journal of Archaeological Science: Reports* 9 (October): 293–308.

Golden, Charles, Andrew K. Scherer, A. René Muñoz, and Zachary Hruby. 2012. "Polities, Boundaries, and Trade in the Classic Period Usumacinta River Basin." *Mexicon* 34 (1): 11–19.

Golden, Charles, Andrew K. Scherer, A. René Muñoz, and Rosaura Vasquez. 2008. "Piedras Negras and Yaxchilan: Divergent Political Trajectories in Adjacent Maya Polities." *Latin American Antiquity* 19 (3): 249–74.

Graña-Behrens, Daniel. 2006. "Emblem Glyphs and Political Organization in Northwestern Yucatán in the Classic Period (A.D. 300–1000)." *Ancient Mesoamerica* 17 (1): 105–23.

Grube, Nikolai, and Ruth J. Krochock. 2011. "Reading Between the Lines: Hieroglyphic Texts from Chichén Itzá and Its Neighbors." In *Twin Tollans: Chichén Itzá, Tula, and the Epiclassic to Early Postclassic Mesoamerican World*, edited by Jeff Karl Kowalski and Cynthia Kristan-Graham, 157–93. Rev. ed. Washington, D.C.: Dumbarton Oaks Research Library and Collection.

Grube, Nikolai, Alfonso Lacadena, and Simon Martin. 2003. "Chichén Itzá and Ek Balam: Terminal Classic Inscriptions from Yucatán." In *Notebook for XXVIIth Maya Hieroglyphic Forum at Texas*, pt. 2, 1–105. Austin: University of Texas.

Hahn, Lauren D., and Geoffrey E. Braswell. 2012. "Divide and Rule: Interpreting Site Perimeter Walls in the Northern Maya Lowlands and Beyond." In *The Ancient Maya of Mexico: Reinterpreting the Past of the Northern Maya Lowlands*, edited by Geoffrey E. Braswell, 264–81. New York: Routledge.

Hammond, Norman. 1974. "The Distribution of Late Classic Maya Major Ceremonial Centers in the Central Area." In *Mesoamerican Archaeology: New Approaches*, edited by Norman Hammond, 313–34. Austin: University of Texas Press.

Hanson, Craig A. 2008. "The Late Mesoamerican Village." PhD diss., Tulane University, New Orleans.

Hirth, Kenneth G. 2016. *The Aztec Economic World: Merchants and Markets in Ancient Mesoamerica*. Cambridge: Cambridge University Press.

Houck, Charles Weston, Jr. 2004. "The Rural Survey of Ek Balam, Yucatán, Mexico." PhD diss., Tulane University, New Orleans.

Houston, Stephen D. 1999. "Classic Maya Religion: Beliefs and Practices of an Ancient American People." *Brigham Young University Studies* 38 (4): 43–72.

Hutson, Scott. 2014. "Regional Integration Involving Ucí and Its Causeway." In *The Archaeology of Yucatán*, edited by Travis Stanton, 243–53. Oxford: Archaeopress.

Hutson, Scott R. 2015. "Adapting LiDAR Data for Regional Variation in the Tropics: A Case Study from the Northern Maya Lowlands." *Journal of Archaeological Science* 4 (December): 252–63.

Iannone, Gyles. 2010. "Collective Memory in the Frontiers: A Case Study from the Ancient Maya Center of Minanha, Belize." *Ancient Mesoamerica* 21 (2): 353–71.

Johnson, Scott A. J. 2012. "Late and Terminal Classic Power Shifts in Northern Yucatán: The View from Popola." PhD diss., Tulane University, New Orleans.

Johnson, Scott A. J. 2018. "Rulers Without Borders: The Difficulty of Identifying Polity Boundaries in Terminal Classic Yucatán and Beyond." In *Landscapes of the Itza: Archaeology and Art History at Chichén Itzá and Neighboring Sites*, edited by Linnea Wren, Cynthia Kristan-Graham, Travis Nygard, and Kaylee Spencer, 109–37. Gainesville: University Press of Florida.

Jones, Siân. 1997. *The Archaeology of Ethnicity: Constructing Identities in the Past and Present*. London: Routledge.

Jordan, Keith. 2016. "From Tula Chico to Chichén Itzá: Implications of the Epiclassic Sculpture of Tula for the Nature and Timing of the Tula-Chichén Contact." *Latin American Antiquity* 27 (4): 462–78.

Kaufman, Terrence. 2001. "The History of the Nawa Language Group from the Earliest Times to the Sixteenth Century: Some Initial Results." https://www.albany.edu/pdlma/Nawa.pdf.

Kepecs, Susan M. 1999. "The Political Economy of Chikinchel, Yucatán, Mexico: A Diachronic Analysis from the Pre-Hispanic Era Through the Age of Spanish Administration." PhD diss., University of Wisconsin–Madison.

Kepecs, Susan M. 2011. "Chichén Itzá, Tula, and the Epiclassic/Early Postclassic Mesoamerica World System." In *Twin Tollans: Chichén Itzá, Tula, and the Epiclassic to Early Postclassic Mesoamerican World*, edited by Jeff Karl Kowalski and Cynthia Kristan-Graham, 95–113. Rev. ed. Washington, D.C.: Dumbarton Oaks Research Library and Collection.

Kepecs, Susan M., and Marilyn A. Masson. 2003. "Political Organization in Yucatán and Belize." In *The Postclassic Mesoamerican World*, edited by Michael E. Smith and Francis F. Berdan, 40–44. Salt Lake City: University of Utah Press.

Kowalski, Jeff Karl, and Cynthia Kristan-Graham, eds. 2011. *Twin Tollans: Chichén Itzá, Tula, and the Epiclassic to Early Postclassic Mesoamerican World*. Rev. ed. Washington, D.C.: Dumbarton Oaks Research Library and Collection.

Kurjack, Edward B., and E. Wyllys Andrews V. 1976. "Early Boundary Maintenance in Northwest Yucatán, Mexico." *American Antiquity* 41 (3): 318–25.

Lacadena García-Gallo, Alfonso. 2004. "The Glyphic Corpus from Ek' Balam, Yucatán, México." Foundation for the Advancement of Mesoamerican Studies, Inc., Crystal River, Fla. http://www.famsi.org/reports/01057/01057LacadenaGarciaGallo01.pdf.

Lincoln, Charles E. 1986. "The Chronology of Chichén Itzá: A Review of the Literature." In *Late Lowland Maya Civilization: Classic to Postclassic*, edited by Jeremy A. Sabloff and E. Wyllys Andrews V, 141–96. Albuquerque: University of New Mexico Press.

Lincoln, Charles E. 1991. "Ethnicity and Social Organization at Chichén Itzá, Mexico." PhD diss., Harvard University.

Lothrop, Samuel K. 1952. *Metals from the Cenote of Sacrifice, Chichén Itzá, Yucatán*. Memoirs of the Peabody Museum of Archaeology and Ethnology Harvard University 10, no. 2. Cambridge, Mass.: Peabody Museum, Harvard University.

Love, Bruce. 2019. "Corpus Volume 9: Ichmul de Morley, Panels 1 and 2, Yucatán, Mexico." *Contributions to Mesoamerican Studies*, November 3. https://brucelove.com/corpus/corpus-volume-009.

Lundy, Heather Darlene. 2016. "Architecture and Placemaking at a Northern Maya City: Ek' Balam and the Question of Style." PhD diss., Florida State University, Tallahassee.

Manahan, T. Kam, Traci Ardren, and Alejandra Alonso Olvera. 2012. "Household Organization and the Dynamics of State Expansion: The Late Classic-Terminal Classic Transformation at Xuenkal, Yucatán, Mexico." *Ancient Mesoamerica* 23 (2): 345–64.

Marcus, Joyce. 1976. *Emblem and State in the Classic Maya Lowlands: An Epigraphic Approach to Territorial Organization*. Washington, D.C.: Dumbarton Oaks Research Library and Collection.

Marken, Damien B., Stanley P. Guenter, and David A. Freidel. 2017. "He's Maya, but He's Not My Brother: Exploring the Place of Ethnicity in Classic Maya Social Organization." In *"The Only True People": Linking Maya Identities Past and Present*, edited by Bethany J. Beyyette and Lisa J. LeCount, 187–217. Boulder: University Press of Colorado.

Martin, Simon. 2020. *Ancient Maya Politics: A Political Anthropology of the Classic Period, 150–900 CE*. Cambridge: Cambridge University Press.

Martin, Simon, and Nikolai Grube. 2008. *Chronicle of the Maya Kings and Queens: Deciphering the Dynasties of the Ancient Maya*. 2nd ed. New York: Thames and Hudson.

Masson, Marilyn A., and David A. Freidel. 2013. "Wide Open Spaces: A Long View of the Importance of Maya Market Exchange." In *Merchants, Markets, and Exchange in the Pre-Columbian World*, edited by Kenneth G. Hirth and Joanne Pillsbury, 201–28. Washington, D.C.: Dumbarton Oaks Research Library and Collection.

Masson, Marilyn A., and Carlos Peraza Lope. 2014. *Kukulcan's Realm: Urban Life at an Ancient Mayapán*. Boulder: University Press of Colorado.

Mathews, Peter. 1991. "Classic Maya Emblem Glyphs." In *Classic Maya Political History: Hieroglyphic and Archaeological Evidence*, edited by T. Patrick Culbert, 19–29. Cambridge: Cambridge University Press.

McAnany, Patricia A. 2013. "Artisans, *Ikatz*, and Statecraft: Provisioning Classic Maya Royal Courts." In *Merchants, Markets, and Exchange in the Pre-Columbian World*, edited by Kenneth G. Hirth and Joanne Pillsbury, 229–54. Washington, D.C.: Dumbarton Oaks Research Library and Collection.

Morley, Sylvanus G. 1928. *Research in Middle American Archaeology.* Year Book 27, 1927–28. Washington, D.C.: Carnegie Institute of Washington.

Morris, Earl H., Jean Charlot, and Ann Axtell Morris. 1931. *The Temple of the Warriors at Chichén Itzá, Yucatán.* 2 vols. Publication 406. Washington, D.C.: Carnegie Institution of Washington.

Okoshi Harada, Tsubasa, Ana Luisa Izquierdo, and Lorraine Williams-Beck. 2006. *Nuevas perspectivas sobre la geografía política de los mayas.* Mexico City: Instituto de Investigaciones Filológicas, Centro de Estudios Mayas, Universidad Nacional Autónoma de México.

Parker, Bradley J. 2006. "Toward an Understanding of Borderland Processes." *American Antiquity* 71 (1): 77–100.

Peniche May, Nancy, Lauren D. Hahn, and Geoffrey E. Braswell. 2009. "Excavaciones de la UCSD en Chichén Itzá: La gran nivelación y la muralla." Informe de la temporada de campo 2009 al Proyecto Chichén Itzá, University of California, San Diego.

Pérez de Heredia, Eduardo. 2010. "Ceramic Contexts and Chronology at Chichén Itzá, Yucatán, Mexico." PhD diss., La Trobe University, Melbourne.

Pérez de Heredia, Eduardo, and Péter Biró. 2018. "K'ak' Upakal K'inich K'awil and the Lords of the Fire: Chichén Itzá During the Ninth Century." In *Landscapes of the Itza: Archaeology and Art History at Chichén Itzá and Neighboring Sites*, edited by Linnea Wren, Cynthia Kristan-Graham, Travis Nygard, and Kaylee Spencer, 65–108. Gainesville: University Press of Florida.

Proskouriakoff, Tatiana. 1962. "Civic and Religious Structures at Mayapan." In *Mayapan, Yucatan, Mexico*, by H. E. D. Pollock, Ralph L. Roys, Tatiana Proskouriakoff, and A. Ledyard Smith, 88–164. Publication 619. Washington, D.C.: Carnegie Institution of Washington.

Puleston, Dennis E. 1974. "Intersite Areas in the Vicinity of Tikal and Uaxactun." In *Mesoamerican Archaeology: New Approaches*, edited by Norman Hammond, 303–11. London: Duckworth.

Puleston, Dennis E. 1983. *The Settlement Survey of Tikal.* University Museum Monograph 48. Philadelphia: University of Pennsylvania Museum of Archaeology and Anthropology.

Quezada, Sergio. 1993. *Pueblos y caciques yucatecos, 1550–1580.* Mexico City: Colegio de México.

Quezada, Sergio. 1998. "Political Organization of the Yucatecan Mayas During the Eleventh to Sixteenth Centuries." In *Maya Civilization*, edited by Peter Schmidt, Mercedes de la Garza, and Enrique Nalda, 469–81. New York: Thames and Hudson.

Quezada, Sergio. 2014. *Maya Lords and Lordship: The Formation of Colonial Society in Yucatán, 1350–1600.* Translated by Terry Rugeley. Norman: University of Oklahoma Press.

Restall, Matthew. 1997. *The Maya World: Yucatec Culture and Society, 1550–1850.* Stanford: Stanford University Press.

Ringle, William M. 1990. "Who Was Who in Ninth-Century Chichén Itzá." *Ancient Mesoamerica* 1 (2): 233–43.

Ringle, William M. 2004. "On the Political Organization of Chichén Itzá." *Ancient Mesoamerica* 15 (2): 167–218.
Ringle, William M. 2009. "The Art of War: Imagery of the Upper Temple of the Jaguars, Chichén Itzá." *Ancient Mesoamerica* 20 (2): 15–44.
Ringle, William M. 2014. "Plazas and Patios of the Feathered Serpent." In *Mesoamerican Plazas: Arenas of Community and Power*, edited by Kenichiro Tsukamoto and Takeshi Inomata, 168–92. Tucson: University of Arizona Press.
Ringle, William M. 2017. "Debating Chichén Itzá." *Ancient Mesoamerica* 28 (1): 119–36.
Ringle, William M., and George J. Bey III. 1992. "The Center and Segmentary State Dynamics: African Models in the Maya Lowlands." Paper presented at the Segmentary State and the Classic Lowland Maya: A "New" Model for Ancient Political Organization conference, Cleveland State University, Cleveland.
Ringle, William M., and George J. Bey III. 2001. "Post-Classic and Terminal Classic Courts of the Northern Maya Lowlands." In *Royal Courts of the Ancient Maya*, vol. 2, *Data and Case Studies*, edited by Takeshi Inomata and Stephen D. Houston, 266–307. Boulder, Colo.: Westview Press.
Ringle, William M., and George J. Bey III. 2008. "Preparing for Visitors: Political Dynamics on the Northern Plains of Yucatán." Paper delivered at the VI Mesa Redonda de Palenque: Homenaje a Ian Graham, Palenque, Mexico.
Ringle, William M., and George J. Bey III. 2009. "The Face of the Itzas." In *The Art of Urbanism: How Mesoamerican Kingdoms Represented Themselves in Architecture and Imagery*, edited by William L. Fash and Leonardo López Luján, 329–83. Washington, D.C.: Dumbarton Oaks Research Library and Collection.
Ringle, William M., and George J. Bey III. 2012. "The Late Classic to Postclassic Transition Among the Maya of Northern Yucatán." In *The Oxford Handbook of Mesoamerican Archaeology*, edited by Deborah L. Nichols and Christopher A. Pool, 385–404. Oxford: Oxford University Press.
Ringle, William M., George J. Bey III, Tara Bond-Freeman, Craig A. Hanson, Charles W. Houck, and J. Gregory Smith. 2004. "The Decline of the East: The Postclassic Transition at Ek Balam, Yucatán." In *The Terminal Classic in the Maya Lowlands: Collapse, Transition & Transformation*, edited by Arthur Demarest, Don Rice, and Prudence Rice, 485–516. Boulder: University Press of Colorado.
Ringle, William M., George J. Bey III, Tara M. Bond-Freeman, Charles W. Houck, J. Gregory Smith, and Craig A. Hanson. 2003. "El proyecto Ek Balam: Una perspectiva regional, 1986–1999." *Los Investigadores de la Cultura Maya* 11 (2): 392–405.
Ringle, William M., Tomás Gallareta Negrón, and George J. Bey III. 1998. "The Return of Quetzalcoatl: Evidence for the Spread of a World Religion During the Epiclassic Period." *Ancient Mesoamerica* 9 (2): 183–232.
Ringle, William M., George J. Bey III, and Carlos Peraza Lope. 1991. "An Itzá Empire in Northern Yucatán? A Neighboring View." Paper presented at the 47th Annual Meeting of the International Congress of the Americanists, New Orleans.
Roys, Ralph L. 1957. *The Political Geography of the Yucatán Maya*. Publication 613. Washington, D.C.: Carnegie Institution of Washington.

Sabloff, Jeremy A., and William L. Rathje. 1975. "The Rise of a Maya Merchant Class." *Scientific American* 233 (4): 72–82.
Schele, David. 2000. "The Linda Schele Drawings Collection." Foundation for the Advancement of Mesoamerican Studies, Inc., Crystal River, Fla. http://research.famsi.org/schele.html.
Schele, Linda, and David A. Freidel. 1990. *A Forest of Kings: The Untold Story of the Ancient Maya*. New York: William Morrow.
Schele, Linda, and Peter Mathews. 1998. *The Code of Kings: The Language of Seven Sacred Maya Temples and Tombs*. New York: Scribner.
Schortman, Edward M., Patricia A. Urban, and Marne Ausec. 2001. "Politics with Style: Identity Formation in Prehispanic Southeastern Mesoamerica." *American Anthropologist* 103 (2): 312–30.
Shafer, Harry J., and Thomas R. Hester. 1991. "Lithic Craft Specialization and Product Distribution at the Maya Site of Colha, Belize." *World Archaeology* 23 (1): 79–97.
Shaw, Justine M. 2008. *White Roads of the Yucatán: Changing Social Landscapes of the Yucatec Maya*. Tucson: University of Arizona Press.
Smith, J. Gregory. 1998. "Riding the Fence in Yucatán: Politics, Ethnicity, and Identity in the Chichén Itzá–Ek Balam Borderlands." Paper presented at the First Annual Graduate Symposium, University of Pennsylvania, Philadelphia.
Smith, J. Gregory. 2000. "The Chichén Itzá-Ek Balam Transect Project: An Intersite Perspective on the Political Organization of the Ancient Maya." PhD diss., University of Pittsburgh.
Smith, J. Gregory. 2019. "The History of the Ichmul de Morley Ballplayer Panels." *Contributions to Mesoamerican Studies*, November 26. https://brucelove.com/research/contribution-009/.
Smith, J. Gregory, and Tara M. Bond-Freeman. 2009. "Floor Plans and Potsherds: A Comparison of Domestic Architecture in the Chichén Itzá-Ek Balam Region of Northern Yucatán, Mexico." Paper presented at the 74th Annual Meeting of the Society for American Archaeology, Atlanta.
Smith, J. Gregory, and Tara M. Bond-Freeman. 2018. "In the Shadow of Quetzalcoatl: How Small Communities in Northern Yucatán Responded to the Chichén Itzá Phenomenon." In *Landscapes of the Itza: Archaeology and Art History at Chichén Itzá and Neighboring Sites*, edited by Linnea Wren, Cynthia Kristan-Graham, Travis Nygard, and Kaylee Spencer, 138–170. Gainesville: University Press of Florida.
Smith, J. Gregory, William M. Ringle, and Tara M. Bond-Freeman. 2006. "Ichmul de Morley and Northern Maya Political Dynamics." In *Lifeways in the Northern Maya Lowlands*, edited by Jennifer P. Mathews and Bethany A. Morrison, 155–72. Tucson: University of Arizona Press.
Smith, Michael E. 1996. *The Aztecs*. Malden, Mass.: Blackwell.
Smith, Michael E. 2003. "Small Polities in Postclassic Mesoamerica." In *The Postclassic Mesoamerican World*, edited by Michael E. Smith and Francis F. Berdan, 35–39. Salt Lake City: University of Utah Press.
Smith, Michael E. 2014. "The Aztecs Paid Taxes, Not Tribute." *Mexicon* 36 (1): 19–22.

Smith, Robert E. 1971. *The Pottery of Mayapan, Including Studies of Ceramic Material from Uxmal, Kabah, and Chichén Itzá*. Papers of the Peabody Museum 66. Cambridge, Mass.: Peabody Museum of Archaeology and Ethnology, Harvard University.

Smith, Robert E., and James C. Gifford. 1965. "Pottery of the Maya Lowlands." In *Archaeology of Southern Mesoamerica*, pt. 1, edited by Gordon R. Willey, 498–534. Austin: University of Texas Press.

Stanton, Travis, Traci Ardren, Nicolas Barth, Juan Fernandez-Diaz, Patrick Rohrer, Dominique Meyer, Stephanie Miller, Aline Magnoni, and Manuel Pérez. 2020. "'Structure' Density, Area, and Volume as Complementary Tools to Understand Maya Settlement: An Analysis of Lidar Data Along the Great Road Between Cobá and Yaxuna." *Journal of Archaeological Science: Reports* 29 (February): 102178.

Taube, Karl A. 1992. *The Major Gods of Ancient Yucatán*. Studies in Pre-Columbian Art and Archaeology 32. Washington, D.C.: Dumbarton Oaks Research Library and Collection.

Taube, Karl A. 1994. "The Iconography of Toltec Period Chichén Itzá." In *Hidden Among the Hills: Maya Archaeology of the Northwest Yucatán Peninsula*, edited by Hanns J. Prem, 212–46. Acta Mesoamericana 7. Möckmül, Germany: Verlag Von Fleming.

Thompson, J. Eric S. 1970. *Maya History and Religion*. Norman: University of Oklahoma Press.

Tokovinine, Alexandre. 2011. "People from a Place: Re-Interpreting Classic Maya Emblem Glyphs." In *Ecology, Power, and Religion in Maya Landscapes*, edited by Christian Isendahl and Bodil Liljefors Persson, 91–106. Acta Mesoamericana 23. Markt Schwaben, Germany: Verlag Anton Saurwein.

Tokovinine, Alexandre, and Dmitri Beliaev. 2013. "People of the Road: Traders and Travelers in Ancient Maya Words and Images." In *Merchants, Markets, and Exchange in the Pre-Columbian World*, edited by Kenneth G. Hirth and Joanne Pillsbury, 169–200. Washington, D.C.: Dumbarton Oaks Research Library and Collection.

Vail, Gabrielle. 2000. "Pre-Hispanic Maya Religion: Conceptions of Divinity in the Postclassic Maya Codices." *Ancient Mesoamerica* 11 (1): 123–47.

Vargas de la Peña, Leticia, and Víctor R. Castillo Borges. 2014. "Las construcciones monumentales de Ek'Balam." In *The Archaeology of Yucatán*, edited by Travis Stanton, 377–394. Oxford: Archaeopress.

Vlcek, David T., and William L. Fash Jr. 1986. "Survey in the Outlying Areas of the Copan Region, and the Copan-Quirigua 'Connection.'" In *The Southeast Maya Periphery*, edited by Patricia A. Urban and Edward M. Schortman, 102–13. Austin: University of Texas Press.

Volta, Beniamino, and Geoffrey E. Braswell. 2014. "Alternative Narratives and Missing Data: Refining the Chronology of Chichén Itzá." In *The Maya and Their Central American Neighbors: Settlement Patterns, Architecture, Hieroglyphic Texts, and Ceramics*, edited by Geoffrey E. Braswell, 356–402. New York: Routledge.

Volta, Beniamino, Nancy Peniche May, and Geoffrey E. Braswell. 2018. "The Archaeology of Chichén Itzá: Its History, What We Like to Argue About, and What We Think We Know." In *Landscapes of the Itza: Archaeology and Art History at Chichén Itzá and Neighboring Sites*, edited by Linnea Wren, Cynthia Kristan-Graham, Travis Nygard, and Kaylee Spencer, 28–64. Gainesville: University Press of Florida.

Voss, Alexander W., and Markus Eberl. 1999. "Ek Balam: A New Emblem Glyph from Northeastern Yucatán." *Mexicon* 21 (6): 124–31.

Voss, Alexander W., and H. Juergen Kremer. 2000. "K'ak'-u-pakal, Hun-pik-tok' and the Kokom: The Political Organization of Chichén Itzá." In *The Sacred and the Profane: Architecture and Identity in the Southern Maya Lowlands*, edited by Pierre R. Colas, 149–81. Acta Mesoamericana 10. Markt Schwaben, Germany: Verlag Anton Saurwein.

Willey, Gordon R., and Richard M. Leventhal. 1979. "Prehistoric Settlement at Copan." In *Maya Archaeology and Ethnohistory*, edited by Norman Hammond, 75–103. Austin: University of Texas Press.

Williams-Beck, Lorraine A. 2001. "Rethinking Maya Political Geography." Foundation for the Advancement of Mesoamerican Studies, Inc., Crystal River, Fla. http://www.famsi.org/reports/98058/98058WilliamsBeck01.pdf.

Wren, Linnea, Cynthia Kristan-Graham, Travis Nygard, and Kaylee Spencer, eds. 2018. *Landscapes of the Itza: Archaeology and Art History at Chichén Itzá and Neighboring Sites*. Gainesville: University Press of Florida.

Wren, Linnea, Kaylee Spencer, and Travis Nygard. 2018. "To Face or to Flee from the Foe: Women in Warfare at Chichén Itzá." In *Landscapes of the Itza: Archaeology and Art History at Chichén Itzá and Neighboring Sites*, edited by Linnea Wren, Cynthia Kristan-Graham, Travis Nygard, and Kaylee Spencer, 258–87. Gainesville: University Press of Florida.

CHAPTER 6

Crossing the Last Maya Boundary

The Central Line of the Military Campaign, 1899–1904

ALEJANDRA BADILLO SÁNCHEZ

In 1847, Maya people from the north, south, and east of the Yucatán Peninsula began an armed movement known as the Caste War. The uprising began in towns near Valladolid such as Tihosuco, Tepich, and Chichimilá but then spread to other places. The causes of this war stemmed from a series of misdeeds that had been brewing since the Spanish conquest. By the nineteenth century, Maya in the area suffered from the loss of their lands, abuse of colonial authorities, and high tax collection, among other things. Additionally, there was a divisive political atmosphere in Yucatán between two groups that fought for political power and attempted to impose their ideals. Miguel Barbachano led the more conservative-leaning group, while the second was under Santiago Méndez, who embodied more liberal ideas. Each of the political contenders had supporters among the civilian, military, and Maya populations, although politicians attempted to curry favor with the Maya by promising to give them a tax exemption if they joined their campaigns (Careaga Viliesid 2016, 2:286–95; Dumond 2005, 129–30, 134–37; Reed 2007, 62; Rugeley 2009, 58–59).

The war lasted until the first years of the twentieth century, waxing and waning from tense periods between Maya peoples and the local authorities to periods of apparent tranquility. Early in the conflict, Maya rebels dominated a large part of the Yucatán Peninsula, especially the eastern, central, and southern parts of the territory (Rugeley 2009, 59). Governor Santiago Méndez, upon seeing that he was about to lose Mérida due to strategic attacks, resigned his position and left his post to Lieutenant Governor Miguel Barbachano (Paoli Bolio 2015, 18). Nevertheless, the strength of the Maya was diminished in the early 1850s due to rivalries and disorganization among the different Maya groups. They also suffered from inadequate supplies and ammunition, leading some Maya leaders to consider negotiations with the government to lay down their arms. However, the conditions were not favorable to Indigenous peoples and the war raged on (Rugeley 2009, 59).

The war was revitalized with the veneration of the Talking Cross shrine in the town of Chan Santa Cruz in the eastern-central part of the peninsula (Dumond 2005, 271). In October 1851, Juan de la Cruz announced the existence of the Talking Cross cult, which built a wooden temple with a thatch roof around the cross (Careaga Viliesid 2016, 2:303). The oracle of the Talking Cross (voiced by ventriloquist Manuel Nahuat) encouraged the continuation of the war and established Chan Santa Cruz as the capital of the eastern Maya (Careaga Viliesid 1998, 30; 2016, 2:300–303). This also resulted in Chan Santa Cruz becoming the focus of attention and attack by Mexican authorities.

Mexican authority went through several stages during the war, from the establishment of the Second Federal Republic in the middle of the nineteenth century to passing through a dictatorship, the Second Empire, and finally the Porfiriato period in the 1870s. Each government launched new military offensives, but none had an impact until 1899, when Porfirio Díaz launched the "Military Campaign of Yucatán," entrusting General Ignacio A. Bravo as its head (Careaga Viliesid 1998, 46). Planning for this military campaign began in 1895 and 1896, due to disputes over the exploitation of land and natural resources (Badillo Sánchez 2019, 161–72).

I examine this period through the lens of historical archaeology, based on several seasons of fieldwork (starting in 2005) with the Cochuah Regional Archaeological Survey (CRAS) project led by Dr. Justine M. Shaw. CRAS focuses on the study of cultural heritage in the ancient region of Cochuah. I document and analyze the modification of colonial-era ranches and haciendas during the Caste War, focusing on the last part of the Caste War when the Military Campaign of Yucatán acted against Maya peoples in 1899. The Maya territory was transformed into a warlike landscape under the Díaz regime as it consolidated the country as a nation-state. The Díaz government used the military to appropriate civilian spaces and established military architecture within Maya rebel territory. This helped unveil the "Theater of

War" and the military actions that took place within the region to regain control of the conflict zone (Badillo Sánchez 2019, 180–99).

The Last Maya Boundary: Coveted Territory

Prior to the nineteenth century, the Yucatán Peninsula was a broad territory of rich natural resources with jungles and mangroves, the sea on the east and west coasts, and Guatemala and British Honduras to the south. The distribution and availability of natural resources and forest wealth benefited the Maya population, providing subsistence and the production of goods for trade. However, this wealth also created economic competition and triggered political disputes across that vast territory (Villalobos 1993, 21).

The Maya living space of the nineteenth century was the result of a long historical process that dates back to the sixteenth century. In this Spanish colony, the economic focus was on extracting resources in the eastern-central part of the peninsula. The Spanish ruled in the southeast, while the border area was precarious, as it was exploited by English colonists from British Honduras. The English based their economy on the cutting and exploitation of timber, including cedar, mahogany, *palo de tinte*, and chicozapote (Badillo Sánchez 2019, 55). Along coastal routes, they could connect British Honduras with Quintana Roo and the northern coast of the State of Yucatán. Timber resources were also floated down inland rivers to the coast. Shortly after the creation of these trade routes, the district (now state) of Campeche separated from Yucatán and the political division of the peninsula shifted to states. Additionally, the colonial expansion in the peninsula was conditioned by new exploitation interests. For the British monarchy, obtaining and exporting timber was an activity of great economic importance and woodcutting was the colony's largest industry in the 1890s (Wilson 1897).

English colonists regularly entered Mexican territory and Maya lands. Mexicans also moved into the unoccupied border area with the Guatemalan territory for the exploitation of hardwoods. In the northern part of the peninsula, Spanish colonizers cultivated henequen and sugar cane, while in Campeche and the southern part of Peto, they raised livestock. Yet there were still regions inhabited by the Maya beyond the reach of the English and Spanish monarchies. A map of Yucatán in 1861 shows its five districts: Mérida, Valladolid, Izamal, Campeche, and Tekax. An area was designated "Monte Despoblado" (Unoccupied Territory) in the eastern part of the state, and other territories were occupied by the "Indians of the South" and "Indians of the East" (Suárez y Navarro 1861). However, these regions in the southeast of the Yucatán Peninsula and into Belize and Guatemala began to be targeted, in order for extractors to collect chicle from the Chicozapote tree (*Manilkara sapota*) located in regions where Indigenous Maya people lived (Bracamonte y Sosa 2000, 157).

Authorities commonly removed Maya from "unoccupied" areas where, in fact, they had lived for centuries (Bracamonte y Sosa 2000, 156). Laws aimed at colonialist expansion can be traced to December 2, 1825, when the "colonization of vacant lands" was instituted. The connotation of "vacant lands" was strategically used to obtain *legal* access to the land while also justifying the idea of dispossession of "barbarians" because "the Indians did not have the necessary aptitude to manage their own affairs, hence their use of the lands was limited" (173, 175). This policy ignored the Indigenous tradition of ejidos or communal lands and enabled privatization.[1] It also affected people who then had to be integrated as workers onto the ranches or farms. Thus, between 1840 and 1847, many of the so-called vacant lands north of Peto, in Tihosuco, Valladolid, and Tizimin, transferred ownership.

This was the catalyst of the rebellion, sparking significant conflict. After the cruelest years of the beginning of the war (1847–53), the Yucatán government redesignated the "vacant" zone on maps to be the territory of the "rebellious eastern Indians" in the area, including Chan Santa Cruz, the "pacified Indians" toward the south, and the "peaceful Indians" in the northern part of the peninsula (Fremont 1861). The term *rebel* began to be used to criminalize the Maya armed movement, thus justifying the war that the Díaz government waged against them (Ministerio de Justicia e Instrucción Pública 1883). This validated the dispersal of Indigenous groups and allowed the state to focus on control and hegemonic power through a "justified" military occupation of the area (Badillo Sánchez 2019, 26–70).

Once this border of the "rebel" Maya was delineated, the complaints by non-Indigenous landowners began to pour in to acquire the "vacant" lands, leading to a transformation of land tenure. The arable lands passed into the hands of the *hacendados*, and other lands were distributed to businessmen

---

1. These concessions and permits did not provide land ownership but did grant broad rights for the use of the natural resources, excluding Indigenous peoples (Bracamonte y Sosa 2000, 173, 175).

and other areas with "low demographic density." According to the authorities, the Indigenous labor was colonized and taken on as wage earners or servants. As a result of this dispossession, some Maya retreated to the jungle or the eastern mountain region, and there was a general dismantling of Indigenous communities (Bracamonte y Sosa 2000, 163). On July 22, 1863, a new law was issued stipulating that the vacant lands became the property of the nation. This allowed for the presence of "deslindadoras" and colonizing companies in regions near Maya rebel territory (173, 175).[2] In the following years, sociopolitical changes led to territorial planning and an attempt to define and establish the southern border of Mexico (Macías Richard 1997, 32).

The Chan Santa Cruz Maya maintained an affable relationship with the English of British Honduras, who gave them permission to work the lands on the Mexican side in exchange for arms, gunpowder, and ammunition from the colony (Sweet Escott 1893; Wihelm 1997, 17, 18). In 1883, Porfirio Díaz encouraged colonization and the exploitation of forest concessions in the eastern jungles of the peninsula as a way to suppress the rebel Maya (Bracamonte y Sosa 2000, 173). Logging companies were expanded, mostly in the eastern rebel territory (Macías Richard 1997, 12), and companies such as El Cuyo y Anexas were dedicated to agricultural and forestry exploitation and the extraction of palo de tinte for the world market (Bracamonte y Sosa 2000, 173). The East Coast Colonizing Company took over more territory in the north and in the Peto region (174), and the concessions continued to expand in British Honduras, including the commercial house Felipe Ibarra Ortoll and Company, from Ascension Bay to the Río Hondo (Villalobos González 1993, 91–92). As the government sold land parcels, it used the money to deal with insolvency issues or compensate the soldiers of the Yucatecan army (Rugeley 1996, 124). The new inhabitants on farms and haciendas complained that the land was not sustainable for intensive subsistence crops. They failed to maintain the traditional system of land rotation, in which the land was allowed to rest, and livestock further damaged the land. With the Indigenous economy in shambles, many Maya had to depend on haciendas to survive (Bracamonte y Sosa 2000, 156, 160).

---

2. The companies were dedicated to measuring, valuing, and dividing the vacant lands to award them to foreign immigrants or nationals for the purpose of colonization (Gómez de Silva Cano 2016, 81).

By the 1890s, land controlled by the rebel Maya had become economically and politically important due to its strategic location in the border area, its natural wealth of timber resources, and the Maya labor force. Local authorities in Yucatán, the government of Porfirio Díaz, and the British monarchy all coveted control of the region and its natural resources (Bracamonte y Sosa 2000, 173; Wilson 1897). Porfirio Díaz resolved to take control by force and expand his power over the disputed territory by implementing a large-scale campaign using the Federal Army, the Yucatán National Guard, and the National Navy (the Marine branch of the Army). Planning began in 1895, with a network of military construction that gradually crossed the limit of the territory of the rebel Maya from the west (Badillo Sánchez 2019, 172–79).

Crossing the Boundary: Military Operation of Central Lines

The military campaign officially began in October 1899 and terminated around 1904. There were four operation fronts in the peninsula. Three were by land—the North Line, the Central Line, and the Southern Line—and a fourth was a maritime operational front that was extended along the entire eastern coast, known as the Eastern Line of Yucatán and the Río Hondo (Badillo Sánchez 2019, 172–79). Each of the operational fronts covered an extensive area of the peninsula, and a total of sixty military points were built. In the North Line, three forts and at least thirteen camps were built. In the South Line, they built a fortification and eleven camps extending from the British Honduras border near the Bacalar Lagoon to the north.[3] In the East Line, they established at least seven camps between Chetumal Bay and Puerto Morelos. A Naval station and customs post were established in Chetumal Bay, an exclusive port for the use of the Mexican government in Cozumel. They also established an anchorage in the Banco Chinchorro to provide service to warships, steamers, and other vessels participating in the campaign. This included the ships of the "Río Hondo Flotilla," which were concentrated in the border area between the Mexican territory and British Honduras (Bravo and De la Vega 1903). Lastly, in the Central Line, they established eight forts, four checkpoints, a central railway station, and eight camps. In 1895, in the village

---

3. It is not specified in the document, but "fortification" possibly refers to the eighteenth-century fortress of San Felipe de Bacalar, located on the shores of the lagoon and adapted to the needs of the 1899 military campaign.

of Peto, General Lorenzo Garcia oversaw the development of the Central Line, with the recognition that this would cross directly into the heart of the "rebel territory," ultimately reaching Chan Santa Cruz in May 1901.

The earliest construction of the Central Line was at the Fort at Tzonotchel (Fort no. 1). Tzonotchel was a small town whose central plaza walls formed an irregular perimeter (Avalos 1895). Inside, there were private houses and pole-and-thatch structures that housed the troops and officers as well as corrals for livestock and pack animals. There were also houses for the general in chief and transport officers that were protected by a fence, as well as a pole-and-thatch shed that protected the well that supplied water for the troops, the village inhabitants, and the mules. Between 1900 and 1901 they next fortified Peto, which was protected by the construction of eight walls that blocked access to the main streets. The barracks were located in the central plaza, in addition to office areas and rooms to house the battalions, ammunition, and armament deposits (Badillo Sánchez 2019, 182).

I studied the architecture of the military forts through photographs by Pedro Guerra from 1901 (Guerra 1901), architectural plans, and archaeological work. Using old maps, I was able to locate Fort Cepeda Peraza, Fort Calotmul, Fort Ichmul, Fort Balche, Fort Sabán, Fort "Okop," and Fort Hobompich; some smaller buildings or posts like "El Pozo" and "La Aguada"; and camps such as Santa María, Tabí, and Nohpop (Badillo Sánchez 2019).

The settlement patterns at some of the sites revealed the type of architecture that the military implemented to maintain its positions and protect itself from Maya fighters. For example, Fort Cepeda Peraza, the best-preserved site, used a cruciform floor plan with a circular tower located in the center, three sheds with thick masonry walls lined with benches (that could have been roofed with pole-and-thatch), and a long, sinuous staircase with a pair of masonry benches on the sides (figure 6.1). Just outside the fort, on the right side, there was a masonry tank measuring approximately 2 × 4 m that contained rainwater or water from the San Mateo cenote (Badillo Sánchez 2019, 184).

The next major construction was Fort Calotmul, located in the town of Calotmul, which still contained ancient Maya structures. The fort was made of limestone blocks (likely reused from the ancient constructions), with a circular floor plan, 35 m in circumference and 10 m high.[4] Fort Ichmul was built in a small town of the same name. This fort and at least one military

---

4. The work was conducted under General Severo del Castillo and General Lorenzo García in 1895 and 1899 (Bravo and De la Vega 1903).

FIGURE 6.1 Main access to Fort Cepeda Peraza (photograph by Alejandra Badillo Sánchez).

post were built into the ancient Maya acropolis dating to the Terminal Classic (AD 900), which was also the source for the stone used to build them. The structures rose 11 m above the main square and the layout mimicked the ancient structures found on the acropolis (Flores and Normark 2004, 2005). There was also a military post, located on a hill approximately 13 m high, with a square floor plan and surrounded by a perimeter wall (figure 6.2). The height of the structures allowed the military to keep constant surveillance of the nearby areas. The plaza level included a church, barracks, and a central hospital as well as several houses for the medical corps.

The head of the military campaign, General Lorenzo García, advanced with his troops toward the southeast of Ichmul, where he built Fort Balche, located on the modern ejido of Sacalaca. An archaeological survey showed that the fort was adapted to an eighteenth-century colonial ranch and reinforced with trenches located on the perimeter, a bastion, and at least four surveillance zones (figure 6.3) (Badillo Sánchez and Flores 2018).

Around 1850, only a few inhabitants remained in the small town of Sabán due to the violence of the war. The military occupied the town on January 12,

FIGURE 6.2 Pool inside Fort Ichmul, located on the top of the acropolis (photograph by Alejandra Badillo Sánchez).

1900, when it constructed Fort Sabán. The twenty-second battalion installed an infirmary, and houses were modified to be used as lodgings for officers and their families, troops, and merchants. Sources indicate that there were telegraph and telephone offices and that the central church was used as a warehouse, post office, and lodging for the warehouse guard. The town was surrounded by a perimeter barricade of logs and branches that made outside access nearly impossible (Bravo and De la Vega 1903).

Following the creation of Fort Sabán, General Ignacio Bravo took over as the head of the military campaign and established Fort Okop, the most important fortification on the Central Line. General Aureliano Blanquet was in charge of the construction, which was built in two phases. We have documented a quadrangular fort with bastions on each corner, allowing the military to watch roads that led to the towns of Sabán and Soyolá. The walls were nearly a meter thick and are still visible. A small fort with an irregular floor plan, meter-thick walls, two bastions, and a narrow entrance was built on top of a hill (figure 6.4) over ancient Maya constructions dating from AD 600–800 (Badillo Sánchez et al. 2010). The ancient stones served as raw materials for the larger fort as well.

FIGURE 6.3 Central part of Fort Balche, originally a colonial ranch (photograph by Alejandra Badillo Sánchez).

Many military leaders lived at Fort Sabán and thus it was heavily fortified. Archaeological documentation noted thick, lime-plastered masonry walls standing 3 m tall. The walls included small openings that allowed soldiers to watch for outsiders and to shoot weapons. It is also the only fort surrounded by a protective moat, which was 2.5 m wide, 1.75 m deep, and could only be crossed by wooden drawbridges at each of the two entrances (Badillo Sánchez 2015). The exterior of the fort was equipped with a livestock pen with a stone wall and a shooting range that was lined with trunks and fallen branches to protect from outside attacks (Pezo 1900). A historic photo shows several pole and thatch structures that were occupied by the troops and their commander as well as a kitchen with several ovens.[5] In another section of the fort, there was a well and an arsenal storage area. Excavations yielded many alcoholic bottles used for red wine, beer, tequila, and rum.[6] We believe that

---

5. There were four areas, two with a semicircular masonry oven, and two that were used for either food preparation or processing meat (Badillo Sánchez 2019, 220).

6. Typology is based on the Historic Glass Bottle Identification & Information website, accessed February 13, 2023, https://sha.org/bottle/index.htm.

this was the only fort in which a ration of alcohol was provided daily, as we did not find the quantity or diversity of bottles at the other forts.

The final fort built was Hobompich, which is described as having pole-and-thatch barracks for troops and a corral for the livestock (Bravo and De la Vega 1903). Although we do not see evidence of stones today, all the other forts of the Central Line included them, and we expect this would have been the same. Furthermore, because this fort was the last of its kind on the Central Line, it was closest to the city of Chan Santa Cruz. It was in this fort where General Bravo's troops stayed for a few days before taking Chan Santa Cruz (Badillo Sánchez 2019, 182–90).

In general, these eight forts had walls approximately 1 m wide and up to 3 m high, with sheltered entrances or narrow entrances that may have been protected by wooden doors. Although only one fort had a moat, the others were surrounded by barricades of logs or branches. They also had bastions that were used for surveillance in the elevated areas. These aspects all reveal the high degree of danger that the authorities attributed to the rebel Maya.

Additionally, there were associated military posts and camps along the central line that served to monitor and assist the advance of the military. These included posts such as Uaimax, the well near the ranch of Xkanil, the aguada (water storage) near the ancient city of Yo'okop, and Chuncab (Badillo Sánchez 2019, 182–90). These posts were built on a quadrangular or rhomboidal floor plan and on elevated spaces. For example, Post "C" of the aguada was placed on top of a Prehispanic structure in the ancient city of Yo'okop. The military built a protective wall out of ancient stones and a staircase with protective walls on both sides to be able to access the top (figure 6.5). Inside, we expect that they used pole-and-thatch constructions. While troops were often posted at the forts for at least five years, these temporary posts were abandoned after they had assisted with the advancement of troops (Bravo 1900).

We also know that the National Guard was housed at the Santa María camp in the Central Line, which also included a pole-and-thatch hospital. The Tabí camp was built in the plaza of an ancient Maya precinct, where pole-and-thatch houses were built to house troops, an infirmary, a bakery with an oven, and a warehouse for food storage. We also identified the largest structure in our survey, a 1 m tall wall built of ancient stones and covered with a pole-and-thatch roof. This was built around a pole-and-thatch house on top of a stone platform. Access to the structure was restricted by staggered logs that were placed over a collapsed stairway of the ancient mound. The camp was protected by an 800 m long wall that stood 1 m wide by 1.20 m high.

FIGURE 6.4 Current state of Fort Okop. The perimeter moat and water well are still visible (photograph by Alejandra Badillo Sánchez).

FIGURE 6.5 The southeast wall of the La Aguada Post (photograph by Alejandra Badillo Sánchez).

Lastly, the town of Nohpop was located near the rebel Maya capital of Chan Santa Cruz, and they established the last camp on top of a 5 m high structure in the center of an ancient plaza. The military constructed a wattle-and-daub house with a thatch roof, one of which served as a barracks, as well as three small roads.

Finally, after a year and a half of advancing the military campaign, General Bravo led the military of the Central Line into Chan Santa Cruz. Upon entry into the village, they found four houses occupied by locals and Chinese merchants. They renamed the town "Santa Cruz de Bravo" and modified the structures to suit the needs of military authorities. Thus, the former Maya rebel capital housed a hospital, and they converted the church into artillery barracks. The masonry huts with thatch roofs were converted into officer housing for the leaders of the sixth and thirteenth battalions. Others housed the officers' families and the troops. Additionally, several pole-and-thatch structures were adapted to protect a well, a tank for the laundry, and a pen for the mules.

In the village of Vigía along the coast at Ascension Bay, another detachment was created to connect Santa Cruz with the coast. The Decauville train tracks that had been used for agro-industrial production (see Mathews, this volume) were reused by the military to distribute food, war supplies, personnel transport, and pack animals (Badillo Sánchez 2019, 190). Along this same route, they established camps and military posts, such as San Isidro, Cenote Puerto, and Xunantunic. They also built a central railway station and three secondary stations (A, B, and C) with telephone booths, lodging for the military leaders and troops, kitchens, warehouses, an infirmary (at Station A), and pens for pack animals and livestock. There were also privately owned trading houses and halls designated as "rooms for blacks" for the railroad workers (Bravo and De la Vega 1903).

The military establishments created the necessary infrastructure for military officers, their families, and the troops as well as for the mules and other pack animals. The Central Line of Operations is strategically connected with the Eastern Line at the Bay of Ascension at "General Camp Vega" as well as with the South Line (Badillo Sánchez 2019, 190). The government of Mexico dedicated significant resources to support the Central Line military campaign to overtake the Maya of Chan Santa Cruz.

Deciphering the Crossing: Architecture and Archaeology of the Military Occupation

Since the Central Line campaign was the result of the governmental actions against the Maya rebellion, understanding the type and location of the checkpoints and forts in Yucatán provides insight into the strategy of the campaign (Badillo Sánchez 2019, 157–266). Archaeological fieldwork was conducted to establish the settlement patterns common to the Central Line operations at the forts of Balche (Badillo Sánchez and Flores 2018; Kaeding 2005) and Okop (Badillo Sánchez 2012, 2015; Badillo Sánchez et al. 2010; Martos Lopez 1998) as well as military posts such as "El Pozo" and "La Aguada" (Badillo Sánchez and Flores 2014), among others (Badillo Sánchez, Flores, and Borges 2018). I was able to document architectural floor plans, military architectural features such as balustrades and thick walls, and a pattern of reusing ancient stonework and taking advantage of elevated surveillance points.

I also visited archives in Yucatán such as the General Archive of the State of Yucatán, the General Archive of the Nation in Mexico City, the Historical Archives of the Secretariat of the National Defense, the Historical Archives of the National Navy of Mexico, the Manuel Orozco and Berra Map Library, and the Archives and Record Service in Belmopan, Belize, to obtain relevant documents, maps, and photographs. These resources revealed the complexity and variety of military architecture.

I found that historical documents between 1900 and 1903 provide little information on the architecture of military sites; however, with the help of archeological surveys, old photographs, and maps, I found that the construction materials varied according to the area. Along the southern section of the Central Line and along the coast, the military used wooden planks. This was in contrast to the stone constructions used across the entire Central Line, where they also used guano palms or sheets of zinc for roofs of pole-and-thatch constructions.

In general, the military facilities accommodated relatives who accompanied military men fighting in the campaign. Documents reveal that the accommodations included sleeping quarters, bathrooms, kitchens, bakeries, food storage facilities, corrals, office areas, hospitals, schools, trading posts, telegraph booths, and telephones (Bravo and De la Vega 1903).

Using archival sketches and photographs from the time of military occupation, I was able to fill in some gaps in the material remains and written documents (Roca et al. 2014, 97). Two sketches in particular revealed how the military fortified the towns and villages to defend itself against Maya attacks. In Peto, thick walls were used to protect the streets and main access points. In other cases, long perimeter walls were built to defend entire villages, such as the one built at Tzonotchel. I also analyzed photographs from the 1901 album that registered the visit of Governor General Francisco Canton Rosado of Yucatán State and was able to learn about the construction of the Nohpop camp, the interior of the camps, and the officer barracks at Tabí and Santa María. I also learned that in several towns, existing constructions were adapted as barracks, warehouses, cellars, hospitals, cavalries, and shelters, including at Ichmul, Sabán, and Santa Cruz de Bravo.

By combining these materials with archaeological research, I identified three ways in which the military transformed the peninsula's geography and resources to its advantage in the Central Line military campaign (Badillo Sánchez 2019, 180–99). First, the military used readily available materials, such as limestone blocks from ancient Maya cities whose structures were either destroyed or partially dismantled. Temples, acropoli, and plazas were transformed into forts, military posts, and camps, such as the forts at Balche, Okop, Ichmul, and Cepeda Peraza, the post at La Aguada, and the camp of Tabí and Nohpop. Second, it made simple adaptations or modified the function of the existing contemporary buildings according to the needs of the military company. Thus, at Peto, Tzonotchel, Ichmul, and Sabán, some of the rooms of the houses became hospitals or offices, while other buildings with administrative functions were adapted as barracks. Additionally, at Fort Balche, the big house at the hacienda was converted into lodging for the military chief. Lastly, the church of Chan Santa Cruz was converted to a warehouse and artillery barracks when the Federal Army occupied the town. A third pattern was the construction of trenches, moats, and protective walls. At the village of Peto, the military built barricades with barbed wire, while in some camps in Ascension Bay, it created navigation channels at the ports of embarkation and disembarkation at Cozumel and even dredged an ancient channel for the navigation of Mexican warships in Xcalak in Chetumal Bay. These transformations demonstrate the magnitude of influence that the Central Line military campaign had on Yucatecan infrastructure in order to carry out the objectives of the government of Porfirio Díaz. The forts of the Central Line, together with the construction of the other three lines of operation (North, South, and East), formed a panopticon system (Badillo Sánchez 2019, 199–206) of military architecture. With extreme vigilance, the military was able to advance troops and the Mexican government was able to regain control of the territory and the people. The establishment of military architecture in the area disrupted the daily lives of the Maya fighters and civilians. Thus, the architecture is a material representation of the violence that transformed the geography and modified the sociopolitical organization of the peninsular territory by 1902.

Boundary Changes: Transforming a Maya Territory to the Federal Territory of Quintana Roo

As a result of the 1899 campaign, the military established forts, camps, barracks, and military posts into a string of settlements that were no more than 10 km apart. This allowed it to communicate efficiently by traveling over paths as well as with telegraphs and telephones. This transformed the Maya territory into a military environment and ascribed the territory with new meaning: sacred churches became barracks, houses became hospitals, and ancient Maya ceremonial precincts became checkpoints or were destroyed to be used as raw construction material. In addition, new paths were opened in the jungle, forming connections that had never existed before because of the high degree of danger that authorities perceived of the rebel Maya.

The intention of the government was to establish its power over the territory and its inhabitants by applying a policy of "Indian reduction" (Orla 1898). It hoped that through this network of military architecture, it would restrict the rebel Maya, leading to their withdrawal or surrender. The military architecture allowed the government to promote a powerful presence of the armed forces in a region that had been previously inaccessible. This symbolized that the government was bringing forth "progress" through the Díaz administration. In May 1901, federal troops entered the town of Chan Santa Cruz, resulting in the rebel Maya retreating to the east, leaving the town abandoned. Similarly, those Maya not directly participating in the war migrated to other parts to avoid the violence of the war.

This military campaign spurred a political division in the State of Yucatán: what authorities had previously identified as an "uninhabited territory" in the eastern part of the state was later defined as "rebel territory." This was in contrast to the Maya of southern Campeche, which the government recognized as "peaceful." While Campeche was left intact, on November 24, 1902, Porfirio Díaz ordered the creation of the federal territory of Quintana Roo in a "temporary manner so as not to generate discord between the Government of Yucatán and that of the Center" (Orla 1898, 6, translation mine). This panopticon system focused on isolating and containing the Maya population, reducing the rebels, forcing them to work on haciendas and ranches or ultimately displacing Maya inhabitants into reservations (Badillo Sánchez 2019, 199–206). The government set aside "free Indian property," which were lands for subsistence farming. This would also remove Maya populations far from the border with Guatemala and Belize, restricting the economic powers of the English colony (Sierra Méndez al General Porfirio Díaz 1901, 103).

The Maya of the federal territory of Quintana Roo lived under the presence of military personnel until the summer of 1904. Many Maya people had fled from their homes to take refuge in their cornfields, in the forest, or in other areas far from the danger that the military occupation represented. They had lost their lands, their homes, their "places of memory,"[7] and their area of undeniable wealth, and the local government relocated them to restricted areas to keep them under control. The State of Yucatán became fragmented, and much of the usable land that would have been used

---

7. Natural or artificial spaces are characterized by having a material appearance while also containing symbols and functions with meanings for a large group of people (Nora 2008, 35).

for the extraction of commodities and raising cattle was taken away (Sierra Méndez al General Porfirio Díaz 1896, 6). This geopolitical transformation created the sense that the Maya were living under siege with the constant fear of being captured. The strategy of government control was reflected in the omnipresent military architecture that helped contain and reduce the rebel Maya (Badillo Sánchez 2019, 269–307).

Finally, Maya resistance against the emergence of the nation-state to "defend their autonomy and the right to dispose of their forests" (Macías Richard 1997, 7) diminished as the military blocked trade routes used to access arms and supplies. The network of military fortifications from the military campaign prevented the Maya from organizing, reducing their threat in the area. The material remnants of the military presence that lie in the jungle today are an indication of government power against the Maya in the late nineteenth and early twentieth centuries.

Acronyms of Consulted Archival Collections

AHGE-SRE   Archivo Histórico Diplomático Genaro Estrada de la Secretaría de Relaciones Exteriores
AH-SEDENA   Archivo Histórico de la Secretaría de la Defensa Nacional
BA&RS   Belize Archives & Record Service
B-UANL   Biblioteca de la Universidad Autónoma de Nuevo Leon
BY-SEDECULTA   Biblioteca Yucatanense de la Secretaría de la Cultura y las Artes de Yucatán, Mérida, Yucatán
CPD-UIA   Colección Porfirio Díaz, de la Biblioteca Francisco Xavier Clavijero de la Universidad Iberoamericana
MMOyB-SAGARPA   Mapoteca Manuel Orozco y Berra de la Secretaría de Agricultura, Ganadería Desarrollo Rural, Pesca y Alimentación

Archival Sources

Avalos, A. 1895. Teniente Coronel de Ingeniería, *Plano de la fortificación de Sonotchel, Peto*. Octubre de 1895. CPD-UIA, L40/C6/D00031.

Bravo, Ignacio A. 1900. General en Jefe al General de División de Guerra. Baluarte no. 7, Enero 12. Operaciones Militares, Campaña de Yucatán, 1900. AH-SEDENA, XI/481.4/14739.

Bravo, Ignacio (general de División), and José María De la Vega (general de brigada). 1903. *Relación que manifiesta las construcciones hechas por cuenta del gobierno federal en yodos los puntos es esta zona ocupados por fuerzas del mismo así como las que se hallan en obra y herramientas que existen.* Campamento General Vega, Quintana Roo, 12 de diciembre, 1903. AH-SEDENA, Expediente XI/481.4/14738.

Fremont, H. 1861. *Plano de la Península de Yucatán.* MMOyB-SAGARPA, 22-OYB-7264-A.

Guerra, Pedro. 1901. *Album del recuerdo de la visita del General Francisco Cantón Rosado a Chan Santa Cruz.* BY-SEDECULTA, Sección Fototeca.

Ministerio de Justicia é Instrucción Pública, Sección Primera, Benito Juarez President Constitucional de los Estados Unidos Mexicanos, a sus Habitantes. Congreso de la Unión. 1883. Libro III, Título Decimocuarto. *"Delitos Contra la Seguridad Interior,"* Capítulo I, *Rebelión, en código penal para el Distrito Federal y territorio de la Baja California sobre delitos del fuero común, y para toda la República sobre delitos contra la Federación.* Librería de Donato Miramonte, Chihuahua. B-UANL.

Orla, Francisco. 1898. Encargado de negocios de Guatemala pregunta a Ministro de Relaciones Exteriores Ignacio Mariscal. 8 de diciembre. AHGE-SRE, 11-9-37.

Pezo, A. 1900. Oficial mayor encargado de la Secretaría al General Jefe de la 12a Zona Militar. México, enero 15. Operaciones Militares, Campaña de Yucatán, 1900. AH-SEDENA, XI/481.4/14739.

Sierra Méndez, Manuel, al Sr. General Don Porfirio Díaz. 1896. *Memorandum relativo á la creación de un territorio federal en Yucatán, México, Junio.* Operaciones Militares, Quintana Roo, 1901–1909. AH-SEDENA.

Sierra Méndez, Manuel, al Sr. General Don Porfirio Díaz. 1901. *Informe que el que suscribe rinde al Sr. Secretario de Guerra y Marina sobre puntos referentes á la elección del territorio federal en Yucatán.* México, 14 de Diciembre. Operaciones Militares, Quintana Roo, 1901–1909. AH-SEDENA.

Suárez y Navarro, Juan. 1861. *Plano de Yucatán.* Material gráfico en Francisco Sosa Serapio, *Ensayo histórico sobre las Revoluciones de Yucatán desde 1840 hasta 1864,* en 5 tomos v., ed. Rodríguez Losa Salvador (Mérida: Universidad Autónoma de Yucatán, 1990).

Sweet Escott, E. B. 1893. Administrador del Gobierno de la Colonia de Belice al Marqués de Ripon K. G. 20 de septiembre. BA&RS, R123-II.

Wilson, D. 1897. "Confidencial, 20 de agosto de 1897, a J. Chamberlain, the House." BA&RS, R123-II.

Works Cited

Badillo Sánchez, Alejandra. 2012. "Historias que convergen a través de los objetos: Fortín de Yo'okop, Operaciones 1 y 2." In *Reporte final de la Temporada de campo 2012 del Proyecto de Reconocimiento Arqueológico de la Región de Cochuah,* edited by Justine M. Shaw, 24–59. Eureka, Calif.: College of the Redwoods.

Badillo Sánchez, Alejandra. 2015. "Two Places in Time: A Constructed Landscape in the Northwestern Region of Yo'okop." In *The Maya of the Cochuah Region: Archaeological and Ethnographic Perspectives on the Northern Lowlands,* edited by Justine M. Shaw, 213–33. Albuquerque: University of New Mexico Press.

Badillo Sánchez, Alejandra. 2019. "Rumbo al aorazón de la tierra Macehual: La campaña militar de Yucatán contra los Mayas 1899–1904." PhD diss., Centro de Investigaciones y Estudios Superiores en Antropología Social.

Badillo Sánchez, Alejandra, and Alberto G. Flores. 2014. "Mapping of the Post of La Aguada (Miliary Post C)." In *Final Report of the 2014 Field Season, Cochuah Regional Archaeological Survey*, edited by Justine M. Shaw, 228–36. Eureka, Calif.: College of the Redwoods.

Badillo Sánchez, Alejandra, and Alberto G. Flores. 2018. "Revisitando Xbalche, en busca del 'Fuerte No. 5 de Balche.'" In *Reporte final de la Temporada de campo 2018 del Proyecto de Reconocimiento Arqueológico de la Región de Cochuah*, edited by Justine M. Shaw, 111–21. Eureka, Calif.: College of the Redwoods.

Badillo Sánchez, Alejandra, Bryce Davenport, Justine M. Shaw, and Alberto Flores. 2010. "Un espacio dos lugares: De Mayas y militares; el paisaje construido en el Noreste de la región de Yo'okop." In *Reporte final de la Temporada de campo 2010 del Proyecto de Reconocimiento Arqueológico de la Región de Cochuah*, edited by Justine M. Shaw, 13–47. Eureka, Calif.: College of the Redwoods.

Badillo Sánchez, Alejandra, Alberto Flores, and Jorge Borges. 2018. "Sobre el camino: ¿Puesto militar? En el antiguo camino, Rumbo a Saban." In *Reporte final de la Temporada de campo 2018 del Proyecto de Reconocimiento Arqueológico de la Región de Cochuah*, edited by Justine M. Shaw, 102–6. Eureka, Calif.: College of the Redwoods.

Bracamonte y Sosa, Pedro. 2000. "La jurisdicción cuestionada y el despojo agrario en el Yucatán del siglo XIX." *Revista Mexicana del Caribe* 5 (10) 150–79.

Careaga Viliesid, Lorena. 1998. *Hierofanía combatiente: Lucha, simbolismo y religiosidad en la Guerra de Castas*. Mexico City: Universidad de Quintana Roo.

Careaga Viliesid, Lorena. 2016. *Invasores, exploradores y viajeros: La vida cotidiana en Yucatán desde la óptica del Otro, 1834–1906*. 2 vols. Mérida: Secretaría de la Cultura y las Artes de Yucatán.

Dumond, Don E. 2005. *El machete y la cruz: La sublevación de campesinos en Yucatán*. Mexico City: Centro de Estudios mayas, IIF-UNAM.

Flores, Alberto G., and Johan Normark. 2004. "Ichmul y sus Alrededores." In *Reporte final del Proyecto Arqueológico de la Región de Cochuah, Temporada de campo 2004*, edited by Justine M. Shaw, 60–77. Eureka, Calif.: College of the Redwoods.

Flores, Alberto G., and Johan Normark. 2005. "Between Mounds and Sacbeob: Investigations in Ejido of Ichmul." In *Final Report of the 2005 Field Season, Cochuah Regional Archaeological Survey*, edited by Justine M. Shaw, 7–24. Eureka, Calif.: College of the Redwoods.

Gómez de Silva Cano, Jorge J. 2016. *El derecho agrario mexicano y la Constitución de 1917*. Mexico City: Secretaría de Gobernación, Secretaría de Cultura, Instituto Nacional de Estudios Históricos de las Revoluciones de México, UNAM, Instituto de Investigaciones Jurídicas.

Kaeding, Adam. 2005. "Xbalche." In *Reporte Final de la Temporada de Campo 2005 del Proyecto de Reconocimiento Arqueológico de la Región de Cochuah*, edited by Justine M. Shaw, 138–52, Eureka, Calif.: College of the Redwoods.

Macías Richard, Carlos. 1997. *Nueva frontera mexicana: Milicia, burocracia y ocupación territorial en Quintana Roo, 1884–1902*. Colección Sociedad y Cultura en la Vida de Quintana Roo 3. Mexico City: Universidad de Quintana Roo/CONACYT.

Martos Lopez, Luis Alberto. 1998. *Reporte de los Trabajos de Reconocimiento y Levantamiento Planimétrico, Llevados a Cabo en Fortín de Yokob, Quintana Roo*. INAH, February.

Nora, Pierre. 2008. *Les lieux de mémoire*. Paris: Ediciones Trilce.

Paoli Bolio, Francisco José. 2015. *Historia gráfica de la Guerra de Castas Yucatán*. Mérida: Editorial Dante.

Reed, Nelson. 2007. *La Guerra de Castas*. Mexico City: Ediciones Era.

Roca, Lourdes, Felipe Morales Leal, Carlos Hernández Marines, and Andrew Green. 2014. *Tejedores de imágenes: Propuestas metodológicas de investigación y gestión del patrimonio fotográfico y audiovisual*. Mexico City: Laboratorio Audiovisual de Investigación Social, Instituto Mora.

Rugeley, Terry. 1996. *Yucatán's Maya Peasantry and the Origins of the Caste War*. Austin: University of Texas Press.

Rugeley, Terry. 2009. *Rebellion Now and Forever: Mayas, Hispanics, and Caste War Violence in Yucatán, 1800–1880*. Stanford: Stanford University Press.

Villalobos González, Martha H. 1993. "Las concesiones forestales en Quintana Roo a fines del Porfiriato." *Relaciones Estudios de Historia y Sociedad* 14 (53): 87–112.

Wihelm, Burkhard, ed. 1997. *¿Indios rebeldes? El fin de la Guerra de Castas en Yucatán vista por El Estandarte de San Luis Potosí*. San Luis Potosí: Lascasiana.

CHAPTER 7

All in All, It's (Not) Just Another Brick in the Wall

Examining the Diverse Functions of Wall Architecture in Western Belize

JAIME J. AWE AND SHAWN G. MORTON

> Walls are interesting because they are physical and symbolic sites of inclusion and exclusion that mark the inside from the outside.
> *William A. Callahan, "The Politics of Walls"*

Walls and wall-like features represent ubiquitous forms of architecture across the lowland Maya landscape. Traditionally in the central Maya lowlands, the largest of these architectural features, particularly where they stand alone, have been interpreted as fortifications, defensive barricades, and evidence for increasing militarism in the Classic and Postclassic periods. In this chapter, we pull together relevant literature and primary archaeological research concerning masonry walls in western Belize to highlight their diversity of purposes. While recognizing evidence that favors interpretations for defensive or militaristic use of walls elsewhere, here we discuss the evidential bases for ritual, political, and socioeconomic purposes, and we argue that walls can serve to both bind and divide social groups.

Maya Warfare and Defensive Features: A Brief Overview

In the 1940s and 1950s, preeminent archaeologists Sylvanus G. Morley (1946, 70) and J. Eric S. Thompson (1959) painted a picture of the ancient Maya as a peaceful people whose ruler priests were primarily concerned with the arts, astronomy, and the pursuit of esoteric knowledge. To scholars of the time, still reeling from the horrors of World War II, the peace-loving Maya were the antithesis of the violent and warlike Aztecs. So pervasive was this view that, as David Webster (2002, 338) subsequently noted, despite mounting evidence to the contrary, the "peaceful Maya" perspective continued to dominate scholarship well into the 1960s. What was particularly incomprehensible is that this position persisted despite the fact that Giles Healey had published his photographs of the polychrome murals at Bonampak in 1946 that presented the violent side of Maya history. As Mary Miller (1986) and other iconographers also remarked, the murals in Room 2 of Structure 1 at Bonampak provided one of the most vivid portrayals of ancient Maya warfare and human sacrifice, with captives cast upon the steps of a temple, grimacing in pain, blood dripping from severed fingers or extracted nails. These scenes certainly should have served to disabuse early scholars of their dogma of the Maya as a peace-loving culture.

Even before the publication of Healey's photographs of the Bonampak murals, Spanish conquistadors and clerics had also recorded considerable evidence of Maya militarism and defensive features. Much of this information was noted in the first dispatches of Hernán Cortés to Emperor Charles V (Blacker and Rosen 1962), in Bernal Díaz del Castillo's (1962) volume on the conquest of New Spain, in Juan de Villagutierre Soto-Mayor's (1983, 294) report on the conquest of the Itza, and in Diego de Landa's *Relación de las cosas de Yucatán*. In Alfred M. Tozzer's (1941, 123) translation of the latter, for example, Landa reported: "In the roads and defiles [passageways], the enemy placed defenses filled with archers, and made of sticks and wood and usually of stone. After the victory they took the jaws off the dead bodies and with the flesh cleaned off, they put them on their arms. In their wars they made great offerings of the spoils, and if they made a prisoner of some distinguished man, they sacrificed him immediately, not wishing to leave anyone alive who might injure them afterwards." The "defenses" of "sticks and wood" described by Landa almost certainly refer to the use of palisades by the Yucatec Maya, and his stone walls were likely part of defensive earthworks.

Subsequent discoveries in the 1960s and 1970s, such as the wall on the northern periphery of Tikal (Puleston and Callender 1967), the moat at Becán (Webster 1976a, 1976b), and the recognition that much of Chichén Itzá's art had a militaristic theme, provided what seemed to be additional evidence for widespread Maya militarism. This was followed by a series of articles published by David Webster (1976a, 1976b, 1977, 2000, 2002), in which he provided more compelling evidence for the construction of defensive earthworks across the Maya area, to solidly establish the fact that like in other subregions of Mesoamerica, internecine warfare was as important a part of Prehispanic Maya culture as was maize agriculture.

Understandably, the years following Webster's insightful publications saw the pendulum on Maya militarism swing 180 degrees. Contrary to the Morley and Thompson view of the 1940s and 1950s, several researchers began to promote warfare as the primary (or at least important) catalyst for the rise, successes, and subsequent failure of many polities across the Maya lowlands (see, e.g., Aoyama and Graham 2015; Brown and Stanton 2003; Chase and Chase 1989; Dahlin 2000; Demarest et al. 1997; Golden et al. 2008; Inomata 1997; McKillop 2004; Palka 2001; Rice and Rice 1981). Some Mayanists went so far as to suggest that "even small communities, agricultural fields, and water sources were fortified" with defensive walls during the Late to Terminal Classic period (Demarest 1997; Demarest et al. 1997; McKillop 2004, 194). In the case of the Late Classic site of Dos Pilas in Guatemala, Arthur A. Demarest and his colleagues (1997) further argued that defensive walls were hastily constructed over existing buildings with stones scavenged from even the most impressive of elite architecture. A similar argument was subsequently made by Bruce Dahlin (2000) for some sites in the Yucatán Peninsula. At Chunchucmil and Cuca, for example, Dahlin suggests that, in a desperate effort to protect the cities from invaders, work gangs rapidly constructed defensive walls out of cut stones that were scavenged from existing causeways, buildings, and dry-laid stone walls known as *albarradas*.

Interestingly, Webster (1978, 1993) had previously noted the presence of defensive walls at several sites in the Yucatán Peninsula; however, unlike Dahlin, he argued that the walls were not constructed as a response to immediate danger and that the walls were actually remodeled over time. Despite these differing opinions, these publications all served to highlight the fact that almost all Terminal Classic to Postclassic sites in Yucatán contained walled features. Acknowledging that defense is the most likely explanation for many of these features, careful scrutiny reveals that there is considerably greater diversity in the function of walls at many Maya lowland sites than can be accounted for by any single motivation.

Nondefensive Walled Features in the Yucatán Peninsula

During their survey of Uxmal, Alfredo Barrera Rubio (1978) and colleagues from the Instituto Nacional de Antropología e Historia (INAH) relocated a wall that John Lloyd Stephens and Frederick Catherwood had reported in the 1840s (Stephens 1841, 422). Barrera Rubio (1978, 229) notes that "the wall has an irregular elliptical plan," it partly encircles the site epicenter, and it was likely constructed during the Terminal Classic period (AD 800–1000). While the Uxmal wall was initially considered defensive in nature (Andrews 1997), more recent assessments suggest that "the wall system . . . appears to have been created more to control pedestrian traffic than to defend the site" from imminent danger (Hutson 2010, 52). In published surveys of the great Central Mexican metropolis of Teotihuacan, we can clearly see similar walls to the north of the Avenida that, while serving only poorly as defensive structures, would have served admirably to control the flow of traffic (Millon 1973). As we note later in this chapter, the use of walls to control the flow of pedestrian traffic, or to limit access to more exclusive spaces, is relatively common in cave sites (Moyes 2012, 2020, this volume).

Most surface sites in the Yucatán Peninsula also have extensive networks of albarradas. Rather than functioning as defensive barriers, albarradas served as boundary walls, and their primary function seems to have been to demarcate and enclose discrete socioeconomic units, household space, or "houselots" (Batún-Alpuche, this volume; Hutson 2010; Magnoni 1995; Magnoni, Hutson, and Dahlin 2012). At some centers, such as Chunchucmil, albarradas range between 0.4 and 1.25 m high, they "enclose and demarcate most houselots," and on average they enclose spaces of about 4,400 m^2 (Hutson 2010, 52). Scott Hutson (52) further notes that Cobá and Mayapán contain some of the best examples of albarradas in Yucatán and that they are "common in the Postclassic period (1000–1521 CE) but rare in earlier times." Households have often been interpreted as microcosms of larger systems of organization, such as the polity. Indeed, this idea stands as one of the most ancient—in Western thought being espoused by Aristotle, and in Eastern thought by Confucius. Yet, in the loosely structured settlements that characterize much of the Classic lowland Maya world, the specific constituents of any one household can be frustratingly difficult to define. The presence of albarradas thus allows us to define bound groups of social and economic actors, significant for understanding both the micro- and macrolevels of the society in question.

Walls can bind in other ways as well. As parts of walkways or *andadores* (Benavides Castillo 1981; Goñi Motilla 1993; Magnoni, Hutson, and Dahlin 2012; Vargas, Santillan, and Vilalta 1985), low stone walls in the Yucatán were also used to tie together larger social groups. An example of these andadores was recorded by Jeffrey B. Glover, Dominique Rissolo, and Jennifer P. Mathews (2011, 200) at Vista Alegre in northern Quintana Roo. This andador is 1.4 km in length and links the site core of Vista Alegre with a large temple 1.4 km to the south. At Chunchucmil, Alice Magnoni, Scott Hutson, and Bruce Dahlin (2012, 316) apply the name of *chichbes* to walls, which themselves are described as "narrow, raised causeways (less than 1m high and 0.5–3m wide)." They also note that unlike *sakbe'ob* (raised roads), these chichbes tend "to wind around residential groups similar to albarradas." Furthermore, chichbes are often used in conjunction with, or as part of, albarradas to demarcate boundaries and enclose houselots (316).

Mayapán, which served as one of the last major capitals of the Yucatán Peninsula, is unquestionably one of the best sites at which to examine the diverse functions of walls in the Maya world. In addition to having a defensive barrier or wall encircling the city (Shook 1952; Webster 1976b, 366), the site contains extensive networks of albarradas, chichbes, andadores, and causeways (Bullard 1954; Hare, Masson, and Russell 2014; Smith 1962). This same pattern is evident at Tulum, which, like Mayapán, is primarily identified as a fortified site (Hutson 2010; Magnoni 1995). Within the walls of Mayapán, a Carnegie Institution of Washington survey in 1951–55 also documented twenty-nine cenotes, three of which were partly encircled by low stone walls that served to restrict access to the wells (Smith 1962, 210). According to Edwin M. Shook (1952, 249–50), at least one of the wells, the Cenote Itzmal Ch'en, is known to have been the site of annual rain ceremonies in the past. The use of walls around these cenotes, therefore, was not intended for defense but rather to restrict access to a sacred landscape used for ritual purposes.

Stone walls that served nondefensive purposes have also been reported in northern Petén, Guatemala. At Naachtun, for example, a survey by Philippe Nondédéo and Antoine Dorison (2019, fig. 13) recorded numerous stone walls in association with agricultural terraces. The walls run perpendicular to the terraces and extend from the base to the summit of terraced slopes. According to Nondédéo and Dorison (2019, 17), the walls were likely used to manage water resources or as pathways facilitating access to and from the terraced fields. Scott L. Fedick et al. (2000, 131–52) recorded wall features in the Yalahau region in Yucatán that served similar purposes to those suggested at Naachtun. Note that Arlen F. Chase and Diane Z. Chase (1998, fig. 6) have made similar observations closer to our region of focus in this chapter, at Caracol, Belize.

Wall Features in Western Belize

Our ongoing investigations in western Belize have recorded a variety of walls and wall-like features at the sites of Cahal Pech, Lower Dover, Lower Barton Creek, Xunantunich, and Tipan Chen Uitz (figure 7.1). Like many of the wall features in the Yucatán Peninsula, which are architecturally diverse and served a variety of functions, we argue here that the context and morphology of these features in western Belize strongly suggest that many had little to do with defense or militarism.

Cahal Pech

At Cahal Pech, which is located in the upper Belize River valley, we recorded three low walls in the site's epicenter (figure 7.2). Two of these walls are located in Plaza G, and the third wall is in Plaza C. The first Plaza G wall was constructed between the northeast corner of Structure G1 and the southwest corner of Structure G2. This wall is 1.40 m long, 0.65 m wide, and 0.5 m high. The wall also has a small cavity at its base, designed to work as a drain for water to flow out of Plaza G. The second wall is located at the northwest corner of Plaza G, between Structures F2 and B5. It measures 1.62 m long, ranges between 60 and 65 cm wide, and was originally about 50 cm high. Unlike the southeastern wall, this southwestern wall was constructed of both cut limestone blocks facing west and crude boulders facing east into Plaza G. For both walls, the cut stone appears to have been scavenged from the western and southern façade of Structures G2 and B5. We came to this conclusion when horizontal exposure of the two structures noted that they were missing many of the facing stones from the frontal walls of the building platforms. Our discovery of evidence for peri-abandonment habitation at the summit of Structure G2 and a peri-abandonment deposit on the flanks of Structure G2 (Awe, Ebert, et al. 2020) also suggest that the walls were likely constructed during the last occupation of the plaza during the Terminal Classic period. The height and small size of the walls further suggest that they likely functioned as albarradas, that is, to enclose living space in Plaza G during the final years of occupation in the site core.

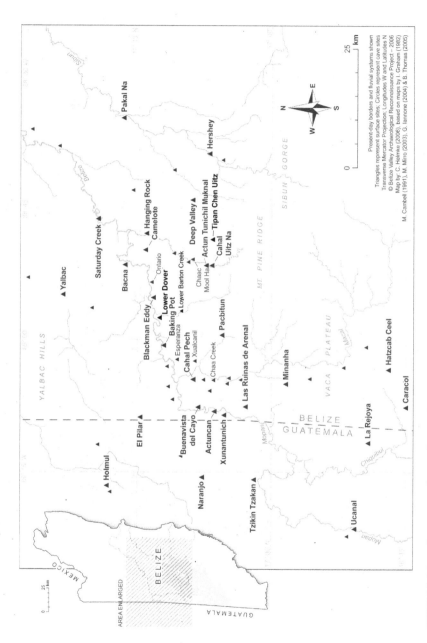

FIGURE 7.1 Map of western Belize with sites discussed in the text (map by Christophe Helmke).

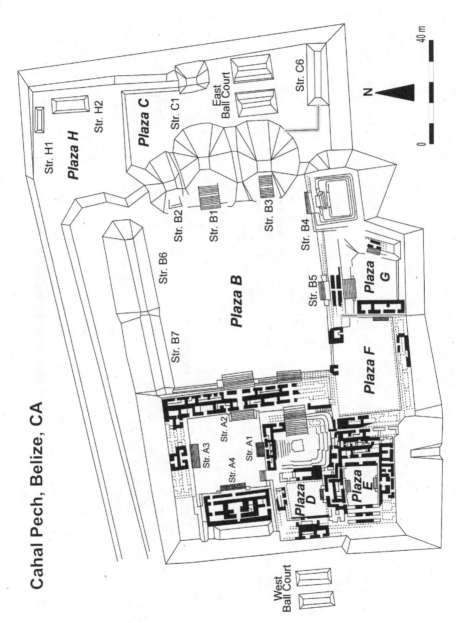

FIGURE 7.2 Map of Cahal Pech epicenter showing the location of walls (plan by Mark Campbell and Claire Ebert).

All in All, It's (Not) Just Another Brick in the Wall 195

FIGURE 7.3 Stone wall in Plaza C at Cahal Pech (photograph by Jaime Awe).

The wall in Plaza C is considerably longer than those in Plaza G (see figures 7.2 and 7.3). It extends 5.2 m west from Structure C6, then turns at a right angle and extends northward for 28 m before it ends at the southeastern base of Structure B1, the central pyramid of the site's Eastern Triadic Shrine (aka E-Group). The width of the Plaza C wall ranges between 80 and 90 cm, and it is approximately 30–34 cm in height. The inner and outer faces of the wall were constructed of cut limestone blocks, four to five courses high, that were mortared together and appear to have been scavenged from the northern façade of Structure C6. Like the case in Plaza G, we came to this conclusion when our horizontal exposure of the northern façade of Structure C6 revealed that most of its facing stones were missing and had been removed at the end of the Classic period.

Our investigations in Plaza C and Plaza H further indicate that the Plaza C wall was constructed during the Terminal Classic, either during the last phase of occupation or when the site was reoccupied following a short period of abandonment (Awe et al. 2017; Awe, Ebert, et al. 2020). During this final and brief period of occupation, small platforms with pole-and-thatch buildings were constructed directly over earlier Late Classic buildings in Plaza H. Other activities associated with this final phase of occupation include the construction of the low walls described in this chapter; the placement of intrusive burials on several structures across the site core; peri-abandonment ritual deposits in Plazas A, B, and G; the removal and repositioning of stone monuments from Plaza B to Plaza C; and the construction of a crude altar in the center of Plaza C (Awe, Ebert, et al. 2020). When we consider the location of the lone wall vis-à-vis the contemporaneous pole-and-thatch buildings in Plaza C, it is readily apparent that the wall could not have been constructed for defensive purposes. If it was, it would have failed as a barrier to Plazas C and H, which could have been easily accessed from the north, west, and east sides of the site core. Given these characteristics, we can conclude that the wall in Plaza C served to enclose space that was used during the final occupation of the Cahal Pech site core.

Lower Dover

The site of Lower Dover is located on the southern banks of the Belize River, approximately 15 km east-northeast of Cahal Pech (see figure 7.1). During our initial survey of the Lower Dover site core (Guerra and Morton 2012), we recorded two lines of stones, approximately 1.20 m apart, that appeared to be a low wall or part of a causeway that extended for approximately 63 m from the southwestern corner of Structure A5 to the southeastern corner of Structure B14 (figure 7.4). The length of the feature was later confirmed by further clearing of the thick secondary foliage in 2011. That same summer, we excavated a 3 m section of the feature to determine its function and mode of construction. These investigations confirmed that the feature was a wall that measured 63 m long by 1.2 m wide, and with an average height of 48 cm above the last plaza floor (Guerra and Arksey 2012, 119). The wall is also faced with cut limestone blocks, four to six courses high. To the north of the wall, there are two long and low (approximately 20 cm high) platforms (Structures B15 and B16) that likely supported perishable buildings. Along with the wall to the south, Structure A5, and the ballcourt to the east, the northern buildings enclosed a level area between Plazas A and B. With the construction of the wall and two buildings, access into the enclosure was thereafter limited to a very narrow opening between Structures B15 and B16, and a passageway between Structures A5 and B16. Our excavations of the

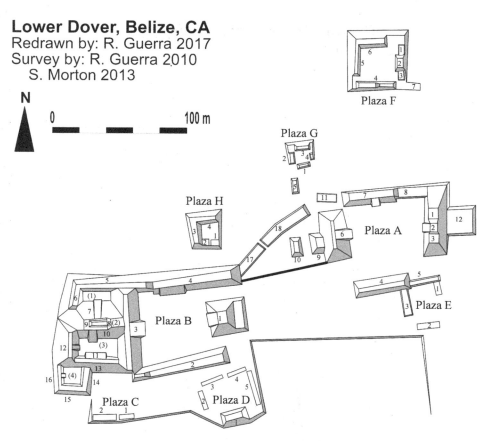

FIGURE 7.4 Site core plan of Lower Dover (plan by Rafael Guerra and Shawn G. Morton).

two platforms and wall further determined that all three architectural features were contemporaneous, dating to the Terminal Classic period. Given this configuration, we concluded that the wall served as the southern border of an enclosure that included at least two residential buildings, and that it likely functioned as an albarrada rather than a defensive feature.

Lower Barton Creek

Lower Barton Creek is a minor center that is located approximately 6 km upstream from Lower Dover (see figure 7.1). The site core features three courtyards constructed on a small hill and in a north–south alignment (fig-

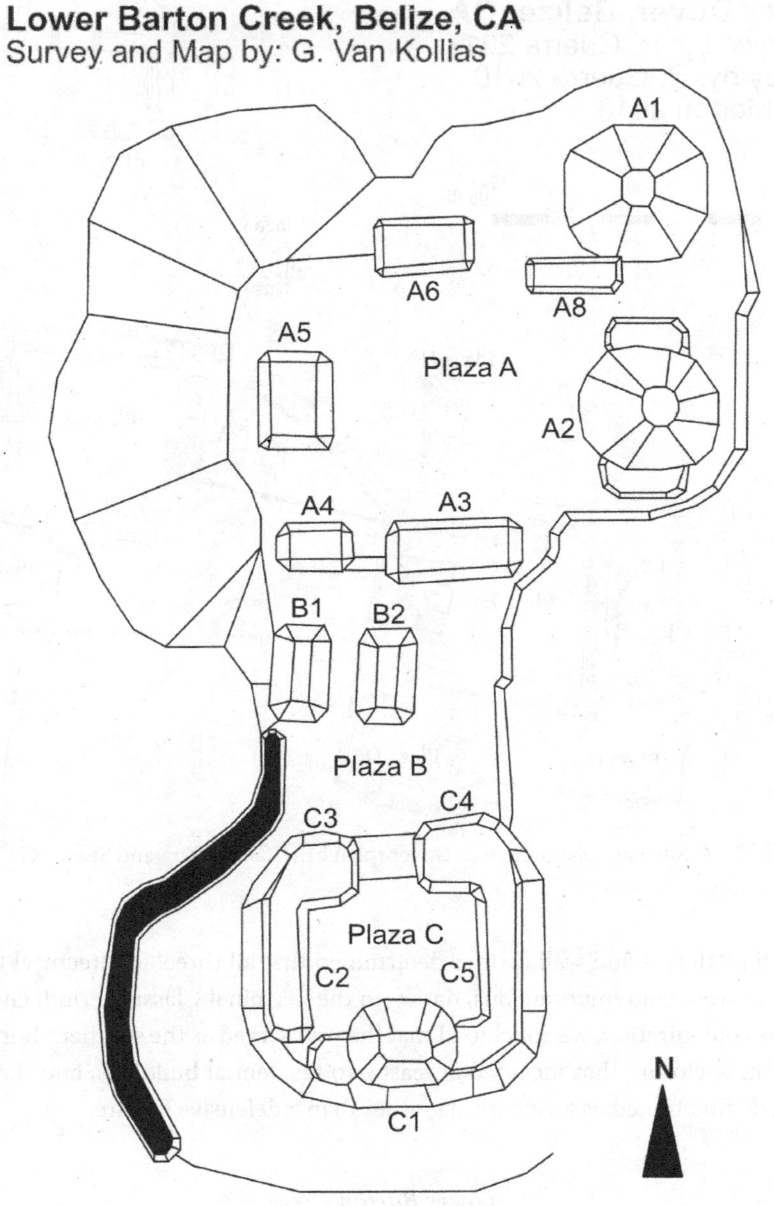

FIGURE 7.5 Site core plan of Lower Barton Creek (drawn after Kolias 2016).

ure 7.5). At the north end, Plaza A contains an eastern triadic shrine (Structure A2), a second large pyramidal mound, and five building platforms. The central courtyard, Plaza B, has two flanking mounds that served as the site's ballcourt. At the south end of the site core, Plaza C is an elevated palace complex with several residential buildings. Several meters to the west of Plaza C, there is a long, low, and curvilinear wall that commences just southwest of the palace complex, curves around the western base of the latter, and terminates at the southern base of the ballcourt. The wall is approximately 100 m long by 1.5 m wide and appears to have been "designed to direct people around the palatial complex, obviously a highly restricted area, through the ballcourt, and into Plaza A, the largest and most public Plaza" at the site (Kolias 2016, 73–75). Like at Cahal Pech, Xunantunich (see next section), and Lower Dover, we found no evidence to suggest that the wall at Lower Barton Creek served defensive purposes. In contrast, the wall appears to have been purposely constructed to direct the flow of traffic, or ingress, into the site center from the south.

Xunantunich

The epicenter of Xunantunich contains three large courtyards, Plazas A-I, A-II, and A-III, that are bordered by the largest monumental architecture at the site. Within this core area of Xunantunich there is also a low masonry wall in the northeastern corner of Plaza A-I (figure 7.6). A small section of the wall was excavated by the Xunantunich Archaeological Project in the mid-1990s (Jamison 2010) and then completely excavated and conserved in 2016 by the Xunantunich Archaeology and Conservation Project under the direction of Jaime J. Awe. These investigations revealed that the wall extends from the southeastern corner of Structure A1 to the northwestern base of the Structure A3 central stairway. Along with Structures A2 and A4, Structure A3 forms the site's Eastern Triadic Shrine.

The Xunantunich site core wall is 12.6 m long, 0.75–0.90 m wide, and 0.44 m high. Both sides of the wall are faced with cut limestone blocks that were likely scavenged from the east side of Structure A1, or from Structures A3 or A13. Our horizontal excavation of the latter buildings and the east side of Structure A1 noted that large sections of their façades had been stripped of their facing stones sometime during or after the abandonment of the site in the Terminal Classic period (Awe, Helmke, et al. 2020).

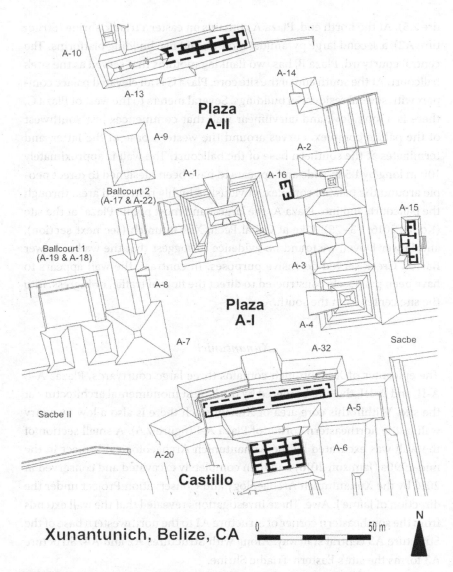

FIGURE 7.6 Site core plan of Xunantunich (drawn after Jamison 2010).

According to Thomas R. Jamison (2010, 130), during the early facet of the Late Classic Hats' Chaak phase, Plazas A-I and A-II actually made up a single large courtyard. The construction of Structure A1 in the latter part of the Hats' Chaak phase (or the latter part of the Late Classic period) subsequently cut this large courtyard in two, creating Plazas A-I and A-II. Jamison (2010,

130) contends that this action "began the process of focusing ritual activities in Plaza A-I and restricting access to that newly emphasized space." He also suggests that the low wall was constructed not too long after the construction of A1, and that "this wall may have supported a perishable structure or formed a more symbolic boundary" (130). While we concur with Jamison that the wall most certainly served to restrict access into Plaza A-I from Plaza A-II, we found no evidence indicating that it supported any perishable structure, and we disagree with his dating of this feature to the Late Classic Hats' Chaak phase. As we noted previously, the wall was almost certainly constructed of cut stones that were scavenged from earlier buildings, including Structure A1. Furthermore, the wall is clearly associated with several low platforms that were constructed at the base of Structures A2, A3, and A4. Our excavations of these platforms recovered several Terminal Classic burials and deposits (Audet 2006; Awe 2008; Awe, Helmke, et al. 2020) that suggest that, like the wall, they are associated with peri-abandonment activities and modifications that took place during the Terminal Classic Tsak' phase. This conclusion is further supported by the fact that the eastern end of the wall terminates at the central stairway of the central structure of the site's Eastern Triadic Shrine or "E-Group." It is inconceivable that the main stairway of the central structure of the site's triadic shrine would have been partially blocked when it was still in use.

To test whether there were other walls blocking the northwest, southeast, and southwest access points into Plaza A-I, we decided to excavate all three access points into this major courtyard. None of our excavations located another wall, suggesting that the lone wall at the northeastern corner of Plaza A-I most likely did not serve defensive purposes. Alternatively, our investigations indicate that, like at Cahal Pech, the Xunantunich wall solely served the purpose of closing access into Plaza A-I from the northeast, thus functioning like an albarrada or for directing the flow of traffic from Plaza A-II to A-I through Ballcourt 2 to the west.

Tipan Chen Uitz

Tipan Chen Uitz (figure 7.7) is located in an upland region of dissected karst, east of the Roaring Creek (see figure 7.1). Research carried out by the Central Belize Archaeological Survey (CBAS) project that began in 2009 indicates that the site was built largely during the Late Classic period and that it is

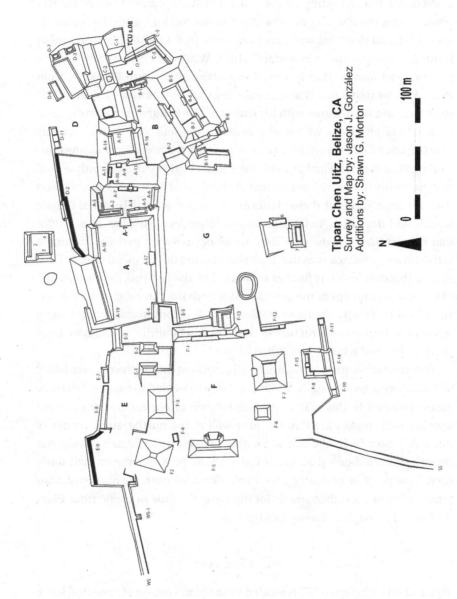

FIGURE 7.7 Site core plan of Tipan Chen Uitz (drawn after Jason J. González).

defined by a particular architectural style unique to this subregion (Morton, Wrobel, and Andres 2019). As with similar sites, such as Lower Dover, it provides another good reason to resist the temptation of facile arguments that link walls directly to warfare.

One of the first features of Tipan's monumental core that became apparent during initial scouting of the site in 2009 was its position atop a high point in the local terrain. In many instances, the natural bedrock upon which Tipan was constructed approaches the living surface of the site (and, in some cases, may have risen above finished plazas). Based on the presence of natural bedrock high up in Plaza C only a meter below the surface, it is similarly apparent that the builders of Tipan took advantage of this topography to facilitate rapid construction, and it seems likely that many of the buildings on site are heavily underpinned by natural formations. This aspect of Tipan's site plan results in having a "perched" appearance of significant foreboding when viewed from the outside—an appearance heightened, in fact, by steep platform faces and even a short section of sheer 4 m high cliff face, particularly along the northern margin of the site. The survey by Jason González revealed a series of long, low, narrow structures (in most cases, less than 1 m in height and 2–3 m thick) that surmounted many plaza edges across the site, and again, particularly along its northern margin.

In 2010, CBAS co-director Christopher R. Andres initiated excavations on one of these structures, Structure D-2, on the northern margin of Plaza D (Andres 2011, 49–56). In a relatively large horizontal excavation (2 m north–south by 6 m east–west), Andres revealed that Structure D-2 was built atop the surface of Plaza D and consisted of a coarse rubble core held in place by a mere two courses of cut limestone blocks. A superior alignment of cut stone blocks, not quite in the center of the platform and approximately 1 m shy of the northern edge of Plaza D, further embellished the structure. Some of these blocks were set vertically and stood up to 40 cm above the platform surface, making the total height of the masonry structure less than 1 m above the plaza surface. The structure was initially suggested to have served as support for a defensive palisade wall, perhaps driven through the structure and into the core of the plaza below, though Andres notes that no evidence of projectile points was found in association (cf. Demarest et al. 1997, 234, for an example from the Petexbatún), and no evidence of burning was uncovered. Further, in contrast to the Petexbatún examples, it seems clear that Structure D-2 was not an ad hoc construction of materials culled from surrounding buildings but was a formal (and likely, plastered) element of Tipan's monumental core (Andres 2011, 53–54). It is worth noting that no evidence for a palisade was recovered, with the search for telltale post molds stymied by loose rubble core and abundant disturbance from roots.

Whether a palisade wall was present or not, it is clear that Tipan's builders spent a significant amount of effort in constructing *something* along the margins of many of the site's plazas. Even without a palisade, these structures would have effectively diverted casual traffic to more formal points of entry, such as the site's several causeways or through a gap to the north of Tipan's ballcourt. But were they defensive? We would suggest that they were not. Low structures such as Structure D-2 effectively restricted access to the northern site plazas and cumulatively to the acropolis on the site's east end; however, at this point, we have little evidence for similar control on the site's southern margin, with few observed obstacles to Plaza G or Plaza F and through this, to the rest of the site. Structures such as D-2 would seem like poor performers at defense if attackers could simply walk around them. Is there a better explanation?

As with the examples presented here, perhaps structures like D-2 served a sociopolitical purpose rather than a defensive one. Andres et al. (2011) have noted that the approach from Plaza A to the apical courtyard of Tipan's acropolis would have required passing through three separate portals. Controlling the visual field during this approach appears to have been important to the elite at Tipan; as each door is offset laterally from the previous, one is never afforded a view extending beyond the next space. Awe (2008) has argued similar visual and spatial control at Cahal Pech, Xunantunich, and Caracol. Perhaps it is this principle, rather than defense, that best explains the access-limiting features of Tipan's monumental core. Conceivably, their most important purpose was to shield the view of the various plazas that they bind and, in turn, the activities of those acting within them from outside observation.

Walls in Cave Sites

In the late 1890s, while exploring Actun Spukil in Yucatán, Henry Mercer (1896, 26–27) noted that the entrance to an inner chamber of the cave was partly "blocked with a wall of loose stones." Just beyond the entrance to this partly blocked chamber, Mercer and his companions discovered "forty-six stone water-dishes." In spite of this discovery, Mercer (1896, 27) concluded that the walls were used as blinds for hunting birds and animals that frequented the cave entrance, an interpretation that was later questioned by Thompson (1959, 128) in his introduction to a reprint of the Mercer book. Eduard Seler (1901) notes that access to the inner chamber of a cave near Quen Santo, Guatemala, was constricted by two stone walls and that the enclosed space "may have concealed a priest who acted as the mouthpiece of an oracle" (Thompson 1959, 122). Thompson (1959, 122) further notes that stone walls in Quen Santo Cave were deliberately used to narrow passages that provided access into the innermost chamber of the cave, and that it contained two "stone idols," incense burners, urns, and jaguar effigy vessels. More recent work in both the highland and lowland Maya subregions indicates that stone walls are common features in subterranean sites (Bonor 1989; Brady 1989; Ferreira 2019; Helmke 2009; Moyes 2006, 2012, 2020, this volume; Peterson 2006) and that the primary purpose of these walls was for limiting access into sacred space. One of the few exceptions to this rule is a proposal by James E. Brady and Pierre R. Colas (2005, 152–55), who suggest that victorious armies often terminated the caves of vanquished enemies by closing off their entrances with stone walls.

Like the Guatemalan highlands and the Yucatán Peninsula, western Belize has hundreds of caves, most of which contain stone walls and evidence of architectural modifications. For the sake of brevity, we provide a few key examples of the contexts, forms, and proposed functions of these subterranean walls.

British Museum archaeologist Adrian Digby was among the first researchers to record stone walls in the caves of western Belize. In a report of his research at Las Cuevas in 1957, Digby (1958, 274–75, fig. 7) wrote that about "100 yards [91 m] from the entrance" there was a long stone wall constructed of crude boulders that separated an inner chamber from the main entrance to the cave. Beyond this major wall there were a series of "enclosures outlined with upright stones" and another wall with a narrow doorway that led "into a series of inner chambers with glistening white stalactites and stalagmites" and large amounts of broken pottery littering the floor (Thompson 1959, 126). The Las Cuevas Archaeological Reconnaissance project, under the direction of Holley Moyes, recently produced detailed maps of Las Cuevas and recorded three walls within the tunnel system (Moyes 2012, 2020). It is likely that the wall noted by Digby corresponds to Wall 1, located at the rear of the Entrance Chamber. The wall spans the tunnel opening, and a small constructed doorway restricts the entrance to Chamber 1. Wall 2, a formally constructed wall with a doorway, is located deep within the tunnel system and restricts access between Chambers 6 and 7. Wall 3 is located at the entrance to Chamber 8. The wall has been damaged by looters but originally spanned from the floor to the ceiling, completely blocking the entrance, thus forcing ritual participants to enter Chamber 8 via a small constructed crawl space on the far side of the room. Moyes (2020) suggests that while these small entrances directed pedestrian traffic in specified ways, they may also have created meaning within the context of the cave's cosmological associations. Alexander Hamilton Anderson, the first Archaeological Commissioner of Belize, also claimed to have observed a small "grotto" in Las Cuevas where access had been restricted by a stone wall. Thompson (1959, 126) notes that "the grotto, which would have made an ideal shrine, was further walled off by artificial masonry to the left as one entered." More recent research by Holley Moyes (2012) was unable to confirm the presence of these walls, thus Anderson's previous interpretations remain dubious and unsubstantiated. In spite of that, a recent multiregional Belize Cave Research Project, under the direction of Moyes and Awe, noted that more than half of the seventy-five cave sites they investigated in western Belize contained architectural features, including "walls, doorways, blockages, terraces, steps, platforms, and anomalous features" (Moyes 2020, 319). In the case of the cave walls, Moyes (2020, 319) concludes that they were "used to create enclosed spaces or limit accessibility by closing off alcoves and niches or blocking rooms or tunnels." Moyes (2020, 320) further notes that, besides restricting access to some chambers, the walls also served to channel the movement of ritual practitioners, occlude vision, and diminish sound.

In the 1960s, David M. Pendergast of the Royal Ontario Museum investigated several cave sites in the vicinity of Las Cuevas that also contained stone walls. In Actun Balam, for example, Pendergast (1969, 8) reports that the furthest chamber from the entrance, designated as Chamber E, "is less than a meter in height and about 3.5 by 7 meters, [and] is barely large enough to admit a single person of moderate size." In spite of these characteristics, access to the small chamber was even more restricted by an 85 cm thick wall. The latter was constructed of crude rocks mortared together with mud and "pierced" by a narrow 71 cm high by 55-31 cm wide doorway. According to Pendergast (1969, 8), "the presence of the wall suggests that the area was of some special importance to the ancient Maya." He adds that artificial walls are a common feature of caves in western Belize and that they generally serve to demarcate space or limit access to smaller chambers.

In Eduardo Quiroz Cave, Pendergast (1971) recorded stone walls in five of the six chambers of the cave. The first wall, constructed of crude, dry-laid, limestone blocks, served to "close off a small, low-ceilinged niche" in "the outer area of Chamber 1" (Pendergast 1971, 9–10). Chambers 2 and 3 contained the greatest evidence for artificial modification at the site. A wide "slit" connecting the two chambers was closed off by a wall made of large boulders. Thereafter, access between the two chambers was only possible via a small doorway that penetrated the wall. Another stone wall between Chambers 5 and 6 "was built to reduce the size of an already uncomfortably small passageway" (Pendergast 1971, 10). The morphology and location of the walls in Eduardo Quiroz Cave led Pendergast (1971, 113) to conclude that they had been constructed to "create a simple division within a chamber" and to "enhance already existing divisions, presumably to increase the remoteness of the inner chambers" for ceremonial purposes.

Dorie Reents-Budet and Barbara MacLeod (1997) discovered similar types of walls during their investigation of subterranean sites in the Caves Branch River valley. They note that in an area of massive ceiling breakdown in Petroglyph Cave, the Maya constructed a small circular platform beneath a giant rock designated as Nohoch Tunich, then enclosed the area around the platform with a masonry wall. Reents-Budet and MacLeod (1997, 90) suggest that, in addition to darkening the space around the platform, the wall served to "restrict access and create privacy and boundaries for ceremonial space."

In the Sibun Valley, Polly A. Peterson (2006) recorded numerous artificial stone walls in several caves and rockshelters. At Actun Ibach, Peterson (2006, 61, fig. 2.20) mapped twenty artificial stone walls in the cave. Some of these walls served to seal off seven of the eighteen entrances to the cave, while others sealed off small chambers or directed the flow of traffic to inner chambers. At Ek' Waynal, also known as Many Walls Cave, Peterson (2006, 84) noted that a large wall was "constructed on the northern side of the eastern chamber" to block "access to the Usrey Valley entrance to the cave." Following her study of the various stone walls in the caves of the Sibun Valley, Peterson (2006, 264) concluded, "Where there were two caves that connected valleys, one of them was closed off with an artificial wall. If there were two ways into a cave, one side was blocked.... The constructed walls, thus function either to direct movement through the landscape by blocking passage in certain directions, serve as boundaries demarcating use areas, block light or wind, or terminate use of the space." With the exception of defensive purposes, the functions of cave walls noted by the aforementioned speleo-archaeological investigations thus reflect the same diversity as those noted at surface sites in western Belize and the Yucatán Peninsula.

The Social Functions of Walls

The Berlin Wall and the Great Wall of China are certainly two of the most iconic, and best-known, walls ever built by humans. First constructed in 1961, the Berlin Wall subsequently underwent at least three major modifications. In its final stage, the wall stretched some 160 km and was a massive, 3.6 m high, steel and concrete structure (Eghigian 2007). For twenty-eight years, the Berlin Wall effectively separated East and West Berlin, until it was finally brought down on November 9, 1989. Imposing though it was, and despite its iconic stature, this renowned wall served neither defensive nor ritual purposes. Instead, it represented one of the most famous symbols of an ideological divide. As William A. Callahan (2018) notes, East Germans perceived the wall as a barrier blocking their access or escape to the west, or as a tangible separation between "its morally superior socialist 'experiment' from West Berlin's morally corrupt capitalist" path. In contrast, others perceived the wall as the symbolic boundary between democracy (good) and communism (evil). In the end, and regardless of one's bias, both perspectives serve to confirm that the Berlin Wall's primary function was ideological rather than a physical object barring East Berliners' access to the west.

In the case of the Great Wall of China, the prevailing assumption is that this 20,000 km long structure was specifically erected by the Ming dynasty as a defensive barricade to keep out northern barbarians from invading Chinese settlements in the south. What most people don't realize, however, is that the Great Wall is not continuous. It actually consists of "dozens of discontinuous and overlapping walls, built at different times, by different peoples, for different purposes" (Callahan 2018 471). Furthermore, despite its presence, southern China was eventually still invaded from the north.

Interestingly, Callahan (2018, 458) argues that the Great Wall provides us with a good example of "how walls vary in meaning temporally: a century ago the Great Wall was understood in China as a monument to the wastefulness of tyrannical emperors, and/or as a useless ruin that didn't border anything.

Now in the twenty-first century it is taken for granted that the Great Wall is morally good as a symbol of peace that benefits humanity." This symbolic aspect of the Great Wall is also applicable to the past, particularly if we consider that, like the Berlin Wall, it represented two distinct cultural realities. In the case of China, the Great Wall served as a tangible divide between the "civilized south" (China) and the "barbaric north" (Mongolia).

In many respects, the border wall that the Donald Trump administration proposed to construct along the U.S.–Mexico border shares a similar ideological value to that of the Berlin Wall and the Great Wall of China. When we listen to the rhetoric that pervades the public media, it is very apparent that the northern side of the proposed wall is associated by some with "safety, law, and sovereignty," while the southern side of the wall "marks danger, violence, and anarchy" (Callahan 2018, 461). In this sense, many walls can be associated with what R. B. J. Walker (1993) refers to as an inside/outside dichotomy. Depending on one's perspective, the inside is always associated with good, order, and civilization. The outside, in contrast, is associated with lawlessness, immorality, and chaos. Whatever the case may be, we can certainly conclude that, given advanced military technology, most modern walls, including that proposed on our southern border, serve negligible defensive purposes. They simply serve to divide different ideologies and to separate "us" from "them."

Returning to the Maya world, we previously noted that almost every discussion on the use of walls for defensive purposes has focused some attention on Mayapán. What is ironic is that this site provides one of the best examples of the multipurpose use of walls in the Maya area. This was clearly noted by a Light Detection and Radar (LiDAR) survey of Mayapán (Hare, Masson, and Russell 2014) that identified several types of walls at the site. These features include the wall encircling the core of the city, and hundreds of albarradas, chichbes, and the walls encircling three of the city's twenty-nine cenotes. At Mayapán, therefore, it is obvious that the Maya used walls not only for defensive purposes but also for demarcating household spaces (albarradas), delineating walkways (chichbes and andadores), and controlling access to sacred space (cenote walls and cave walls).

In comparison with the Yucatán Peninsula, stone walls are considerably less common in the Belize River Valley. Of the various functions proposed, at least in this context, none of the walls that we have investigated at surface sites in western Belize appear to have served defensive purposes. Their morphology, context, and associated cultural remains all indicate that they either functioned as albarradas, for controlling access, or for directing the flow of traffic into and out of site cores. While some might think that this situation represents exceptions to the rule, this is really not the case. As Robert J. Sharer and Loa P. Traxler (2005, 143) note, "most Maya centers ... developed without fortifications, which indicates that for most of their history, the ancient Maya did not practice large-scale warfare for conquest or other political ends, but instead limited conflict among polities, both in scale and in scope." At the same time, we are very much aware that "the presence or absence of walls in the archaeological record implies neither the presence nor the absence of war *per se*" (Arredondo Leiva 2010, 351). What we argue here is that not all walls at Maya sites were created equally and that it sometimes behooves us to temper our exuberance and assumptions when trying to determine the significance of walls in the archaeological record. Consider, for example, the earthen wall to the north of Tikal. Shortly after its discovery, Dennis Puleston and Donald W. Callender Jr. (1967, 48) argued that the 9.5 km long earthworks served as fortifications designed to defend the northern border of Tikal, and for "protecting the agricultural resources upon which they ultimately depended." Forty years after Puleston and Callender first published the "Great Tikal Earthwork," David Webster and his colleagues (2007) revisited the feature to determine its extent and form, and hypothesized a defensive function. Following their comprehensive study, Webster et al. (2007, 61) concluded, "We are struck by how often provisional and guarded conjectures by the original researchers became accepted wisdom." They added, "We should no longer assume the following: (1) That the earthworks represent fortifications (at least finished ones). (2) That there is a southern earthwork; someone might discover one someday, but until then this earthwork is an archaeological will-o-the-wisp. (3) That the earthworks were built in Early Classic times, or that they can be associated with specific events in Tikal's history as reconstructed from art and epigraphy."

Conclusion

In this chapter, we note that following the pendulum swing of the 1970s, archaeologists have often elevated defense and the effects of internecine warfare to the primary interpretation explaining the presence of walls and earthworks at Maya sites. While there is no doubt that some walls at some sites served these purposes, our study of stone walls at both surface and subterranean sites in western Belize indicates that the Maya also constructed these architectural features for a variety of nondefensive purposes. Alternative functions include the use of walls to demarcate household space or property, to direct the flow of traffic into and out of private or public space, and to restrict access to ceremonial space. In other cases, walls also serve as tangible symbols for demarcating ideological divisions. In this sense, they represent physical and symbolic systems of inclusion and exclusion and serve to mark the inside from the outside. On the inside, they facilitate ties that bind a family, corporate group, or community together. On the outside, they represent walls that divide us from them.

Works Cited

Andres, Christopher R. 2011. "The 2010 Architectural Investigations at Tipan Chen Uitz Cayo District, Belize." In *The Caves Branch Archaeological Survey Project: A Report of the 2010 Field Season*, edited by Christopher R. Andres and Gabriel D. Wrobel, 41–126. Occasional Report 2. Oxford: Belize Archaeological Research and Education Foundation.

Andres, Christopher R., Gabriel D. Wrobel, Jason J. González, Shawn G. Morton, and Rebecca Shelton. 2011. "Power and Status in Central Belize: Insights from the Caves Branch Archaeological Survey Project's 2010 Field Season." *Research Reports in Belizean Archaeology* 8:101–13.

Andrews, George F. 1997. *Pyramids and Palaces, Monsters and Masks: The Golden Age of Maya Architecture: Architectural Survey at Uxmal.* Vol. 1. Lancaster, Calif.: Labyrinthos Press.

Aoyama, Kazuo, and Elizabeth Graham. 2015. "Ancient Maya Warfare: Exploring the Significance of Lithic Variation in Maya Weaponry." *Lithics: The Journal of the Lithic Studies Society* 36:5–17.

Arredondo Leiva, Ernesto. 2010. "Archaeological Investigations of a Walled Compound at Naachtun, Peten, Guatemala: Architecture, Politics and Warfare." PhD diss., La Trobe University, Bundora, Victoria, Australia.

Audet, Carolyn M. 2006. "The Political Organization of the Belize Valley: Evidence from Baking Pot, Xunantunich, and Cahal Pech." PhD diss., Vanderbilt University, Nashville, Tenn.

Awe, Jaime J. 2008. "Architectural Manifestations of Power and Prestige: Examples from Classic Period Monumental Architecture at Cahal Pech, Xunantunich and Caracol, Belize." *Research Reports in Belizean Archaeology* 5:159–74.

Awe, Jaime J., Claire E. Ebert, Carolyn Freiwald, and Kirsten Green. 2017. "The Dead Do Tell Tales: Unravelling the Case of Cahal Pech's John or Jane Doe." *Research Reports in Belizean Archaeology* 14:213–26.

Awe, Jaime J., Claire E. Ebert, Julie A. Hoggarth, James J. Aimers, Christophe Helmke, John Douglas, and W. James Stemp. 2020. "The Last Hurrah: Examining the Nature of Peri-Abandonment Deposits and Activities at Cahal Pech, Belize." *Ancient Mesoamerica* 31 (3): 175–87.

Awe, Jaime J., Christophe Helmke, James J. Aimers, Claire E. Ebert, Julie A. Hoggarth, and W. James Stemp. 2020. "Applying Regional, Contextual, Ethnohistoric, and Ethnographic Approaches for Understanding the Significance of Peri-Abandonment Deposits in Western Belize." *Ancient Mesoamerica* 31 (3): 109–26.

Barrera Rubio, Alfredo. 1978. "Settlement Patterns in Uxmal Area, Yucatán, Mexico." Paper presented at the 43rd Annual Meeting of the Society for American Archaeology, Tucson, Ariz.

Benavides Castillo, Antonio. 1981. "Cobá y Tulum: Adaptación al medio ambiente y control del medio social." *Estudios de Cultura Maya* 13:205–22.

Blacker, Irwin R., and Harry M. Rosen. 1962. *Conquest: Dispatches of Cortez from the New World*. Universal Library. New York: Grosset and Dunlap.

Bonor, Juan L. 1989. *Las cuevas mayas: Simbolismo y ritual*. Madrid: Instituto de Cooperación Iberoamericana, Universidad Complutense de Madrid.

Brady, James E. 1989. "An Investigation of Maya Ritual Cave Use with Special Reference to Naj Tunich, Peten, Guatemala." PhD diss., University of California, Los Angeles.

Brady, James E., and Pierre R. Colas. 2005. "Nikte Mo' Scattered Fire in the Cave of K'ab Chan:e': Epigraphic and Archaeological Evidence for Cave Desecration in Ancient Maya Warfare." In *Stone Houses and Earth Lords: Maya Religion in the Cave Context*, edited by Keith M. Prufer and James E. Brady, 149–66. Boulder: University Press of Colorado.

Brown, M. Kathryn, and Travis W. Stanton. 2003. *Ancient Mesoamerican Warfare*. Walnut Creek, Calif.: AltaMira Press.

Bullard, William R., Jr. 1954. "Boundary Walls and House Lots at Mayapan." *Current Reports* 13:234–53.

Callahan, William A. 2018. "The Politics of Walls: Barriers, Flows, and the Sublime." *Review of International Studies* 44 (3): 456–81.

Chase, Arlen F., and Diane Z. Chase. 1989. "The Investigation of Classic Period Warfare at Caracol, Belize." *Mayab* 5:5–18.

Chase, Arlen F., and Diane Z. Chase. 1998. "Scale and Intensity in Classic Period Maya Agriculture: Terracing and Settlement at the 'Garden City' of Caracol, Belize." *Culture and Agriculture* 20 (2): 60–77.

Dahlin, Bruce. 2000. "The Barricade and Abandonment of Chunchucmil: Implications for Northern Maya Warfare." *Latin American Antiquity* 11 (3): 283–98.

Demarest, Arthur A. 1997. "The Vanderbilt Petexbatún Regional Archaeological Project 1989–1994: Overview, History, and Major Results of a Multidisciplinary Study of the Classic Maya Collapse." *Ancient Mesoamerica* 8 (2): 209–27.

Demarest, Arthur A., Matt O'Mansky, Claudia Wolley, Dirk Van Tuerenhout, Takeshi Inomata, Joel Palka, and Hector Escobedo. 1997. "Classic Maya Defensive Systems

and Warfare in the Petexbatún Region: Archaeological Evidence and Interpretations." *Ancient Mesoamerica* 8 (2): 229–54.
Díaz del Castillo, Bernal. 1962. *The Conquest of New Spain*. Translated by J. M. Cohen. London: Penguin Books.
Digby, Adrian. 1958. "A New Maya City Discovered in British Honduras: First Excavations at Las Cuevas and an Underground Necropolis Revealed." *The Illustrated London News*, February 15.
Eghigian, Greg. 2007. "Homo Munitus: The East Germans Observed." In *Socialist Modern: East German Everyday Culture and Politics*, edited by Katherine Pence and Paul Betts, 37–70. Ann Arbor: University of Michigan Press.
Fedick, Scott L., Bethany A. Morrison, Bente Juhl Andersen, Sylviane Boucher, Jorge Ceja Acosta, Jennifer P. Mathews. 2000. "Wetland Manipulation in the Yalahau Region of the Northern Maya Lowlands." *Journal of Field Archaeology* 27 (2): 131–52.
Ferreira, Becky. 2019. "1,000-Year-Old Pristine Mayan Artifacts Found in Sealed 'Jaguar God' Cave." Motherboard, March 8. https://motherboard.vice.com/en_us/article/8xyezp/1000-year-old-mayan-artifacts-found-in-sealed-jaguar-god-cave.
Glover, Jeffrey B., Dominique Rissolo, and Jennifer P. Mathews. 2011. "The Hidden World of the Maritime Maya: Lost Landscapes Along the North Coast of Quintana Roo, Mexico." In *The Archaeology of Maritime Landscapes*, edited by Benjamin L. Ford, 195–216. New York: Springer.
Golden, Charles, Andrew K. Scherer, A. René Muñoz, and Rosaura Vasquez. 2008. "Piedras Negras and Yaxchilan: Divergent Political Trajectories in Adjacent Maya Polities." *Latin American Antiquity* 19 (3): 249–74.
Goñi Motilla, Guillermo Antonio. 1993. "Solares Prehispánicos en la Península de Yucatan." PhD diss., Escuela Nacional de Antropología e Historia, Mexico City.
Guerra, Rafael, and Marieka Arksey. 2012. "The 2011 Excavations at the Major Center of Lower Dover." In *The Belize Valley Archaeological Reconnaissance Project: A Report of the 2011 Field Season*, vol. 17, edited by Julie A. Hoggarth, Rafael A. Guerra, and Jaime J. Awe, 108–20. Belize: Institute of Archaeology.
Guerra, Rafael, and Shawn G. Morton. 2012. "2011 Survey at Lower Dover." In *The Belize Valley Archaeological Reconnaissance Project: A Report of the 2011 Field Season*, vol. 17, edited by Julie A. Hoggarth, Rafael A. Guerra, and Jaime J. Awe, 105–7. Belize: Institute of Archaeology.
Hare, Timothy, Marilyn Masson, and Bradley Russell. 2014. "High-Density LiDAR Mapping of the Ancient City of Mayapán." *Remote Sensing* 6 (9): 9064–85.
Helmke, Christophe G. B. 2009. "Ancient Maya Cave Usage as Attested in the Glyphic Corpus of the Maya Lowlands and the Caves of the Roaring Creek Valley, Belize." PhD diss., Institute of Archaeology, University of London.
Hutson, Scott. 2010. *Dwelling, Identity, and the Maya: Relational Archaeology at Chunchucmil*. Lanham, Md.: AltaMira Press.
Inomata, Takeshi. 1997. "The Last Day of a Fortified Classic Maya Center: Archaeological Investigations at Aguateca, Guatemala." *Ancient Mesoamerica* 8 (2): 337–51.

Jamison, Thomas R. 2010. "Monumental Building Programs and Changing Political Strategies at Xunantunich." In *Classic Maya Provincial Politics: Xunantunich and Its Hinterlands*, edited by Lisa J. LeCount and Jason Yaeger, 122–44. Tucson: University of Arizona Press.

Kolias George Van, III. 2016. "Investigating the Maya Polity at Lower Barton Creek, Cayo, Belize." MA thesis, Northern Arizona University, Flagstaff.

Magnoni, Aline. 1995. "Albarradas at Chunchucmil and in the Northern Maya Area." BA thesis, Institute of Archaeology, University College of London.

Magnoni, Aline, Scott R. Hutson, and Bruce H. Dahlin. 2012. "Living in the City: Settlement Patterns and the Urban Experience at Classic Period Chunchucmil, Yucatán, Mexico." *Ancient Mesoamerica* 21:313–43.

McKillop, Heather. 2004. *The Ancient Maya: New Perspectives*. New York: W. W. Norton.

Mercer, Henry C. 1896. *The Hill Caves of the Yucatán: A Search for Evidence of Man's Antiquity in the Caverns of Central America*. Philadelphia, Pa.: J. B. Lippincott.

Miller, Mary E. 1986. *The Murals of Bonampak*. Princeton, N.J.: Princeton University Press.

Millon, René. 1973. *Urbanization at Teotihuacan, Mexico*. Vol. 1, *The Teotihuacan Map*. Austin: University of Texas Press.

Morley, Sylvanus G. 1946. *The Ancient Maya*. Stanford: Stanford University Press.

Morton, Shawn G., Gabriel D. Wrobel, and Christopher R. Andres. 2019. "The Centre on the Edge: Polity Development on the Frontier of the Belize Valley." *Research Reports in Belizean Archaeology* 16:201–12.

Moyes, Holley. 2006. "The Sacred Landscape as a Political Resource: A Case Study of Ancient Maya Cave Use at Chechem Ha Cave, Belize, Central America." PhD diss., State University of New York at Buffalo.

Moyes, Holley. 2012. "Constructing the Underworld: The Built Environment in Ancient Mesoamerican Caves." In *Heart of Earth: Studies in Maya Ritual Cave Use*, edited by James E. Brady, 95–110. Bulletin 23. Austin, Tex.: Association for Mexican Cave Studies.

Moyes, Holley. 2020. "Capturing the Forest: Ancient Maya Ritual Caves as Built Environments." In *Approaches to Monumental Landscapes of the Ancient Maya: A Legacy of Human Occupation*, edited by Brett A. Houk, Barbara Arroyo, and Terry G. Powis, 313–34. Gainesville: University Press of Florida.

Nondédéo, Philippe, and Antoine Dorison. 2019. "Operación I.5: Análisis Preliminar de la imagen LiDAR." In *Proyecto Peten-Norte Naachtun 2015–2018: Informe de la octava temporada de campo 2018*, edited by Philippe Nondédéo, Dominique Michelet, Johann Begel, and Lillian Garrido, 15–26. UMR 8096-CNRS. Paris: Laboratoire "Archeologie des Ameriques" Université Paris 1 Panthéon-Sorbonne.

Palka, Joel W. 2001. "Ancient Maya Defensive Barricades, Warfare, and Site Abandonment." *Latin American Antiquity* 12 (4): 427–30.

Pendergast, David M. 1969. "The Prehistory of Actun Balam, British Honduras." Art and Archaeology Occasional Paper 16. Royal Ontario Museum, Toronto.

Pendergast, David M. 1971. "Excavations at Eduardo Quiroz Cave, British Honduras (Belize)." Art and Archaeology Occasional Paper 21. Royal Ontario Museum, Toronto.
Peterson, Polly A. 2006. "Ancient Maya Ritual Cave Use in the Sibun Valley, Belize." PhD diss., Boston University.
Puleston, Dennis, and Donald W. Callender Jr. 1967. "Defensive Earthworks at Tikal." *Expedition* 9 (30): 40–48.
Reents-Budet, Dorie, and Barbara MacLeod. 1997. "The Archaeology of Petroglyph Cave, Cayo District, Belize." Manuscript on file, Department of New World Archaeology, Royal Ontario Museum, Toronto.
Rice, Don S., and Prudence M. Rice. 1981. "Muralla de Leon: A Lowland Maya Fortification." *Journal of Field Archaeology* 8 (3): 271–88.
Seler, Eduard. 1901. *Die Alten Ansiedelungen von Chaculá, im Distrikte Nenton des Departments Huehuetenango der Republik Guatemala.* Berlin: Verlag von Dietrich Reimer.
Sharer, Robert J., and Loa P. Traxler. 2005. *The Ancient Maya.* 6th ed. Stanford: Stanford University Press.
Shook, Edwin M. 1952. *The Great Wall of Mayapan.* Washington, D.C.: Carnegie Institution of Washington.
Smith, A. Ledyard. 1962. "Residential and Associated Structures at Mayapan." In *Mayapan, Yucatan, Mexico*, by H. E. D. Pollock, Ralph L. Roys, Tatiana Proskouriakoff, and A. Ledyard Smith, 165–319. Washington, D.C.: Carnegie Institution of Washington.
Stephens, John L. 1841. *Incidents of Travel in Central America, Chiapas and Yucatan.* Edited by Frederick Catherwood. New York: Harper and Bros.
Thompson, J. Eric S. 1959. "The Role of Caves in Maya Culture." *Mitteilungen aus dem Museum für Völkerkunde im Hamburg* 25:122–29.
Tozzer, Alfred M., trans. 1941. *Landa's Relación de las cosas de Yucatán.* Peabody Museum of Archaeology and Ethnology 18. Cambridge, Mass.: Harvard University.
Vargas, Ernesto, Patricia S. Santillan, and Marta Vilalta. 1985. "Apuntes para el análisis del patrón de asentamiento de Tulum." *Estudios de Cultura Maya* 16:55–83.
Villagutierre Soto-Mayor, Juan de. (1701) 1983. *History of the Conquest of the Province of the Itza.* Edited by Frank E. Comparato. Culver City, Calif.: Labyrinthos.
Walker, R. B. J. 1993. *Inside/Outside: International Relations as Political Theory.* Cambridge: Cambridge University Press.
Webster, David. 1976a. *Defensive Earthworks at Becan, Campeche, Mexico.* Middle American Research Institute 41. New Orleans: Tulane University.
Webster, David. 1976b. "Lowland Maya Fortifications." *Proceedings of the American Philosophical Society* 120 (5): 361–71.
Webster, David. 1977. "Warfare and the Evolution of Maya Civilization." In *Origins of Maya Civilization*, edited by Richard E. W. Adams, 335–73. Albuquerque: University of New Mexico Press.

Webster, David. 1978. "Three Walled Sites of the Northern Maya Lowlands." *Journal of Field Archaeology* 5 (4): 375–90.

Webster, David. 1993. "The Study of Maya Warfare: What It Tells Us About the Maya and What It Tells Us About Maya Archaeology." In *Lowland Maya Civilization in the Eighth Century A.D.*, edited by Jeremy A. Sabloff and John S. Henderson, 415–44. Washington, D.C.: Dumbarton Oaks Research Library and Collection.

Webster, David. 2000. "The Not So Peaceful Civilization: A Review of Maya War." *Journal of World Prehistory* 14 (1): 65–119.

Webster, David. 2002. *The Fall of the Ancient Maya: Solving the Mystery of the Maya Collapse*. London: Thames and Hudson.

Webster, David, Timothy Murtha, Kirk D. Straight, Jay Silverstein, Horacio Martinez, Richard E. Terry, and Richard Burnett. 2007. "The Great Tikal Earthwork Revisited." *Journal of Field Archaeology* 32 (1): 46–64.

CHAPTER 8

Two Tales of a City

The Sakbe'ob at Yo'okop from the Viewpoints of Elites and Commoners

JUSTINE M. SHAW AND ALBERTO G. FLORES COLIN

Maya *sakbe'ob* (causeways) have traditionally been considered to be architectural features that function as "ties that bind" important spatial locations and the denizens of those places. They would have required the collective participation of various kin groups, socioeconomic classes, and communities (see Shaw 2008; Vallejo-Cáliz and Hutson, this volume). In the northern lowlands, major systems include the roads linking Ucí, Kancab, Ucanha, and Cansahcab (Hutson and Welch 2014), the wide-flung architectural groups of Chichén Itzá (Cobos and Winemiller 2001), and the Cobá–Yaxunah 100 km *sakbe* forming part of the former's extensive road system (Folan et al. 2009; González and Stanton 2013; Stanton et al., this volume). In the Cochuah region of west-central Quintana Roo, the sites of Ichmul and Yo'okop have multiroad systems, and individual causeways have been located at other sites; these too have been thought of as important functional and symbolic geopolitical links (Flores Colin 2015, 2019; Shaw 2008).

The fact that those in power at so many Maya sites in different places and during varied time periods invested in causeways supports their binding function. The energetics invested in sakbe'ob (Abrams 1994; Abrams and Bolland 1999) could have been put into temples, palaces, or the formalization of plazas, but roads were often chosen by those empowered to make decisions and control labor. Daniel Vallejo-Cáliz and Scott R. Hutson (this volume) discuss rural integration along the causeways in their study area. Rather than marking boundaries, they seem to have attracted settlement, establishing and maintaining integration between Ucí and its hinterland.

Stanton and colleagues' (this volume) Light Detection and Radar (LiDAR) study of Cobá has revealed high values for area density at many of the termini, although both the area and the volume of architecture drop off sharply away from these areas. In the Cochuah region, this binding function is also recognized, with causeways connecting several types of physical spaces and an increase in construction at newly joined nodes (Shaw 2008). Interestingly, at both Cobá (Stanton et al., this volume) and the sites in the Cochuah region, it is only the termini themselves that possess a marked increase in architectural density, but in the Ucí study (Vallejo-Cáliz and Hutson, this volume), the entire length of the roads seemed to attract an increased amount of architecture. This may be because the latter's causeways were built relatively early in the sequence of the region, giving them time to attract more construction, whereas the former two imposed roads onto their settlement patterns rather late in their occupations.

At the same time, much like walls (Awe and Morton, this volume), sakbe'ob potentially served a second, divisive set of functions. This politically and spatially inclusive feature may have also been intrusive for the commoners called upon to build, maintain, and live among the roads. They would have had little-to-no say about their placement or concerning potential rules about when and where sakbe'ob nonelites could access causeways. It could have been a burden to those obligated to construct and maintain a feature that passed through their neighborhood. The dual inhabitants/workers may have lost part of their land through "eminent domain," they may have been banned from using or crossing the sakbe'ob through an official decree, and they might not have appreciated processions and accompanying spectators invading their neighborhood. In that sense, the impact and interpretation of a causeway would have varied not only with one's geographical location but also with one's social position.

An Overview of Research at Yo'okop and the Discovery of Its Sakbe'ob

Located in the contact-period province of Cochuah (Roys 1965), approximately 12 km southeast of the modern pueblo of Sabán and 2 km northwest of Dzoyola in west-central Quintana Roo (figure 8.1), Yo'okop had been the subject of several informal studies prior to our current program of research. "The first archaeological party ever" to visit the site, also known as Okop or

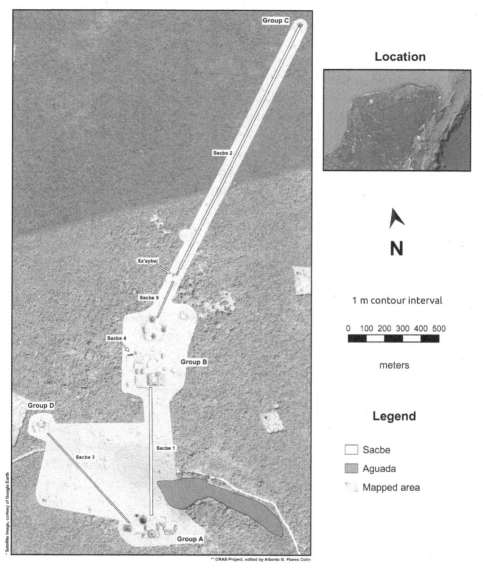

FIGURE 8.1 Plan map of Yo'okop (created by Alberto G. Flores Colin, Justine M. Shaw, and Dave Johnstone).

La Aguada, consisted of journalist Gregory Mason and Herbert Spinden, of the Peabody Museum at Harvard University (Mason 1926). The pair traveled through the region with the assistance of *chicleros* in 1926, remarking on the devastation that remained following the recent conclusion of the Caste War (Wren and Nygard 2015).

Under the auspices of the Carnegie Institution of Washington, Gustav Strömsvik, Harry E. D. Pollock, and Heinrich Berlin made a brief stop at Yo'okop, following a few days at the nearby site of Ichmul, in 1954. Strömsvik and Berlin returned three months later to spend several more days documenting some of the major architecture and monuments at Yo'okop (Strömsvik, Pollock, and Berlin 1955). They were the first to note the existence of one of the site's sakbe'ob (Sakbe 1).

Reginald Wilson, a missionary doctor, along with aviation pilots Jack Walker and Bill Clapp, made repeated visits to Yo'okop between 1966 and 1972 in order to locate and record additional monuments, document the existence of Sakbe 2, and survey Groups A and B. This resulted in Wilson's 1974 publication, which expanded on the work begun by the Carnegie Institution. Sensitive to concerns about foreigners removing archaeological remains from elsewhere in the Maya region, no excavations were conducted, and no artifacts were removed in the course of their visits (Wren and Nygard 2015).

Archaeological focus didn't return to Yo'okop until 1998, when Mexico's Instituto Nacional de Antropología e Historia (INAH) conducted basic reconnaissance and made some surface collections at the site. That same summer, Justine Shaw and Dave Johnstone visited the site and the nearby community of Sabán in order to assess the potential for long-term research. Three seasons of fieldwork focused exclusively at Yo'okop began in 2000 and additional work as part of the Cochuah Regional Archaeological Survey from 2003 until the present has revealed much more of the site's features, including the location of three additional sakbe'ob (Shaw 2015).

The Layout of the Site of Yo'okop

Yo'okop consists of four primary groups of monumental architecture (Groups A, B, C, and D) linked by five sakbe'ob, including a smaller, unfinished roadway on the western edge of Group B (figure 8.1). These groups are composed of monumental architecture, with some structures reaching more than 20 m in height, in addition to numerous smaller mounds, a ballcourt, platforms, and other residential structures such as foundation braces (Shaw, Johnstone, and Krochock 2000, 17). Although the settlement is extensive, and there are many vestiges that have not been mapped yet, on several surface surveys we've observed that the settlement extends mainly toward the west (Flores Colin 2010).

The four primary causeways serve to connect the fringes of the large architecture in each group rather than continuing into the cores of the groups. While much of the surrounding terrain is flat, Group A is perched atop a long ridge that continues well beyond Yo'okop itself, through the Fortin de Yo'okop, 2 km to the northwest. Immediately to the south-southeast of Group A is a water catchment feature, known as an *aguada*, that was modified in ancient times through linear features within the water and cut stones along portions of its edge. Like the higher portion of the Fortin de Yo'okop, the high ridge above the aguada, to the east of the mapped portion of Group A, was reoccupied and modified during the Caste War (see Badillo Sánchez, this volume). According to the results of more than twenty excavations, both horizontal exposures and 2 × 2 m test pits, we know that the site had an occupation that spans from the Middle Formative to the Terminal Classic, although there is evidence of Postclassic shrines in various parts of the site (Flores Colin 2015, 68–88). Most of Yo'okop's visible architecture is from either the Terminal Classic or in some cases the Postclassic because these were the final periods of site occupation within the four main groups. The 718 m long Sakbe 1, cut by the modern road between Sabán and Dzoyola, crosses the relatively flat terrain to the south of Group B.

This part of the site has otherwise little architecture, as the deeper soils here were potentially reserved for agricultural purposes. Within this zone, there is a collapsed section where a portion of the causeway has fallen into a *sascabera* (mine for soft limestone easily crushed into powder) that predated the road's construction as well as a Postclassic altar atop the sakbe. Just south of the modern road cut, beyond where the Early Classic Altar 1 was placed atop the Terminal Classic roadway during the Postclassic, Sakbe 1 climbs the sharp natural slope up to the northern portion of Group A. Its terminus is the plaza north of the Group's tallest structure (the "Castillo"), with the road's eastern edge remaining more well defined for a greater distance than the western side. For much of the length of Sakbe 1, a straight course is maintained and its height of about 60 cm remains fairly constant with larger cut-stone blocks of up to three courses in height defining its edges.

Near its termini in both Groups A and B, the height is decreased with the road grading into the plaza surface. No steps or ramps have been detected along its course.

Sakbe 2 and Sakbe 5 link the northern edge of Group B with the lone platform and pyramidal structure composing Group C. Along their 1,800 m course, the height of both roads is close to ground level in some sections and up to 4.4 m tall in other locations (figure 8.2), which serves to maintain a constant grade. Originally it was thought that this road was built in two sections. However, based on their construction styles and their widths, it was concluded that the span consisted of two different roads, with Sakbe 2 potentially being an extension of Sakbe 5. The latter causeway, Sakbe 5, connects Group B to the Xa'aybeh complex, which is composed of a small platform and a pyramidal structure, while Sakbe 2 connects the Xa'aybeh complex to Group C itself. The former is 7 m wide, while the latter is 10 m wide and taller. Between the two causeways is a 5 m long gap with no construction material, potentially once bridged by perishable materials. While there was a small hamlet nearby until the 1970s that could have removed the stone from the sakbe, it is striking that all stone, including gravel, cobbles, and larger stones, is absent from this gap. Sakbe 2 has two semidetached platforms with several foundation braces that could be later additions on its top, and it is lined by at least sixteen sascaberas. About 800 m from the start of the roadway, in the stretch of greatest height, is a vaulted passage that would have permitted movement beneath the causeway.

Sakbe 3, which was located during the 2000 field season along with Group D (see figure 8.1), is also bisected by the modern Sabán–Dzoyola road. Running 690 m north-northwest to south-southeast, it maintains a relatively constant grade with heights of around a meter over much of its course; near the road cut, it attains a height of more than 2 m. As with Sakbe 1, where deeper soil is present, there are apparently architecture-free zones along the sides of the road that may have been used for agriculture. Portions with bedrock near the surface boast residential architecture ranging from vaulted structures to simple foundation braces. In this zone between the major groups, geological features rather than proximity to causeways seem to have determined where structures were erected. This may be due to the relatively late date of the Terminal Classic constructions, emplaced when settlement patterns were well established, or their lack of impact on the location of other architecture. The absence of architecture near Yo'okop's sakbe'ob contrasts markedly

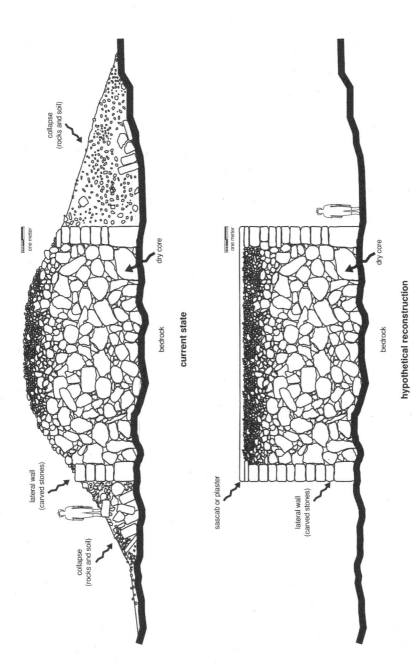

FIGURE 8.2 Sakbe 2 at its maximum height (created by Alberto G. Flores Colin and Justine M. Shaw).

with Vallejo-Cáliz and Hutson's (this volume) research, where LiDAR data revealed settlement density along the Ucí–Kancab and Ucanha–Cansahcab causeways to be six times higher than the settlement density between sites not connected by roads.

The unfinished Sakbe 4 on the western edge of Group B never reached 30 m in length and appears to have been intended to only connect architecture within the group itself. The western portion of the road is filled with cobbles, although it's not clear that gravel or finer components that would have comprised the surface were ever added. Halfway along the length of Sakbe 4, parallel side walls and two perpendicular internal lines of stones are visible, with only part of the material that would have comprised the fill being present. A further unfinished section is present at the eastern terminus. As the internal divisions that are visible do not appear to provide structural support to a road that is generally just one course of stones high, they may have served to divide the road into portions that were the responsibilities of distinct population units, analogous to the historic *fagina* system in which residents were obligated to perform unpaid labor for their municipality (Redfield 1941, 176–80; Redfield and Villa Rojas [1934] 1962, 30; Villa Rojas 1945, 75–76). The unfinished nature of Sakbe 4 is different from features at other sites, such as Ucí's Causeway 6—which seems to stop short of its logical destination but boasts replastered surfaces—or the Ucí–Kancab and Ucanha–Canshacab causeways, whose termini have been obliterated by modern occupations (Vallejo-Cáliz and Hutson, this volume).

Yo'okop's entire road system is believed to date to the Terminal Classic based on more than sixteen excavations, the age of the features connected by sakbe'ob, the unfinished nature of Sakbe 4 directly visible on a plaza surface in a major group, and stratigraphic relationships with associated features. However, the roads were not necessarily built as a single planned program. If the denser and more varied architecture in the elevated part associated with the site's aguada is perceived as the site's core, then the system appears to be radial; such systems emphasize a single core where roads originate, like that of Cobá (Cobos and Winemiller 2001, 284). However, conceiving of the various groups, or at least Groups A, B, and D, as multiple cores whose function and importance changed through time, then it could be perceived as more linear, with a "kink" to connect to Group D (Shaw 2008). Linear systems are used in sites with roughly equivalent groups, multiple important loci with functional distinctions or shifting temporal emphases. Sayil's system (Tourtellot and Sabloff 1994; Tourtellot, Sabloff, and Carmean 1992) is typical of linear sakbe systems with a north–south roadway that connects major architectural complexes from the Great Palace to the South Palace, passing through a vaulted portal (Shaw 2008, 96).

Analysis of Morphology and Destination Context

In order to obtain a better understanding of the function of the roadways, it is necessary to conduct an analysis of all the attributes of the roads at an entire site (table 8.1). Based on this, it can be assumed that they were thought of in the same way as other monumental constructions, due to the work involved in their construction and their overall volume. They had the aim of allowing the simultaneous movement of several rows of persons at the same time, with the clear intention of separating them from the surface of the ground. Additionally, such roads served to permit pedestrians to move directly, without obstacles or distractions, from one end to the other, which is evidenced by the rectilinear course of the causeways.

Although the morphological attributes of the roads give some indication of the intentionality with which they were constructed, it is also necessary to extend the analysis to the areas or constructions that the roads connect. Thus, Yo'okop's causeways were analyzed according to the type of context in each terminus area. This proposed type of study has been named the "analysis of destination contexts" (Flores Colin 2015, 433–44). In this analysis, roadways are not considered as individual features but instead in terms of the two termini areas located at their ends that are joined by each road. This permits the road and its termini to be conceived of as a minimum unit of analysis, bound together as a single unit. This can help us understand the functions of these constructions as a whole. A terminus area is an immediate zone at the beginning or end of a roadway, regardless of whether it is an open area, a construction, or any other feature. In the case of Yo'okop, using the analysis of the destination contexts, it is observed that not all the roads end in identical contexts. Instead, there is a diversity of terminus areas that are composed of four elements: major plaza, minor plaza, range structures, and pyramidal structures.

The major plazas are those that have several access points, have a larger overall physical space, and therefore would likely have been public in nature with a greater capacity to host people. The smaller plazas would have been

TABLE 8.1 Morphological analysis of sakbe'ob at Yo'okop

Name	Width (m) max/min	Length (m)	Height (m) max/min	Course (°) (both directions)	Volume (m³)	Time period
Sakbe 1	13	718	.50/.70	20/200	5,600.4♦	Terminal Classic
Sakbe 2	10	1,550	.20/4	48/228	32,550•	Terminal Classic
Sakbe 3	7	690	.1/2	160/340	5,071.5•	Terminal Classic
Sakbe 4	4.9/3.2	30	0/.2	106/286	12.15•	Terminal/Early Classic
Sakbe 5	7	250	2*	44/224	1,750•	Terminal Classic

Note: * = Average; ♦ = calculated with a height of 0.70 m; • = calculated with the average height, all using the minimum distance as reference.

more reduced in capacity, as they consisted of more restricted spaces with controlled entrances that made them more private. The activities conducted here would have been more intimate in nature, as the spaces were reserved for a smaller number of attendees. They were perhaps only accessible for religious and/or political leaders or for a kin group (G. Andrews 1977, 37–38; Gendrop 2007, 162; Hammond 1982, 242; Inomata 2006b, 192–95; Parmington 2011, 13; Wagner, Box, and Kline Morehead 2013, 5–7).

Range structures are constructions that have a rectangular shape and differ from the most common housing platforms because of the height of the platforms on which they are placed. Well-cut stones were used in their constructions and they had, in most cases, a frontal stairway (Liendo 2002, 76; Montmollin 1989, 51). This type of construction was generally composed of rows of contiguous rooms placed "in a series" with different arrangements to access each room (G. Andrews 1977, 43–46; Harrison 2000, 185–86, 2001b; Parmington 2011, 10–12). Range structures are usually located in civic-religious areas, so it has been assumed that they were the headquarters of the elites or had civic-administrative functions, although it is likely that they did not have permanent residential functions (Liendo 2002, 76; Montmollin 1989, 51).

Pyramidal structures are buildings that had a conical shape, that is, a very wide base and a smaller summit, which might have been crowned by a temple. These constructions can be formed by one or several staggered levels and have a quadrangular, rounded, circular, or compound base (Gendrop 2007, 160, 197). The temple at the top is often part of the same construction project, although sometimes there are modifications or later constructions.

In any case, it is common that these buildings are called pyramid-temples, since they are part of the same complex (G. Andrews 1977, 39–43). Generally, within sites, the pyramidal temples are the tallest constructions or those with the greatest volume, and it has been presumed that their functions are religious, for the worship of gods or ancestors, or they are funerary mausoleums for the main rulers of the sites (Harrison 2001a, 226; Parmington 2011, 11–12; Webster 1998, 36). The summit temples are generally small and may have one or more rooms, which generally offer limited access. Some contain smaller shrines or sanctuaries, where only one or two persons could have entered at the same time (G. Andrews 1977, 39–46). That is why it is assumed that these pyramidal temples had a private character, reserved only for the leaders or the ritual specialists and those participating in the ceremonies that were performed in these precincts (Schele and Mathews 1998, 29).

There are different combinations of these four types of structures and spaces in the terminus areas of Yo'okop's roadways. For example, Sakbe 1 and Sakbe 3 form the first destination context, which includes a larger plaza with several access points, within which the largest constructions of the site are located. At the other end, there is a smaller plaza with one range structure, which, although not aligned with the roadway, possesses the greatest dimensions of the group. Additionally, these range structures do not have their front facing the sakbe but instead are aligned in another direction (figure 8.3).

The second destination context identified for the Yo'okop causeways includes Sakbe 2 and Sakbe 5, which have pyramidal structures at their southwestern end, while the northeastern terminus is a minor plaza with a pyramidal structure. In addition, another trait they possess is that one of the pyramidal structures is oriented with its front toward the sakbe, while the construction at the other end faces another direction (opposite or lateral, relative to the sakbe). Furthermore, at its northeastern terminus, the two contiguous sakbe'ob arrive directly at (or within a few meters of) the pyramidal structure, without an intermediate plaza between both constructions, while at the other end there is a minor plaza of minor dimensions. Another similarity shared by the terminus areas of these roadways is that one of the pyramidal structures exceeds 10 m in height, while those at the other end are smaller (see figure 8.3).

Only Sakbe 4 corresponds with the last group of destination contexts of the Yo'okop roadways. However, because this road seems to have been left

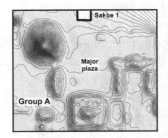
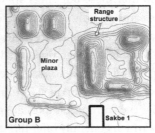

**Destination context 1
Sakbe 1, termini areas**

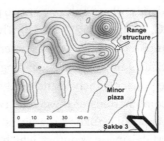
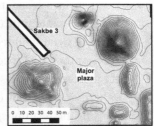

**Destination context 1
Sakbe 3, termini areas**

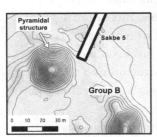
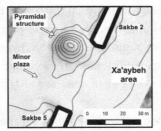
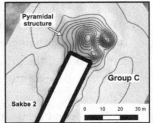

**Destination context 2
Sakbe 2 and 5, termini areas**

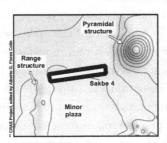

**Destination context 3
Sakbe 4, termini areas**

1 m contour interval

FIGURE 8.3 Types of destination contexts of the sakbe'ob at Yo'okop (created by Alberto G. Flores Colin).

unfinished, in addition to its short length (barely 30 m), its analysis is more problematic than the rest of the causeways. The roadway links a minor plaza with a range structure at one end and another area that includes a pyramidal structure with no plaza between the two ends. In addition, this type of context shows that the range structures and plazas are not aligned with the roadway but that the course of the road was designed to touch the sides of these features. Thus, we propose that these types of destination context combinations are related to the function of the terminus areas as well as to the groups that are linked at a larger scale. Each type of destination context must have involved different activities, directly related to each type of terminus area.

In the case of the first destination context (Sakbe 1 and 3), which is made up of the sakbe'ob that led from a larger plaza to a minor plaza with a range structure, it is likely that they had a more public function, perhaps related to activities such as trade, ceremonies, religious festivities, and other events that involved a multitude of people; this relates to the larger constructions and larger open spaces at the site (G. Andrews 1977, 37; Gendrop 2007, 162; Inomata 2006a; 2006b, 192–95; Parmington 2011, 13; Wagner, Box, and Kline Morehead 2013, 5–7). At the other extreme, the minor plazas had the same type of functions as the larger squares, although with a less public character since, due to their size, they allowed a smaller number of participants (G. Andrews 1977, 37–38; Arancón García 1992, 32; Gendrop 2007, 157; Hammond 1982, 242). In the case of Sakbe 1, the northern terminus is both the minor plaza and the acropolis; the minor plaza very much looks like what could be construed as a market area (King 2015).

As range structures have been interpreted as the seats of political power or constructions where administrative matters were carried out (Harrison 2000, 185; 2001b; Liendo 2002, 76; Montmollin 1989, 51), the minor plazas with the range structures would have been related to elite administrative/residential activities, while the major plazas would be associated with a religious/ceremonial/economic function. In addition to the population in general, the persons involved in the activities related to these spaces would have been the local leaders and/or elites who resided and/or performed administrative tasks in the smaller plazas with range structures.

As for the examples of the second destination context, exemplified by Yo'okop's Sakbe 2 and Sakbe 5, formed by a minor plaza with a pyramidal structure connected directly to another pyramidal structure, it can be inferred that the roads played host to activities related to religious cults since that was the general function of the temples built on top of the pyramids (G. Andrews 1977, 39–46; Gendrop 2007, 160, 197; Parmington 2011, 11–12). Additionally, many of the temples were mausoleums where important persons were buried and potentially remembered and revered through these buildings (Harrison 2001a, 226; McAnany 1995, 22–26; 1998; Schele and Mathews 1998; Webster 1998, 36).

Therefore, if this was the case, in this type of destination context the roadways would have linked areas with strictly religious functions, related to the pyramidal constructions; this differed from the roads of the previous destination context, which were related to wider spaces and more public use. The number of people who could have had access to these pyramidal constructions would have been very low. At the other end of this context type, there was a smaller square; it would have had a less public or semipublic nature since these spaces had a lower capacity to contain the attendees. This was unlike what would have happened in the previous context, where the larger squares could have accommodated a large number of people. Using this same argument, with the other extreme of this type of context, where only a pyramidal structure would be found, access would have been more restricted since the roads end directly in these constructions. It is evident that not all the pedestrians near the roadway would have access to the top of the temple-pyramids.

The last type of context, the destination context formed by Sakbe 4, composed of a square with a range structure connected to a pyramidal structure, would have had a semipublic character (minor plaza with range structure) linked to a private one (pyramidal structure). Likewise, the functions of these spaces and constructions, the range structure with the minor plaza, could have included elite civic/administrative functions, while the pyramidal structure must have had a religious function. If this was the case, the function of this type of context was related to the political and religious spheres at the same time. Table 8.2 summarizes some characteristics of the destination contexts, such as their accessibility and their possible functions.

In sum, based on the morphological analysis and the type of destination contexts, it can be assumed that the roadways together with their terminus areas had specific and differentiated functions. In addition to linking spaces in which different activities took place, the roads physically and symbolically connected these places. In the following sections, we will discuss how the

TABLE 8.2 Destination contexts of Yo'okop's Sakbe'ob

Type of destination context	Accessibility	Possible function	Causeways
Major plaza connecting a minor plaza with a range structure	Public-semipublic	Political	Sakbe 1 Sakbe 3
Pyramidal structure connecting a minor plaza with a pyramidal structure	Private-semipublic	Religious	Sakbe 2 Sakbe 5
Minor plaza with a range structure connecting a pyramidal structure	Semipublic-private	Political-religious	Sakbe 4

roadways, with their possible differentiated functions, were used by the elites of the group as well as the consequences and effects that they caused in other segments of society.

Sakbe'ob for Elites at Yo'okop

From the viewpoint of an archaeologist analyzing the routes of causeways on maps, it seems obvious that their role is that of connection (Shaw 2008). As William Folan (1991, 224) states, they "represent a twenty-four-hour, twelve-month-a-year communication network" for "the transportation of goods and services from near and far thereby providing a near-perfect element to any forest-bound communication network." They provide passage to and between marketplaces (Dahlin and Ardren 2002), water features (Folan 1977; Witschey 1993), palaces (Pollock 1954), and ritual architecture (Kristan-Graham 2001), among other things. Roadways, likewise, served to link and include others politically through boundary maintenance (Kurjack 1977) and referencing other polities in the mimicry of their settlement templates (Ashmore 1991). Functions would have also included the integration of kin and corporate social groups within and between sites (Kristan-Graham 2001), through the activities that may have taken place on and around the roads and the visual and physical ties between the spaces they possessed.

However, all these possible functions were related and/or regulated by the leading groups or the elites of the site, as evidenced by the type of areas and/or structures that the roadways connect: main plazas with monumental architecture, elite groups, range structures, or pyramids. This pattern is observed in many sites, including Calakmul, Caracol, Cobá, Izamal, and

Chichén Itzá, among others (Chase and Chase 2001; Folan 1977; Folan, Marcus, and Miller 1995; Maldonado 1995). In very few cases, Maya roads were built to connect areas of production or with specific resources with habitational buildings, in order to improve the pedestrian surface to provide optimal movement of the population, as is the case with many sidewalks, streets, or avenues in modern cities. One of the few examples of this would be four roads at Calakmul, which connect housing complexes with quarry deposits and lithic workshops as well as two of the largest water features at the site (Folan, Marcus, and Miller 1995, 19; Folan et al. 2001, 56–60). Another similar case would be some roads at the site of Muyil that were built to easily cross flood zones and transport passersby to nearby lagoons (Witschey 1993, 185). Nevertheless, formal causeways do not lead to cultivation areas or link commoner housing areas with each other; instead, roads avoid connecting these types of points other than the fact that, in general, two spaces are connected. Causeways sometimes cut through structures or go over them, ignoring other adjacent constructions and even nearby sites (Flores Colin 2015, 441–42), as in the case of Sakbe 3 at Yo'okop (Shaw 1998).

According to Ross Hassig (1990, 39; 2006, 57), contrary to the logic of today's highways, where layouts favor major destinations, such as cities or other sites of first-rate economic importance, and try to avoid intermediate points that lack relevance, Prehispanic pedestrian paths tend to pass through everything from the largest to the smallest population centers, privileging local traffic. Footpaths provided services for pedestrians, such as supplies, security, accommodation, or a greater exchange of goods. Thus, many Prehispanic pedestrian paths aimed to connect the most possible points in their vicinity as well as link the most active and populated areas within each site. In the case of the sakbe'ob of Yo'okop, based on a morphological analysis, the objective seems to have been the opposite; the intention was to connect only the elite groups, establishing a spatial continuity between them, and, at the same time, to create a hierarchy of spaces and segment the settlement.

For example, Groups A and B, formed mainly by public architecture, were linked to Group D, which seems to have served less of a public and more of a domestic function for elites. According to this interpretation, the difference between Groups A and D would not be hierarchical but would belong to a functional order. In any case, the roadways would have served to demonstrate, physically, the links established by the elites or rulers between the four groups of Yo'okop (Shaw 2008, 160–64).

Sakbe 2 and Sakbe 5 together can be an additional example since they are the result of the symbolic management of the space established by the elite because they lead to isolated pyramidal structures that possibly served as mausoleums for important personages of the site. Furthermore, both constructions pass through areas where there seems to be no immediately adjacent population. In addition, they connect highly restricted spaces, with space for only a small, select group of people (Shaw and Flores Colin 2009, 145–49).

Another feature that indicates the intention of the elites when building roads is accessibility since they lack obvious entrances or exits for pedestrians along their routes, with the exception of a small stairway for Sakbe 3 that seems to be a contemporaneous feature. This lack of access translates to the fact that, practically, the causeways could only be accessed at specific points and not just at any part of the route since, once atop the road, you could not exit or enter midway. This would have meant that the movement of pedestrians was designed to go from one end to the other, leading pedestrians directly from one elite area to the other. There was no direct access from the roadway to other constructions, although these were located in the vicinity.

While some sections of the causeway would have allowed access to features by taking a step higher than normal, sections that are 1–4 m high would have required a ladder, rope, or other perishable construction to enter or exit the road (see figure 8.2). In addition, it is possible that the character or status of the causeways was restricted, or access would have only been allowed on certain occasions, and the lack of formal entrances/exits could be evidence of this. The case of Sakbe 2 (Shaw and Flores Colin 2009, 147) could be a good example of this since its high sides along a good part of its route would have made access impossible. This may be indicated by the presence of a vaulted passage that crosses through/under the road. This element is another feature that suggests access to causeways was not allowed to all passersby, indicating that at least part of the flow of pedestrians had to pass under this construction rather than atop it, even though a set of staircases would have been less challenging to engineer. In sum, the morphology of the sakbe'ob, the type of points they connect, and their accessibility are indicators that the roadways were built specifically to satisfy the will of the elites and leaders instead of having been designed to have a functional character for the commoners.

Another consequence of the existence of the causeways and perhaps not planned by the elites is related to the integration/disintegration that sakbe'ob

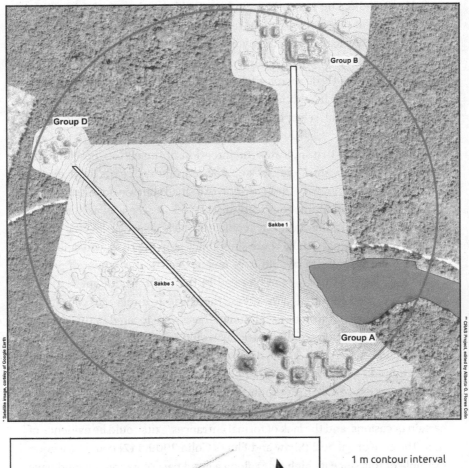
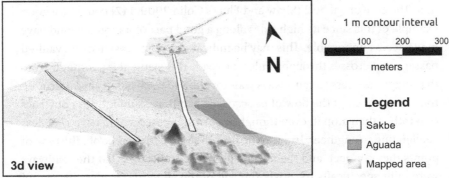

FIGURE 8.4 Area between Sakbe 1 and Sakbe 3 (created by Alberto G. Flores Colin, Justine M. Shaw, and Dave Johnstone).

caused in certain sectors of the settlement. Although the roadways served to bind together the monumental groups of the site, at the same time they created a segmentation in the space outside these groups and within the interior of the settlement, resulting in various distinct sectors, which could have benefited some more than others. For example, the area between Sakbe 1 and Sakbe 3 would have been framed between these constructions, creating an area with greater integration with respect to Groups A, B, and D, while the zones outside both roads would have been separated from this sector by these constructions. Inhabitants would only have direct access to one or two groups and not to the three (figure 8.4). This arrangement could have resulted in a situation in which this area had a more central and privileged character; this is reflected in that this is one of the parts of the site where most vaulted structures have been registered. It is also more nucleated, while outside this zone the settlement is more dispersed.

In contrast, the presence of Sakbe 2 and Sakbe 5 would have separated the northeast and northwest parts of the site, making the transit from one to another more difficult or lengthy (unless one was able to cross over the causeway or through the vaulted passage). This would have conditioned the movement from north to south and vice versa. If this was so, the northern part of the site would have been divided, perhaps creating social differences in the inhabitants of both areas (figure 8.5). In non-systematic surveys to the east and west of Sakbe 2 and Sakbe 5, the presence of structures or foundations of structures has not been evidenced near the roads (Flores Colin 2015, 371–76), so it is thought that there were no inhabitants in these parts of the site. If this was the case, perhaps the presence of these two roads was inhibiting the construction of buildings in this section since it would have been difficult to go from one side to another without making a detour of several hundred meters. This was the case even during the Terminal Classic, a period when the site grew to the east and west of the area between Groups A, B, and D, reaching its maximum extent.

In addition to this and considering that all the roads were built in the Terminal Classic, they likely represent a project of urbanization of the site created by the elites of this period. Contrary to modern urbanization projects that at least take the needs and wants of the populace into account to some degree, this was probably the result of a more specialized and stratified society that manipulated the distinction of spaces to accentuate elite privileges in front of the rest of the group. In this sense, the construction of all

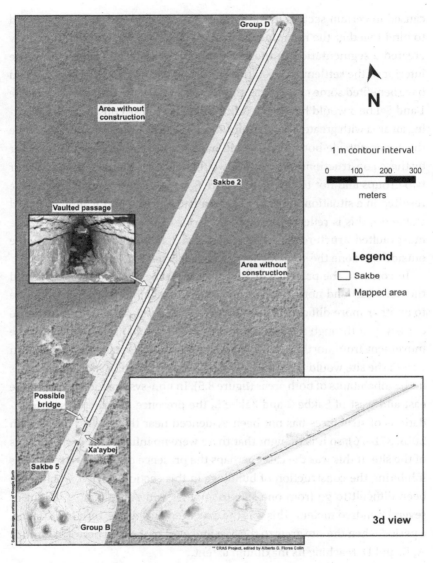

FIGURE 8.5 Plan of Yo'okop's Sakbe 2 and Sakbe 5 (created by Alberto G. Flores Colin, Justine M. Shaw, and Dave Johnstone).

the roads in this short period would have been the result of a consolidation of power by elites applied to the built space of the site.

In sum, from the point of view of the elites, the roads represented a form of organization of the space, a way to express their hierarchy and reinforce symbols of control and power over the population. It bound together the elite architecture and its privileged occupants, providing a means for a limited number of people to traverse space atop wide, elevated walkways. However, this story was not experienced in the same way for all sectors of Yo'okop's society.

Sakbe'ob for Commoners at Yo'okop

From the point of view of the commoners, the roads of Yo'okop would have had a series of very different connotations. Those able to compel laborers to create these monumental features, built at tremendous labor and material costs, likely envisioned many of the previously discussed integrative outcomes of the construction projects. Yet it is important to remember that the vast majority of the inhabitants of Yo'okop were not the elites who planned the roadways and most benefited from their existence. Neither were they archaeologists, observing the clear and obvious ties created through intersite and intrasite causeways through maps and aerial images. Instead, on a day-to-day level, the experience of living around monumental roads as a commoner may have been a negative one that called for mitigation in some cases.

One of the first ways that commoners would have been actively impacted by causeways was during their construction, work that was likely accomplished by them. The divisions within Yo'okop's unfinished Sakbe 4 imply that the work to build even this relatively short roadway was divided in some way, with different social groups being responsible for building particular segments. This work to quarry, transport, build, and then maintain the roads could have been compensated or uncompensated, voluntary or forced. However, historic and ethnographic sources indicate that labor for infrastructure construction and other community projects was commonly obtained through obligatory fagina labor (Halperin 1975; Re Cruz 1996; Richmond 2015; Rugeley 1996). Forced labor projects regularly included both the construction and maintenance of roads, with only individuals who lived in frontier zones or in privileged social or economic positions able to escape up to six months of annual service (Richmond 2015, 50, 101). The potentially burdensome fagina obligation was a significant factor in maintaining support in Cruzob (followers of the "talking cross") communities for the prolonged Caste War (Richmond 2015, 111). More generally, the fagina was resented in that it served as a mechanism to prevent upward socioeconomic mobility, giving peasants substantially less time to devote to their milpas (slash-and-burn agricultural fields) or other economically important work (Re Cruz

1996, 94), yet was commonly required to be considered a village citizen and retain associated benefits (Re Cruz 1996, 88; Redfield and Villa Rojas [1934] 1962, 78–79). If the construction of Yo'okop's causeways was mandated in a similar manner, the imposition of the major Terminal Classic building program would have been a significant burden for commoners. Sakbe 4's unfinished condition may indicate that commoners had reached their limits, leaving the zone they inhabited subject to control or rebellion. Alternately, failure to complete the road could merely mean that conditions had deteriorated to such a degree that those in charge of the roadway's construction had to prioritize other concerns, like the erection of a set of very late, hastily built fortifications found in the southwestern part of Group B.

Once a causeway was constructed, it may be that as ritual space (Palka 2014), sakbe'ob were off-limits to the very commoners who built them, during processions (Inomata and Coben 2006; Sanchez 2007; Shaw 2008; Tozzer 1941) or potentially at all times. Elites demonstrated their power publicly in their ability to organize and take part in processions limited to privileged individuals (Sanchez 2007, 42), literally looking down on those who built the roads and lived in the neighborhoods bisected by them. Extending rituals in the form of processions could have simultaneously created a sense of *communitas* (Morton 2012, 142; Turner 1966), while reinforcing the unequal roles and power structure of the society. Expending so much time and energy to build a reminder of the impotence inherent in commoner status may have been resented by those at the bottom of the social hierarchy.

In considering sakbe'ob, particularly monumental causeways like those of Yo'okop, it is also important to think about them not just as extended, potentially sacred ritual spaces but also as roads. A good deal of study has taken place on the impact of modern roads, particularly highways, on nearby residents. While issues such as noise and air pollution produced by vehicles are not relevant, a number of other areas of concern are worth considering when thinking about what it might have been like to live in a neighborhood bisected by a sakbe. Karst Geurs, Wouter Boon, and Bert Van Wee (2009) define the social impacts of transport as "changes in transport sources that (might) positively or negatively influence the preferences, well-being, behaviour or perception of individuals, groups, social categories and society in general (in the future)." They and others (e.g., Markovich and Lucas 2011) stress the need to look at not only environmental and economic impacts—emphasized by many transport researchers today—but also the social impacts of roadways. Although causeways lacked motorized vehicles, the construction of a monumental causeway may have included the social impacts of stress incurred in anticipating what the impact of the road will be for those immediately adjacent, severance/social cohesion, barriers and diversions, forced relocation, visual quality, and an elevated noise level and nuisance factors (Markovich and Lucas 2011, 8–9).

Prior to the actual building of a sakbe, it is likely that those whose land and preexisting constructions lay in or near its path had some knowledge about what would take place but not details about what the exact course, appearance, or impact would be. Whether or not they agreed with the plan, the straight course of the causeways implies that something like eminent domain (Reynolds 2010) or outright land seizure was used to maintain the course desired by those in command. Such powerlessness, especially with uncertain outcomes, could have potentially been quite stressful. Even in modern societies where public information meetings to disclose plans are held, some residents opposed to all or parts of a potential plan report becoming increasingly stressed with expectations of how their lives might be impacted (Hamersma et al. 2017).

When a sakbe was put through a residential area and cultural practices and/or the physical characteristics of the road created a barrier that had to be circumnavigated, community or social severance could have resulted (Foley et al. 2017; James, Millington, and Tomlinson 2005, 24; Jones and Lucas 2012; Markovich and Lucas 2011, 27–28). While such a barrier may be real or perceived, it could have resulted in a lower quality of life as former neighbors were less able to interact, share resources, or engage in group labor activities. At the very least, residents were forced to adapt to the barrier effect by shifting those with whom they had their most regular interactions, potentially redefining what they considered to be their neighborhood to include a larger territory on their side of the barrier (Egan et al. 2003, 1466). The inclusion of the arched passage in Yo'okop's Sakbe 2, the steps along Sakbe 3, and the presence of steps along roads at other sites (including the Ichmul–Xquerol sakbe in the CRAS study area and the sakbe'ob at Dzibilchaltun; see E. Andrews and E. Andrews 1980) may have been attempts to mitigate the degree to which roadways obstruct pedestrian flow. However, at Yo'okop, the small set of steps on one causeway, the arched passage, and the gap that may represent a perishable "bridge" are the only known mitigation measures, meaning that following the completion of the causeways, large swaths of the site became cut off from easy access to each other. This physical blockade would have been felt along the portions of Sakbe 2, Sakbe 3, and Sakbe 5 that were elevated a meter or more. Sakbe 1 could have been physically crossed as its height was only that of a tall step, but it is possible that, at least during ritual events, cultural taboos would have prevented this.

Unlike modern highways that can conceivably be planned to go around existing architecture and other culturally important features, a key component of environmental impact studies required by the National Historic Preservation Act (Falk and Andrzejewski 2016) and the National Environmental Policy Act (Bronstein et al. 2005) in the United States, most sakbe'ob, including those of Yo'okop, connect two locations in a straight line. It is quite possible that residences and other key features may have been built over, forcing inhabitants to relocate (Herring 2012). This impact would have been potentially less common for Sakbe 1 and Sakbe 3, as portions of each pass through zones with deeper soils with little construction, potentially reserved for agriculture. At the same time, those who used the land to grow food would have still lost valuable territory, permanently diminishing the quantity of food that they could produce. This would have been felt to a greater degree if inhabitants were engaged in shifting agriculture that required fields to be left fallow for years. By the time the causeways were built in the Terminal Classic, if land were given in compensation for what was lost, available territory may have been quite some distance from the site core. Modern governments that use eminent domain often find themselves criticized by both affected parties and others who resent unilateral intervention (Zuck 2007). Sean-Shong Hwang, Yue Cao, and Juan Xi (2011) point out that there are social, economic, and health impacts for individuals forced to relocate, including adapting to a new place of residence, the act of moving itself, securing a postmigration livelihood, and reduced social networks and social support systems.

Although many may have seen the gleaming white roads as beautiful architecture, it should not be assumed that the "visual quality" (Geurs, Boon, and Van Wee 2009; Markovich and Lucas 2011) created through road construction was seen as an improvement by all. Rather than looking at vegetation or constructions of their choosing, those living adjacent to the causeway would have gazed directly on a stone wall up to 4 m high. Studies of modern, vehicle-lined streets have shown that nearby residents find them to be "visually claustrophobic" (Bayley et al. 2004, 449) and an "aesthetic degradation" (Wright and Curtis 2002, 146).

A final set of consequences when a causeway is built through an inhabited zone include an elevated noise level and increased nuisance factors. While lacking the extreme noise levels of motorized vehicles, activities taking place on the sakbe—potentially including processions and increased foot traffic—would introduce more noise and people who might not otherwise have been present into the affected neighborhood. It may have been similar to the impact of living along a popular parade route, providing excellent access to events but potentially bringing undesirable outsiders and activities (Bryan 2004; Ramirez 1998). The impact of nonlocals, both on the causeway and drawn to events taking place atop the road, would have varied with sociodemographic factors such as gender, economic status, age, and health status (Foley et al. 2017; Jones and Lucas 2012). For some, events would have been a welcome diversion, making adjacency a positive, but others may have felt the need to remain indoors for personal safety or preference as once-private space became public. This would have begun when the sakbe'ob were being built and work crews entered the area but could have become a common, if not constant, issue depending on how the roads were used and who was allowed to travel on them. Once in use, modern transportation infrastructure tends to lead to population growth and redistribution (Kasraian et al. 2016), although it's not clear that those of Yo'okop did this, due to either their relatively late construction date and/or the very different types of "traffic" on them.

Thus, for commoners, the construction, maintenance, and continued presence of sakbe'ob should not be assumed to be a universal positive. Impacts ranged from decreased economic productivity to physical severance and loss of privacy. They were not in a position of power to block the construction, potentially even less empowered than those voicing concerns about highway construction today (e.g., Hamersma et al. 2017). However, at Yo'okop and other Maya sites, causeways were built from the Middle Formative through the Postclassic. This indicates that their overall value, at least for the elites who were able to direct their construction, outweighed the repercussions of any animosity generated among the adjacent inhabitants.

Conclusion

In this chapter, we have shown how the roads could have been seen from at least two perspectives—the elites and the commoners. The morphological analysis of these roads as well as their destination contexts and their accessibility suggest that although these constructions served to tie together certain areas, at the same time they represented a series of barriers that limited the pedestrian interaction and quality of life with the rest of the site and obligated residents into an increased workload to build and maintain the causeways. The response to the query about causeways being links or barriers is multifaceted, dependent on who tells the story. In addition, the causeways created an integration and spatial disintegration of the sites, as exemplified by the axial analysis of Yo'okop, where the inclusion of several areas was privileged and others were excluded, which could have contributed to establishing and accentuating the segmentation of the society.

There is still much to know about the causeways of Yo'okop as well as this settlement in general; however, we can agree that the presence of the sakbe'ob did not mean the same for all sectors of society. The study of the causeways from these perspectives helps us better understand that the inhabitants of a site and their lived experiences cannot be characterized as homogeneous. There was a diversity within them, and the monumental constructions and the physical modification of the landscape benefited or impacted residents asymmetrically, creating at least two tales from one city. In short, just as the imposition of a modern highway may elicit a range of positive and negative reactions from stakeholders, it should be understood that the construction, use, and evolution of sakbe'ob would have been received and experienced by the inhabitants of Yo'okop and other sites in varied ways based on their social status, spatial location, economic privilege, social connections, personality, gender, age, and other factors.

Works Cited

Abrams, Elliot M. 1994. *How the Maya Built Their World: Energetics and Ancient Architecture*. Austin: University of Texas Press.

Abrams, Elliot M., and Thomas W. Bolland. 1999. "Architectural Energetics, Ancient Monuments, and Operations Management." *Journal of Archaeological Method and Theory* 6 (4): 263–91.

Andrews, E. Wyllys, IV, and E. Wyllys Andrews V. 1980. *Excavations at Dzibilchaltun, Yucatan, Mexico*. Middle American Research Institute 48. New Orleans: Tulane University.

Andrews, George F. 1977. *Maya Cities: Placemaking and Urbanization*. Norman: University of Oklahoma Press.

Arancón García, Ricardo. 1992. "La plaza generadora del espacio urbano mesoamericano." *Cuadernos de Arquitectura Mesoamericana* 16 (17):29–40.

Ashmore, Wendy. 1991. "Site-Planning Principles and Concepts of Directionality Among the Ancient Maya." *Latin American Antiquity* 2 (3): 199–226.

Bayley, Mariana, Barry Curtis, Ken Lupton, and Chris Wright. 2004. "Vehicle Aesthetics and Their Impact on the Pedestrian Environment." *Transportation Research Part D: Transport and Environment* 9 (6): 437–50.

Bronstein, Daniel, Dinah Baer, Bryan Hobson, Joseph Dimento, and Sanjay Narayan. 2005. "National Environmental Policy Act at 35." *Science* 307 (5710): 674.

Bryan, Dominic. 2004. "Parading Protestants and Consenting Catholics in Northern Ireland: Communal Conflict, Contested Public Space, and Group Rights." *Chicago Journal of International Law* 5 (1): 233–50.

Chase, Arlen F., and Diane Z. Chase. 2001. "Ancient Maya Causeways and Site Organization at Caracol, Belize." *Ancient Mesoamerica* 12 (2): 273–81.

Cobos, Rafael, and Terance L. Winemiller. 2001. "The Late and Terminal Classic-Period Causeway Systems of Chichen Itza, Yucatan, Mexico." *Ancient Mesoamerica* 12 (2): 283–92.

Dahlin, Bruce, and Traci Ardren. 2002. "Modes of Exchange and Regional Patterns: Chunchucmil, Yucatan." In *Ancient Maya Political Economies*, edited by Marilyn A. Masson and David A. Freidel, 249–84. Walnut Creek, Calif.: AltaMira Press.

Egan, Matt, Mark Petticrew, David Ogilvie, and Val Hamilton. 2003. "New Roads and Human Health: A Systematic Review." *American Journal of Public Health* 93 (9): 1463–71.

Falk, Cynthia, and Anna Andrzejewski. 2016. "Peopling Preservation: A Forum in Honor of the Fiftieth Anniversary of the National Historic Preservation Act of 1966." *Buildings & Landscapes* 23 (2): 1–5.

Flores Colin, Alberto G. 2010. "Bajo el follaje del olvido: Periferías y nuevos sitios en los ejidos de Sacalaca y Saban." In *Reporte Final del Proyecto de Reconocimiento Arqueológico de la Región de Cochuah, Temporada 2010*, edited by Justine M. Shaw, 262–78. Eureka, Calif.: College of the Redwoods.

Flores Colin, Alberto G. 2015. "Antiguas calzadas mayas: Estudio comparativo de los Sacbeob de Ichmul, San Felipe y Yo'okop, tres sitios de la Región de Cochuah." BA thesis, Escuela Nacional de Antropología e Historia, Mexico City.

Flores Colin, Alberto G. 2019. "Al final del camino: Movilidad y poder en torno al Sacbe 1 de San Felipe, Quintana Roo." PhD diss., Universidad Autónoma de Yucatán.

Folan, William. 1977. "El Sacbé Coba-Ixil: Un camino maya del pasado." *Nueva Antropología* 2 (6): 30–42.

Folan, William. 1991. "Sacbes of the Northern Maya." In *Ancient Road Networks and Settlement Hierarchies in the New World*, edited by Charles D. Trombold, 222–29. Cambridge: Cambridge University Press.

Folan, William J., Laraine A. Fletcher, Hau Jacinto May, and Lynda Florey Folan. 2001. *Las ruinas de Calakmul, Campeche, México: Un lugar central y su paisaje cultural*. Mexico City: Centro de Investigaciones Históricas y Sociales, Universidad Autónoma de Campeche.

Folan, William J., Armando Anaya Hernandez, Ellen R. Kintz, Laraine A. Fletcher, Raymundo González Heredia, Jacinto May Hau, and Nicolas Caamal Canche. 2009. "Coba, Quintana Roo, Mexico: A Recent Analysis of the Social, Economic, and Political Organization of a Major Maya Urban Center." *Ancient Mesoamerica* 20 (1): 59–70.

Folan, William J., Joyce Marcus, and W. Frank Miller. 1995. "Verification of a Maya Settlement Model Through Remote Sensing." *Cambridge Archaeological Journal* 5 (2): 277–83. https://doi.org/10.1017/S0959774300015067.

Foley, Louise, Richard Prins, Fiona Crawford, David Humphreys, Richard Mitchell, Shannon Sahlqvist, Hilary Thomson, and David Ogilvie. 2017. "Effects of Living near an Urban Motorway on the Wellbeing of Local Residents in Deprived Areas: Natural Experimental study." *PLoS One* 12 (4): E0174882.

Gendrop, Paul. 2007. *Diccionario de arquitectura mesoamericana.* Mexico City: Editorial TRILLAS.

Geurs, Karst, Wouter Boon, and Bert Van Wee. 2009. "Social Impacts of Transport: Literature Review and the State of the Practice of Transport Appraisal in the Netherlands and the United Kingdom." *Transport Reviews* 29 (1): 69–90.

González, Tatiana Loya, and Travis W. Stanton. 2013. "Impacts of Politics on Material Culture: Evaluating the Yaxuna-Coba Sacbe." *Ancient Mesoamerica* 24 (1): 25–42.

Halperin, Rhoda. 1975. "Administered Land and Labor: A Case for Mexican Political Economy." PhD diss., Brandeis University, Waltham, Mass.

Hamersma, Marije, Eva Heinen, Taede Tillema, and Jos Arts. 2017. "The Development of Highway Nuisance Perception: Experiences of Residents Along the Southern Ring Road in Groningen, The Netherlands." *Land Use Policy* 61 (February): 553–63.

Hammond, Norman. 1982. *Ancient Maya Civilization.* New Brunswick, N.J.: Rutgers University Press.

Harrison, Peter D. 2000. *The Lords of Tikal: Rulers of an Ancient Maya City.* New York: Thames & Hudson.

Harrison, Peter D. 2001a. "La arquitectura maya en Tikal, Guatemala." In *Los Mayas: Una civilización milenaria,* edited by Nikolai Grube, 218–31. Bergamo, Italy: Könemann.

Harrison, Peter D. 2001b. "Thrones and Throne Structures in the Central Acropolis of Tikal as an Expression of the Royal Court." In *Royal Courts of the Ancient Maya,* vol. 2, *Data and Case Studies,* edited by Takeshi Inomata and Stephen D. Houston, 74–101. New York: Westview Press.

Hassig, Ross. 1990. *Comercio, tributo y transportes: La economía política en el Valle de México en el siglo XVI.* Mexico City: Alianza Editorial Mexicana.

Hassig, Ross. 2006. "Rutas y caminos de los Mexicas." *Arqueología Mexicana,* no. 81: 54–59.

Herring, Neill. 2012. "Red State Irony: Property Rights Enlisted in Class Struggle for the Environment." *Monthly Review* 63 (11): 49–57.

Hutson, Scott R., and Jacob A. Welch. 2014. "Sacred Landscapes and Building Practices at Uci, Kancab, and Ucanha, Yucatan, Mexico." *Ancient Mesoamerica* 25 (2): 421–39.

Hwang, Sean-Shong, Yue Cao, and Juan Xi. 2011. "The Short-Term Impact of Involuntary Migration in China's Three Gorges: A Prospective Study." *Social Indicators Research* 101 (1): 73–92.

Inomata, Takeshi. 2006a. "Plazas, Performers, and Spectators: Political Theaters of the Classic Maya." *Current Anthropology* 47 (5): 805–42.

Inomata, Takeshi. 2006b. "Politics and Theatricality in Mayan Society." In *Archaeology of Performance: Theaters of Power, Community, and Politics*, edited by Takeshi Inomata and Lawrence S. Coben, 187–221. Lanham, Md.: AltaMira Press.

Inomata, Takeshi, and Lawrence S. Coben. 2006. *Archaeology of Performance: Theaters of Power, Community, and Politics*. Archaeology in Society Series. Lanham, Md.: AltaMira Press.

James, Emma, Anya Millington, and Paul Tomlinson. 2005. *Understanding Community Severance*. Pt. I, *Views of Practitioners and Communities*. Wokingham: Transport Research Laboratory.

Jones, Peter, and Karen Lucas. 2012. "The Social Consequences of Transport Decision-Making: Clarifying Concepts, Synthesizing Knowledge and Assessing Implications." *Journal of Transport Geography* 21 (March): 4–16.

Kasraian, Dena, Kees Maat, Dominic Stead, and Bert Van Wee. 2016. "Long-Term Impacts of Transport Infrastructure Networks on Land-Use Change: An International Review of Empirical Studies." *Transport Reviews* 36 (6): 772–92.

King, Eleanor M., ed. 2015. *The Ancient Maya Marketplace: The Archaeology of Transient Space*. Tucson: University of Arizona Press.

Kristan-Graham, Cynthia. 2001. "A Sense of Place at Chichén Itzá." In *Landscape and Power in Ancient Mesoamerica*, edited by Rex Koontz, Kathryn Reese-Taylor, and Annabeth Headrick, 317–69. Boulder, Colo.: Westview Press.

Kurjack, Edward. 1977. "Sacbeob: Parentesco y desarrollo del estado maya." In *XV Mesa Redonda*, vol. 1, *Mesoamérica y áreas circunvecinas*, 217–30. Guanajuato, Mexico: Sociedad Mexicana de Antropología.

Liendo, Stuardo Rodrigo. 2002. *La organización de la producción agrícola en un centro maya del clásico: Patrón de asentamiento en la región de Palenque, Chiapas, México*. Translated by Rodríguez Concepción Obregón. Mexico City: Instituto Nacional de Antropología e Historia / University of Pittsburgh.

Maldonado Cárdenas, Rubén. 1995. "Los sistemas de caminos del Norte de Yucatán." In *Seis ensayos sobre antiguos patrones de asentamiento en el área Maya*, edited by Vargas Pacheco Ernesto, 68–92. Mexico City: Instituto de Investigaciones Antropológicas, Universidad Nacional Autónoma de México.

Markovich, Julia, and Karen Lucas. 2011. "The Social and Distributional Impacts of Transport: A Literature Review." Working Paper no. 1055. Transport Studies Unit, School of Geography and the Environment, University of Oxford.

Mason, Gregory. 1926. "Explorers Start for Maya Jungle." *New York Times*, March 7, 27.

McAnany, Patricia A. 1995. *Living with the Ancestors: Kinship and Kingship in Ancient Maya Society*. Austin: University of Texas Press.

McAnany, Patricia A. 1998. "Ancestors and the Classic Maya Built Environment." In *Function and Meaning in Classic Maya Architecture*, edited by Stephen D.

Houston, 271–98. Washington, D.C.: Dumbarton Oaks Research Library and Collection.

Montmollin, Olivier de. 1989. *The Archaeology of Political Structure: Settlement Analysis in a Classic Maya Polity.* Cambridge: Cambridge University Press.

Morton, Shawn G. 2012. "Ritual Procession and the Creation of Civitas Among the Ancient Maya: A Case Study from Naachtun, Guatemala." *Canadian Journal of Archaeology* 36 (1): 141–65.

Palka, Joel W. 2014. *Maya Pilgrimage to Ritual Landscape: Insights from Archaeology, History, and Ethnography.* Archaeologies of Landscape in the Americas Series. Albuquerque: University of New Mexico Press.

Parmington, Alexander. 2011. *Space and Sculpture in the Classic Maya City.* Cambridge: Cambridge University Press.

Pollock, H. E. D. 1954. "The Southern Terminus of the Principal Sacbe at Mayapan—Group Z-50." *Current Reports* 37:529–49.

Ramirez, Anthony. 1998. "Neighborhood Report: Upper East Side; Let It Rain on Parades, Residents Say." *New York Times*, October 4.

Re Cruz, Alicia. 1996. *The Two Milpas of Chan Kom: Scenarios of a Maya Village Life.* SUNY Series in Anthropology of Work. Albany: State University of New York Press.

Redfield, Robert. 1941. *The Folk Culture of the Yucatan.* Chicago: University of Chicago Press.

Redfield, Robert, and Alfonso Villa Rojas. (1934) 1962. *Chan Kom: A Maya Village.* Chicago: University of Chicago Press.

Reynolds, Susan. 2010. *Before Eminent Domain: Toward a History of Expropriation of Land for the Common Good.* Studies in Legal History. Chapel Hill: University of North Carolina Press.

Richmond, Douglas W. 2015. *Conflict and Carnage in Yucatán: Liberals, the Second Empire, and Maya Revolutionaries, 1855–1876.* Tuscaloosa: University of Alabama Press.

Roys, Ralph L. 1965. *Ritual of the Bacabs.* Civilization of the American Indian Series. Norman: University of Oklahoma Press.

Rugeley, Terry. 1996. *Yucatan's Maya Peasantry and the Origins of the Caste War.* Austin: University of Texas Press.

Sanchez, Julia L. J. 2007. "Procession and Performance: Recreating Ritual Soundscapes Among the Ancient Maya." *World of Music* 49 (2): 35–44.

Schele, Linda, and Peter Mathews. 1998. *The Code of Kings: The Language of Seven Sacred Maya Temples and Tombs.* New York: Simon and Schuster.

Shaw, Justine. 1998. "The Community Settlement Patterns and Residential Architecture of Yaxuná, from A.D. 600–1400." PhD diss., Southern Methodist University, Dallas.

Shaw, Justine. 2008. *White Roads of the Yucatan: Changing Social Landscapes of the Lowland Maya.* Tucson: University of Arizona Press.

Shaw, Justine, ed. 2015. *The Maya of the Cochuah Region: Archaeological and Ethnographic Perspectives on the Northern Lowlands.* Albuquerque: University of New Mexico Press.

Shaw, Justine M., and Alberto G. Flores Colin. 2009. "El sacbe 2 de Yo'okop: Un camino hacia los muertos." In *XIX Encuentro Internacional: Los Investigadores de la Cultura Maya*, 2:137–53. Mexico City: Universidad Autónoma de Campeche.

Shaw, Justine M., Dave Johnstone, and Ruth Krochock. 2000. *Final Report of Proyecto Arqueológico Yo'okop's 2000 Field Season*. Eureka, Calif.: College of the Redwoods.

Strömsvik, Gustav, Harry E. D. Pollock, and Heinrich. Berlin. 1955. *Exploration in Quintana Roo*. Year Book 53, July 1, 1953–June 30, 1954. Washington, D.C.: Carnegie Institution of Washington.

Tourtellot, Gair, and Jeremy A. Sabloff. 1994. "Community Structure at Sayil: A Case Study of Puuc Settlement." In *Hidden Among the Hills: Maya Archaeology of the Northwest Yucatan Peninsula*, edited by Hanns J. Prem, 71–91. Möckmühl, Germany: Von Flemming.

Tourtellot, Gair, Jeremy A. Sabloff, and Kelli Carmean. 1992. "Will the Real Elite Please Stand Up? An Archaeological Assessment of Maya Elite Behavior in the Terminal Classic Period." In *Mesoamerican Elites: An Archaeological Assessment*, edited by Diane Z. Chase and Arlen F. Chase, 80–98. Norman: University of Oklahoma Press.

Tozzer, Alfred M., trans. 1941. *Landa's Relación de las cosas de Yucatán*. Peabody Museum of Archaeology and Ethnology 18. Cambridge, Mass.: Harvard University.

Turner, Victor. 1966. *The Ritual Process: Structure and Anti-Structure*. Lewis Henry Morgan Lectures. Ithaca, N.Y.: Cornell University Press.

Villa Rojas, Alfonso. 1945. *The Maya of East Central Quintana Roo*. Carnegie Institution of Washington Publication 559. Baltimore: Lord Baltimore Press.

Wagner, Logan, Hal Box, and Susan Kline Morehead. 2013. *Ancient Origins of the Mexican Plaza: From Primordial Sea to Public Space*. Austin: University of Texas Press.

Webster, David. 1998. "Classic Maya Architecture." In *Function and Meaning in Classic Maya Architecture*, edited by Stephen D. Houston, 5–47. Washington, D.C.: Dumbarton Oaks Research Library and Collection.

Wilson, Reginald. 1974. "Okop: Antigua Ciudad Maya de Artesanos." *INAH Boletín Epoca* 2 (9): 3–14.

Witschey, Walter Robert Thurmond. 1993. "The Archaeology of Muyil, Quintana Roo, Mexico: A Maya Site on the East Coast of the Yucatan Peninsula." PhD diss., Tulane University, New Orleans.

Wren, Linnea, and Travis Nygard. 2015. "The State of Research in the Cochuah Region of Quintana Roo." In *The Maya of the Cochuah Region: Archaeological and Ethnographic Perspectives on the Northern Lowlands*, edited by Justine M. Shaw, 25–40. Albuquerque: University of New Mexico Press.

Wright, Chris, and Barry Curtis. 2002. "Aesthetics and the Urban Road Environment." *Municipal Engineer* 151 (2): 145–50.

Zuck, John. 2007. "Kelo v. City of New London: Despite the Outcry, the Decision Is Firmly Supported by Precedent—However, Eminent Domain Critics Still Have Gained Ground." *University of Memphis Law Review* 38 (1): 187–230.

CHAPTER 9

Changing Perspectives on Ancient Maya Neighborhoods and Houselots at Xnoha in Northwest Belize

THOMAS H. GUDERJAN, C. COLLEEN HANRATTY,
AND JOSHUA J. KWOKA

In this chapter, we use Light Detection and Radar (LiDAR) data combined with terrestrial verification to show that the Maya at the site of Xnoha in northwestern Belize had large, well-defined neighborhoods that we internally divided into houselots. Houselots were defined by the construction of Linear Stone Boundary Markers (LSBM), contained one or more residential structures, and show clear patterning of prehistoric activities. Primarily because of the vagaries of the archaeological record, scholars of the ancient Maya have given the topics of neighborhoods, households, and land tenure too little attention. Especially in the heavily forested southern Maya lowlands, traditional methods of terrestrial mapping of residential structures have been extremely time-consuming. Compounding this is that the ephemeral nature of many residences means they are often not noted in any survey methodology. Consequently, archaeological evidence for neighborhood and houselot boundaries has generally been a matter of educated guesswork. As a result, higher-level constructs such as Thomas W. Killion's houselot model (1990) have been difficult to empirically test. Similarly, surveys appropriate to define neighborhood boundaries have been rare. Land tenure studies are particularly difficult without significant advances in our understanding of neighborhoods and houselots. However, recent LiDAR surveys that are able to cover large areas have been improving this data deficiency.

Our team has been intensively investigating the ancient Maya of northwest Belize since 1990, focusing broadly on topics as diverse as Maya urban organization (Guderjan 2007) and wetland agricultural systems (Beach et al. 2019). Although the site of Xnoha was located in 1990 (Guderjan 1991), mapping of the central precinct and quadridirectional transects was not conducted until 2002–5 (González 2013; Lohse 2013). Renewed fieldwork began in 2012 (Guderjan et al. 2016) and included a 2016 LiDAR mission that enabled us to identify new features in the central precinct and identify at least four topographically bounded neighborhoods (Guderjan, Kwoka, and Hanratty 2019; Kwoka et al. 2021).

We used recent LiDAR data from Xnoha that show spatial dividers on the landscape to examine the integration of Maya households and neighborhoods into Maya cities. Our 2016 LiDAR survey revealed an extensive network of previously undocumented Linear Stone Boundary Markers.[1] These linear piles of river gravel and clays were carried to the uplands to demarcate houselots and thus inform us of houselot size and function, neighborhoods, and land tenure. Dating the construction of these LSBMs is still uncertain, but ceramics from the excavation of a single associated residential building date to the Late Classic period (AD 600–850; Guderjan, Kwoka, and Hanratty 2019). The inclusion of radiometric dating in future studies will be essential to determining if houselots and associated features (walls, rock piles, etc.) were contemporaneous.

We then compared the neighborhoods of Xnoha with a model we developed at the nearby site of Blue Creek, grounded in Immanuel Wallerstein's World Systems Theory (Guderjan 2007). The Xnoha data enable us to build upon the Blue Creek model and enhance our understanding of Maya houselots and neighborhoods. Additionally, we were aided by data from studies

---

1. The data from this report derive from the July 2016 LiDAR survey flown by the Northwest Belize LiDAR Consortium, which consists of the National Science Foundation (BCS nos. 1550204, 0924501, 0924510, S. Luzzadder-Beach and T. Beach, PIs; CNH no. 1114947, N. Brokaw, PI); the University of Texas College of Liberal Arts; the C. B. Smith Sr. Centennial Chair in US-Mexico Relations; the Beach Geography and the Environment Labs at UT Austin (T. Beach and S. Luzzadder-Beach, directors); the Center for Archaeological and Tropical Studies at UT Austin and the Programme for Belize Archaeological Project (F. Valdez Jr., director); the Center for Social Science Research at the University of Texas at Tyler and the Maya Research Program (T. Guderjan, director); the Institute of Archaeology (Belize); and the National Center for Airborne Laser Mapping at the University of Houston. Protocols for this survey were the standards set by the National Center for Airborne Laser Mapping (NCALM) that have been consistently applied for archaeological surveys in Middle America. Two large blocks were surveyed; the 40 km^2 Xnoha block and the 200 km^2 PfB/MRP block. The information from this report derives from the Xnoha block.

of contemporary houselots from the Yucatec village of Yaxunah (Bascopé and Alcocer Puerto, this volume; Hernández Álvarez, this volume) to better understand prehistoric houselot activities.

Walls as Spatial Dividers Carrying Social Meaning

Walls can serve as functional and/or symbolic barriers as well as convey social structures and emic perceptions of a society's racial or class norms and the fears of those they are attempting to keep out (see Awe and Morton, this volume). State-level polities have long used walls to divide people who are difficult to govern from those who are governable. At the state level, walls can also represent the unifying values and visions of their builders. Other state-level efforts manifest the cultural values and visions of society. For example, the NASA moon effort of the 1960s and 1970s was as much a social centroid and nationalistic symbol as it was a technological achievement. Certainly, the Donald Trump administration hoped that a wall between the United States and Mexico would be symbolic of values that united and motivated its supporters. By contrast, the Ronald Reagan administration sought to remove the Berlin Wall to reunify East and West Germany. Importantly, thinking about public works projects as expressions of nationalism makes us consider the efforts undertaken to build such projects as expressions of social unification. Rather than wonder how so many people were conscripted into building something, we are better off thinking about the strength and importance of the socially shared values that led to the construction of such projects. Wall building for state-level societies also requires the consensus to expend resources and a shared understanding of both the utility and symbolic meaning of the wall.

However, the focus of this chapter is to examine walls at the household level, where their efficacy requires a socially shared understanding of their meaning, of who owns them, who builds them, and whose responsibility it is to maintain them. There must also be a socially shared understanding of the behavioral expectations of those who do not own the walls and associated enclosed spaces. In most U.S. cities, zoning and other legal requirements have wooden property fences facing out and the side with the upright posts as the inside of the owner's side. This codification tells us who is intended to be kept out, who wishes other people were kept out, and whose responsibility it is to maintain the structure that keeps us out. Since many of us who are kept out have similar symbolism at our own homes, we respect the "keep out" symbolism as part of a code of mutual responsibility. Such walls do not need to be functional physical or visual barriers to be effective. Typical six-foot wooden fences are easily scaled. More expensive stone and metal fences are even more easily breached.[2] Many fences are only symbolic and are not visual barriers at all. Instead, they communicate the essentials of "mine" versus "yours" of land tenure. As long as all members of society understand the rules and behave accordingly, the structure of society is inviolate and secure. When someone understands the rules and does not behave accordingly, they are criminalized and punished. Consequently, walls in the archaeological record are artifacts whose meaning is related to how ancient peoples constructed their social space. Walls inform us about the view of the landscape, land tenure, and ownership of their builders.

Jaime J. Awe and Shawn G. Morton (this volume) describe walls at several sites in western Belize that functioned to either surround residential spaces or restrict access to public spaces. While some prehistoric walls at Tikal, Uxmal, and Becan were royally commissioned public projects, others, such as the *albarradas* (walls) of Buena Vista, Cozumel (Batún-Alpuche, this volume), Chunchucmil (Hutson and Welch 2016, 2017), Cobá (Folan, Kintz, and Fletcher 1983; Folan et al. 2009; Stanton et al., this volume), Playa del Carmen (Silva Rhoads and del Carmen Hernández 1991), and Ambergris Caye (Guderjan and Garber 1995), were likely constructed as vernacular architecture to define private property. These houselots have modern analogs in the *solares* (exterior spaces within albarradas) of contemporary communities such as Yaxunah (Bascopé and Alcocer Puerto, this volume; Hernández Álvarez, this volume).

Modeling Maya Cities and Their Neighborhoods

Many of our investigations at the Maya center of Blue Creek have focused on understanding the spatial arrangement of the city and the integration of its neighborhoods (i.e., Guderjan 2007; Guderjan, Baker, and Lichtenstein 2003; Guderjan and Hanratty 2006). Blue Creek is a medium-sized center with a central precinct consisting of two plazas at the top of the 100 m Bravo

---

2. This was demonstrated by the founding director of Belize's Institute of Archaeology at the senior author's former home in San Antonio, Texas.

Escarpment, overlooking the rich agricultural lands below. Royal or high-status elites lived in the central precinct while nonroyal elites lived in the nearby Kin Tan neighborhood (Guderjan and Hanratty 2006). Above the escarpment, there are hilltops covered with the remains of ancient neighborhoods that are separated by high-quality, upland soils most likely used for agriculture. Below the escarpment are expanses of ditched agricultural fields with adjacent residences for lower-status people who likely were the workers in the ditched agricultural fields (Guderjan 2016). Surrounding the central precinct are numerous neighborhoods located on hilltops and topographic rises separated from each other by unoccupied agricultural land.[3] Each neighborhood is unique, although all have a central place or focal node (figure 9.1). Most importantly, the internal stratification and differential access to exotic goods within each component indicate that each had its own internal mode of local leadership and that those modes were not identical across components. It is also important to note that neighborhoods at Blue Creek do not have LSBM's defining houselot boundaries.

In some Blue Creek neighborhoods, such as Kín Tan, local leadership consisted of the authority of multigenerational lineages that controlled large holdings of agricultural lands (Guderjan 2007; Guderjan and Hanratty 2006; Guderjan, Lichtenstein, and Hanratty 2003). Similar power structures probably existed in other Blue Creek neighborhoods such as Nukuch Muul and Rosita. However, such multigenerational lineages do not seem to have existed at Chan Cahal and Sayap Ha, where the existence of neighborhood central places such as shrines indicate that these communities were internally integrated with their own public places and leadership. Leadership and authority seem to have been achieved by individuals during their lifetimes rather than ascribed to a lineage from their ancestors (Guderjan 2007). Thus, there were multiple modes of local leadership in the neighborhoods of Blue Creek. Further, the central precinct straddles the top of the 100 m tall Bravo Escarpment, and the elites who controlled the large, grand, public places of the central precinct also most likely controlled the large agricultural resources available below the escarpment. How can the existence of these apparently conflicting structures of power, legitimacy, and authority be reconciled?

---

3. In various publications, we have referred to neighborhoods as residential groups, residential components, residential communities, and barrios. In all cases at Blue Creek, we are referring to the same entities.

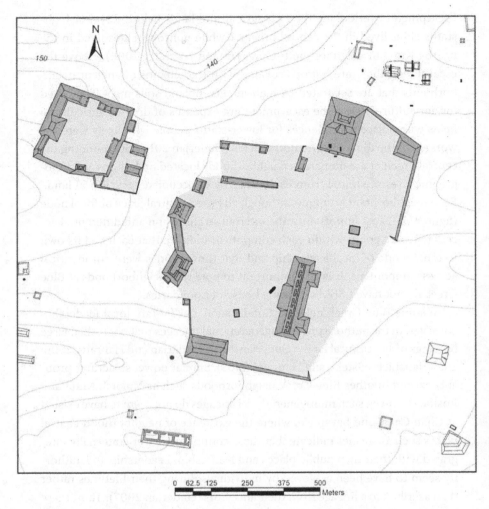

FIGURE 9.1 Map of central precinct of Xnoha (map by Marc Wolf, courtesy of Maya Research Program).

World Systems Theory (WST) is a framework for understanding human interaction and how that interaction leads to the creation and maintenance of power, legitimacy, and authority (Wallerstein 1974). It has helped scholars understand the structures of power, legitimacy, and authority in the contemporary world and in ancient societies (Chase-Dunn and Hall 1991; Peregrine 1991; Peregrine and Feinman 1996). Wallerstein's initial evaluation of core–periphery relations was an argument that there would be permanency in the relationship between the core and the periphery due to their economic interaction. In the ancient Maya world, interlineage relationships were dynamic; for example, the relationship between the nonroyal elites of Kín Tan and the royal elites of the central precinct area was not static. But WST directs us to examine the relationships and interactions among people and institutions. Institutionalized structures of power, legitimacy, and authority, such as the central precinct and Kín Tan, simply could not coexist unless they were mutually supportive of each other. We view interaction among multigenerational lineages as the central cause for those lineages to have become powerful and then to maintain and enhance this power.

For example, when the adult male found buried in Sayap Ha Burial 2 was living, a member of the ruling elite likely gave him the elaborate, carved, and inlaid shells bearing images of scribes and the carved bone "bib-head" that would otherwise evoke royalty that accompanied his grave (Guderjan 2007). This, like the case of the Trobriand trading partner (Malinowski 1922), increased his authority and certainly enhanced his loyalty. However, the enhanced status did not have a multigenerational impact. At least there was no discernable multigenerational impact in any archaeologically visible manner. On the other hand, there were multigenerational impacts at Kín Tan that most likely consisted of numerous interactions between the lineages of Kín Tan and the central precinct (Guderjan and Hanratty 2006).

Thus, it was not simply the authority of the rulers over the commoners that explains the integrity of Blue Creek or the power, legitimacy, and authority of the ruling elite of the core area. Instead, power and authority are derived from the interaction among local leadership within each residential component and the ruling elites of the core area. The archaeological markers of these structures are easily seen. For example, we find complex residences and public sacred spaces within residential components that are larger and more elaborate than others within that neighborhood. Further, we see connectivity between residential components and the core area such as roads.

Neighborhoods at Blue Creek were tethered to the ruling lineages of the central precinct through complexities of political economy and interaction among leaders (Guderjan 2007). If this is true, then they should also exhibit archaeological signatures of this sort of interaction. Despite the general lack of relevant data, several sites do have these patterns. For example, outlying central places that are probably surrounded by unrecorded residential components are architecturally linked to the central precinct. In the Belize Valley at sites such as Cahal Pech, causeways sometimes, but not always, connect such termini groups to the site core (Cheetham 2004). It is not clear whether these ritual buildings are central places for residential components as seen at Blue Creek, but they probably are. Stanton and his colleagues make a similar argument for Cobá in this volume.

Another such case is the large, Classic period site of Dzibanche in southern Quintana Roo, which is situated on an erosional remnant "island" surrounded by a very large bajo and its high-quality soils (Nalda and Balanzario 2005). A causeway leads north from Dzibanche approximately 2 km to a small site, Kinich Na, which consists of a large temple complex surrounded by a group of relatively small, elite residences. Kinich Na was the home of an important lineage that was part of the Dzibanche polity and probably functioned to consolidate Dzibanche's authority over the northern sector of the bajo. Current LiDAR data show these to be parts of a large city rather than discrete settlements.

A related pattern is seen at the Becan-Xpuhuil-Chicanna complex also in southern Quintana Roo, less than 100 km north of Blue Creek. The central precinct of Becan is surrounded by a large moat with five crossings. Only 1 km to the south is Chicanna, a small center with elite residential compounds, and temples and ritual spaces are smaller than those of Becan. Lastly, Xpuhuil, 4 km east of Becan, has compounds of elite residences and a three-towered pyramid. Two towers face east, the direction of the Xpuhuil elite residences, defining the ritual space for Xpuhuil. However, the third tower faces west and has an ornate façade designed to mark the large terminus of the causeway from Becan. While incorporated into larger polities, Kinich Na, Chicanna, and Xpuhuil all have the political authority and economic bases to build large and complex masonry residences and large public monumental architecture. These, like the causeway termini buildings at Baking Pot in Belize, represent central places for components of larger polities and the homes for the lineages that control them. Further, the ruling lineages of the core area are connected to the people of the outlying residential components through social and political ties to the local elite lineages.

At Blue Creek, the same structural and functional interrelationships are seen. Except for U Xulil Beh, each residential component has its central place that often includes a complex lineage residence more prestigious than the rest (Guderjan 2007; Guderjan, Baker, and Lichtenstein 2003). In the cases of Kín Tan, Nukuch Mul, Rosita, Chan Cahal, and Sayap Ha, lineages in each component or community formed relationships through political economies with the ruling lineages of the core area. In the case of U Xulil Beh, it appears that the community was settled late in Blue Creek's history, possibly to exploit additional agricultural resources. Further, we lack evidence for internal stratification, a central place, or a lineage that is regularly articulated with the lineages of the core area. If this model of cities composed of local neighborhoods with leadership maintained by multigenerational interaction with the ruling elites has validity, it should be testable in other situations. We now examine how these principles may be applied to the nearby site of Xnoha.

Testing the Model at Xnoha: Discovery and Description of the Linear Stone Boundary Markers

Recently, aerial LiDAR has revealed a complex of linear stone features bounding houselots at the Maya site of Xnoha (Guderjan, Kwoka, and Hanratty 2019; Guderjan et al. 2016; Guderjan et al. 2020; Kwoka et al. 2021). Xnoha's central precinct includes a large pyramid-plaza complex with a nearby hilltop acropolis complex. Royal Early Classic stucco masks have been found on two buildings. However, the first known constructions at Xnoha were two Late Formative shrines that continued to be used through the Classic period. The central precinct of Xnoha consists of a large, irregularly shaped plaza approximately 150 m southwest-northeast and 100 m southeast-northwest. The east side of the plaza is well defined by a 70 m long-range building, Structure 1, with uncarved stelae on both east and west sides. The south and west sides of the plaza are defined by the pyramidal Structures 2 and 3. The north side of the plaza is marked by Structure 10, the tallest and most complex building.

Approximately 50 m northwest of the plaza is an elevated acropolis complex dominated by the Structure 4 pyramid on its west side. Structure 4 is notable due to the presence of anthropomorphic masks adorning both sides of the frontal staircase. Approximately 100 m east of the plaza is the Eastern Elite Residential Group (EERG), notably the Str. 79 Group, which is anchored symbolically to a somewhat isolated shrine (Structure 77) built in the Late Formative and never modified. In a roughly parallel setting approximately 100 m west of the plaza, the Western Elite Residential Group (WERG) is a

Classic-period elite residential group with another Late Formative shrine (Structure 100), on the south end of the group. Current evidence is that this shrine, too, had not been modified after construction.

Xnoha's central precinct is situated on top of a karstic, erosional remnant hill about 1 km south of the Rio Hondo. On the south, east, and west sides, the remnant gradually slopes down 40 or more meters. On the north side, there is a precipitous cliff. About 1 km to the west is a small, relatively isolated wetland that has not yet been visited. During the rainy season, this overflows to a drainage area immediately north of the central precinct and then drains to the Rio Hondo. These are all normally dry drainages, though some can have heavy energy floods in the rainy season.

Xnoha's location is also the highest point between the Bajo Alacranes and the Bravo Escarpment and represents the largest center between the two. Rainy season water spills from the Bajo Alacranes into the same Rio Hondo drainage. The common usage for this drainage is the Rio Azul or Blue Creek, following the thinking that the Rio Azul of Guatemala, which flows past the same-named site, continues to flow into Belize to become the Mexico–Belize border. The area around Xnoha's central precinct is heavily dissected, leaving large hilltops 20–30 m above the surrounding lowlands. The central precinct is located on one of these hilltops, and four others, very roughly to the north, east, west, and south, are marked by dense Maya occupation (figures 9.2 and 9.3).

FIGURE 9.2 LiDAR surface model of Xnoha, including Northern and Western Neighborhoods (courtesy of Maya Research Program).

FIGURE 9.3 Excavated Linear Stone Boundary Marker (photograph by Thomas Ruhl, courtesy of Maya Research Program).

In July 2016, the Northwest Belize LiDAR Consortium conducted a 39.8 km^2 LiDAR survey of the study region. The resulting data, which were collected with Teledyne Optech's Titan multiwave LiDAR (Fernandez Diaz et al. 2014), were interpolated to produce 50 cm resolution bare-earth terrain models. A digital survey of the LiDAR data was initiated in 2018, using Esri's ArcGIS platform. This process proceeded by creating an inventory of structures and spatially discrete landscape features, such as small reservoirs and cave entrances, using point shapefiles. These were then digitized, along with linear stone features, resulting in a series of polygon and line shapefiles. Identification of archaeological features was facilitated by blending multiple raster visualizations generated with Relief Visualization Toolbox and by use of the Red Relief Image Map (RRIM) technique developed by Tatsuro Chiba, Shin-ichi Kaneta, and Yusuke Suzuki (2008). The RRIM technique can enhance the visibility of small topographic features. For the study loci, ground truthing proceeded by uploading data generated by the digital LiDAR survey to a Trimble Geo 7x Global Navigation Satellite System (GNSS). Data fidelity was assessed along two axes—whether or not structures and archaeological features identified in the digital survey were present, and the degree of match (area, height, etc.) between digitized structures and those surveyed in the field.

We have now documented 83.4 linear km or approximately 41,700 cm of these features (Guderjan, Kwoka, and Hanratty 2019; Kwoka et al. 2021). By comparison, a 100 m tall pyramid with a 100 × 100 m base would have a volume of 30,000 m^3. We have documented approximately 216 ancient structures in the Western Neighborhood, which encompasses 7,300 m^2. If each structure was a residence, the population estimate for the Western Neighborhood could be in the range of 1,200 people, using an estimate of 5.6 persons per residence (e.g., Culbert and Rice 1990). If all four neighborhoods were equally populous and there were a few hundred people in the central precinct as indicated by several years of excavations, there would have been approximately 6,000 persons living in the central 6 km^2 of Xnoha. Importantly, this does not account for "invisible" settlement, which could raise the numbers considerably (e.g., Pyburne 1990, among others). This compares favorably to urban population densities in larger cities like Tikal and Seibal (Culbert et al. 1990; Tourtellot 1990). This density is also well within the range postulated for peri-urban growth zones in highly populated areas of Petén, Guatemala. At present, we have identified 2,409 structures within the 40 km^2 survey block, for a structure density of 60.5/km^2. For comparison, this figure exceeds regional structure density figures for some of the major Classic period (AD 300–850) sites, including El Perú-Waka', Tintal, Uaxactun, Xultun, and El Zotz (Canuto et al. 2018, table 4).

Similar features have been found elsewhere, notably Chunchucmil in northwest Yucatán (Hutson 2016), near Playa del Carmen (Silva Rhodes and del Carmen Hernández 1991), Isla Cozumel (Batún-Alpuche, this volume), and Ambergris Caye (Guderjan and Garber 1995) (see figure 9.1). In each of these cases, the wall structures or albarradas consist of stacked, cut-stone blocks. They can be as low as a few courses or taller than 3 m. Contemporary albarradas at Yaxuná are much taller and present a physical and visual barrier. By contrast, the Xnoha LSDMs are low, rounded, linear piles of small limestone and chert rocks and do not alone present barriers to human transit (figure 9.3). This allows three possible interpretations: (1) they were only symbolic, spatial boundary markers; (2) they may be the remnant component of compound boundaries that incorporated a floral component such as trees or shrubs; or (3) they may be pathways as well as spatial markers. Like Justine M. Shaw and Alberto G. Flores Colin's (this volume) observation that causeways also can become spatial dividers, we will only focus on their function as boundary markers.

A fundamental challenge to the boundary wall interpretation is the muted elevation profile (i.e., 20–50 cm), as they were easily crossed by the authors while conducting fieldwork. Possible explanations for the discrepancy between morphology and function are that they served as foundations for vegetation stands (Becker 2001, 433) or supported pole-and-thatch walls similar to those documented by Laraine A. Fletcher (1983, 94, fig. 6.2) at Cobá in the 1980s. Alternatively, the demarcation of space may have been the primary function rather than the impediment of physical movement. Support for this hypothesis is provided by recent work at Chunchucmil, where linear stone features functioned as pathways and/or boundary markers (Hutson and Magnoni 2017, 39–43). It should be noted that although terraces have a clear agricultural function, they can also serve as expressions of human territoriality by marking space as restricted. Indeed, multifunctionality is a core attribute of linear stone features, and the ancient Maya employed both feature classes to demarcate houselot boundaries.

Solares: What Happens Within the Walls

Yaxunah and its neighbor Chan Kom are traditional Maya villages in the northern part of the Yucatán Peninsula. A family's walled houselot, including a one-room house and activity areas, is controlled by them and publicly perceived to be theirs. Solares are the domain of the women of Yaxunah, while men control more remote fields (Bascopé 2005, 135–37, Bascopé and Alcocer Puerto, this volume; Hernández Álvarez, this volume). Yaxunah solar walls are used to delineate the space between households; however, they are much taller than the Xnoha LSBMs (up to 3 m) and provide a more formidable physical and visual barrier.

In the Western Neighborhood at Xnoha, there are approximately 216 residential houselots, each with a mean enclosed space of 1.8 acres. We view these as ancient solares where most household activities occur. Grace Lloyd Bascopé and Elias Alcocer Puerto (this volume) and Héctor Hernández Álavarez (this volume) tell us that the wide range of household activities would be expected to be spatially patterned. It is likely that similar activities also occurred in Xnoha solares and that there would be a clear spatial pattern to the archaeological evidence for these activities. Interestingly, Xnoha solares are significantly larger than those of Yaxunah, which have a mean size of fewer than 0.5 acres.

To test whether spatial patterning of activities could be ascertained within Xnoha houselots, we selected two cases, AL17 and AL18, for intensive study. In each case, we ground-truthed the LiDAR information, confirming both LSBMs and aboveground prehistoric structures. Test pitting of both structures yielded Early Classic dates. Additionally, we conducted systematic shovel testing to identify distribution patterns of artifact deposition and conducted soil phosphate tests across the ground surface of each houselot. As we expected from the Yaxunah data, both artifact distribution and phosphate levels were highly variable and the distributions were spatially patterned (figures 9.4 and 9.5). These data strongly support the interpretation that the LSBMs demarcated solares or residential houselots as seen in Yaxunah today.

Qualitative soil Pav values were measured for 117 samples obtained from contiguous houselots AL17-2 and AL17-3. Results indicate an overall deficiency in Pav, as 78 percent of samples produced depleted or deficient values (Kwoka, Ruhl, and Eshleman 2018). While no surplus values were recorded for either houselot, AL17-4 had almost double the amount of adequate and sufficient values. Sufficient values were concentrated in three areas, ranging in size from 32 to 375 m^2, located in close proximity (i.e., 2–6 m) to structures. Houselot AL17-3 also had three areas with sufficient Pav values, though they covered much smaller areas of 25–53 m^2. One of these abuts the back of the large residential compound, while the others were located at distances of 10–12 m from the edge of the structure's basal platform. An additional 117 soil samples were collected from the houselot AL18-1 (Kwoka 2019). Survey transects were extended 5–10 m beyond the eastern and northern houselot boundary walls to explore the possibility that these areas were used for refuse disposal (Hutson and Welch 2016). In contrast to the AL17 area, adequate to surplus Pav values were recorded for 59 percent of the samples. Ten areas with sufficient surplus values were identified with areas between 10 and 1,366 m^2. As with houselot AL17-2, high Pav values were recorded for a zone running along the back of two residential struc-

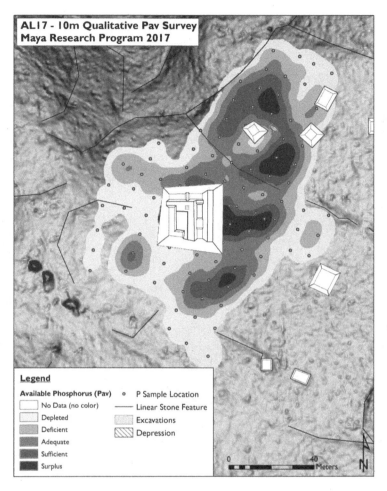

FIGURE 9.4 Map of results of phosphorus survey of AL17 compound, Xnoha (map by Joshua J. Kwoka, courtesy of Maya Research Program).

tures. Other areas with elevated Pav values were located either adjacent to structures or at a distance of 10–18 m.

Neighborhood Cohesion and Wealth Inequality

In addition to residences, neighborhoods may include temples, markets, administrative buildings, and other spaces that function as focal nodes (Hutson 2016, 71; Kintz 1983). Focal nodes promote neighborhood cohesion by serving as arenas of face-to-face interaction (Hutson 2016, 80). Archaeological

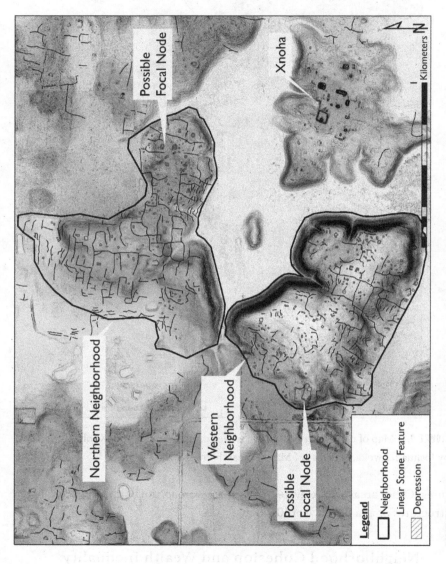

FIGURE 9.5 Image of AL18 showing LSBMs, structures, and phosphate distribution (map by Joshua J. Kwoka, courtesy of Maya Research Program).

(Kintz 1983) and ethnographic (Vogt 1976) data indicate focal nodes need not be centrally located. The neighborhoods at Blue Creek exhibit this characteristic. Focal nodes are places of power that are located differently in each neighborhood (Guderjan 2007, 2013). Scott R. Hutson (2016, 85) suggests that focal node types may be indicative of the mechanisms and degree of neighborhood integration. For example, Jason Yaeger (2000, 2010) has argued that at San Lorenzo, Belize, two elite residences functioned as focal nodes by hosting community feasts. These face-to-face interactions reified neighborhood wealth and status inequalities by displaying disproportionate amounts of exotic goods by the hosts. In contrast, Megan Peuramaki-Brown (2013, 582) suggests that the Buena Vista focal node, which consisted of a nonresidential building and an associated patio, may have strengthened social bonds by serving as a venue for public rituals that facilitated the comingling of community inhabitants.

Both neighborhoods in the Xnoha region contain potential focal nodes in the form of structures or platforms that are substantially larger than the surrounding settlement (see figure 9.1). A houselot within the Northern neighborhood contains two elite patio groups, one of which appears to have an eastern shrine, structures that are often associated with ancestor veneration (McAnany 1995, 102). In the Western neighborhood of Xnoha sits a large two-tiered platform with a surface area of 7,348 m^2. Using the standard estimate of 5.6 inhabitants per structure (Santley 1990; see also Hutson and Welch 2016, 106), the 216 structures of the Western Neighborhood would represent a population of 1,210. As archaeological studies of ancient Maya populations poorly account for both vacant and invisible houses, this figure is likely an underestimation but could also be an overestimation. However, using this figure, the platform exceeds the threshold of 1–3.1 m^2/person necessary to accommodate all neighborhood residents simultaneously (Inomata 2006, 812), with a ratio of 6.07 m^2/person, or 1.99 m^2/person using just the upper tier. Recalling the examples cited in the preceding paragraph, this focal node morphology and function variation could indicate inter-neighborhood differences in social and economic integration.

Houselots and Land Tenure

Classic Maya land tenure is poorly understood (McAnany 1995, 65), with models relying primarily on ethnohistoric and ethnographic data (Collier 1975; Netting 1982, 1993; Restall 1997; Vogt 1976; Wisdom 1940). Within the northern Maya lowlands, it is clear that concepts of restricted land-use rights and inheritance were in place before the Spanish entrada. Ethnohistoric documents contain multiple references to land surveys (McAnany 1995, 84) and titles (Roys 1939, 265; 1943, 37; 1967, 64–65). Joyce Marcus (1982, 254) draws on linguistic evidence to argue for the antiquity of this practice, citing the Yucatec Mayan word *ah ppiz k'aan* for a specialist who measured fields. Perhaps the strongest evidence for private land tenure in the Maya Classic period is provided by the networks of boundary walls that appear to mark houselots, similar to contemporary Maya solares (Batún-Alpuche 2009, this volume; Hutson 2016).

Beginning with William R. Bullard Jr. (1952), comparisons between archaeological houselots and contemporary Maya solares have long been made for Late Classic and Postclassic sites in the northern lowlands and Río Bec region (Dunning 2004; Eaton 1975; Folan, Kintz, and Fletcher 1983; Folan et al. 2009; Freidel and Sabloff 1984; Hutson 2016; Kurjack 1974; Lemonnier and Vannière 2013; Thomas 1974; Turner 1979). If archaeological and contemporary houselot boundary walls were functionally equivalent, then this would demonstrate the existence of a land tenure system based on restricted land use rights. Multiple lines of evidence support this interpretation. Cross-culturally, there is a link between the amount of labor invested in landscape modification and the system of land tenure; large labor inputs are positively correlated with restricted use rights (Adler 1996). The 83.4 linear km of terraces and boundary walls at Xnoha represent a substantial labor investment in the creation and maintenance of the landesque capital (a landscape that serves economic, social, and ritual purposes). Such an investment indicates planned future use, which can only be guaranteed by the presence of a system that restricts the use and transfer rights (Earle 2000, 49). Furthermore, ethnographic studies of Maya peoples (Collier 1975; Netting 1993) have demonstrated an association between intensive agricultural production, land inheritance, and the emergence of private property (Earle 2000, 43). Based on these factors and the preceding discussion of land and wealth, there is strong evidence to suggest that a system of restricted land tenure was in place by at least the Early Classic period. We support Patricia A. McAnany's (1995, 68) view that Classic Maya land tenure likely represented a continuum based on environment and distance to settlement, with use rights becoming less restrictive the further one moved away from intensively cultivated infield houselots.

Conclusion

The 2016 LiDAR survey of Xnoha provides new data that enable us to test models of Maya city organization developed elsewhere. Models grounded in WST that were developed from Blue Creek and settlement data from other Maya cities lead us to understand that Maya cities were composed of multiple neighborhoods, each with its focal nodes. Each appears to also be controlled by multigenerational lineages that interact with the royal multigenerational lineages of a city's central precinct. The focal places of these neighborhoods were controlled by local elites and sometimes incorporated significantly large monumental architecture. In some cases, such as Xpuhuil and Becan, the causeways that connected the neighborhoods to the central precinct terminated at the monumental architecture, the focal node, of the neighborhood.

At Blue Creek, neighborhoods could be distinguished from one another due to the topography of hills separated by low-lying, high-quality agricultural lands. At Xnoha, hilltops again are where neighborhoods are located. However, the LiDAR data from Xnoha gave us the advantage of identifying LSBMs that bound houselots. Since we can now identify houselots that are otherwise invisible, we have been able to construct a more nuanced view of the neighborhoods, houselot size, variability within neighborhoods, and population density. By examining contemporary analogs, particularly at Yaxunah, we are building a picture of the activities and functions that occurred within houselots and the spatial patterning of those activities and functions. This chapter is not an endpoint but a waypoint in our research. As we continue our multitiered and multifaceted research, we will be seeking to integrate household archaeology with a better understanding of neighborhood structure and variability and how neighborhoods combine to construct urban areas around central places ruled by royal elites.

Acknowledgments

The authors thank our collaborators in the Blue Creek Archaeological Project, the Northwest Belize LiDAR Consortium, especially Juan Fernandez Diaz of NCALM at the University of Houston, and the staff of the Institute of Archaeology of Belize. We also thank our friends in Blue Creek, Orange Walk, Belize, for tolerating us for three decades.

Works Cited

Adler, Michael A. 1996. "Land Tenure, Archaeology, and the Ancestral Pueblo Social Landscape." *Journal of Anthropological Archaeology* 15 (4): 337–71.

Bascopé, Grace Lloyd. 2005. "The Household Ecology of Disease Transmission: Childhood Illness in a Yucatán Maya Community." PhD diss., Southern Methodist University, Dallas.

Batún-Alpuche, Adolfo Iván. 2009. "Agrarian Production and Intensification at a Postclassic Maya Community, Buena Vista, Cozumel, Mexico." PhD diss., University of Florida, Gainesville.

Beach, Timothy, Sheryl Luzzadder-Beach, Thomas Guderjan, Fred Valdez Jr., Juan Carlos Fernandez-Diaz, Sara Eshleman, and Colin Doyle. 2019. "Ancient Maya Wetland Fields Revealed Under Tropical Forest Canopy by Laser Scanning and Multiproxy Evidence Reveal." *Proceedings of the National Academy of Sciences* 116 (43): 21469–77.

Becker, Marshall J. 2001. "Houselots at Tikal, Guatemala: It's What's Out Back That Counts." In *Reconstruyendo la ciudad maya: El urbanismo en las sociedades antiguas*, edited by Andrés Ciudad Ruiz, María Josefa Iglesias Ponce de León, and Maria del Carmen Martínez, 427–60. Madrid: Sociedad Española de Estudios Mayas.

Bullard, William R., Jr. 1952. "Residential Property Walls at Mayapan." *Current Reports* 3:36–41.

Canuto, Marcello A., Francisco Estrada-Belli, Thomas G. Garrison, Stephen D. Houston, Mary Jane Acuña, Milan Kováč, Damien Marken, et al. 2018. "Ancient Lowland Maya Complexity as Revealed by Air-Borne Laser Scanning of Northern Guatemala." *Science* 361 (6409): 0137.

Chase-Dunn, Christopher, and Thomas Hall. 1991. *Core/Periphery Relations in Precapitalist Worlds*. Boulder, Colo.: Westview Press.

Cheetham, David. 2004. "The Role of 'Terminus Groups' in Lowland Maya Site Planning: An Example from Cahal Pech." In *The Ancient Maya of the Belize Valley: Half a Century of Archaeological Research*, edited by James F. Garber, 125–48. Gainesville: University Press of Florida.

Chiba, Tatsuro, Shin-ichi Kaneta, and Yusuke Suzuki. 2008. "Red Relief Image Map: New Visualization Method for Three-Dimensional Data." *International Archives of the Photogrammetry, Remote Sensing and Spatial Information Sciences* 38, pt. B2: 1071–76.

Collier, George A. 1975. *Fields of the Tzotzil: The Ecological Bases of Tradition in Highland Chiapas*. Austin: University of Texas Press.

Culbert, T. Patrick, Laura J. Kosakowski, Robert E. Fry, and William Haviland. 1990. "The Population of Tikal, Guatemala." In *Precolumbian Population History in the Maya Lowlands*, edited by T. Patrick Culbert and Don S. Rice, 103–22. Albuquerque: University of New Mexico Press.

Culbert, T. Patrick, and Don S. Rice. 1990. *Precolumbian Population History in the Maya Lowlands*. Albuquerque: University of New Mexico Press.

Dunning, Nicholas P. 2004. "Down on the Farm: Classic Maya 'Homesteads' as 'Farmsteads.'" In *Ancient Maya Commoners*, edited by J. C. Lohse and F. Valdez Jr., 97–116. Austin: University of Texas Press.

Earle, Timothy. 2000. "Archaeology, Property, and Prehistory." *Annual Review of Anthropology* 29 (October): 39–60.

Eaton, Jack D. 1975. "Ancient Agricultural Farmsteads in the Río Bec Region of Yucatán." *Contributions of the University of California Archaeological Research Facility* 27: 56–82.

Fernandez-Diaz, Juan Carlos, William E. Carter, Ramesh L. Shrestha, Craig L. Glennie. 2014. "Now You See It . . . Now You Don't: Understanding Airborne Mapping LiDAR Collection and Data Product Generation for Archaeological Research in Mesoamerica." *Remote Sensing* 6 (10): 9951–10001.

Fletcher, Laraine A. 1983. "Linear Features in Zone 1: Description and Classification." In *Cobá: A Classic Maya Metropolis*, edited by William J. Folan, Ellen R. Kintz, and Laraine A. Fletcher, 89–102. New York: Academic Press.

Folan, William, Ellen Kintz, and Laraine Fletcher, eds. 1983. *Cobá: A Classic Maya Metropolis*. New York: Academic Press.

Folan, William J., Armando Anaya Hernandez, Ellen R. Kintz, Laraine A. Fletcher, Raymundo González Heredia, Jacinto May Hau, and Nicolas Canche. 2009. "Cobá, Quintana Roo, Mexico: A Recent Analysis of the Social, Economic, and Political Organization of a Major Maya Urban Center." *Ancient Mesoamerica* 20 (1): 59–70.

Freidel, David A., and Jeremy Sabloff. 1984. *Settlement Patterns on Cozumel*. New York: Academic Press.

González, Jason J. 2013. "Domestic Landscapes, Power, and Political Change: Comparing Classic Maya Communities in the Three Rivers Region of Northwestern Belize (A.D. 600–1000)." PhD diss., Southern Illinois University, Carbondale.

Guderjan, Thomas H. 1991. *Maya Settlement in Northwestern Belize: The 1988 and 1990 Seasons of the Rio Bravo Archaeological Project*. Culver City, Calif.: Labyrinthos.

Guderjan, Thomas H. 2007. *The Nature of an Ancient Maya City: Resources, Interaction, and Power at Blue Creek, Belize*. Tuscaloosa: University of Alabama Press.

Guderjan, Thomas H. 2016. *The Ancient Maya City of Blue Creek, Belize: Wealth, Social Organization, and Ritual*. British Archaeological Reports, International Series S2796. Oxford: BAR.

Guderjan, Thomas H., Jeff Baker, and Robert Lichtenstein. 2003. "Environmental and Cultural Diversity at Blue Creek." In *Heterarchy, Political Economy and the Ancient Maya*, edited by Vernon Scarborough, Fred Valdez Jr., and Nicholas Dunning, 77–91. Albuquerque: University of New Mexico Press.

Guderjan, Thomas H., and James F. Garber. 1995. *Maya Maritime Trade, Settlement and Populations on Ambergris Caye, Belize*. Lancaster, Calif.: Labyrinthos.

Guderjan, Thomas H., and C. Colleen Hanratty. 2006. "A Thriving Non-Royal Lineage at Blue Creek: Evidence from a Sequence of Burials, Caches and Architecture." *Acta Mesoamericana* 19:37–46.

Guderjan, Thomas H., Colleen Hanratty, Brie Deschenes, Hollie Lincoln, Morgan Moodie, Alexander Parmington, Hannah Plumer, Carlos Quiroz, Justin Telepak, and Marc Wolf. 2016. "Understanding Xnoha: Temporal and Spatial Dynamics." *Research Reports in Belizean Archaeology* 13:317–27.

Guderjan, Thomas H., Joshua J. Kwoka, and Colleen Hanratty. 2019. "LiDAR Reveals Stone Boundary Markers Surrounding Ancient Maya Houselots in Belize." *Mexicon* 41 (4): 96–97.

Guderjan, Thomas H., Joshua J. Kwoka, Colleen Hanratty, Timothy Beach, Sheryl Luzzadder-Beach, Samantha Krause, Sara Eshleman, Thomas Ruhl, and Colin Doyle. 2020. "Early Onset Anthropocene: Control of the Landscape by the Ancient Maya in Northwestern Belize." *Research Reports in Belizean Archaeology* 17:105–17.

Guderjan, Thomas H., Robert J. Lichtenstein, and C. Colleen Hanratty. 2003. "Elite Residences at Blue Creek, Belize." In *Maya Palaces and Elite Residences*, edited by Jessica Joyce Christie, 13–45. Austin: University of Texas Press.

Hutson, Scott R. 2016. *The Ancient Urban Maya: Neighborhoods, Inequality, and Built Form*. Gainesville: University Press of Florida.

Hutson, Scott R., and Aline Magnoni. 2017. "The Map of Chunchucmil." In *Ancient Maya Commerce: Multidisciplinary Research at Chunchucmil*, edited by Scott R. Hutson, 27–50. Boulder: University of Colorado Press.

Hutson, Scott R., and Jacob Welch. 2016. "Neighborhoods at Chunchucmil." In *The Ancient Urban Maya: Neighborhoods, Inequality, and Built Form*, by Scott R. Hutson, 97–138. Gainesville: University Press of Florida.

Inomata, Takeshi. 2006. "Plazas, Performers, and Spectators: Political Theaters of the Classic Maya." *Current Anthropology* 47 (5): 805–42.

Killion, Thomas W. 1990. "Cultivation Intensity and Residential Site Structure: An Ethnoarchaeological Examination of Peasant Agriculture in the Sierra de los Tuxtlas, Veracruz, Mexico." *Latin American Antiquity* 1 (3): 191–215.

Kintz, Ellen R. 1983. "Neighborhoods and Wards in a Classic Maya Metropolis." In *Cobá: A Classic Maya Metropolis*, edited by William J. Folan, Ellen R. Kintz, and Laraine A. Fletcher, 179–90. New York: Academic Press.

Kurjack, Edward B. 1974. *Prehistoric Lowland Maya Community and Social Organization: A Case Study at Dzibilchaltun, Yucatán, Mexico*. Middle American Research Institute 39. New Orleans: Tulane University.

Kwoka, Joshua J. 2019. "AL18: Excavations of Ancient Maya Houselots." In *The 27th Annual Report of the Blue Creek Archaeological Project*, edited by Thomas H. Guderjan and C. Colleen Hanratty, 97–106. Tyler: Maya Research Program and Center for Social Science Research, University of Texas.

Kwoka, Joshua J., Thomas H. Guderjan, Sara Eshleman, Thomas Ruhl, Justin Telepak, Timothy Beach, Sheryl Luzzadder-Beach, Will McClatchey, and Grace Bascopé. 2021. "A Multimethod Approach to the Study of Classic Maya Houselots and Land Tenure: Preliminary Results from the Three Rivers Region, Belize." *Journal of Archaeological Science-Reports* 38:1030–49.

Kwoka, Joshua J., Thomas Ruhl, and Sara Eshleman. 2018. "AL17: Investigations of Ancient Maya Houselots." In *The 26th Annual Report of the Blue Creek Archaeological Project*, edited by Thomas H. Guderjan and C. Colleen Hanratty, 81–92. Tyler: Maya Research Program and Center for Social Science Research, University of Texas.

Lemonnier, Eva, and Boris Vannière. 2013. "Agrarian Features, Farmsteads, and Homesteads in the Río Bec Nuclear Zone, Mexico." *Ancient Mesoamerica* 24 (2): 397–413.

Lohse, Jon C. 2013. *Classic Maya Political Ecology: Agrarian Resource Management, Political Change, and Class Histories in Upper Northwestern Belize*. Los Angeles: Cotsen Institute for Archaeology, University of California.

Malinowski, Bronisław. 1922. *Argonauts of the Western Pacific*. New York: Dutton.

Marcus, Joyce. 1982. "The Plant World of the Sixteenth and Seventeenth Century Maya." In *Maya Subsistence: Studies in Memory of Dennis E. Puleston*, edited by K. V. Flannery, 239–73. New York: Academic Press.

McAnany, Patricia A. 1995. *Living with the Ancestors: Kinship and Kingship in Ancient Maya Society*. Austin: University of Texas Press.

Nalda, Enrique, and Sandra Balanzario. 2005. "Kohunlich and Dzibanché: The Last Years of Research." *Mexican Archaeology* 13 (76): 42–47.

Netting, Robert McC. 1982. "Territory, Property, and Tenure." In *Behavioral and Social Science Research: A National Resource*, edited by Robert McC Adams, Neil J. Smelser, and Donald J. Treiman, 446–502. Washington, D.C.: National Academy Press.

Netting, Robert McC. 1993. *Smallholders, Householders*. Stanford: Stanford University Press.

Peregrine, Peter. 1991. "Prehistoric Chiefdoms on the American Mid-Continent: A World System Based on Prestige Goods." In *Core-Periphery Relations in Precapitalist Worlds*, edited by Christopher Chase-Dunn and Thomas Hall, 191–211. Boulder, Colo.: Westview Press.

Peregrine, Peter N., and Gary M. Feinman. 1996. *Pre-Columbian World Systems*. Madison, Wis.: Prehistory Press.

Peuramaki-Brown, Meaghan. 2013. "Identifying Integrative Built Environments in the Archaeological Record: An Application of New Urban Design Theory to Ancient Urban Spaces." *Journal of Anthropological Archaeology* 32 (4): 577–94.

Pyburn, K. Anne. 1990. "Settlement Patterns at Nohmul-Preliminary Results of Four Excavation Seasons." In *Precolumbian Population History in the Maya Lowlands*, edited by T. Patrick Culbert and Don S. Rice, 183–98. Albuquerque: University of New Mexico Press.

Restall, Matthew. 1997. *The Maya World: Yucatec Culture and Society, 1550–1850*. Stanford: Stanford University Press.

Roys, Ralph L. 1939. *The Titles of Ebtun*. Publication 505. Washington, D.C.: Carnegie Institution of Washington.

Roys, Ralph L. 1943. *The Indian Background of Colonial Yucatán*. Publication 548. Washington, D.C.: Carnegie Institution of Washington.

Roys, Ralph L. 1967. *The Book of Chilam Balam of Chumayel.* Norman: University of Oklahoma Press.

Santley, Robert S. 1990. "Demographic Archaeology in the Maya Lowlands." In *Precolumbian Population History in the Maya Lowlands*, edited by T. Patrick Culbert and Don S. Rice, 325–44. Albuquerque: University of New Mexico Press.

Silva Rhoads, Carlos, and Concepción María del Carmen Hernández. 1991. *Estudios de patrón del asentamiento en Playa del Carmen, Quintana Roo.* Colleccíon Científica, Serie Arqueología 321. Mexico City: Instituto Nacional de Anthropología e Historía.

Thomas, Prentice M. 1974. *Prehistoric Maya Settlement Patterns at Becan, Campeche, Mexico.* Middle American Research Institute 45. New Orleans: Tulane University.

Tourtellot, Gair. 1990. "Population Estimates for Preclassic and Classic Seibal, Peten." In *Precolumbian Population History in the Maya Lowlands*, edited by T. Patrick Culbert and Don S. Rice, 83–102. Albuquerque: University of New Mexico Press.

Turner, Billie Lee, II. 1979. "Prehispanic Terracing in the Central Maya Lowlands: Problems of Agricultural Intensification." In *Maya Archaeology and Ethnohistory*, edited by Norman Hammond and Gordon R. Willey, 103–15. Austin: University of Texas Press.

Vogt, Evon Z. 1976. *Tortillas for the Gods.* Cambridge, Mass.: Harvard University Press.

Wallerstein, Immanuel. 1974. *The Modern World-System: Capitalist Agriculture and the Origins of the European World Economy in the Sixteenth Century.* New York: Academic Press.

Wisdom, Charles. 1940. *The Chorti Indians of Guatemala.* Chicago: University of Chicago Press.

Yaeger, Jason. 2000. "The Social Construction of Communities in the Classic Maya Countryside: Strategies of Affiliation in Western Belize." In *The Archaeology of Communities: A New World Perspective*, edited by Marcello-Andrea Canuto and Jason Yaeger, 123–41. London: Routledge.

Yaeger, Jason. 2010. "Landscapes of the Xunantunich Hinterlands." In *The Classic Maya Provincial Politics: Xunantunich and Its Hinterlands*, edited by Lisa J. LeCount and Jason Yaeger, 233–49. Tucson: University of Arizona Press.

CHAPTER 10

Prehistoric *Albarradas* at the Site of Buena Vista, Cozumel

ADOLFO IVÁN BATÚN-ALPUCHE

During the past fifty years of Maya studies, the agricultural base that supported precontact populations has become a major topic of debate. This interest originated after a number of archaeological investigations showed that ancient Maya peoples were not limited to slash-and-burn cultivation to sustain their cities, as previously believed. Instead, they employed a variety of agricultural techniques related to the highest levels of production through the use of terraces, raised fields, demarcated fields, house orchards (*solares*), and irrigation canals, among others (Adams 1982; Alexander 2000; Fedick 1996; Gómez-Pompa, Salvador Flores, and Sosa 1987; Harrison and Turner 1978, 1983; Healy et al. 1983; Killion 1992; Liendo Stuardo and Vega Correa 2018; Pohl 1990; Siemens and Puleston 1972). Understanding how production was organized in these modified landscapes and how houselots were distributed to optimize production requires further investigation.

In the Yucatán Peninsula, ancient agricultural techniques were employed, modifying different geographical features such as *bajos* (seasonal wetlands), hill slopes, *rejolladas* (land depressions), and swamps. The abundant limestone characterizing the peninsula was the most common material employed to transform the landscape and demarcated suitable cultivation areas. During the Late Postclassic period (AD 1200–1518), a commercial market society emerged on the east coast of the peninsula to meet the demand for the cultivation of crops and the production of agricultural commodities (Rathje and Sabloff 1973, 227; Sabloff and Freidel 1975; Sierra Sosa and Robles Castellanos 1988).

This chapter presents the results of an archaeological settlement pattern study conducted for dissertation research, at the site of Buena Vista in Cozumel, Mexico, in 2002 and 2003 (Batún-Alpuche 2009). The main goal was to identify the vestiges of landscape modifications at the site indicating agrarian land use and agricultural production and their related task group residences (houselots). The basic theoretical model guiding my research was that of "settlement ecology," which is designed to study agrarian settlements investigating the relationship between population and agricultural practices in their ecological setting (Killion 1992; Stone 1996).

Cozumel

The island of Cozumel is located 16 km from the northeastern coast of the Yucatán Peninsula. During the Late Postclassic period, the island served as the main port located along the long-distance canoe trade route that followed the coast of Yucatán between Honduras and Tabasco. Cozumel's importance as a sacred pilgrimage center is also mentioned in ethnohistorical sources (Roys et al. 1940). Thirty-three archaeological sites are known on Cozumel, the largest being San Gervasio in the north-central region of the island (figure 10.1). San Gervasio is formed by six architectural complexes and numerous domestic features covering an area of 3.14 km^2. After the arrival of Spanish invaders, the Maya cities of Cozumel were integrated into an autonomous political entity with its capital city located in San Gervasio (Sabloff and Freidel 1975, 401; Sierra Sosa and Robles Castellanos1988, 2).

One of the most remarkable features reported previously on Cozumel is an extensive limestone wall system that covers all but a small portion of the island's surface, dividing the land into irregular field plots (Arnold and Frost 1909; Escalona Ramos 1946; Freidel and Leventhal 1975, 67–68; Freidel and Sabloff 1984; Sanders 1956; Sierra Sosa and Robles Castellanos 1988). The most elaborate forms of stone walls demarcating fields were reported around two main sites: Buena Vista and Chen Cedral (Freidel and Sabloff 1984).

Buena Vista

The site of Buena Vista is situated 18 km south of San Gervasio. It is laid above a low natural ridge located 1.5 km inland, paralleling the southeastern coast of the island. The site core is composed of a complex of agglu-

FIGURE 10.1 Main archaeological sites on the island of Cozumel, Quintana Roo, Mexico (drawn by Tina Ross after the original map created by Adolfo Batún-Alpuche).

tinate platforms, some of which have standing vestiges of masonry buildings, but others were most probably used to support perishable structures (figure 10.2). The main platform on the site was constructed by artificially leveling the natural elevation. It covers about 7 hectares and its height varies from 2 to 7 m. At its northern end, another platform was built to support a central plaza group.

Surrounding the main platform are four groups of "shrines" connected by *sakbe'ob* (raised roads) to the central precinct as well as several other small

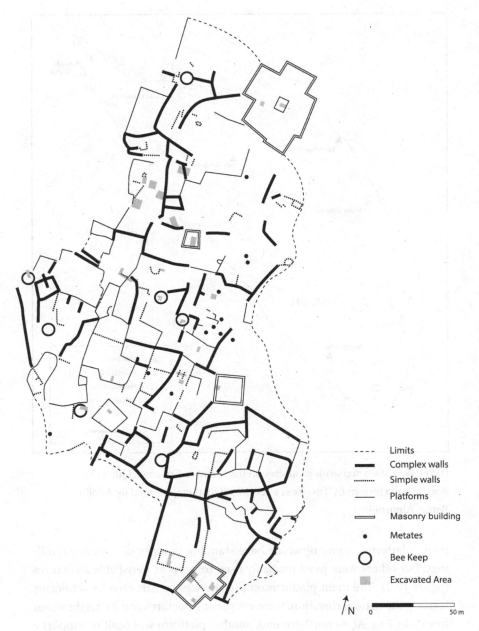

FIGURE 10.2 Buena Vista core, showing distribution of structures and stone walls (drawn by Tina Ross after the original map created by Adolfo Batún-Alpuche).

platforms and structures. Beyond the central-site core is an extensive network of field walls, or *albarradas*, that vary in size. There are single-course rubble walls with an estimated standing height of 1 m, to walls with rubble and gravel cores, and dry-laid masonry retainers standing more than 2 m high by 2 m wide. Such massive and simple walls occur in an apparently random fashion, enclosing lots of different sizes. Similar walled systems have been noted at the ancient sites of Tulum (Vargas Pacheco 1996), Cobá (Fletcher 1983), Xamanha (Silva Rhoads and Hernandez 1991), Rancho Ina (Terrones Gonzáles 1990, 1994), Chunchucmil (Vleck 1978), Mayapán (Bullard 1952, 1954), and Xcaret (Andrews 1990).

The Buena Vista Archaeological Project (BVAP) investigated the organization of agrarian production at the site during its last period of occupation corresponding to the Late Postclassic (AD 1250–1518). During 2002 and 2003 and funded by the Foundation for the Advancement of Mesoamerican Studies, Inc. (FAMSI) (Batún-Alpuche 2004), archaeological survey and mapping were undertaken in the Buena Vista peripheral area, to study the distribution of archaeological features and the ecological setting surrounding the site core (figure 10.3). Our survey included a total of 5.2 km² that was centered at the site's monumental plaza. The survey included mapping of all archaeological and topographic signatures found within 50 m wide *brechas* (survey transects) and the detailed mapping of sectors of the site, which by its concentration of archaeological vestiges and associated topography were chosen as representing different forms of micro-environmental adaptations.

The Ecological Setting at Buena Vista

Topographic information registered during survey and mapping was used to generate a digital elevation model of the project area, which in turn with the aid of satellite images, aerial photographs, and soil and vegetation data was combined to generate a land cover map. Four distinct microenvironmental zones were registered, including (1) the *akalche* zone, covering 13 percent of the surveyed area; (2) the *tzekel* zone, covering 15 percent; (3) the broken ridges zone, covering 39 percent; and (4) the upland zone, covering 33 percent. The akalche zone is a low depression area located at the southeastern corner of the survey area. It is a seasonally inundated zone characterized by reddish-brown vertisol soil and vegetation of the low, thorny, semidecidu-

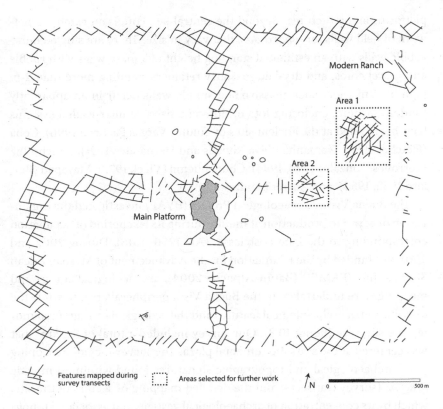

FIGURE 10.3 Survey area of the Buena Vista Archaeological Project in 2003 (drawn by Tina Ross after the original map by Adolfo Batún-Alpuche).

ous forest. The tzekel zone occupies the northeast section of the study area and is dominated by shallow lithosol stony soils with a high occurrence of limestone outcrops. Vegetation is predominantly dry, low-deciduous forest with abundant thorny bushes and cacti. The broken ridges area is defined by a broken topography formed by low ridges about 3–4 m high and 50–100 m wide and flat areas between ridges about 100 m wide. This is the largest zone and is located across the central part of the survey area. The soil on the ridges is dark and deep with a high concentration of organic material, and the flat bottomlands between ridges have abundant karstic depressions, known locally as *huay'as*, and rejolladas, where rich organic soil accumulates. Vegetation in this area is composed of low deciduous and medium semi-evergreen forests. The upland zone occupies the entire west section of the project area. This zone has the highest elevation in southern Cozumel; vegetation here has been defined as medium to high semi-evergreen forest, including large ramón trees (*Brosimum alicastrum*), chicozapote (*Manilkara zapota*), and kopo (*Ficus tecolutensis*), among other large tree species. Soils in this area are deep and dark with abundant limestone, known locally as *chichluums*.

The Buena Vista Demarcated Lots

Four different types of dry-laid stone walls were identified demarcating lots in Buena Vista: (1) simple walls, consisting of a line of boulders (30–40 cm in diameter) up to about a meter; (2) slab-based walls, with large slabs (60–120 cm diameter) forming the base of the wall and completed with boulders up to about 1.5 m; (3) large walls, formed by a ridge of boulders 1–2 m wide, about 60–70 cm high; and (4) massive walls, about 2 m wide by 2 m high with retainer walls holding a core of rubble and gravel. A total of 229 complete wall-demarcated lots were mapped, obtaining a representative sample of lots in each microenvironmental zone. Demarcated lots range from small lots of approximately 377 m^2 to large lots of about 11,000 m^2. Likewise, some of the lots in Buena Vista contain the remains of ancient dwellings and ancillary structures, but other lots have no structures inside. Further description of demarcated areas is provided in the next section after contextualizing other features in Buena Vista.

Archaeological Features of Buena Vista

During this project, 591 features other than stone walls were registered at Buena Vista, including large platforms, masonry structures, remains of perishable and semiperishable structures, and ancillary and special function features. Documented features were identified and classified into five general classes and variants based on previous typologies established in the area (Freidel and Sabloff 1984; Sierra Sosa and Robles Castellanos 1988; Vargas 1992). A total of 372 features were identified as regular structures, of which 238 were classified as domestic structures or dwellings, all having at least one habitable area of 18 m^2. Thirty-eight percent of these structures have a circular form, whereas the rest are square, rectangular, or irregular in shape.

Special Features

Special features include peculiar structures such as apiaries and ramps, and other nonstructures like *chultunes* (underground storage chambers), sakbe'ob, *sascaberas* (limestone quarries), wells, *metates* (grinding stones), and monoliths. Thirty-seven circular apiaries were registered in Buena Vista. Surprisingly, this was more than the number found at San Gervasio, although more than double the area surveyed at San Gervasio (Sierra Sosa and Robles Castellano 1988, 110). The typical apiary is a dry-laid stone circular structure enclosing an area ranging from 20 m^2 to 100 m^2. Most of these structures have low rectangular platforms in their interior, cylinder-like stones, and a variate number of circular stone disks (Batún-Alpuche 2004, 2005, 2020). Some apiaries were found in isolation, but most are in clusters of two or three apiaries. The largest group included seven apiaries in the southwest section of the study area.

Six short and narrow sakbe'ob were found in Buena Vista; these linear features were 1.5–2 m wide. Three sakbe'ob connected structures, probably temples, to the core platform; two connected temples with rejolladas; and in one case, it was not possible to determine its origin without further excavation. Other important special modified features were registered during the survey that can be classified as procurement and/or cumulative features: 55 rejolladas, 2 sascaberas, 56 huaya'as, 11 small cenotes (natural underground reservoirs), and about 120 rough wells.

The Nature of the Demarcated Lots

As mentioned previously, the largest construction work implemented in Cozumel and Buena Vista in particular during the Late Postclassic period was a large and continuous wall demarcation system covering most of the island surface. In Buena Vista, large portions of this wall system are still standing, delineating the land into discrete parcels of different sizes and forms. Previous research on the site indicated great diversity in the form, construction technique, and size of walls demarcating these parcels. As noted, structures were distinguished from demarcated lots. The demarcated lot was the basic analytical unit employed in this study to analyze the infield agrarian landscape at Buena Vista. The BVAP documented a sample of 229 completely demarcated lots and 388 additional fragments of demarcation walls ranging from 5 to 50 m long. The complete catalog of structures and demarcated lots is presented in the appendixes of my dissertation (Batún-Alpuche 2009).

The catalog of demarcated lots includes the central geographic UTM coordinates of each lot, their map quadrant location, general information on their form and construction technique, their perimeter and area measurements, and the number and type of karstic and settlement features enclosed in each lot. During the mapping process, great diversity was documented in the form and size of demarcated lots and also on the settlement and natural features within demarcated parcels; however, the form and construction technique employed on a large sample of walls was more difficult to determine without excavation of these features.

Next, I will present formal categories of demarcated lots and the range of variation on their dimensions. I also describe the distinct techniques of construction observed in various segments of the wall system and how the majority of walls were documented in this study. One of the first characteristics of demarcated lots in Buena Vista showing great variation is the Plainview form. Based on Plainview form, lots in Buena Vista were classified into four general categories: (1) rectangular lots, (2) trapezoid lots, (3) irregular non-convex lots, and (4) non-angular lots. From the total sample of 229 demarcated lots, 37 were classified as rectangular lots, 76 as trapezoid lots, 48 as irregular non-convex lots, and 68 as non-angular lots.

Rectangular lots have a very regular rectangular form. They are usually oriented approximately 30° northeast parallel to the coastline. The majority of these lots are vacant, showing no evidence of archaeological structures. Rectangular lots have an average area of 3,907 m^2, with the largest lot having an area of 8,700 m^2 and the smallest an area of 377 m^2. Trapezoid lots are very irregular in form. Sometimes one of the segments is much longer than their parallel and the lot takes a quasi-triangular form. These lots enclose an average area of 2,950 m^2. The largest trapezoid lot encloses an area of approximately 11,000 m^2, whereas the smallest encloses an area of only 424 m^2.

Irregular non-convex lots have a very irregular geometric form, looking as if an extension was made to an original irregular or rectangular lot to add on adjacent patches of land. On average, these irregular lots enclose an area of 3,700 m^2, but the largest of these lots demarcates an area of 11,400 m^2. Non-angular lots are the smallest type of lots in the sample. They have no intersection of walls but contain a continuous wall enclosing an irregular area that apparently extends to incorporate complete karstic features into their enclosed area. Non-angular lots measure an average of 1,400 m², but small non-angular lots of approximately 200 m² were recorded. The largest lot of this form encloses an area of 4,200 m².

The Buena Vista Land Use Pattern

Analysis of archaeological features within and between microenvironmental zones in Buena Vista revealed a differential land-use pattern. The akalche zone has a low density of features, with only eleven identified as dwellings, and most of the fields are demarcated with simple walls enclosing areas of about 723.21 m² to 7,017 m². Most of the walls function as dikes or dams to control water recession in temporarily inundated areas. The tzekel zone has the highest density of structures in the area, with seventy-two identified as dwellings. Demarcated lots are small with an average area of 1,771 m², and the predominant walls are massive in combination with simple walls. In the broken ridges zone, large walls at the edge of ridges function basically as retaining terraces, while simple walls were used to demarcate cultivable fields located at the low areas among ridges. Simple walls also enclosed rejolladas and fields adjacent to apiaries.

The broken ridges zone has the greatest number of apiaries registered in Buena Vista, with houselots including an average area of 2,300 m². The largest fields in Buena Vista are about 4,000 m². In this zone, eighty-three dwellings were documented. In the upland zone, fields are demarcated by simple walls and slab-based walls, and most of them have small wells carved in the limestone, probably used for pot irrigation in cultivable fields. The density of registered dwellings in this area is about three dwellings per hectare—the lowest in Buena Vista—and the proportion of demarcated lots with structures to lots with no structures is about one lot with at least one dwelling to every four vacant lots. A total of fifty-nine dwellings were identified in this zone.

The Buena Vista Settlement Agroecology

I adopted a settlement agroecological approach, which considers the importance of cultural and environmental factors in agricultural practices and settlement decisions, as the most appropriate means to investigate agrarian production systems and settlement structure in agrarian communities. Under this theoretical framework, the site's settlement pattern is considered the direct result of both the ecological nature of agricultural activities and the social relations involved in them (Stone 1996, 5). Local environmental conditions can present constraints to the ecology of agrarian practices, which have to be overridden before bringing otherwise marginal lands into production. However, agrarian settlements are not simple artifacts of ecology; cultural and historical factors are also important to explain variability in rural settlements (Stone 1996, 11).

Preliminary observation of Buena Vista's agrarian ecology indicates a complex pattern of agrarian production and intensification at the site. Although microenvironmental areas documented in each zone were not of the same size, we noted some differences and similarities. Local microenvironmental zones present variate conditions and suitability for agrarian production; however, the entire study area was demarcated by stone walls, indicating that independent of land capability, the land was employed intensively for different purposes.

A close observation of demarcated lots looking at construction techniques, dimensions, and associated features revealed that stone walls accomplished different functions in different areas. In the akalche area, stone walls work as water-controlling devices to manipulate water recession and create planting surfaces at the end of the rainy season when the area is inundated. In the broken ridges area, large walls form terraces and control soil runoff to create cultivable areas most associated with dwellings and beekeeping structures, creating solares and bee gardens (Batún-Alpuche 2005, 2020). This area also has the largest number of rejolladas in Buena Vista—most likely employed for cultivation of special crops—as indicated by the stone wall demarcation of these karstic features. The uplands area has the largest demarcated fields and some of the most productive soils in the area. Water requirements for cultivation were supplied by means of a large number of wells carved in the limestone. The tzekel area contains the poorest soils in Buena Vista and was heavily populated. Lots in the tzekel area are small, but they are demarcated with the most elaborate and elevated wall system, appearing to protect some special resources while working as windbreaks.

Conclusion

Mapping and survey in Buena Vista revealed a diverse and intensive system of production in the site during the Late Postclassic period. Buena Vista's inhabitants farmed all available land in the area, including land not suitable for milpa cultivation. Here it is important to consider that the study area does not represent the site limits or the limits of the wall system. Stone walls extend over the study area for several kilometers to the south, north, and west. The wall network has been noted in aerial observation as covering a minimum of 75 percent of the island surface (Freidel and Sabloff 1984, 86–87), representing an immense agrarian network.

Although identification of what was cultivated in demarcated fields needs further investigation, it can be noted that the uplands and broken ridges areas have rich organic soils suitable for maize cultivation; however, the tzekel and the akalche areas are poor zones for maize cultivation. During our survey, numerous plants, probably cultivated in these areas in precontact times, were observed growing wild, including wild cotton, copal trees, calabash trees, cactus, and palm trees. Likewise, rejolladas and *waya'as as* (natural soil deposits) may have been used in the past to cultivate special valuable trees such as cacao.

Using the number of documented dwellings at Buena Vista and a minimum of five persons per dwelling produces an estimated population of 1,190 persons. If we take into account that only 40 percent of the area was mapped and add the remaining 60 percent, this estimate can be raised to 2,975 in 4 km^2 or 7 persons/hectare. This is a moderate assessment, considering the study area is the core central zone of the settlement and its immediately adjacent areas. It is likely that the number of people living at Buena Vista caused no stress to their available land and food production; but on the other hand, they may have exceeded the level of subsistence production, and the surplus could have been used to supply other communities on the island and for the market.

Moreover, the extensive area demarcated with stone walls in Cozumel, in contrast with the population of the entire island, is estimated to be about 10,000 inhabitants (Freidel and Sabloff 1984, 178) and was probably used to produce far more agricultural crops and commodities than what they needed for subsistence. At this point, it is time to start looking at Cozumel's intensive agrarian system as a productive strategy to supply trading demands most probably motivated by the large number of pilgrims visiting the island.

Also, the pattern of houselots, documented in each microenvironmental zone, indicates that the distribution, size, and form of houselots were related to the nature of agrarian activities in each zone, including necessary labor for production or the size of activity groups. In the tzekel zone, houselots were small in a densely populated zone. The size and complexity of walls and the number of ancillary features were also dense, suggesting large task groups working in specialized productive activities. In the akalche zone, which was periodically inundated, the scarcity of drylands may be the cause of the low density of houselots.

In the houselots in the broken ridges zone, there was a high concentration of beekeeping activities, which were likely an extended family task. There were a large number of apiaries strategically located near flowering species and milpa. In the uplands area, where the richest soil is located, we find the lowest density of houselots and the highest density and largest field lots. Milpa cultivation most likely took place in these walled areas, requiring the work of the nuclear family most of the year, with a spike in activity during the harvesting period. The settlement ecology model provides us with a key hypothesis to analyze settlement patterns in agrarian settings. During the Late Postclassic period, the site of Buena Vista presents a complex distribution pattern of agrarian houselots and field lots, which would have required complementary agrarian activities. A deeper understanding requires further archaeological investigation, including detailed excavation of houselots in all microenvironmental zones.

Acknowledgments

I would like to thank the Foundation for the Advancement of Mesoamerican Studies, Inc. (FAMSI) and the Consejo Nacional de Ciencia y Tecnología (CONACYT) for funding my investigation in Buena Vista, and the Instituto Nacional de Antropología e Historia (INAH) for facilitating the permits to conduct research in Cozumel.

Works Cited

Adams, Richard E. W. 1982. "Ancient Maya Canals, Grids and Lattices in the Maya Jungle." *Archaeology* 35 (6): 22–35.

Alexander, Rani T. 2000. "Patrones de asentamiento agregados en el sudoeste de Campeche: Una visión desde la Isla Cilvituk." *Mesoamerica* 21 (39): 359–91.

Andrews, Anthony P. 1990. "The Role of Ports in Maya Civilization." In *Vision and Revision in Maya Studies*, edited by Flora S. Clancy and Peter D. Harrison, 159–67. Albuquerque: University of New Mexico Press.

Arnold, Channing, and Frederick Frost. 1909. *American Egypt: A Record of Travel in Yucatan*. London: Hutchinson.

Batún-Alpuche, Adolfo Iván. 2004. "Maya Settlement Pattern and Land Use in Buena Vista, Cozumel, Mexico." Report submitted to the Foundation for the Advancement of Mesoamerican Studies, Inc., Crystal River, Fla.

Batún-Alpuche, Adolfo Iván. 2005. "The Cozumel Maya Bee Gardens." Paper presented at the Southeast Conference on Mesoamerican Archaeology and Ethnohistory (SECMAE), Tampa, Fla.

Batún-Alpuche, Adolfo Iván. 2009. "Agrarian Production and Intensification at a Postclassic Maya Community, Buena Vista, Cozumel, Mexico." PhD diss., University of Florida, Gainesville.

Batún-Alpuche, Adolfo Iván. 2020. "The Archaeology of Intensive Beekeeping in Postclassic Yucatán." *The Mayanist* 2 (1): 39–56.

Bullard, William R., Jr. 1952. "Residential Property Walls at Mayapan." *Current Reports* 3:36–44.

Bullard, William R., Jr. 1954. "Boundary Walls and House Plots at Mayapan." *Current Reports* 13:234–53.

Escalona Ramos, Alberto. 1946. "Algunas ruinas prehistóricas en Quintana Roo." *Boletín de la Sociedad Mexicana de Geografía y Estadística* 61 (3): 513–628.

Fedick, Scott L. 1996. *The Managed Mosaic: Ancient Maya Agriculture and Resource Use.* Salt Lake City: University of Utah Press.

Fletcher, Laraine A. 1983. "Linear Features in Zone 1: Description and Classification." In *Cobá: A Classic Maya Metropolis*, edited by William J. Folan, Ellen R. Kintz, and Laraine A. Fletcher, 89–102. New York: Academic Press.

Freidel, David, and Richard Leventhal. 1975. "The Settlement Survey." In *A Study of Changing Pre-Columbian Commercial Systems: The 1972–1973 Season at Cozumel, Mexico*, edited by Jeremy Sabloff and William L. Rathje, 60–76. Cambridge, Mass.: Peabody Museum of Archaeology and Ethnology, Harvard University.

Freidel, David, and Jeremy Sabloff. 1984. *Cozumel Late Maya Settlement Patterns.* New York: Academic Press.

Gómez-Pompa, Arturo, José Salvador Flores, and Victoria Sosa. 1987. "The 'Pet Kot': A Man-Made Tropical Forest of the Maya." *Interciencia* 12 (1) 10–15.

Harrison, Peter D., and B. L. Turner II. 1978. *Pre-Hispanic Maya Agriculture.* Albuquerque: University of New Mexico Press.

Harrison, Peter D., and B. L. Tuner II. 1983. *Pulltrouser Swamp: Ancient Maya Habitat, Agriculture, and Settlement in Northern Belize.* Austin: University of Texas Press.

Healy, Paul F., John D. H. Lambert, J. T. Armason, and Richard J. Hebda. 1983. "Caracol, Belize: Evidence of Ancient Maya Agricultural Terraces." *Journal of Field Archaeology* 10 (4): 397–410.

Killion, Thomas. 1992. *Gardens of Prehistory: The Archaeology of Settlement Agriculture in Greater Mesoamerica.* Tuscaloosa: University of Alabama Press.

Liendo Stuarco, Rodrigo, and Felipe Vega Correa. 2018. "Técnicas agrícolas en el área de Palenque: Inferencias para un estudio sobre la organización política de un señorío maya del Clásico." *Arqueología*, no. 23: 3–24.

Pohl, Mary DeLand. 1990. *Ancient Maya Wetland Agriculture: Excavation on Albion Island, Northern Belize.* Boulder, Colo.: Westview Press.

Rathje, William, and Jeremy Sabloff. 1973. "A Research Design for Cozumel, Mexico." *World Archaeology* 5 (2): 221–31.

Roys, Ralph L., France V. Scholes, and Eleanor B. Adams. 1940. *Report and Census of the Indians of Cozumel.* Publication 523. Washington, D.C.: Carnegie Institution of Washington.

Sabloff, Jeremy, and David Freidel. 1975. "A Model of a Pre-Columbian Trading Center." In *Ancient Civilization and Trade*, edited by Jeremy Sabloff and C. C. Lamberg-Karlovsky, 369–408. Albuquerque: University of New Mexico Press.

Sanders, William T. 1955. "An Archaeological Reconnaissance of Northern Quintana Roo." *Current Reports* 24:179–222.

Siemens, Alfred, and Dennis Puleston. 1972. "Ridged Fields and Associated Features in Southern Campeche: New Perspectives on the Lowland Maya." *American Antiquity* 37 (2): 228–39.

Sierra Sosa, Thelma Noemí, and Fernando Robles Castellanos. 1988. "Investigaciones arqueológicas en San Gervasio, Isla de Cozumel." In *Cozumel, un encuentro en la historia*, edited by Eva Saavedra Silva and Jorge Sobrino Sierra, 1–13. Mexico City: Fondo de Publicaciones y Ediciones de Quintana Roo.

Silva Rhoads, Carlos, and Concepción María del Carmen Hernández. 1991. *Estudios de patrón de asentamiento en Playa del Carmen, Quintana Roo.* Mexico City: Colección Científica, Instituto Nacional de Antropología e Historia.

Stone, Glenn Davis. 1996. *Settlement Ecology: The Social and Spatial Organization of Kofyar Agriculture.* Tucson: University of Arizona Press.

Terrones Gonzáles, Enrique. 1990. "Proyecto Salvamento Arqueológico Rancho Ina, Quintana Roo." *Mexicon* 12 (5): 89–92.

Terrones Gonzáles, Enrique. 1994. "Apiarios Prehispánicos." *Boletín de la Escuela de Ciencias Antropológicas* 20 (117): 43–57.

Vargas de la Peña, Leticia. 1992. "Estudio de la arquitectura pública de San Gervasio, Cozumel." BA thesis, Universidad Autónoma de Yucatán, Mérida.

Vargas Pacheco, Ernesto. 1996. *Tulum: Organización político y territorial de la costa oriental de Quintana Roo.* Mexico City: Instituto de Investigaciones Antropológicas, Universidad Nacional Autónoma de México.

Vleck, David. 1978. "Muros de delimitación residencial en Chunchucmil." *Boletín de la Escuela de Ciencias Antropológicas de la Universidad de Yucatán*, no 28: 55–64.

CHAPTER 11

An Ethnoecological View of the Evolution of *Solares*

A Yucatán Maya Houselot Case Study

GRACE LLOYD BASCOPÉ AND ELIAS ALCOCER PUERTO

The physical location of the *solar* (yard or houselot) surrounding the home and outbuildings in rural areas in Yucatán has played a strategic role in sustaining the Maya family for millennia. In good years, it complements the products of the milpa (cornfield) with a suite of plants that, due to water requirements and wildlife predation, would not survive in the outfield setting. Today, both native and nonnative plants in the solar provide home remedies, enriching nutritional supplements, and a variety of spices that enliven daily cuisine. The solar also contains space for small animal husbandry. The proximity of the solar garden to the table means small animals—chickens, turkeys, pigs—can consume vegetable matter not otherwise used by the family, making this system more energy efficient and sustainable. In years of environmental stress, endemic species grown in the solar and adapted to drought have been essential to family survival, and today, nonnative species introduced to the solar have a better chance of withstanding stressors because of watering and another close tending.

We explore evolving uses of the solar and its place in supplementing the diets of families in Yaxunah, a small Yucatec Mayan–speaking community in the central part of Yucatán. We find that government policies and the forces of global capitalist consumer economics impact the work carried out in the solar and include changes in the traditional place the solar garden has had on the nutritional status of the family. We conclude that as village members are being integrated into a wider regional fabric, diminishing the traditional uses of the solar can negatively impact the health of the family and reduce the number of native plants and other plant species in the environment.

Investigations of *Solares* in Yucatán

The literature shows that, in the Yucatán Peninsula, solares help maintain species diversity and are a sustainable nutritional resource for families. However, both the makeup of the family unit and its economic status impact the overall number of plants found within the solar and the number of introduced ornamentals and nonnative edible flora. Easy access to the city of Mérida, the capital and urban center of Yucatán, also plays a role in the number and types of species found in solares.

Traditional Maya agroforestry (the milpa/solar garden complex) has helped maintain a high degree of species diversity in Yucatán (Toledo et al. 2008), and the region contains high plant endemism (Ibarra-Manríquez 1996; see also Scales and Marsden 2008). Alfredo Barrera-Rubio (1980) reports that of the ninety-two tree and shrub-sized species most commonly present in Yucatán solar gardens, 61 percent come directly from the native flora of the peninsula, 13 percent are Neotropical but not found in the wild flora of the immediate area, and only 26 percent are plants introduced after the sixteenth century.

In the small town of Yaxcaba (the *cabecera*, roughly equivalent to a county seat of the municipio, the government entity to which Yaxunah belongs), Heriberto E. Cuanalo de la Cerda and Rogelio R. Guerra Mukul (2008) explored the possibility that household structure was a key factor in determining solar garden creation, maintenance, and the number of components a garden contained. Of the thirty-one home gardens surveyed, all had fruit trees of varying types but chiefly citrus. A total of 71 percent also contained other edible vegetables and 58 percent contained ornamental plants. Eighty-four percent had fowl, and 71 percent had pigs. The findings demonstrated clearly that household structure impacted the size and complexity of the home garden in two key ways: (1) households with small children had fewer elements in their gardens, and (2) households in which the male head of household did not migrate had more nutrition-giving components (Cuanalo de la Cerda and Guerra Mukul 2008).

In Pomuch, a town in the western part of the State of Yucatán, Wilbert Santiago Poot-Pool et al. (2012) found that economic stratification played a significant role in differences in home garden production. Their investigations showed that wealthier families preferred herbaceous ornamentals and planted fruit trees for occasional use. Poorer community members showed a preference for native flora and planted in higher densities. The researchers concluded that economics impacted the conservation of species diversity, with poorer families making the greater contribution to the retention of native plants (Poot-Pool et al. 2012).

Victor Rico-Gray et al. (1990) studied home gardens in two villages in Yucatán—one near Mérida and one, Tixcacaltuyub, in the same municipio as Yaxunah. Their findings showed that in the gardens of the more urbanized community, ornamental plants and commercial fruit trees were common. The size of the home garden in the rural community depended on the number of family members able to tend it, and the Tixcacaltuyub garden owners either planted or tolerated the growth of more native species than did more urbanized owners (Rico-Gray et al. 1990). This conforms with the findings of Adelaido Vara (1980), who studied "urbanization events" (the coming of electricity, tap water, and paved roads) in Yaxcaba and their effect on solar gardens and found that more nonnative fruit trees were introduced immediately after these modernizing changes.

José A. Alayón-Gamboa and Francisco D. Gurri-García (2008, 395) reported that "tropical home gardens are ecologically sustainable systems that not only generate household savings on food, medicine and spice expenditures, but provide subsistence agriculturalists with supplementary income and improve the nutritional quality of the families' diet." Energy, protein, minerals, and vitamins gained from home garden plants may not be found in milpa crops (Niñez 1985).

Alayón-Gamboa and Gurri-García (2008) studied the dynamics of home garden production in the municipio of Calakmul in Campeche. They noted that many subsistence farmers were in the process of converting to more agribusiness strategies—planting commercial crops and raising cattle for profit. They reported that households engaged in commercial activities purchased more nonrenewable and renewable energy, while those relying on subsistence agriculture used renewable energy for fields and home gardens. Alayón-Gamboa and Gurri-García (2008) found that commercial crop growers had smaller home gardens with fewer nutritional plants. They concluded that subsistence-shifting agriculture (the milpa), home garden production, and small animal husbandry guard the family in times of crop failure (see Alayón-Gamboa 2014a; Chi-Quij et al. 2014; Dine et al. 2019; and Terán and

Rasmussen 2009 on crucial supplements to the cornfield from the home garden), offer savings in food investments, provide nutritional supplement variety, and maintain higher biodiversity (Alayón-Gamboa and Gurri-García 2008). They conclude that by recycling the biomass they create into family members and animal husbandry, they use little nonrenewable energy in this production and, thus are more sustainable and more efficient than commercial croppers (Alayón-Gamboa and Gurri-García 2008).

Xa'an, or sabal palm (*Sabal yapa* Wright ex Becc. and *Sabal mexicana* Mart.), endemic to the lowland Maya region of Mesoamerica, has been used for roof thatching for more than three thousand years (see Caballero 1994). In a 2006 study, Andrea Martínez-Ballesté, Carlos Martorell, and Javier Caballero investigated the impact of how this plant fared in households that became more market-oriented. They found that as families focused more on acquiring rather than producing goods, the need for palm leaves diminished and the impetus to plant the trees declined. More traditional families, those relying heavily on the milpa/solar subsistence complex, continued to use their home gardens to grow leaves sufficient for their home and outbuilding needs (Martínez-Ballesté, Martorell, and Caballero 2006), thus contributing to their household economy and helping maintain a small component of the native environment.

Mariana Y. Hernández, Pedro A. Macario, and Jorge O. López-Martínez (2017, 125) invoked the concept of food sovereignty evolved from "the international peasants' movement" actions at the World Food Summit in 1996. The authors explored the potential for the long-term sustainability of the agro-environment in three communities within the Calakmul Biosphere Reserve in the State of Campeche, Mexico, on the Yucatán Peninsula. The biosphere not only contains the World Heritage Site of Calakmul but also is a biodiversity "hot spot" the country is particularly eager to maintain (Haenn 2000; see also Zizumbo et al. 2011). Hernández, Macario, and López-Martínez (2017) found that by combining labor from the family unit and the heat of the sun, a traditional agroforestry system (the milpa/solar complex) is energy efficient and sustainable over long periods when compared with more recently adopted farming practices employing technological methods (see also Alayón-Gamboa 2014b; Altieri 1999). They showed that 55 percent of the food consumed by villagers came from this combination of solar gardens, milpa, and animal husbandry, and 33 percent came from the solar garden exclusively (Hernández, Macario, and López-Martínez 2017).

In sum, this literature shows that the solar, with its garden and space for animal husbandry, contributes to the nutritional and medicinal needs of the family, offers variety in the daily diet, and potentially generates revenue through the sale of small animals raised there. Native plants in the solar can be more resistant to periods of environmental stress and provide a safety net for its inhabitants when milpa crops fail. Family composition impacts the structure and size of the solar. Small children require time-consuming care, time that otherwise might be spent in increasing the size and complexity of the solar garden. The presence of the male head of household can mean the garden gets more attention than would be the case if he migrated for work. Finally, solares of less wealthy families and those continuing to use more traditional means of cropping prove to rely less on nonrenewable energy and thus to be more sustainable over time (the use of homegrown palm thatch rather than commercial roofing materials is an example). These families tend to favor more native plants, thereby contributing to the ongoing natural biodiversity in the region.

Study Methodology

The two authors of this chapter have visited the community of Yaxunah for both short and extended stays every year for a combined total of forty-eight years. During this time, we have been involved in participant observations in virtually every aspect of village and family life; entered into countless informal conversations and interviews; taken social censuses and inventories of resources; conducted formal interviews, generally using open-ended questionnaire methods; and, based on these, have produced one undergraduate thesis, one master's thesis, and one doctoral dissertation. Subsequently, we have continued to engage in numerous small research projects in Yaxunah and now are involved in ongoing education and development projects at the behest of community members.

The Yaxunah Ejido and Village

Yaxunah is a village and an ejido, corporately held land surrounding the community itself. To fully understand the place of solares or houselots for families of Yaxunah, it is important to have a somewhat broader view of the environmental and legal entities that surround them. The ejido has 139 certified members (*ejidatarios*) who own the land jointly and equally share usufruct rights to plant cornfields and harvest firewood and other products of the forests. By federal law, the ejido is closed—meaning no new certifications of ownership can be issued. Ejido membership can only be inherited—passed to one son (or widow or daughter, if no son exists) in the subsequent generation. However, other, younger sons, not eligible to be ejidatarios, still have rights to petition the ejido assembly for permission to work a plot of land, harvest firewood, and so forth. These second sons, however, can neither vote in the ejido governing assembly nor hope to gain full ejidatario rights.

Under the 1917 federal constitution that created the ejido system, fifty hectares of land were set aside within each ejido and designated as village or township proper. Houselots with their solares cannot be built outside this designated village space. In Yaxunah, the community is laid out in the familiar Spanish-style grid pattern seen throughout Latin America, with a plaza in the center, important buildings surrounding it (e.g., the *comisaria* [town hall], Catholic church, homes of the oldest community members), and streets radiating away in forty-five small and roughly square blocks. Several homes with their surrounding solares are found in each of these blocks. Community members hold title to their plots inside the village and, unlike the adjoining ejido lands, can sell them if they so desire.

The population stands at 650 and has decreased in the later part of the 2010s. Community members give various reasons for the decline. Chief among these is the necessity to look for more substantial employment than temporary migration permits. Villagers consider that the best ejido lands are already under cultivation—leaving only poor-quality milpa space to second sons. Daughters who marry men not from the village know their husbands can no longer petition for full ejido rights, so they leave for the spouse's home community.

La Milpa—The Cornfield

The cornfield (milpa) and the solar intertwine in providing for the nutritional and other necessities of Maya families. Corn (*Zea mays* L.), squash (*Cucurbita argyrosperma* Huber and *Cucurbita moschata* Dauch), plus beans (*Phaseolus vulgaris* and *Phaseolus lunatus* L.) make up the bulk of milpa crops growing on rotating plots within the ejido. Traditionally, these have been the main sources of vegetable protein and carbohydrates for the family.

Robert S. Carlsen (1997), Robert M. Carmack, Janine Gasco, and Gary H. Gossen (1996), Duncan Earle (1986), Sylvia Terán (2010), Terán and Christian H. Rasmussen (2009), among many others, explain that a universal characteristic in Maya communities is the fact that much that is meaningful and religious, even today, inheres in symbols of the milpa. Sheldon Annis (1987, 10) refers to this as "milpa logic" and states that "the milpa is not only an economically elegant way to produce corn and beans, it is an elegant expression of . . . 'Indianness'" (see Re Cruz 1996 for a similar analysis related specifically to Yucatec Maya).

Even today, having a milpa, being a milpero, is part of the way Yucatec Maya choose to identify themselves. When asking a schoolteacher or a craftsman in the community (men who do not make milpa) where he is going, one might hear the response "I am going to my milpa," meaning "I am going to work" (Bascopé 2005; Re Cruz 1996). However, from 1990 to 2000, the Instituto Nacional de Estadística Geografía e Informática (INEGI) reported that the small portion of the population of the State of Yucatán engaged in agriculture declined by 10 percent (INEGI 1990, 2000). There is no reason to believe this trend has reversed.

Historically, corn production in rural Maya communities in the central region of the State of Yucatán has not been sufficient to meet the year-round needs of the family, and no excess has been available for sale. While land tenure does give families a buffer and allows them to supply some of their own nutritional requirements, time spent away from farming to generate cash revenue becomes increasingly more consuming. Further, older milperos in Yaxunah contend that, since the devastation of Hurricane Gilbert (Gilberto) in 1988, which caused an almost 100 percent crop loss throughout the state (see Clifton 1991), weather patterns have remained erratic and their own long-practiced folk knowledge of when to plant is no longer reliable. They do recognize and acknowledge that climate fluctuations began before the hurricane, but the date has become a shorthand anchor to which they peg impactful changes. From that point, when asked where a man is going, he might say, "I'm going to play the lottery," which is understood to mean "I'm going to plant my milpa."

The Mexican government formally recognizes the importance and precariousness of milpa work by providing a subsidy program called Programa de Apoyos Directos al Campo (PROCAMPO), which gives each farmer 1,600 Mexican pesos per hectare planted in corn. This amount is intended to cover the cost of seed corn, herbicides, insecticides, and fertilizers the milpero might use and to sustain a family until the next crop is harvested. At the state level in Yucatán, PROCAMPO is viewed as an allotment for the rural poor rather than payment for actual numbers of hectares under cultivation. Only certified ejidatarios receive PROCAMPO grants; second sons are not eligible, and, in part, this contributes to their migrating away from the village or turning to craft making and other remunerative activities.

The *Solares* of Yaxunah

There is no true equivalent English word for solar. Words like yard and houselot begin to approximate it, but the solar is much more than the grounds surrounding a habitation or habitations. The solar can be thought of as the playing field on which daily family life unfolds (figure 11.1). It is difficult to know how many solares are in Yaxunah, nor is it important to have an exact number for this work. As of October 2018, there are 268 plots or houselots in the community and there are 188 habitations or family dwellings. Some lots contain more than one habitation, and the families in them might or might not consider their plot to be divided into multiple solares.

Because the general pattern of postmarital residence is patrilocal, in rural Maya communities in Yucatán, young men often stay in their natal homes for years after marriage and may build separate houses in the same solar as their parents. They continue to share all parts of the yard in common. Eventually, the original parental solar may be divided by fences, as brothers' families grow, and their inheritances are more formally parceled (see Rico-Gray et al. 1990). This is demonstrated in the oldest solares. Those in the center of the village nearest the plaza are smaller than those farther away. This parceling of solares also helps account for the fact that several sections of the village are made up of families with the same surname—grandfathers, great uncles, fathers, sons, brothers, uncles, cousins, all budding off yeastlike from the original solares of the founding settlers of their patriline.

Solares are generally roughly rectangular. They are almost invariably fenced by substantial stone walls, either dry stacked or secured with cement. If the solar of a father and son touch, there may not be a fence between them, or the stone fence that does exist may have a large gap through which close family members can freely access the other's property. Otherwise, a solar is inviolable. Except for immediate family, a community member does not

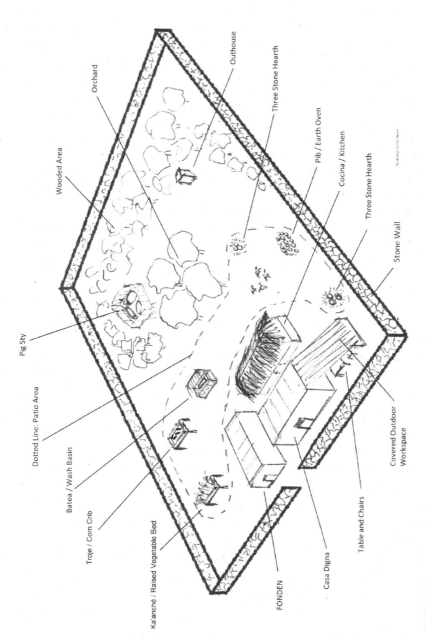

FIGURE 11.1 Model solar (drawing by Daniel Gruen).

enter the solar of another without stopping at the gate or fence, calling out a greeting, and waiting to be acknowledged and invited in. The same greeting ritual is repeated when the visitor steps over the threshold of the dwelling.

The contents of solares vary, but a general pattern has been recognized since preconquest times (Killion 1987, 1990; see Hernández Álvarez 2011 for details on the makeup of a sample of solares in Yaxunah). As a rule, the dwellings in a solar are close to and face the street. Besides living/sleeping quarters, most dwellings have a separate kitchen in the rear (a room that may have been the principal dwelling prior to the construction of one made from commercial materials). The separate kitchen is, in part, to cut down on fire potential, to keep smoke away from sleeping children and others, and to reduce heat in the living quarters. Even today, with 95 percent of families having houses made of commercial materials, almost 100 percent of kitchens are made with traditional pole sides and *huano* (palm thatch) roofs (though some roofs may be patched or covered entirely by oiled corrugated paper shingles).

Because Yaxunah is within the hot and humid Neotropics, for comfort's sake much family life takes place out of doors. This area of activity, the patio section of the solar, can be in front of the main habitation structure but more often is located near and behind the kitchen. Parts of the patio might be roofed with nylon canopy, oiled cardboard shingles, and/or huanos. Often, a table and chairs are located in the shade so meals can be eaten outside even during the rainy season. The patio that extends beyond this shaded area is recognizable because of frequently being swept clean. There may be evidence of small fires around the patio where household trash and leaf litter from the swept area are burned (see Rico-Gray 1990).

As an extension of the domestic living space, the patio is largely considered the province of women. It is her children's playscape, and she is the owner of and is responsible for small animals raised in the solar. Chickens and turkeys may roam the patio freely or there may be fencing for the fowl made from a variety of natural and fabricated materials. By village regulation, her pigs must be penned, and these structures are generally farther back in the solar in an area still filled with trees and brush. Pigs strengthen friendships and relationships with female family members through a *xkex-al*. In this agreement, a woman gives a newly weaned female pig to her trading partner. The recipient then raises the weaner and keeps all but one of its offspring, which she returns to her partner. In this fashion, a woman who has had to sell all her pigs can still get a fresh start. Women report they grow so accustomed to the sounds of pigs that, when few are around, the village seems too quiet and sad. They report that one can tell how well a family and or a village is doing just by looking and listening for pigs.

Pigs do not truly represent a profit. They are fed table scraps, corn with too many weevils, or squash if there is a good crop, but if these items are scarce, their food may need to be supplemented with the purchased meal (growing pigs eat approximately four kilos of corn a day). When this situation becomes untenable, that is, when families must purchase all or most of their own food, pigs will be sold off. It is probably more accurate to consider pigs to be cached resources. They are there in reserve, eating less desirable bits of food the family has produced, until the time arises when the family needs to convert them into cash, as when a child is ill or educational expenses must be paid for.

Larger animals, horses or *boregas* (sheep), are owned by men. These may be tied in the solar during the day but are taken out into the ejido to forage overnight. Though dogs live on the patio and women may feed them, men of the household are considered their owners as they assist men in protecting the milpa and aid in hunting. A few families have ducks. These, too, may be fed by women of the household but belong to the men. They are *mascotas* (pets) and, by village custom, neither their meat nor eggs are eaten by Yaxunenses.

Women grow kitchen condiments and herbal remedies—habanera chilis, green onions, garlic, chives, cilantro, mint, and rue in *ka'ancheob*, containers raised off the ground so chickens, pigs, and so on cannot destroy them (see Vargas 1983). By one count (Bascopé 2005), 87 percent of women in the village had such containers on their patios. In the same study, only 4 percent of women heads of households were found to have no poultry or ka'ancheob in their solares (figure 11.2). A *batea* (wash basin for scrubbing clothes), formerly carved from a large tree trunk but now made of concrete composite, sits toward the back of the patio area under either a tree or a constructed cardboard or plastic roof. Clotheslines are strung throughout the patio. The solar may also contain a *troje* (corn crib) to store seed corn to be used in planting the following year (figure 11.3).

Besides the cooking fire in the kitchen structure, patios invariably have a three-stone hearth where large containers can be accommodated for making celebratory foods or for rendering slaughtered pigs and processing chickens. Often more than one three-stone hearth is placed around the patio if a large family event is planned and more cooking space is required. Besides the hearth, each patio has an area for a *pib*, an underground or pit oven ap-

FIGURE 11.2 *Ka'anché* made from tires and discarded wheelbarrow bed (photograph by Grace Lloyd Bascopé).

FIGURE 11.3 *Troje* (corn crib) storing next year's seed corn (photograph by Grace Lloyd Bascopé).

FIGURE 11.4 Preparing the *pib*, or underground earth oven (photograph by Grace Lloyd Bascopé).

proximately 1.5 m long, used to roast tamales, sweet potatoes, and squash as well as celebratory dishes made from pork, turkey, and occasionally venison. Even when the pib is not in use, it can be spotted as being a rectangular area roughly 1 × 2 m. The area is marked by small bits of charcoal mixed into disturbed soil and fire-cracked rocks left from previous uses (figure 11.4). The area of the solar farthest from the dwelling and patio often maintains an overgrowth of native trees and shrubs, and a small orchard of fruit trees might be placed in this space. Family trash, largely discarded items—tires, broken equipment, glass containers, and the like—may be deposited in this area.

Nutrition and Water Supply

Malnutrition is common in Yucatán (Cuanalo de la Cerda, Cabrera Araujo, and Ochoa Estrada 2007; Cuanalo de la Cerda and Guerra Mukul 2008), with at least one study reporting that more than 50 percent of rural Maya children in the state are chronically undernourished (Ávila-Curiel et al. 1993). Cuanalo de la Cerda and Rafael A. Uicab-Covoh (2005, 2006) contend that government-sponsored home garden programs and those initiated by independent organizations, despite making seeds and saplings readily available at no cost, have had relatively little impact on this ubiquitous nutrition crisis. In a Cuanalo de la Cerda and Guerra Mukul (2008) study, the lack of a year-round adequate water supply was cited as a factor limiting home garden production and animal husbandry. This aligns with a study in Yaxunah by Grace Lloyd Bascopé, Leslie Llado, and Luis Aguirre (2013), in which twenty-five female and/or male heads of households were interviewed using an open-ended questionnaire format. Respondents were asked to provide information on their perceptions about the adequacy of the town water supply, their suggested solutions to any problems they perceived, and the problems if any, that lack of water caused in their own daily lives.

In the summer rainy season, electricity around the state is interrupted when lightning strikes and high winds damage power lines. These outages can last for part of a day to several days, causing the village pump not to function. Water shortages during this period are less critical because of daily rains; plants and animals can continue to survive. If the outage is long, however, cooking and cleaning, bathing, clothes washing, and so forth will become problematic. Because the northern portion of the State of Yucatán is a deciduous rainforest with a marked dry season, maintaining an adequate household water supply becomes problematic for up to six months of the year—a period that can begin as early as November and reach a peak in March and April.

Since the 1960s, Yaxunah has had a deep well, a one-horsepower pump, and a pump house located on the plaza. In turn, the plaza was built beside the cenote, the limestone sinkhole that reaches the water table. This cenote was the chief source of water for all inhabitants until the community was connected to the state electric grid and the well was dug. Interviewees reported that this pump location causes inherent problems in water distribution. The cenote is the lowest point in the surrounding terrain and the entire village slopes toward it. Homes except for those immediately around the plaza are on higher ground—some up to 10 m above the pump house. As the outskirts of the village grow in every direction, the pump works harder to fill the *tinacos* (500 L water barrels) on a roof or water tower in each yard. The pump can be run for two to three hours in the morning each day without becoming overheated. Paying for electricity used to run the pump, even for this short time, becomes a financial strain for many.

Interview respondents stated that problems with adequate water supply occurred because many (50 percent among those surveyed) did not have working float valves to stop water from overflowing when their tinacos were full, and all reported they either had breaks in hoses or loose fittings that also wasted water. All reported that the water system in their own yards could be improved. Lack of funding for clamps, new hoses, and float valves, and the need to pay someone more skilled to do the labor, were reported as major drawbacks to making repairs. Participants were fully aware that the karstic environment of Yucatán meant plumbing equipment—couplings, shower heads, toilet tank fittings, and so on—becomes clogged with calcium deposits almost annually, signifying that repairs and trying to make their own household water system leakproof demanded ongoing labor and attention. In sum, interviewees reported problems with the town water distribution system but also took responsibility for water they felt they caused to be wasted.

Depending on the climate, age and physiology, basic cooking needs, and social and cultural hygiene norms, the World Health Organization sets water sufficiency requirements from 7.5 to 15 L per day per household member. Respondents reported that either they or others they know in the community experienced ongoing intermittent and long-term shortages. Problems that arose from the lack of a sustained year-round water supply were numerous, many potentially impacting health, nutrition, and hygiene. Families nearer the center of the community said they did not make large vegetable gardens, plant fruit trees, or keep more animals for fear they would be criticized for taking water away from those further away. Those on the outskirts of the village reported frequently experiencing water shortages that caused them to delay laundry and other hygiene necessities. One mother's response was typical. "I can only manage to keep three small lemon trees alive during March and

April," she explained, "There just isn't enough water for more. I would like to feed my children, animals, and vegetables, and things I could grow."

A federal government program, Prospera (Fernald, Gertler, and Neufeld 2008), provides small stipends to mothers who bring their children for regular clinic visits and who, themselves, attend regularly scheduled *pláticas* (talks) about various aspects of family health and nutrition. Pláticas often focus on the necessity to use pure water for children especially susceptible to diarrheal diseases. No one can question the need for mothers to understand the benefits that accrue to families when they have access to pure water. Yet in teaching rural poor to look at clean and safe water as a purchasable commodity—as something for which Prospera funds should be spent—rather than as a right simply acquired through citizenship, the need for government spending on a safe and sufficient town water system is obviated. The structural inequality of not having an ample water supply, however, also means that most families, who have listened to and understood the pláticas about the importance of providing children with an adequate and varied diet containing vegetables and fruits, feel frustrated by not being able to grow them. Further, there are negative consequences to teaching citizens to boil water if funds are not available to purchase clean water. As the mode of cooking in the village is with firewood, making water safe by boiling means continued forest destruction and potentially more asthma and other respiratory problems for infants, children, and others in the households—problems health care workers currently attribute to firewood use. In sum, parents purchase water, buy vegetables when they can, and report feeling bad or guilty when they cannot. There is no shortage of clean water within the karstic geology of the peninsula (Bascopé, Llado, and Aguirre 2013; Antonio Paniche, personal communication, 2005), though it must be accessed through deep wells too expensive for individuals to dig and delivered to households by pumps and piping adequate for the population size. With a sufficient town water supply, safe water could be virtually free, and fruits and vegetables adapted to grow in the area could be abundant.

Changing Food Production and Preferences—Threats to the Solar Gardens and Milpa

Jesús Chi-Quej et al. (2011) report that changes in food choices threaten the existence of the solar garden. Odette Pérez Izquierdo et al. (2012) and

Brenda Olvera et al. (2017) explain that as the traditional rural system of individual family production (solar garden, milpa, and animal husbandry [see Alayón-Gamboa 2014b]) declines and the ease of purchasing processed foods increases, health is impacted. Notably, instances of obesity and its complications and Type-2 diabetes mellitus soar, and the age of onset of these diseases continues to fall (Olvera et al 2017). Ironically, by providing money directly to the rural poor, as with Prospera, government social programs designed to ease poverty may be partly responsible for these health downturns, as readily available cash from them may be used to purchase commercially prepared foods of questionable nutritional value (Olvera et al. 2017). Francisco Rosado (2012) contends that when home gardens are lost, an impact on milpa productions follows, and food sufficiency and sovereignty diminish (Terán 2010).

Subsistence *Milperos* No Longer (If Ever They Were)

In a review work, Ute Schüren (2003, 47) urges that we reconceptualize the idea of peasantry—peasants having been defined "as rural cultivators whose most important means of livelihood was subsistence agriculture (understood as production for self-consumption). Their activities were seen as centred around the rural village/community, which was perceived as a relatively homogeneous universe with a distinct culture" (see also Kearney 1996; Leeds 1977; Redfield 1941, 1947). Schüren (2003) explains that, for agriculturalists, even the term *milpero* should be considered a role taken up only during times of actual milpa work. Otherwise, any one person in a rural community—male, female, or children old enough to participate in economic activities—may have various and varied roles.

At any point in the life of a person in Yaxunah, several economic roles play out simultaneously. These change, for all economic actors in the family unit, by the day, week, season, age, family composition, external exigencies, and so forth. Men who have training as masons and masons' helpers migrate to Mérida. Some migrate to Cancún and the Costa Maya, generally to work in hotels on a temporary basis. Other roles taken on by villagers include musician (some work more steadily in the city, while others are hired periodically for saint-day festivals and celebrations both inside the village and in other communities). There are troupes of dancers who perform on the site of Chichén Itzá and at nearby resorts. There is a baker who sells bread inside the village and to neighboring communities and hires others to help him. There are men proficient in plumbing, electrical, charcoal making, and bicycle repair. There are store owners and taxi drivers. Several persons are given a small wage by the *ayuntamiento* (the county) to act as village policemen, to keep the village plaza in good order, and to take the trash, collected in barrels distributed around the community, to the village dump. Each role impacts the importance and use of the solar and the milpa (Lizama Quijano 2007).

As the school semester ends, many of the older middle and high schoolers go to Mérida for temporary work. Their families have long-standing contacts with private homes where girls are employed as nannies and housekeepers. Boys are hired in certain restaurants that provide dormitories for employees. One villager explained lamentingly (personal communication to Bascopé, September 2014), "Once our children put on high school uniforms, they don't return to the milpa; they lose all knowledge of the forest and its plants." During these periods of temporary migration, young people contribute to the economic survival of their families but also learn to navigate the city and become involved in the global capitalist consumer economy, including learning to enjoy and perhaps prefer manufactured foods. Further, this exposure to urban life allows them to gather information about possibilities for technical schooling or entering a public university, a path that might lead to permanent absence from the village.

Some men in the village go on a *batida* (a hunt for deer, javelina, and rabbits) from time to time to supplement the family's protein needs. Didac Santos-Fita, Eduardo J. Naranjo, and José Luis Rangal-Salazar (2012, 2) contend that as Mexican governments "expand development programs introducing new roads, electricity, computers, educational and health services," subsistence hunting will diminish and disappear. A better road system means Yaxunah villagers have increased access to commercially available foodstuffs. Both milpa work and hunting are diminishing (Stearman 2000).

Craft Production—Woodcarving

The commercial activity of craft production is also crowding out traditional milpa work. Rooms in houses, outdoor shelters, and patios are given over to becoming workshops for carvers. Woodchips cover the ground. These may or may not be used as kindling or otherwise burned, or may simply be left to dry as a groundcover. In 2005, a social census by Bascopé revealed that

64 percent of households dedicated some portion of their time to woodcarving. Today, based on a more informal count and conversations with community members, 85 percent of households contain at least one person who works on carving "Maya-esque" masks and wall plaques as a near fulltime occupation. Anuar Patjane Florink (2009) explores how craftspeople of Yaxunah view carving faux-Maya figures pragmatically. They understand that the designs they choose to execute are not representative of themselves as Maya but conform to tourists' expectations of Maya-ness. One family finds it comical that they carve a type of seated, and evidently drunken, figure, dressed in a style of clothes found in northern Mexico. While such a figure is completely foreign to the Yucatán, they are popular memorabilia for tourists visiting the Costa Maya, and the family is content with having this revenue stream.

Men, women, and children carve, sand, and paint these figures. Children, still in school, may spend short periods on this work during the week and as much as fifteen hours on weekends. Despite Prospera stipends, designed to keep children in school through high school, nearly a third of those who finish middle school become involved in full-time craft production. Others finish high school but do not seek further university or technical training, instead choosing to make a more immediate contribution to their family's finances through carving (Alcocer Puerto 2007).

Several men in the community have become middlemen, collecting carvings from others and paying them a wholesale price (Mintz 1956). These are then taken to tourist centers to be sold in bulk for others to distribute. While villagers may make less per item and may complain about this fact, they do not incur the expense of transporting their finished products to market.

Carving involves risks. Knives are kept extremely sharp, and long, tiring hours or distractions can lead to accidents. Both authors have witnessed injuries to legs, palms, fingers, and abdomens, and have taken carvers to clinics in the nearest towns for medical attention. Feeding into the need for cash, craft-producing families explain they purchase televisions, radios, and CD players to help break the boredom that comes from producing the same product over and over, and to help keep the carver(s) awake through long hours and late nights.

Upticks in tourism, for example, cause more family time to be spent in craft production rather than tending the solar or the milpa. This was clearly demonstrated after Hurricane Maria devastated Puerto Rico in September

2017. In the subsequent tourist season, European families, who frequently vacationed in Puerto Rico, chose the Yucatán instead, causing demands for craft goods to soar. Downturns in tourism occur, for example, when the U.S. State Department posts travel warnings for other parts of Mexico or swine flu is reported somewhere in the country. Though these generally do not directly pertain to Yucatán, they are impactful. Further, tourism is, by its very nature, seasonal. U.S. tourists come in summer, winter, and during the weeks of spring break. When tourists are abundant, carvers work ceaselessly. When tourism slows, they are the first in the supply chain to be without work and the last to begin again.

"We are the people of the corn," laments one villager (personal communication to Bascopé, 2000). "We were made of corn, but my children are made of *chakaj* [*Bursera simaruba*, the tree most commonly used in carving]. Because we spend our time carving, they eat French rolls, chips, and cookies. They drink sodas. We don't stop to cook" (figure 11.5).

Both chakaj and *cedro* (*Cedrella odorata*) have virtually disappeared from the Yaxunah ejido and must be purchased and transported from other ejidos.

FIGURE 11.5 Chakaj logs purchased from outside the ejido and ready for carving (photograph by Grace Lloyd Bascopé).

This continues to diminish slim profit margins. The full environmental impact of losing these two important plant species in the ejido and surrounding ecosystem is unstudied and unknown. What is known is that *Bursera simaruba* blooms at a time when little else is in flower in the forest to sustain both wild and commercial honeybees.

Solar and Milpa—A Questionable Future

Statistics show that milpa production is declining in the state of Yucatán, and word-of-mouth information from Yaxunah lends support to this trend (INEGI 1990, 2000). The solar, with its home garden, has been considered the perfect complement to milpa production. The solar garden provides minerals, vitamins, medicinal aids, desired condiments, and protein not found in the traditional milpa. In Yaxunah, these elements, both the milpa and solar food production, are under considerable stress, as is the diet of the village inhabitants. While the male head-of-household may not migrate, his time, and that of his family members, is increasingly taken up in craftwork and in seeking means by which to enter the cash economy, even while staying in the village. Not migrating, for temporary or permanent employment, does not necessarily translate into spending time improving solar food production. For many, the solar has become a workshop rather than a garden.

Even with time for solar garden production and animal husbandry, families do not feel they have an adequate water supply with which to grow the food they might wish. Not being able to grow enough vegetables and fruits for family consumption means these must be purchased when cash is available. Moreover, clean drinking water is not free, and government programs train mothers and other community members that safe water is a commodity to be purchased. The lack of an adequate and safe water system must be considered a form of structural neglect by the government.

As cash is generated by craftwork and through government subsidy programs such as Progresa and PROCAMPO—both designed, in part, to help supplement the diet of families—an unintended consequence is that more manufactured foods, sugars, and processed carbohydrates are consumed. Paved roads make access to such products more easily obtainable—another unintended consequence of government aid. The lack of water for larger home gardens and more animal husbandry and lack of access to processed foods are problematic. Poor diets are shown to lead to obesity and its consequences, malnutrition, and an increase in Type 2 diabetes mellitus (Ávila-Curiel et al. 1993).

Other changes in the solar, in the form of government housing efforts, are welcomed, if somewhat ill-suited to the climate, but this bodes ill for the environment. Manufactured housing materials must be shipped into the village from at least as far as the capital city. Community members become accustomed to these, while materials easily and freely obtained from the ejido are used less often. The sabal palm is not being replanted, for example. Modernization and integration into the wider regional economy are welcome in the village of Yaxunah, although these come with a price often being borne by the health status of community members and by the ecosystem that surrounds it.

Recent Developments

Since this chapter was first written in late 2019, life in Yaxunah has undergone extreme stress. As is true for the rest of the world, Yaxunah has not escaped the ravages of the coronavirus pandemic. A number of villagers have been sickened and a few have died. Craft production is at a complete standstill because tourism has faded away. The nearby archaeological site of Chichén Itzá, which attracts more than 1.5 million visitors annually, was closed in March 2020. It reopened in late September 2020, but it may be a very long time before enough tourists return to the site that merchants will want to purchase goods from the Yaxunah crafters. Villagers are essentially jobless.

Coupled with these ongoing burdens, the village was flooded more severely than its oldest inhabitants can recall. An early season hurricane, Cristobal, began striking the Yucatán Peninsula on June 3, 2020, and shed rain over the area for eight days and nights. Water could not drain into the cenote quickly enough. Homes and solares were waist and shoulder deep in water, their contents waterlogged and damaged. Gardens and small animals in solares were lost (and in the aftermath, if animals had lived, there would not have been food to maintain them). Fencing and many small outbuildings were destroyed.

Corn, beans, and squash in the milpas were flooded and ruined. Water stood in the ejido lands as never before. Some families had enough seed corn to replant, and the government provided seed for others, but milperos report that an insect, one heretofore unknown, destroyed the new plants as they sprouted. The milperos believe this wormlike insect came with the floods.

Starting the last week of September 2020, Tropical Storm Gamma struck the Caribbean side of Yucatán and slowly migrated around the edges and into the Gulf of Mexico, producing more record flooding in the states of the Yucatán Peninsula. The hurricane was devastating. It flooded the whole center of the village as the cenote could not drain all the rain that fell so quickly. Rock walls around solares retained floodwaters and caused water to build up inside houses—in some cases, feet deep. Villagers in lower areas had to move in with neighbors on higher ground or into the primary and secondary school buildings. Home gardens were destroyed and small animals drowned. Initially, having dry firewood, clothing, and blankets for children was a problem. Emergency food and other provisions had to be brought in by larger government entities. Having never experienced such a cascade of difficulties, Yaxunah community members reported being frightened and in shock. For them, it is unclear how and when life can regain some semblance of normalcy.

Works Cited

Alayón-Gamboa, José A. 2014a. "Contribución del huerto familiar a la seguridad alimentaria de las familias campesinas de Calakmul, Campeche." In *El huerto familiar: Un sistema socioecológico y biocultural para sustentar los modos de vida campesinos en Calakmul, Mexico*, edited by José Armando Alayón-Gamboa and Alejandro Morón Ríos, 15–40. Mexico City: El Colegio de la Frontera Sur.

Alayón-Gamboa, José A. 2014b. "Sustentabilidad de la agricultura tradicional y el impacto en su transformación: El caso de Calakmul, Campeche." In *Sociedad y ambiente en Mexico: Áreas naturales protegidas y sustentabilidad*, edited by Miguel Ángel Pinkus Rendón, 211–36. Mexico City: Centro Peninsular en Humanidades y Ciencias Sociales, Universidad Nacional Autónoma de México.

Alayón-Gamboa, José A., and Francisco D. Gurri-García. 2008. "Home Garden Production and Energetic Sustainability in Calakmul, Campeche, Mexico." *Human Ecology* 36 (3): 395–407.

Alcocer Puerto, Elias. 2007. "El ecoturismo cultural dentro de una comunidad maya de Yucatán." MA thesis, Centro de Investigación y Estudios Avanzados, Instituto Politécnico Nacional, Mérida.

Altieri, Miguel A. 1999. "Applying Agroecology to Enhance the Productivity of Peasant Farming Systems in Latin America." *Environment, Development and Sustainability* 1:197–217.

Annis, Sheldon. 1987. *God and Production in a Guatemalan Town*. Austin: University of Texas Press.

Ávila-Curiel, Abelardo, Adolfo Chávez-Villasana, Teresa Shamah-Levi, and Herlinda Madrigal-Fritsch. 1993. "La desnutrición infantil en el medio rural mexicano." *Salud Pública de México* 35 (6): 658–66.

Barrera, Alfredo. 1980. "Sobre la unidad de habitación tradicional campesina y el manejo de los recursos bióticos en el área maya yucatánense. I. Árboles y arbustos de las huertas familiares." *Biotica* 5 (3): 115–28.

Bascopé, Grace Lloyd. 2005. "The Household Ecology of Disease Transmission: Childhood Illness in a Yucatán Maya Community." PhD diss., Southern Methodist University, Dallas.

Bascopé, Grace Lloyd, Leslie Llado, and Luis Aguirre. 2013. "Community Opinion Survey: Adequacy of the Town Water System." Unpublished manuscript in author's possession.

Caballero, Javier. 1994. "Use and Management of Sabal Palms Among the Maya of Yucatán." PhD diss., University of California, Berkeley.

Carlsen, Robert S. 1997. *War for the Heart and Soul of a Highland Maya Town*. Austin: University of Texas Press.

Carmack, Robert M., Janine Gasco, and Gary H. Gossen. 1996. *The Legacy of Mesoamerica: History and Culture of a Native American Civilization*. Upper Saddle River, N.J.: Prentice Hall.

Chi-Quej, Jesús, Gonzalo Galileo Rivas Platero, Isabel Gutiérrez-Montes, Guillermo Detlefsen, José Armando Alayón-Gamboa, and Victor M. Ku Quej. 2011. "Los huertos familiares y su contribución a la seguridad alimentaria en Campeche, Mexico." Paper presented at the 3rd Congreso Latinoamericano de Agroecología, Sociedad Científica Latinoamericana de Agroecología, Universidad Autónoma Chapingo, Mexico City.

Chi-Quej, Jesús, José Armando Alayón-Gamboa, G. Rivas, I. Gutiérrez, G. Detlefsen, and V. Ku-Quej. 2014. "Contribución del huerto familiar a la economía campesina en Calakmul, Campeche." In *El huerto familiar: Un sistema socioecológico y biocultural para sustentar los modos de vida campesinos en Calakmul, Mexico*, edited by José Armando Alayón-Gamboa and Alejandro Morón Ríos, 75–90. Mexico City: El Colegio de la Frontera Sur.

Clifton, Dixon. 1991. "Yucatán After the Wind: Human and Environmental Impact of Hurricane Gilbert in the Central and Eastern Yucatán Peninsula." *Geo Journal* 23 (4): 337–45.

Cuanalo de la Cerda, Heriberto E., Zulema M. Cabrera Araujo, and Ernesto Ochoa Estrada. 2007. "Infant Nutrition in a Poor Mayan Village of Yucatán Is Related to an Energy Deficiency Diet That a Course on Nutrition Could Not Overcome." *Ecology of Food and Nutrition* 46 (1): 37–46.

Cuanalo de la Cerda, Heriberto E., and Rogelio R. Guerra Mukul. 2008. "Homegarden Production and Productivity in a Mayan Community of Yucatán." *Human Ecology* 36 (3): 423–33.

Cuanalo de la Cerda, Heriberto E., and Rafael A. Uicab-Covoh. 2005. "Investigación participativa en la Milpa Sin Quema." *Terra Latinoamericana* 23 (4): 587–97.

Cuanalo-de la Cerda, Heriberto E., and Rafael Alejandro Uicab-Covoh. 2006. "Resultados de la investigación participativa en la Milpa Sin Quema." *Terra Latinoamericana* 24 (3): 401–8.

Dine, Harper, Traci T. Ardren, Grace Lloyd Bascopé, and Celso Gutiérrez Báez. 2019. "Famine Foods and Food Security in the Northern Maya Lowlands: Modern Lessons for Ancient Reconstructions." *Mesoamerican Antiquity* 30 (3): 517–34.

Earle, Duncan. 1986. "The Metaphor of the Day in Quiché Guatemala: Notes on the Nature of Everyday Life." In *Symbols and Meaning Beyond the Closed Community: Essays in Mesoamerican Ideas*, edited by Gary Gossen, 155–72. Albany: SUNY Institute of Mesoamerican Studies.

Fernald, Lia C. H., Paul J. Gertler, and Lynnette M. Neufeld. 2008. "Role of Cash in Conditional Cash Transfer Programmes for Child Health, Growth, and Development: An Analysis of Mexico's Oportunidades." *The Lancet* 371 (9615): 828–37.

Haenn, Nora. 2000. "'Biodiversity Is Diversity in Use': Community-Based Conservation in the Calakmul Biosphere Reserve." America Verde Working Papers 7. The Nature Conservancy, Arlington, Va.

Hernández, Mariana Y., Pedro A. Macario, and Jorge O. López-Martínez. 2017. "Traditional Agroforestry Systems and Food Supply Under the Food Sovereignty Approach." *Ethnobiology Letters* 8 (1). https://doi.org/10.14237/ebl.8.1.2017.941.

Hernández Álvarez, Héctor Abraham. 2011. "Etnoarqueología de grupos domésticos mayas: Identidad social y espacio residencial de Yaxunah, Yucatán." PhD diss., Universidad Nacional Autónoma de México, Mexico City.

Ibarra-Manríquez, G. 1996. "Biogeografía de los árboles nativos de la península de Yucatán: Un enfoque para evaluar su grado de conservación." PhD diss., Universidad Nacional Autónoma de México, Mexico City.

Instituto Nacional de Estadística Geografía e Informática (INEGI). 1990. "Yucatán, resultados definitivos. Datos por localidad. XI Censo General de Población y Vivienda, 1990." Mexico City: INEGI.

Instituto Nacional de Estadística Geografía e Informática (INEGI). 2000. "Yucatán, resultados definitivos. Datos por Localidad. XII Censo General de Población y Vivienda, 2000." Mexico City: INEGI.

Kearney, Michael. 1996. *Reconceptualizing the Peasantry: Anthropology in Global Perspective*. Boulder, Colo.: Westview Press.

Killion, Thomas. 1987. "Agriculture and Residential Site Structure Among Campesinos in Southern Veracruz, Mexico: A Foundation for Archaeological Inference." PhD diss., University of New Mexico, Albuquerque.

Killion, Michael. 1990. "Cultivation Intensity and Residential Site Structure: An Ethnoarchaeological Examination of Peasant Agriculture in the Sierra de los Tuxtlas, Veracruz, México." *Latin American Antiquity* 1 (3): 191–215.

Leeds, Anthony. 1977. "Mythos and Pathos: Some Unpleasantries on Peasantries." In *Peasant Livelihood: Studies in Economic Anthropology and Cultural Ecology*, edited by Rhoda Halperin and James Dow, 227–56. New York: St. Martin's.

Lizama Quijano, Jesús. 2007. *Estar en el mundo: Procesos culturales, estrategias económicas y dinámicas identitarias entre los mayas yucatecos*. Mexico City: Centro de Investigaciones y Estudios Superiores en Antropología Social.

Martínez-Ballesté, Andrea, Carlos Martorell, and Javier Caballero. 2006. "Cultural or Ecological Sustainability? The Effects of Cultural Change on Sabal Palm Management Among the Lowland Maya of Mexico." *Ecology and Society* 11 (2): 27.

Mintz, Sidney. 1956. "The Role of Middlemen in the Internal Distribution System of the Caribbean Peasant Economy." *Human Organization* 15 (2): 18–23.

Niñez, Vera. 1985. "Food Production for Home Consumption: Nature and Function of Gardens in Household Economics." *Archivos Latinoamericanos de Nutrición* 35 (1): 9–29.

Olvera, Brenda, Birgit Schmook, Claudia Radel, and Dominga Austreberta Nazar Beutelspacher. 2017. "Efectos adversos de los programas de apoyo alimentario en los hogares rurales de Calakmul, Campeche." *Estudios Sociales* 27 (49): 13–45.

Patjane Floriuk, Anuar. 2009. "De la milpa a la producción artesanal en serie: Implicaciones socioeconómicas del desarrollo turístico en la región de Chichén Itzá." PhD diss., Universidad de las Américas, Puebla Otoño.

Pérez Izquierdo, Odette, Austreberta Nazar Beutelspacher, Benito Salvatierra Izaba, Sara Elena Pérez-Gil Romo, Luis Rodríguez, María Teresa Castillo Burguete, and Ramón Mariaca Méndez. 2012. "Frecuencia del consumo de alimentos industrializados modernos en la dieta habitual de comunidades mayas de Yucatán, Mexico." *Estudios Sociales* 20 (39): 156–84.

Poot-Pool, Wilbert Santiago, Hans van der Wal, Salvador Flores-Guido, Juan Manuel Pat-Fernández, and Ligia Esparza-Olguín. 2012. "Economic Stratification Differentiates Home Gardens in the Maya Village of Pomuch." *Economic Botany* 66 (3): 264–75.

Re Cruz, Alicia. 1996. "The Two Milpas of Chan Kom: A Study of Socioeconomic and Political Transformations in a Maya Community." PhD diss., State University of New York, Albany.

Redfield, Robert. 1941. *The Folk Culture of Yucatán*. Chicago: University of Chicago Press.

Redfield, Robert. 1947. "The Folk Society." *American Journal of Sociology* 52 (4): 293–308.

Rico-Gray, Victor, Jose G. Garcia-Franco, Alexandra Chemas, Armando Puch, and Paulino Sima. 1990. "Species Composition, Similarity, and Structure of Mayan Homegardens in Tixpeual and Tixcacaltuyub, Yucatán, Mexico." *Economic Botany* 44 (4): 470–87.

Rosado, Francisco. 2012. "Los huertos familiares: Un sistema indispensable para la soberanía y suficiencia alimentaria en el sureste de México." In *El huerto familiar del sureste de Mexico*, edited by R. Mariaca, 350–60. Mexico City: Secretaría de Recursos Naturales y Protección Ambiental del Estado de Tabasco and El Colegio de la Frontera Sur.

Santos-Fita, Dídac, Eduardo J. Naranjo, and José Luis Rangal-Salazar. 2012. "Wildlife Uses and Hunting Patterns in Rural Communities of the Yucatán Peninsula, Mexico." *Journal of Ethnobiology and Ethnomedicine* 8:38.

Scales, Ben R., and Stuart J. Marsden. 2008. "Biodiversity in Small-Scale Tropical Agroforests: A Review of Species Richness and Abundance Shifts and the Factors Influencing Them." *Environmental Conservation* 35 (2): 160–72.

Schüren, Ute. 2003. "Reconceptualizing the Post-Peasantry: Household Strategies in Mexican Ejidos." *European Review of Latin American and Caribbean Studies / Revista Europea de Estudios Latinoamericanos y del Caribe*, no. 75 (October): 47–63.

Stearman, Allyn MacLean. 2000. "A Pound of Flesh: Social Change and Modernization as Factors in Hunting Sustainability Among Neotropical Indigenous Societies." In *Hunting for Sustainability in Tropical Forests*, edited by John G. Robinson and Elizabeth L. Bennett, 233–50. New York: Columbia University Press.

Terán, Sylvia. 2010. "Milpa, biodiversidad y diversidad cultural." In *Biodiversidad y desarrollo humano en Yucatán*, edited by Rafael Durán and Martha Méndez, 54–56. Mérida, Yucatán, Mexico: CICY, PPD-FMAM, CONABIO, SEDUMA.

Terán, Sylvia, and Christian H. Rasmussen. 2009. *La milpa de los mayas*. 2nd ed. Mexico City: Universidad Nacional Autónoma de Mexico.

Toledo, Victor M., Narciso Barrera-Bassols, Eduardo García-Frapolli, and Pablo Alarcón-Chaires. 2008. "Uso multiple y biodiversidad entre los Mayas Yucatecos (México)." *Interciencia* 33 (5): 345–352.

Vara, Adelaido. 1980. "La dinámica de la milpa en Yucatán: El solar." In *Seminario sobre producción agrícola en Yucatán*, edited by Efraín Hernández Xolocotzi and Rafael Padilla y Ortega, 305–41. Mérida, Yucatán, Mexico: Gob. Edo. Yucatán, S.P.P., S.A.R.H., and el Colegio de Postgraduados de Chapingo.

Vargas, Carlos. 1983. "El Ka'anché: Una Práctica Hortícola Maya." *Biotica* 8 (2): 151–73.

Zizumbo, D., P. Colunga, F. May, J. Martínez, and J. Mijangos. 2011. "Recursos Fitogenéticos para la Alimentación y la Agricultura." In *Biodiversidad y desarrollo humano en Yucatán*, edited by Rafael Durán and Martha Méndez, 334–39. Mérida, Yucatán, Mexico: CICY, PPD-FMAM, CONABIO, SEDUMA.

CHAPTER 12

The Identity That Binds and the *Albarradas* That Divide

Residential Space and Ethnoarchaeology in Yaxunah, Yucatán

HÉCTOR HERNÁNDEZ ÁLVAREZ

Within a contemporary Yucatec Maya community, there are multiple and diverse links that unite and barriers that divide people. At the village level, the *albarradas* (low stone walls) are the spatial configurations that divide the residential spaces, while domestic constructions serve as physical means to delimit different family units. On the other hand, collective activities, kinship ties, religious affiliations, shared history, and the management of community organization are some of the mechanisms that promote the social identity of persons who seek to survive the onslaught of modernity. In this sense, residential space acts as a material reference of social relations that symbolizes, mediates, or ascribes social status and differentiation, or reaffirms the kinship relations between members of different domestic groups or between domestic groups and the community. Dwellings and domestic spaces have great significance in defining or positioning the ethnic, political, or religious affiliation of a group. They can also indicate social divisions within a group or with respect to others.

Therefore, I show that the residential spaces, physical dwellings, and domestic material culture are the main references signifying the domestic groups of the contemporary Maya community of Yaxunah, Yucatán. Those material aspects constitute the means through which social identity is negotiated daily. Residences, dwellings, and material possessions are referential entities that act as mediators between the internal coherence of the family unit and are the external link with the community, based on kinship relations, social memory, politics, religion, and their links to the past.

Using data from a sample of contemporary Maya domestic groups, I demonstrate that domestic spaces and material culture play a fundamental role in shaping a community identity by fostering significant social practices and relationships among group members and their community. People experience, create, and reproduce their individual and social identity, maintain traditions, and negotiate positions of authority through a process of conformation and interaction based on material culture, the management of domestic space, and the built environment within the broader community.

Ethnoarchaeology, Domestic Groups, and Social Identity

Ethnoarchaeology is a research approach that uses archaeological interpretation to study the behaviors and material culture of contemporary societies to make analogies about past societies. It is considered the ethnographic study of living cultures from an archaeological perspective (David and Kramer 2001, 2). Since the 1970s, frames of reference have constituted an alternative through which the past could be projected and understood from a network of relational analogies of uniformitarian character (Binford 1967, 2001; Gifford-Gonzalez 1991; Kent 1992). Ethnoarchaeology uses studies on settlement patterns and domestic site structure among actual communities in order to establish frames of reference to structure the domestic model of the past (Alexander and Andrade 2007; Dore 1996; González Ruibal 2001; Kamp 1987; Kent 1992; Lyons 2007; Pierrebourg 1999; Wilk 1983). An example of the fundamental residential unit in the tropical zones of Mesoamerica is the houselot model (Killion 1990). This consists of space delimited by albarradas that contains housing structures surrounded by a patio and garden where waste is deposited. This type of habitation offered adaptive advantages to the Mesoamerican domestic groups, allowing for the best use of space for daily activities, dumping areas, and domestic tasks (Alexander 1999; Arnold 1991; Deal 1998; Pierrebourg 1999; Quintal et al. 2003; Smyth 1990).

In this regard, ethnoarchaeology also shows that the residential space acts as a material reference of social relations, symbolizing, mediating, or ascribing social status. Domestic areas also serve the purpose of differentiating or reaffirming kinship relations between members of different groups or between residential units and the community (González Ruibal 2003). Dwellings and domestic space have great significance when it comes to defining or positioning the ethnic, political, or religious affiliation of a group and can also be an indicator of social divisions within the same group or with respect to others (Alexander and Andrade 2007; González Ruibal 2001; Wilk 1983).

In contemporary nonindustrialized societies, domestic architecture, space, and material culture are some of the main areas in which ideas about order, family, gender, society, power, and the cosmos are embodied (Bourdieu 2000; González Ruibal 2003; Lyons 2009; Wilk 1983). Housing is one of the best ways to demonstrate belonging to a specific community and reinforces the idea of collectivism. But, at the same time, it is also the private refuge of individuals and the place that allows them to differentiate from others. Material culture also plays a central role in shaping the identity of the domestic group by fostering meaningful social practices and relationships among group members and in relation to their community. It is through the process of construction and interacting through material culture, including buildings, space, and things, that "people experience, create and reproduce their individual and social identity, maintain tradition, and negotiate positions of authority" (Lyons 2007, 180).

In the case of Maya domestic groups, ethnoarchaeological research has focused primarily on studies of social organization, residential structure, domestic architecture, handicraft activities, and waste patterns (Alexander and Andrade 2007; Deal 1985, 1998; Dore 1996; Hayden and Cannon 1983; Heidelberg and Rissolo 2006; Hernández Álvarez 2014a; Pierrebourg 1999; Wilk 1983). These studies have contributed to greater knowledge about the morphology and functions of these groups. However, we know little about other types of problems that equally determine domestic groups, such as the negotiation of social identities. Questions regarding gender, status, ritual, and the influence of globalization are also reflected in material culture, the structure of the residential site, and the daily practice of domestic tasks.

Yaxunah, a Community in Constant Change

The town of Yaxunah is a contemporary community of Mayan-speaking peasants located in the central part of the State of Yucatán, 20 km south of the archaeological zone of Chichén Itzá (figure 12.1). As part of a doctoral thesis project, I began to make visits to the town of Yaxunah in 2005 with

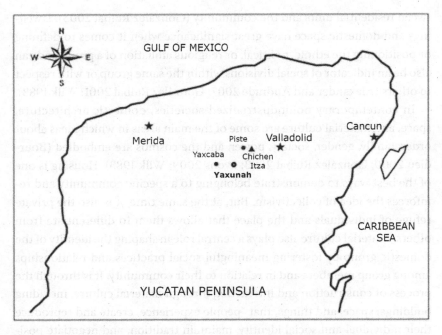

FIGURE 12.1 Map of the northern region of the Yucatán Peninsula with sites mentioned in the text (map by Héctor Hernández Álvarez).

the objective of studying domestic groups, including residential spaces, domestic architecture, and contemporary material culture, as a way of understanding the social identity of the people who live there. Yaxunah constitutes a zone of settlement that has been continuously occupied since Prehispanic times. Its archaeological site was one of the largest and most important of the peninsula since early times and has been the subject of research projects by both national and foreign archaeologists (e.g., Stanton and Ardren 2005; Toscano and Ortegón 2003).

During colonial and historical periods, the settlement included Cetelac, the maize- and livestock-focused hacienda, and a Catholic church constructed in the center of town. Toward 1843, the settlement suffered a period of abandonment due to the Caste War (1847) that affected the Yaxcabá region (Alexander 1999, 2004). In 1920, the town was resettled by peasants who arrived from neighboring towns. At this time, it became an ejido and took on the configuration that we see today (Hernández Álvarez 2014b; Hernández Álvarez and Novelo Rincón 2007).

Initially, the founding families consisted of landless peasants who practiced milpa agriculture and sought to settle on new land to cultivate their fields. From the stories about the origin of the village, preserved by oral tradition, we can perceive a feeling of collective unity when people say, "Here we are all relatives" (Rejón Patrón 1999). These family alliances among the founders encouraged the creation of groups with political and ritual leadership. In addition, this solidarity between the individuals and their families was reinforced by the cooperative work of the milpas and choosing this as the place to settle, as other researchers have demonstrated for the community (Alcocer Puerto 2007; Quintal et al. 2003; Rosales González and Rejón Patrón 2006). This situation tells us about the importance of family ties and the preservation of historical memory for the internal organization of the community of Yaxunah (Hernández Álvarez 2012, 2014b).

Currently, Yaxunah is inhabited by more than six hundred people and occupies an area of approximately 1 km². An ejido commissioner and a municipal commissioner represent the two administrative and political authorities in the town. The board of *ejidatarios* has for many years been the source of mediation for conflicts within the town. Among its functions are the regulation of social activities, the organization of community work, the assignment of ejido land for cultivation, and the distribution of local wage labor. Nuclear families are the predominant residential group in Yaxunah. However, there are several cases of extended families sharing space. Traditionally, the head of the domestic group distributes portions of the family lot among his newly married children so that they can build their own houses. In other cases, newly formed families choose a plot of land close to the family or build their houses on land available outside the village. Thus, multiple families can live on each plot with a system of exchange and reciprocity that encourages shared domestic and productive activities (Rosales González and Rejón Patrón 2006, 1055; see also Bascopé and Alcocer Puerto, this volume).

For many years, the people of Yaxunah lived by cultivating corn, honey, poultry, and other backyard animals and selling the production surplus outside the community. It was not until the 1980s, during an agricultural crisis, that several heads of families were forced to migrate to seek employment in Mérida or Cancún. In addition, Hurricane Gilbert in 1988 left many people financially devastated (Rejón Patrón 1999, 6). We have noticed that a reduction in maize production led to increases in animal husbandry, gardening, and horticulture in Yaxunah houselots and left archaeological evidence that includes norias, wells, water troughs, corrals, pig sties, chicken coops, and remnant fruit trees (Alexander and Hernández Álvarez 2018).

In the 1980s, a U.S.-based archaeological project generated temporary employment for some of the adult males in the community. In addition, since the 1990s, the community has been developing several state-run programs, nongovernmental institutional plans, and local cooperatives like ecotourism tours, handicrafts, culinary tourism, and other heritage-based activities that enhance social identities and bring economic benefits to the community (Alcocer Puerto 2007; Ardren 2018; Ardren and Miller 2020; and Bascopé and Alcocer Puerto, this volume).

The carving of wooden figurines for tourism was one of the projects that was successfully adopted (figure 12.2). They are sold through intermediaries or directly to tourists, mainly in stalls on the grounds of Chichén Itzá and stands and stores in Valladolid. The activity of carving wooden handicrafts has become an alternative source of income for several families in the community. As the chapter by Bascopé and Alcocer Puerto highlights, this has modified the organization of the daily work of men and women as well as the arrangement of their housing spaces.

Finally, differences based on religion have emerged since Protestant denominations penetrated the region. Approximately half of the population practices Catholicism mixed with the traditional Mayan religion, while the other half belongs to one of the Protestant denominations, including Evangelicals, Pentecostals, and Baptists. The contrasting identities based on religious affiliation within the village have manifested in multiple ways. For example, the abandonment of traditional garments in favor of "Protestant" clothing (particularly for women) and the prohibition of alcohol consumption are some of the most evident changes in the town.

Yaxunah's Built Environment: Houselots and Dwellings

My field research in Yaxunah was carried out between 2005 and 2008, with two seasons that covered about twenty weeks in total. During the first phase, I conducted a study of the community-built environment, while during the second phase I focused on a sample of private domestic groups (Hernández Álvarez 2014b). During the first field season (2005–6), I carried out the historical and ethnographic documentation of the community, the systematic mapping of the population, and a detailed record of the total of the

The Identity That Binds and the *Albarradas* That Divide 323

FIGURE 12.2 Yaxunah's domestic household carving wood (photograph by Héctor Hernández Álvarez).

domestic architecture. In this phase, the survey consisted of recording the characteristics of domestic architecture: types of construction materials, predominant forms of plants and ceilings, construction techniques, and the relationship that they maintain with the auxiliary domestic spaces. In addition, a complete topographic map of the town was built, including each one of the *solares* (exterior space within albarradas) and the houses within them (figure 12.3).

During the first phase of research, I registered a total of 277 modern domestic constructions, including houses and kitchens, that were part of the community's built environment. I classified the structures into five types of dwellings according to the materials and forms represented by the houses:

(1) Type I (N=169) are structures that represent the traditional vernacular architecture of the Yucatán Peninsula and Yaxunah. These are pole-and-thatch houses that are rectangular or apsidal in shape, with walls made of perishable, locally derived materials. However, in Yaxunah, some of the

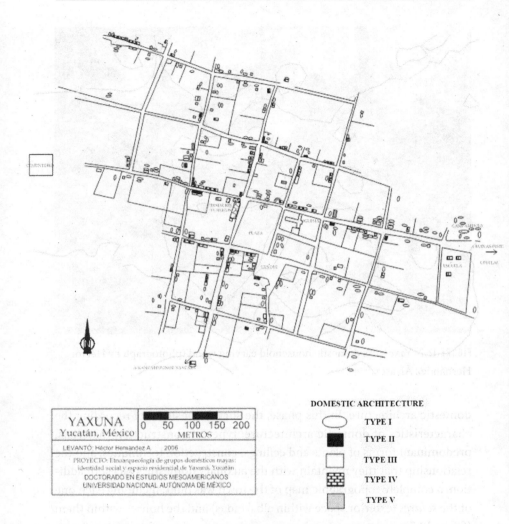

FIGURE 12.3 Yaxunah settlement (drawn by Héctor Hernández Álvarez).

original elements such as the thatch roof, *bajareque* walls, and earthen floors have been altered with the introduction of new materials and construction techniques.

(2) Type II (N=11) are rectangular structures built with stone-based masonry and a cast ceiling.

(3) Type III (N=30) are rectangular structures in the process of construction (often unchanged or abandoned for a long time), with block walls and generally without a roof.

The Identity That Binds and the *Albarradas* That Divide

FIGURE 12.4 Yaxunah domestic architectural types (photographs by Héctor Hernández Álvarez).

(4) Type IV (N=67) correspond to rectangular structures with block walls and a cast ceiling, with masonry foundation and one or multiple rooms.
(5) Type V (N=56) are concrete block houses of 4 × 6 m that were built in 2006 with Fondo de Desastres Naturales (FONDEN) resources (Hernández Álvarez 2010; see also figure 12.4).

During the second field season (2007–8), I sampled thirty houselots to obtain information about the configuration of the domestic group, its residential space, and its residents' material culture. The ethnoarchaeological strategy consisted of (1) the systematic mapping of twenty-one sites and the preparation of sketch plans of the remaining nine, (2) the photographic record and registry of all the material elements of the thirty groups sampled, (3) the survey of each household group and each of the structures of the group, and (4) interviews with the heads of each family to discuss aspects related to the group and its residential space.

The mean occupation of these solares is 4.3 people per houselot. Most are inhabited by nuclear families, although there are extended families of up to eleven members. The heads of the domestic groups stated that their subsistence was based on the cultivation of milpa and other vegetables on ejido lands and on their own gardens. Of these, 50 percent of the sample conduct handicraft activities (carving of wooden figures) to supplement the income of their family. In addition, twenty-four of the twenty-seven male family heads are ejidatarios. With respect to religion, thirteen of the domestic groups surveyed said they are Catholics, while fourteen declared themselves as belonging to Protestant denominations.

To determine the structure of the residential space of Yaxunah, I use the definition of the houselot model proposed by various scholars (Deal 1985; Hayden and Cannon 1983; Killion 1990). We know that, in the Maya area, the domestic space varies with respect to the environmental context, social strategies, and economic possibilities of domestic groups. Therefore, we must be able to observe this diversity and document the rich anthropological information that this form of organization represents.

The Houselot

The primary feature that delimits the peninsular houselots are albarradas: limestone walls that stand around 1 m high and bound the living area. In Yaxunah, the houselots, including those in the postabandonment stage, have an area of 1,948 m^2 on average and present around three large domestic structures and a mean of 4.4 auxiliary structures per lot. On average, the structural area of the sampled houselots was 85.26 m^2.

The Structural Core

The structural core of the houselot is the main residential building. As in many other communities of northern Yucatán, this is composed of one or more multifunctional rectangular or apsidal structures, where domestic activities occur, such as preparation and consumption of food, sleep, handicraft production, and storage of grains and other items. Within the houselot, during successive generations, the diverse productive activities, the consumption patterns, and the deposition, reuse, and dumping of material culture have been spatially patterned within the houselot (figure 12.5). Additionally, houselots are basic units of the reticular pattern of the town, as the structural areas, especially the main houses, are distributed along the streets. Internally, the houses and secondary structures are arranged around a courtyard (patio

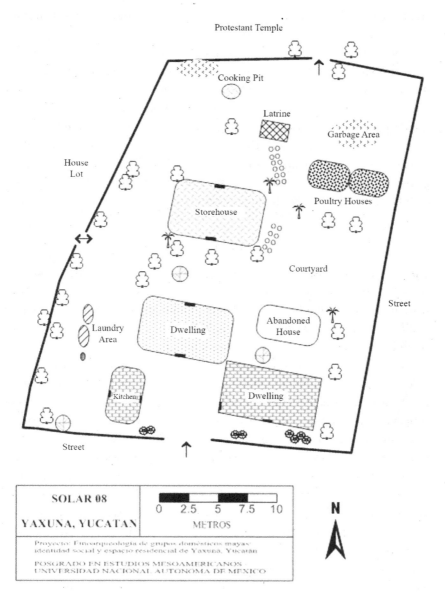

FIGURE 12.5 Houselot 08 plan (drawing by Héctor Hernández Álvarez).

area). Each house has front access to a public street and a rear exit to the interior courtyard.

As I have already pointed out, in general, each lot presents a combination of the five types of houses, described earlier. However, this varies with the homeowner's access to local materials or monetary resources to acquire nonlocal materials or pay masons for construction. Technological innovation in housing obeys complex strategies and circumstances, whether economic, historical, or political. However, regardless of the variability in the constructive environment, the site maintains a typical arrangement that, together with the traditional dwelling, symbolizes social identity and ties the architecture and the domestic space with a sense of communal membership.

The Patio

The patio area consists of various auxiliary features such as poultry houses, corrals, storehouses, and wells, and is where outdoor activities such as woodworking are performed. I also registered the presence of various elements that have been introduced by the FONDEN government programs, such as cement floors, latrines, and cement block houses.

Although a frequently used space, it is swept often and users maintain it as an area cleared of objects and waste. There are fruit trees and ornamental plants, and animals like chickens and turkeys roam freely. It also contains concentrated waste or garbage dumps and a laundry area. Auxiliary structures are behind the buildings and the patio area and are small constructions of perishable materials. These include poultry houses, kitchens, maize storage facilities (Smyth 1990), corrals for animals, *ramadas* (open-sided, thatch-roof work areas), and elevated orchards, made mainly of wood and *huano* (palmetto) leaves or sheets of cardboard. In some cases, we find structures built with cement, stone, and blocks, such as pigsties, poultry coops, laundries, water tanks, ovens, and latrines, which could leave a much more perishable material footprint over time. In Yaxunah, the houselots sample gave us an estimated 465.80 m^2 as the mean area of the courtyards.

The Garden

The *monte* (a distant area from the dwellings that is generally used as a dumping area) and the garden area overlap the patio and generally form a peripheral area of the site characterized by the presence of scattered waste. This zone serves to cover a wide variety of household needs in the back part of the houselots. There they grow a great variety of trees and plants, both cultivated and wild, but we rarely find objects or constructions. These spaces become areas to dispose of and burn woodcarving waste when activities of artisanal production are performed by members of the household. In the monte area, there is also a space used as toilet, and in some cases, weak constructions of sticks and plastic were recorded as physical delimitations of the spaces used as toilets or latrines. In general, the houselots of the community of Yaxunah presented an estimate of 1,493 m^2 for the monte/garden area.

Domestic Groups' Material Culture

Regarding material culture, I did an inventory for each household of the furniture, utensils, electrical appliances, and artifacts present in the thirty residential complexes sampled in Yaxunah. This was complemented with photography and a sketch of the location of the major elements by structure. Material culture among the domestic groups of Yaxunah is quite homogeneous, though there are important distinctions. Furniture is usually limited to a few chairs, benches, plastic or wooden tables, drawers, and cabinets or shelves for storing clothes and other personal items. Beds or armchairs are almost entirely absent, but hammocks are essential objects for all families, constituting an irreplaceable element of the material culture of Maya domestic groups of the Yucatán Peninsula.

Electrical appliances are the most valued goods, including radios, stereos, televisions, fans, blenders, washing machines, VCRs, DVD players, and satellite television systems. However, the most common household artifacts are the tools related to the work of the milpa such as axes, machetes, and *coas* (hand tools for sowing seeds), shotguns for hunting, and utensils for carving handicrafts (knives, scrappers, picks).

Kitchens are considered female spaces and include the three-stone hearth (*k'oben*), which was observed in all cases, as well as tables, chairs, wooden stools for making tortillas, and plastic bottles and buckets for water storage. Pans, pots, and cooking utensils, usually made of metal, are the most common artifacts found in kitchens and were usually hanging on the interior and exterior kitchen walls. Special ceramic vessels used for storing water (*kat*) were only present in two domestic groups. In one case, a stone *metate* (stone tool for maize grinding) was in use, although in other cases, metates were discarded along with objects such as pots, pans, and metal artifacts.

All goods with an estimable monetary value were quantified to understand the economic differences that the domestic material culture could manifest. There is a range that goes from 0 to 10 goods per group, with a mean of 3.7 objects and a mean monetary value of 7,335 Mexican pesos. Most domestic groups had only one or two goods with estimable values. However, in three cases the number of goods and the values estimated are well above average, indicating internal economic differences manifested in the domestic material culture.

Finally, in Yaxunah I also noticed differences in the religious elements present. The absence of articles, images, or areas of worship is notable among those belonging to Protestant denominations, such as Presbyterians and Evangelicals, as well as Jehovah's Witnesses. On the other hand, Catholic families maintain the practice of possessing images of saints, virgins, wooden crosses dressed in huipiles, candles, flowers, and other decorative elements that are displayed on a rectangular table that functions as an altar.

The Structure of Residential Space

The links and barriers between the domestic groups of Yaxunah, their residential space, and the material culture revolved around three questions: (1) What are the main factors that influence the structure of the houselot? (2) How do the differences in the residential space and the material culture of the groups that practice different economic strategies manifest? And finally, (3) What is the relationship between the domestic cycle, material culture, and residential space? To perform the corresponding analysis, I used three nonparametric statistical methods useful for testing hypotheses: the Mann-Whitney U test, the chi-square test, and Spearman's rank correlation coefficient. Table 12.1 summarizes data used in the analyses.

Yaxunah residential groups maintain a subsistence agricultural base, but the analysis of the patterns of the structure of the houselot reveals certain differences. For example, the ethnoarchaeological study conducted by Christopher Dore (1996) in Xculoc, Campeche, indicates that there is variation in the area of the houselot with respect to the number of inhabitants. In Yaxunah, this premise is not discernable. A statistical correlation between inhabitants and houselot area cannot be established ($r = 0.227$; $p < 0.25$;

TABLE 12.1 Variables that structure the residential space at Yaxunah

Variable	Farmers (N=12)	Artisans (N=15)	Catholics (N=13)	Protestants (N=14)	Total (N=27)
Houselot area					
Mean	2,407	1,489	1,668	2,111	1,948
Standard dev.	1,561	752	887	1,550	1,291
Structural area					
Mean	91	79	86	95	85
Standard dev.	79	32	42	36	40
Patio area					
Mean	495	436	405	531	1,273
Standard dev.	305	226	225	288	465
Monte area					
Mean	1,932	1,053	1,262	1,603	1,493
Standard dev.	1,427	648	815	1,437	1,177

Note: All measurements are in square meters.

$\alpha = 0.05$). In some cases, larger residential spaces belong to small domestic groups of an individual or couples without children. Houselots of these families have not been distributed among the descendants and had enough space available. Meanwhile, the opposite is manifested in domestic groups that have many inhabitants and whose space is less than the average of the sample. Those groups represent an advanced stage of the domestic cycle.

With respect to the agricultural and handicraft activities carried out by the domestic groups of Yaxunah, I sought to determine if there is a link between these activities and the space occupied by the houselot. The null hypothesis proposed was that there is no difference in the mean area of land between farmers and artisans. The results of the Mann-Whitney test show that the null hypothesis cannot be rejected ($U = 68$; $p < 0.06$; $\alpha = 0.05$). Therefore, the statistical analysis indicates that there is no significant relationship between the houselot space and the main economic activity carried out by domestic labor when comparing the professions of farmers and artisans. Likewise, I sought to determine if there is any relationship between the mean area of the houselot with respect to Catholic and Protestant families. The null hypothesis proposed that there is no difference in the mean area of the houselot between Catholics and Protestants. The results of the Mann-Whitney test show that the null hypothesis cannot be rejected ($U = 80$; $p < 0.59$; $\alpha = 0.05$). Therefore, the statistical analysis indicates that there is no significant relationship between the space of the houselot and religious affiliation.

On the other hand, other researchers have considered that the residential space is clearly related to the wealth of its occupants (Kamp 1987; Kramer 1979, 1982; Wilk 1983). To corroborate or refute this issue among the Yucatec domestic groups, I chose to perform Spearman's correlation test. The results of Spearman's correlation analysis in the case of goods show that the null hypothesis cannot be rejected because the level of significance was greater than 0.05 ($r = 0.024$; $p < 0.90$; $\alpha = 0.05$). With regard to the monetary valuation of the material goods, a lack of correlation with respect to the houselot area occurs ($r = 0.024$; $p < 0.904$; $\alpha = 0.05$). Therefore, the statistical test indicates that there is no linear relationship between the space of the lot and the wealth of the domestic group exemplified by the number and estimated value of their material assets. Brian Hayden and Aubrey Cannon (1983) similarly concluded a lack of correlation between the goods and the houselot area. This shows us that several correlations about wealth (measured in terms of material culture) do not necessarily meet expectations.

Finally, I documented several narratives related to changes in housing and modifications of the residential space. These changes were all tied to certain stages of the domestic cycle. I also recorded the age of the main structures and their repairs over time. In addition, I have been able to outline the most significant changes that construction technology has undergone over time. This was possible from the register of the materials with which the built environment of the community was used. Perhaps the most significant moment was the construction of FONDEN houses in 2006 (N=56). This event constituted a construction process of such magnitude that it would become notorious in the new configuration of the built environment of the population.

In Yaxunah, the mean age of the domestic groups in the habitation stage (N=27) is 34.18 years, and the number of generations that reside in these groups ranges from one (N=6), mostly two (N=17), and up to three (N=4). Meanwhile, the mean construction age of the principal dwellings is 20.96 years, with a minimum of two to a maximum of seventy-six years per structure. Among the residential units of Yaxunah, the mean age of the inhabitants is moderately and significantly related to the age of construction of their main structures ($r = 0.475$; $p < 0.012$; $\alpha = 0.05$).

In addition, the mean age of residential structures is highly correlated with the size of the structural area ($r = 0.641$; $p < 0.000$; $\alpha = 0.05$) and moderately with the number of material goods (r = 0.418; p <0.030; α = 0.05) and the estimated value of those goods (r = 0.423; p <0.028; α = 0.05). The result of these analyses corroborates the fact that newly formed families have fewer assets than others. In Yaxunah, the accumulation of goods as well as the built space are part of a temporary process that involves consumer decisions and the domestic group life cycle.

Conclusion

The case of Yaxunah has allowed us to better understand how residential space and housing manifest a reference to social identity. Houses at the community level show the variability of housing technology and some implications of the adoption of such technology, as in the case of houses built with resources granted by the government or modified vernacular construction. In addition, there was certain homogeneity in the spatial arrangement of Yaxunah's residential lots, although with some variability in internal elements such as dwellings, auxiliary structures, and material culture. This question could correspond to different situations, such as the form of subsistence of the group, its influence within the community, the stage of the domestic cycle, or affiliation to any of the religions present in the town. The study shows that the factors that promote the maintenance or abandonment of certain elements of social identity are complex and depend on particular processes. As in many of the peninsular Maya communities, this community is experiencing an accelerated cultural change that manifests itself in the material elements of its domestic groups. Therefore, from this ethnoarchaeological study, I have learned that the spatial configuration of the Maya houselot, with its changes and continuities, is a reflection of the way in which peninsular Maya organize their experience in the world and put their daily life into practice. Domestic architecture, residential space, and the associated material culture constitute parameters of construction of a particular reality and are understood as fundamental elements in the expression and negotiation of their identity.

Works Cited

Alcocer Puerto, Elias. 2007. "El ecoturismo cultural dentro de una comunidad maya de Yucatán." MA thesis, Centro de Investigación y Estudios Avanzados, Instituto Politécnico Nacional, Mérida, Yucatán, Mexico.

Alexander, Rani T. 1999. "Mesoamerican House Lots and Archaeological Site Structure: Problems of Inference in Yaxcabá, Yucatán, México, 1750–1847." In *The Archaeology of Household Activities*, edited by Penelope Allison, 78–99. New York: Routledge.

Alexander, Rani T. 2004. *Yaxcabá and the Caste War of Yucatán: An Archaeological Perspective*. Albuquerque: University of New Mexico Press.

Alexander, Rani T., and Sandra Andrade. 2007. "Frontier Migration and the Built Environment in Southwestern Campeche." *Estudios de Cultura Maya* 30:175–96.

Alexander, Rani T., and Héctor Hernández Álvarez. 2018. "Agropastoralism and Household Ecology in Yucatán After the Spanish Invasion." *Environmental Archaeology* 23 (1): 69–79.

Ardren, Traci. 2018. "Now Serving Maya Heritage: Culinary Tourism in Yaxunah, Yucatán, México." *Food and Foodways* 26 (4): 290–312.

Ardren, Traci, and Stephanie Miller. 2020. "Household Garden Plant Agency in the Creation of Classic Maya Social Identities." *Journal of Anthropological Archaeology* 60 (December).

Arnold, Philip, III. 1991. *Domestic Ceramic Production and Spatial Organization: A Mexican Case Study in Ethnoarchaeology*. Cambridge: Cambridge University Press.

Binford, Lewis R. 1967. "Smudge Pits and Hide Smoking: The Use of Analogy in Archaeological Reasoning." *American Antiquity* 32 (1): 1–12.

Binford, Lewis R. 2001. *Constructing Frames of Reference: An Analytical Method for Archaeological Theory Building Using Ethnographic and Environmental Data Sets*. Berkeley: University of California Press.

Bourdieu, Pierre. 2000. *Esquisse d'une théorie de la pratique: récédé de trois études d'ethnologie kabyle*. Paris: Seuil.

David, Nicholas, and Carol Kramer. 2001. *Ethnoarchaeology in Action*. Cambridge: Cambridge University Press.

Deal, Michael. 1985. "Household Pottery Disposal in the Maya Highlands: An Ethnoarchaeological Interpretation." *Journal of Anthropological Archaeology* 4 (4): 243–91.

Deal, Michael. 1998. *Pottery Ethnoarchaeology in the Central Maya Highlands*. Salt Lake City: University of Utah Press.

Dore, Christopher. 1996. "Built Environment Variability and Community Organization: Theory Building through Ethnoarchaeology in Xculoc, Campeche, México." PhD diss., University of New Mexico, Albuquerque.

Gifford-Gonzalez, Diane. 1991. "Bones Are Not Enough: Analogues, Knowledge, and Interpretive Strategies in Zooarchaeology." *Journal of Anthropological Archaeology* 10 (3): 215–54.

González Ruibal, Alfredo. 2001. "Etnoarqueología de la vivienda en áfrica subsahariana: Aspectos simbólicos y sociales." *Archaeoweb* 3 (2).

González Ruibal, Alfredo. 2003. *La experiencia del otro: Una introducción a la etnoarqueología*. Madrid: Akal.

Hayden, Brian, and Aubrey Cannon. 1983. "Where the Garbage Goes: Refuse Disposal in the Maya Highlands." *Journal of Anthropological Archaeology* 2 (2): 117–63.

Heidelberg, Kurt, and Dominique Rissolo. 2006. "Ethnoarchaeology in the Northern Maya Lowlands: A Case Study at Naranjal, Quintana Roo." In *Lifeways in the Northern Maya Lowlands: New Approaches to Archaeology in the Yucatán Peninsula*, edited by Jennifer P. Mathews and Bethany A. Morrison, 187–97. Tucson: University of Arizona Press.

Hernández Álvarez, Héctor. 2010. "Identidad social y cultura material de los grupos domésticos de Yaxuná, Yucatán." In *Identidades y cultura material en la región maya*, edited by Héctor Hernández Álvarez and Marcos Pool Cab, 147–67. Mérida, Yucatán: Universidad Autónoma de Yucatán.

Hernández Álvarez, Héctor. 2012. "Memoria, identidad y espacio residencial de Yaxuná, Yucatán." In *Diálogos sobre los espacios: Imaginados, percibidos y construidos*, edited by Rosario Gómez, Adam Sellen, and Arturo Taracena, 213–35. Mérida, Yucatán: Universidad Nacional Autónoma de México.

Hernández Álvarez, Héctor. 2014a. "Corrales, chozas y solares: Estructura de sitio residencial de la hacienda San Pedro Cholul." *Temas Antropológicos* 36 (2): 129–52.

Hernández Álvarez, Héctor. 2014b. *Etnoarqueología de grupos domésticos mayas: Identidad social y espacio residencial de Yaxunah, Yucatán*. Mexico City: Universidad Nacional Autónoma de México.

Hernández Álvarez, Héctor, and Gustavo Novelo Rincón. 2007. "Una visión diacrónica de la arquitectura doméstica de Yaxuná, Yucatán." *Los investigadores de la Cultura Maya* 15 (1): 279–92.

Kamp, Kathryn. 1987. "Affluence and Image: Ethnoarchaeology in a Syrian Village." *Journal of Field Archaeology* 14 (3): 283–96.

Kent, Susan. 1992. "Studying Variability in the Archaeological Record. An Ethnoarchaeological Model for Distinguishing Mobility Patterns." *American Antiquity* 57 (4): 635–60.

Killion, Thomas W. 1990. "Cultivation Intensity and Residential Site Structure: An Ethnoarchaeological Examination of Peasant Agriculture in the Sierra de los Tuxtlas, Veracruz, México." *Latin American Antiquity* 1 (3): 191–215.

Kramer, Carol. 1979. "An Archaeological View of a Contemporary Kurdish Village: Domestic Architecture, Household Size, and Wealth." In *Ethnoarchaeology: Implications of Ethnography for Archaeology*, edited by Carol Kramer, 139–63. New York: Columbia University Press.

Kramer, Carol. 1982. *Village Ethnoarchaeology: Rural Iran in Archaeological Perspective*. New York: Academic Press.

Lyons, Diane. 2007. "Building Power in Rural Hinterlands: An Ethnoarchaeological Study of Vernacular Architecture in Tigray, Ethiopia." *Journal of Archaeological Method and Theory* 14 (2): 179–207.

Lyons, Diane. 2009. "How I Built My House: An Ethnoarchaeological Study of Gendered Technical Practice in Tigray, Ethiopia." *Ethnoarchaeology* 1 (2): 137–61.

Pierrebourg, Fabienne de. 1999. *L'espace domestique maya: Une approche ethnoarchéologique au Yucatan (Mexique)*. British Archaeological Reports, International Series 764. Oxford: Archaeopress.

Quintal, Ella, Juan Ramón Bastarrachea, Fidencio Briceño, Martha Medina, Renée Petrich, Lourdes Rejón, Beatriz Repetto, and Margarita Rosales. 2003. "Solares, rumbos y pueblos: Organización social de los mayas peninsulares." In *La comunidad sin límites: Estructura social y organización comunitaria en las regiones indígenas de México*, vol. 1, edited by Saúl Millán and Julieta Valle, 291–399. Mexico City: Instituto Nacional de Antropología e Historia.

Rejón Patrón, Lourdes. 1999. "La comunidad de Yaxuná." In *Proyecto INAH Yaxuná: Informe de la Temporada 1998–1999*, 458–72. Mérida: Archaeology Section Archive, Centro INAH Yucatán.

Rosales González, Margarita, and Lourdes Rejón Patrón. 2006. "Las redes que tejen un pueblo: Familias y parentelas en comunidades mayas del oriente y sur de Yucatán." In *Los mayas de ayer y hoy*, vol. 2, edited by Alfredo Barrera and Ruth Gubler, 1052–78. Mérida: Conaculta, Instituto Nacional de Antropología e Historia, Universidad Autónoma de Yucatán.

Smyth, Michael. 1990. "Maize Storage Among the Puuc Maya: The Development of an Archaeological Method." *Ancient Mesoamerica* 1 (1): 51–69.

Stanton, Travis, and Traci Ardren. 2005. "The Middle Formative of Yucatán in Context: The View from Yaxuna." *Ancient Mesoamerica* 16 (2): 213–28.

Toscano, Lourdes, and David Ortegón. 2003. "Yaxuná, un centro de acopio del tributo Itzá." *Los Investigadores de la Cultura Maya* 11 (2): 438–45.

Wilk, Richard. 1983. "Little House in the Jungle: The Causes of Variation in House Size Among Modern Kekchi Maya." *Journal of Anthropological Archaeology* 2 (2): 99–116.

CHAPTER 13

Constructing a World Beneath Quintana Roo

CARMEN ROJAS SANDOVAL, MIGUEL COVARRUBIAS REYNA, AND DOMINIQUE RISSOLO

Cave archaeology has played an increasing role in the study of Maya landscapes and concepts of social space. Once considered peripheral to research objectives focused on major centers, cave investigations became integrated into surface projects in the 1990s at sites like Dos Pilas (Brady et al. 1997). Similarly, single cave reporting transitioned into regional, problem-oriented surveys involving multiple cave sites (e.g., Awe 1998; Bonor Villarejo 1989b; Rissolo 2003). Pioneers like Teobert Maler, Henry Mercer, Edward Thompson, and Román Piña Chan realized the enormous potential that caves had for the study of Maya societies. Spectacular discoveries in caves such as Loltun and Balankanche in Yucatán and Naj Tunich in Guatemala attracted the attention of researchers who began to recognize that caves were an essential part of Maya religious practice (A. Andrews 1981; Bonor Villarejo 1989a; Brady 1989; Piña Chan 1960; Strecker 1981).

Offerings, burials, and rock art are commonly found in caves throughout the Maya area, often invoking concepts of earthly fertility and rain. Though terraces, walls, floors, and altars were constructed in caves across time and space, the central east coast of Quintana Roo is somewhat unique in that the Maya built temples inside caves—temples that were miniature, though often elaborate, counterparts to those found at surface sites like Xelha, Xcaret, and Xamanha. The siting of such structures and features served not only to delimit space within caves but to establish boundaries—both metaphorical and physical—between ceremonial precincts of the surface world and their subterranean analogs.

Caves Along the East Coast of the Yucatán Peninsula

Decades of exploration by cavers and divers along the coastal zone of Quintana Roo have revealed the nature of the caves in this region. Complex and extensive dry and flooded cave systems are common, and many of the systems that were submerged after the end of the Late Pleistocene flow from the interior eastward to the sea. Due to advances in cave-diving techniques and the lure of the region's cenotes (karstic sinkholes), a great many paleontological and archaeological discoveries have been made. The remains of extinct Pleistocene abound, and the study of early human skeletons from submerged caves is revealing much about Paleoamerican life on the Yucatán Peninsula (Chatters et al. 2014; González et al. 2006). The use of the region's many caves and cenotes continued well into the time of the Maya, when they became imbued with symbolic meaning and transformed into places of ritual and veneration.

Caves provided access to water for both humans and animals. It is likely that many skeletons found inside the caves were from individuals in search of water who somehow met their demise in the dark, now submerged tunnels. Although caves can be dark and dangerous, they may have also served as refuges for Paleolithic humans who shared the landscape with massive predators. Since the hunters' prey would also frequent caves in search of water, these humans likely constructed blinds at cave entrances for concealment as they lay in wait. Therefore, certain constructed features inside caves may very well predate the Maya. As the Maya came to populate the landscape, settle in villages, and practice agriculture, the siting of communities—and ultimately larger regal-residential centers—around cenotes and watery cave entrances became widespread. Indeed, caves often provided the only access to fresh water, especially in a region largely devoid of lakes and rivers. Modifications to cave interiors indicate intensive use, which may have also involved hunting and temporary shelter (as was likely the case throughout prehistory).

Likewise, economic activities such as mining were continuous since materials were extracted for construction and the production of pigments. Other resources such as fine sediments in caves were excellent clay sources for the manufacture of pottery, and crystalline calcite was used as temper for ceramic vessels (see Arnold 2005). Like drip water from caves (which was deemed pure by the Maya), other materials from caves could have been accorded the same status (Brady and Rissolo 2006).

Sacred Geography of Caves

Caves were fundamental to the cosmogony of the Maya. Throughout Mesoamerica, there was a shared notion of a universe composed of three fundamental cosmic regions whose ideal materialization was represented by the "cave-pyramid complex" (see Bonor Villarejo 1989a, 6). Architecture—particularly pyramids constructed over caves or caves excavated beneath pyramids—established a link between the underworld and the heavens. The Mesoamerican conception (and particularly that of the Maya universe), with three basic levels framed within the cardinal points, has been made evident through various means and with countless examples. The underworld is the place where life begins and ends, a world of dualities where light and darkness maintain a constant battle and where the solar star enters to make an underground journey and emerge in a new dawn. These ideas were also connected to the validation of divine rulership.

Caves and Cenotes as Funerary Chambers

It has long been thought that the human bones found in caves and cenotes were the result of sacrifices as propitiatory offerings. This may be true in some cases, but contexts have been recorded where individuals were deposited for ritual purposes and with formal funeral treatments, reflecting social aspects of the groups that made them, such as the creation of ancestors appointed to serve as pillars of family lineages. The location of the dead in caves may be related to the intention of bringing them closer to the underworld, where they would reside permanently. The relocation of corpses is a practice that continues in some Maya villages (not in caves but in cemeteries or ossuaries). Still, it appears that indirect interment in caves and cenotes was not an uncommon practice (Rojas Sandoval 2011).

Three probable funerary chambers are currently known in Quintana Roo. In the Calaveras cenote, 14 km north of Cobá, 122 skeletons have been found (Rojas Sandoval 2011). The cenote is within a small Maya site that was founded in the Late Formative / Early Classic and was reoccupied in the Late Postclassic. Human remains belong to the early occupation and offer evidence that the bodies were deposited after death.

The other two examples have not been researched extensively, but evidence indicates functional similarities to the Calaveras cenote. The first one is also at the Cobá area, located 10 km south of the site center, at Mu'ul ich Dzonot (Covarrubias Reyna 2020, 16–17), containing at least nine skeletons and possibly many others hidden under sediment. The second example is known as El Trono near Playa del Carmen, which was associated with the major site of Punta Piedra, where only one skeleton has been found (Rojas Sandoval and Covarrubias Reyna 2017). At both places, evidence of jade dental ornamentation is present, suggesting a high social ranking of interred individuals.

Rain Rites in the Cave Context

As the freshwater of the Yucatán Peninsula lies underground and is largely accessed via caves and cenotes, this may explain the strong relationship between these spaces and rain and rain deities. Although rain ceremonies were not necessarily performed in the caves, we know that ancient Maya collected "virgin water" or *zuhuy ha* from pools in caves and carried it to the surface in ceramic containers. For example, at Balankanche cave in Yucatán state, offerings and invocations were made to the Chaacob and the Chicanes, auxiliary deities who together with the god Chaac brought rain, vital for agriculture. In iconography, these supernatural beings were often associated with serpents, who were often inhabitants of the caves and were associated with lightning. The ophidian origin of these deities possibly dates to the very beginnings of social complexity in Mesoamerica (A. Andrews 1981, 45–47; E. Andrews 1970).

The interment of sacrificial victims in caves and cenotes may have been associated with rain rituals (Rojas Sandoval 2011, 153–54). Agriculture in the northern Maya lowlands was entirely dependent on rainfall, and appeals were made to Chaak, the Maya rain god, for the timely arrival of seasonal rains. During times of drought, the practice of sacrifice dedicated to the rain deities must have intensified.

The relationship between caves and rain can be considered common across Mesoamerica, and rain gods were believed to dwell within caves. It is not uncommon to find iconographic depictions of Chaac seated inside caves or cenotes. Also, artifacts and rock art in caves, in most cases, are associated with rain or water, but perhaps the most valuable offering was human life. In addition to the well-known sacrificial victims found with the Cenote Sagrado at Chichén Itzá, individuals appear to have been sacrificed as part of cave ceremonies, such as in the Actun Tunichil Muknal in Belize, where their remains are associated with pools of water (Moyes 2006, 31–35). Interestingly, both contexts where human sacrifice is involved correspond to the time during which the Late/Terminal Classic drought occurred.

Settlement and Subterranean Space
Distribution and Density

Much less is known about the distribution of archaeological sites in Quintana Roo as compared to the information from the states of Yucatán and Campeche. With a few notable exceptions (e.g., Glover 2006), there have been no large-scale settlement pattern surveys in this region (outside of the developed tourism regions), leaving swaths of the jungle with few archaeological sites located. There are also few financial resources for the use of innovative techniques such as Light Detection and Ranging (LiDAR) to have coverage in these areas, so archaeologists in this region often resort to opportunistic (but reliable) methods of obtaining information about archaeological or paleontological cave sites from other people, including residents, cavers, and divers. Using this information, archaeologists have located settlements with densities exceeding fifteen structures per hectare where these *albarrada* (stone wall) systems are present, whether on the surface or in caves belowground (A. Andrews 1983, 1986; E. Andrews and A. Andrews 1975; Covarrubias Reyna 2017, 2018, 2019a; Martos López 2002; Rojas Sandoval 2015). Although in other areas of the Maya lowlands the presence of albarradas is less common, the density and distribution of domestic settlements are similar to that found in Quintana Roo, where the domestic structures surround the nuclei of public architecture that extend over large areas, including the interior of the caves. Anthony P. Andrews (1986) has called these "macrozones" or areas covered with extensive systems of albarradas and domestic settlements mixed among the larger sites or within caves, which sometimes makes it difficult to discern boundaries between ancient communities. It is common to see these low walls leading to or surrounding cenotes and cave entrances, in addition to water pools located inside them.

The intense Late Postclassic occupation of coastal sites in Quintana Roo is distinguished by a type of architecture known as the "East Coast" style. However, the presence of Late Formative / Early Classic and Late Classic sites such as Cobá and El Naranjal (see Folan, Kintz, and Fletcher 1983; Mathews 1998) in the interior of the territory have caused some researchers to think that the coastal occupation was less intense during these earlier periods (E. Andrews and A. Andrews 1975, 1). However, recent projects are recording new coastal sites, with important occupations dating from these earlier periods (Covarrubias Reyna 2019b; López López and Covarrubias 2018). In the caves of the coastal zone, the most frequently recovered ceramic types also correspond to the Late Formative and Early Classic, with a notable decrease in the Middle, Late, and Terminal Classic (Martos López 2002, 197–98). This demographic concentration on the coast was a response to changes that occurred on the peninsula and in general throughout Mesoamerica, which implies the intensification of maritime trade and interaction (E. Andrews and A. Andrews 1975, 1).

Associations Between Cave Systems and Major Settlements

Since humans began to modify their environment, they also appropriated and interpreted it symbolically. They became intimately connected to the landscape in which they lived and to which they gave meaning consistent with their ideology. Although the coast is a karstic plain with scarce soils and without bodies of surface water, it still offers a favorable landscape for human settlement. With an abundance of cenotes, estuaries with mangroves, and rocky coasts with bays with sandy beaches and diverse coves, it provides access to fresh water and marine resources.

The investigations along the coast have documented evidence of extraordinarily dense occupation during the Late Postclassic, particularly in the vicinity of coves and beaches that enabled access to commercial maritime systems. However, vast sections of the forested interior of central Quintana Roo have not been sufficiently surveyed, and the discovery of new inland sites could change the spatiotemporal concept that currently exists. Cave systems continue to be explored and surveyed, though it is apparent that cenotes and subterranean spaces played an important role in the establishment and identity of Maya communities.

Features

The cave systems of the central coastal region of Quintana Roo have a general orientation from northwest to southeast, and their groundwater flows to the sea. In the case of archaeological studies, we are interested mainly in dry cave systems, since obviously the ancient Maya could not venture into submerged caves. Dry or semiflooded caves can reach considerable horizontal depths (up to 10 km in length) and form parallel to each other. Thanks to collaborations with speleologists and cave surveyors in Quintana Roo—notably Peter Sprouse (personal communication, 2017), who generously shared his cartography of dry caves to complement our archaeological studies—we have found an obvious relationship between these systems and the location and distribution of coastal Maya settlements. We examined three zones south of Playa del Carmen with large coastal settlements that are located at the end of extensive cave systems, where they flow into the sea. This region includes networks of albarradas that, in some cases, are also found inside the caves (figure 13.1). We also consider near-coastal sites, where temples, oratories, altars, and other structures have been documented within the caves—many in an exceptional state of preservation.

Case Studies

Chakalal

Chakalal is an extensive site that was discovered by Herbert Spinden in 1926 and is composed of at least five architectural groups with standing public architecture in the Late Postclassic East Coast style. The first of these groups is located on the shore of a cove of the same name, in what is now called Puerto Aventuras. One temple still has mural paintings in its interior that depict a feathered serpent and a jaguar, and it stands above a cave with fresh water (Mason 1927). The largest settlement is 1.5 km west of the cove and is divided into four groups. The most important in terms of volume is called Group D and consists of at least three pyramidal foundations, one of which reaches 7 m in height. The site core was probably built during the Early Formative or Early Classic, as indicated by surface ceramic sherds of Sierra Red and Huachinango Incised types. The other three groups, A, B, and C, include temples of the Eastern Late Postclassic style (E. Andrews and A. Andrews 1975, 81–83).

The site core of Chakalal covers an approximate area of 42 hectares, and in its interior are a number of caves and cenotes. The habitation zone was likely more extensive, since in another zone 1.5 km to the north, called Taema 1, there are several domestic structures such as foundations and platforms, including Megalithic-type constructions and ceramics that correspond to the Late Formative and Early Classic periods. We also find extensive albar-

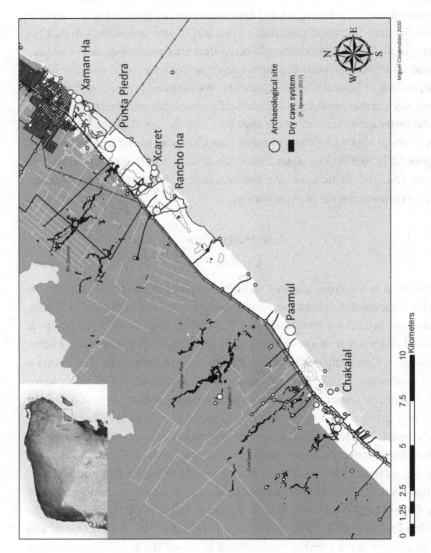

FIGURE 13.1 Coastal region south of modern Playa del Carmen (Xaman Ha) indicating dry cave systems (map by Miguel Covarrubias Reyna).

radas, apiaries, and scarce remnants of Late Postclassic Mama Red–type ceramics (Robles Castellanos 1990). Below this domestic settlement, there are several caves (López López and Covarrubias 2018), one of which is located 1 km north of the main nucleus that reportedly contains an altar. As this cave is located on private property called Pica Piedra, we have not yet been able to verify this (Sprouse, personal communication, 2017). However, approximately 1 km further north of the settlement there is a cave system that extends northwest for about 7 km (figure 13.2).

In this system of caves, called Gavilanes, two underground temples of the East Coast type have been located. The first is called the Templo de la Cueva de los Aluxes, located in a semiflooded area in the twilight zone of the cave. A miniature temple in the East Coast style was built on a natural elevation. The building is characterized by a stuccoed façade, a simple molding, and the remains of blue paint representing two bands. A traditional T-shaped recessed lintel is present as well (figure 13.3). In situ speleothems were integrated into the structure, comprising a portion of the roof and portions of the rear and side walls. It is a small building, 1.15 m high, 1.98 m long, and 1.34 m wide. Within the stuccoed interior of the temple, there is a rectangular altar with a vertically placed stone slab. A wooden beam is also preserved in the roof (Rissolo et al. 2017; Rojas Sandoval 2015).

Inside the cave and behind the temple, there are natural skylights (or karst windows) that allow the entrance of light, where simple walls of a single course of amorphous stones were observed, some of which are parallel, forming "corridors." These "corridors" are common in several caves in the region, and while their probable function is still the subject of some debate, they could have been traps for small animals, or perhaps they could have served a ritual function. Outside the cave, we observed albarradas and some domestic platforms, indicating that the environment was a residential area. Unfortunately, this whole area is being impacted by modern urbanism, affecting other caves and settlement areas, where ceramics from both the Early Classic and the Late Postclassic have also been recovered.

Within the same Gavilanes system but in an uninhabited area 3 km to the northwest of the temple of the Aluxes is a building inside a cave that is perhaps the best conserved of all in the region. It is known as the Oratorio or Ocho Balas Temple and is located just inside the dripline of the cave. It is of greater dimensions and complexity than the previous example but also in the East Coast architectural style (figure 13.4). It was built on a basal platform of

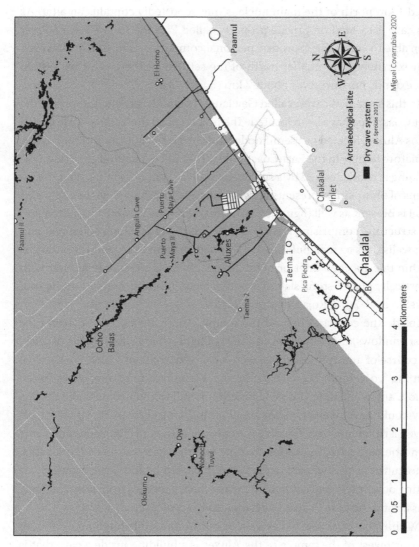

FIGURE 13.2 Cave systems west of modern Puerto Aventuras and the archaeological site of Chakalal (map by Miguel Covarrubias Reyna).

FIGURE 13.3 Miniature temple inside Cueva de los Aluxes (photograph courtesy of Carmen Rojas Sandoval).

FIGURE 13.4 Temple, known as Oratorio or Ocho Balas, inside the cave (photograph courtesy of Dominique Rissolo).

rough masonry, upon which rests a plinth and a stuccoed temple, standing 1.6 m high and 2.8 m². It has a molding of three elements with central fastening on all the façades and with access to the east. Above the inset lintel, there are remains of a stucco sculpture, of which only the legs remain on the molding. On the southwest corner of the roof, there is a simple stone *almena* reminiscent of the Temple of the Wind at Tulum.

The interior is completely stuccoed and has a rectangular bench on the west side as an altar. The flat, beam-and-mortar roof is exceptionally well preserved and can be considered one of the best examples of temple architecture of this type (Rissolo et al. 2016; Rojas Sandoval 2015, 9). Inside the cave are a series of walls and "corridors" as well as another masonry platform similar to that of the temple. At least one other religious structure has been reported inside this cave, but it has not yet been located or studied. In the vicinity of the cave are albarradas, but the nature or extent of associated settlement is yet to be determined. Other caves with underground architecture that may be associated with the Chakalal site are Nohoch Tuyul, Oya, and Olokum, in the Pacto system, 4 km and 5 km northwest of the major site, respectively (Peter Sprouse, personal communication, 2018), as well as Tah Maja, located 2.5 km southwest of the civic ceremonial nucleus. These four sites share stucco altars built on basal platforms of rough masonry with associated steps or miniature stairways.

Paamul

Paamul is a large site with basal pyramids, temples, and other masonry structures that total more than thirty in an area of 4 km² on the rocky coast. It was easily visible from the sea and was recorded as an archaeological site by Karl Berendt as early as 1878 but was first visited by Herbert Spinden in 1926 and subsequently by William Sanders, E. Wyllys Andrews IV, and Michel Peissel (see Mason 1927; E. Andrews and A. Andrews 1975, 77–80; Peissel 1963). The site has a distinctive temple pyramid as well as a round "observatory" and a two-story building similar to the Temple of the Frescoes at Tulum. Several caves, cenotes, albarradas, and *sascaberas* (limestone quarries) are found within the nuclear area (see the partial plan of the site by Terrones, Leira, and Campos 2015).

The extension of the Paamul settlement area has been affected by the coastal highway and modern settlements and is therefore difficult to ascertain. However, like Chakalal, a large cave system is projected from the old city to the northwest, with a length of more than 6 km. Cavers call this system Jaguar Claw, which is associated with several archaeological settlements (figure 13.5). At one point of this system (called "Gil Gamble," which constitutes the southeast entrance to the cave), there is evidence of speleothem breakage and removal.

Approximately 4 km from Paamul is the Metates group; inside the cave are a series of walls dividing various spaces and the presence of a group of *metates* (grinding stones) placed on stone bases as well as abundant surface ceramics, including Chancenote Striated and Tancah Burdo from the Early Formative and Early Classic periods. There is also an anthropomorphic sculpture of a head with the remains of blue paint, approximately 1 m high and 60 cm wide.

Some 700 m to the northwest is a site called Paamul Cave, which is in an area where the system bifurcates into two branches (one to the north and one to the northwest). In an illuminated portion of the cave is a rectangular stuccoed altar with associated fragments of Late Postclassic censers (including types such as Sisal Burdo). In addition to a series of walls and "corridors," there is a small circular cyst near the altar, about 30 cm in diameter.

Following the northwest branch, 1.3 km away, a surface site called Paamul II was built on a cliff above an entrance to the cave. It consists of a monumental core that includes a pyramidal base of approximately 30 m per side and 7 m in height, formed by three overlapping terraces and a rectangular superstructure, with a stairway on the west side. A plaza is defined by two other minor structures on that same side. With the pyramid constructed just above the cave, the arrangement is a clear example of the cave-pyramid complex, representing the three basic levels of the Maya universe (Bonor Villarejo 1989a).

The settlement area around this nucleus has not been determined, but the presence of albarradas was also observed. At 175 m to the northwest, there is another entrance to the cave with a staircase that leads to the interior, where there are rough stone walls restricting several spaces. In the semiflooded section of this cave, there is a circular masonry altar about 2.5 m in diameter and 65 cm high that barely protrudes from the water. It incorporates a speleothem in the form of a column on its west side, protruding from the flat surface of the altar, in front of which a slab was vertically placed (figure 13.6).

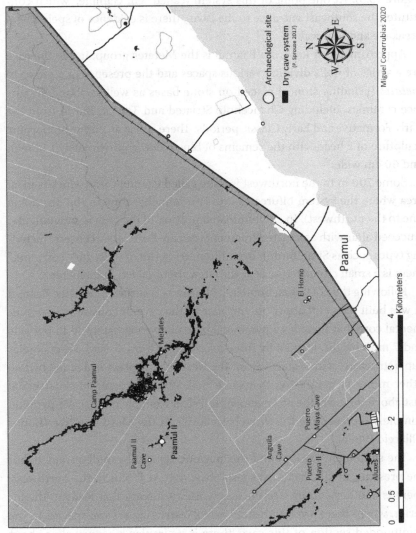

FIGURE 13.5 Cave systems northwest of Paamul (map by Miguel Covarrubias Reyna).

FIGURE 13.6 Circular altar and column in the cave at Paamul II (photograph courtesy of Carmen Rojas Sandoval).

Just in front of the slab were fragments of pottery from a Late Postclassic Chen Mul–type censer. In the northern branch of the cave, 1.2 km from the site Cueva Paamul, we found several rough stone walls and a quadrangular masonry platform 4 m per side and 75 cm in height along the dripline. The platform walls consist of four overlapping courses of roughly carved stones, and on top there is a stuccoed altar of 80 cm per side and 6 cm in height. Within a looter's hole, we observed several Late Postclassic sherds.

We are also aware of another system parallel to this one, about 1,500 m to the north, called Mystic Monkey by cavers, where there is a stuccoed altar with an inset stairway, but we do not know its exact location (Sprouse, personal communication, 2018). In another small cave system located approximately 1 km northwest of Paamul, there is a masonry shrine named El Horno, given its small size and oven-like shape. It is located inside a small cave where a five-step stairway leads to a pool. There is also a rough stone wall behind the structure. The tiny ceremonial structure measures 1.2 m per side and 1 m in height, with the façade and interior covered with stucco and recessed lintel characteristic of the Late Postclassic East Coast style of temple architecture. Inside the structure is a stepped rectangular altar that is 60 cm long, 50 cm wide, and 15 cm high, with a 30 cm high slab placed vertically, consistent with this architectural type; 100 m to the northwest, another cave contains walls and a "corridor."

Punta Piedra

Punta Piedra is probably the largest site in the central section of the coast of Quintana Roo—together with Xcaret, Xamanha, and Rancho Ina—and forms a single urban community. There is confusion regarding this site since initial studies considered it part of Xcaret. Several of the groups located northeast of the cove at Xcaret were identified as belonging to the latter site, specifically those designated as Groups T, U, V, W, X, and Y (E. Andrews and A. Andrews 1975). However, subsequent research has shown that Punta Piedra (Group V) has a much larger and more extensive central precinct than Xcaret or the other sites that were part of this large, urbanized area (Leira Guillermo and Terrones 1982–86).

The cave system of the Río Secreto Park (also known as Sistema Pool Tunich) is approximately 6.2 km long and is notable for its complexity and archaeological features (figure 13.7). Close to the coast, similarly to Punta Piedra and Xcaret, four examples of construction inside caves have been reported in the Q, R, S, and Y groups (E. Andrews and A. Andrews 1975).

Group Q is located approximately 1 km northwest of Xcaret, with a shallow cave that is accessed by a steep passage leading to several chambers and a body of water. About 15 m north of the entrance, in the main chamber, there is a small platform, 2.10 × 2.50 m, with an altar that resembles a throne on top and an inset stairway on the west side. The platform consists of several courses of crudely carved stones that reached 75 cm in height. Both the platform and the altar are stuccoed. Light from the entrance of the cave can illuminate the altar. Associated with this structure were fragments of possible anthropomorphic sculptures of stucco and stone (along with traces of where they had been set onto the altar) as well as fragments of ceramic incense burners (E. Andrews and A. Andrews 1975, 44–45).

Group R was located 1.9 km north-northwest of the Xcaret *caleta* (inlet), where there was a structure near the entrance to the cave that was probably a temple. Inside the cave is a small oratory perfectly preserved in miniature, without a lintel or molding, and with a roof of stone slabs supported by the walls. Inside the oratory is a bench-shaped altar, in the center of which is a depression with the remains of a stucco idol. In the southeast corner of the oratory platform is a stucco sculpture that probably represented a jaguar looking toward the entrance to the cave. There were also two other stucco

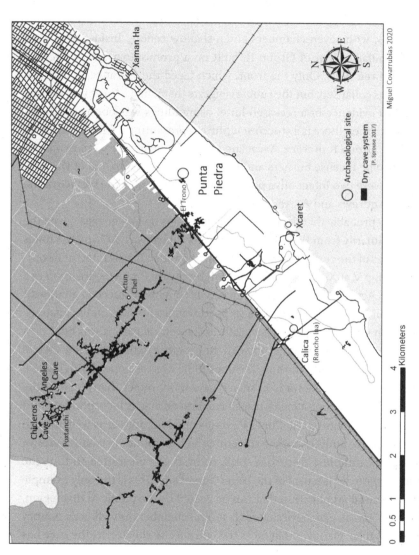

FIGURE 13.7 Archaeological sites of Xcaret and Punta Piedra, and the Pool Tunich Cave System (map by Miguel Covarrubias Reyna).

ornaments atop the roof of the oratory, resembling prickly pear cactus fruit (E. Andrews and A. Andrews 1975, 45–46).

Group S is located approximately 1.8 km north-northwest of the Xcaret caleta, east of Group R. It is a much larger cave than those of the previous two groups, with seven chambers and a shallow cenote. Inside there is an oratory similar to that of Group R, built on a promontory surrounded by water on three sides. Only the front, which faced the entrance, is dry. The building has collapsed, but the rubble suggests that it had a "beehive" vaulted ceiling. No evidence of a recessed lintel or moldings was observed. In the southeast corner, there is a stucco sculpture representing a feline, as was the case of the Group R oratory. Associated with this structure were two complete cup-type incense burners and fragments of others. In one of the later chambers were two intact olive pots, deposited just below the surface of the water (E. Andrews and A. Andrews 1975, 46).

It is very probable that the three previous groups no longer exist, given the damage primarily from the expansion of Federal Highway 307 and the roads and facilities of the current Xcaret amusement park. In the architectural complex of Group V at Xcaret, which is part of the core of Punta Piedra, there is a cave called Actun Merech or El Hemiciclo. It contains a stuccoed altar, with a semicircular plan, consisting of a stepped wall at the ends and a quadrangular bench with a slab placed vertically in the central part. It was built on a platform atop a limestone outcrop, with the entrance to the cave a few meters to the west (Leira Guillermo and Terrones 1982; Martos López 2010, 102–7).

The site of Punta Piedra is in many ways more intact than Xcaret—the latter having undergone a major transformation during its incorporation into a massive amusement park. Punta Piedra is open to tourists as well, though its offerings are modest, and the structures and surrounding landscape have been significantly less disturbed. Still, tourists are permitted to tour the Group Y cave, which is part of the larger Xcaret site. This is the only example of underground architecture that can be visited by the public in this region.

Group Y has an extensive cave with several chambers as well as an oratory on a rectangular platform that faces the entrance to the north. The cave has simple vertical walls—stuccoed and without ornamentation—that when first reported had remains of red paint. The collapsed roof was made of slabs with an inset lintel. Inside there is a bench-type altar. A few meters to the west, there is a petroglyph of an anthropomorphic figure with an oversized phallus (E. Andrews and A. Andrews 1975, 49–50; Terrones and Leira 1984).

Actun Chel, located 3 km northwest of Punta Piedra in the Río Secreto Park, contains an undocumented quadrangular stucco altar (Sprouse, personal communication, 2018). Further northwest, about 6 km from Punta Piedra, is a cave called Ángeles, whose interior structure has also been documented as Shrine X-1 (Rissolo et al. 2017). It is a miniature temple built on a quadrangular base with a three-step stairway, with the façade facing the entrance to the cave and just below a hole that allows light to enter the structure (figure 13.8), similar to the altar of the Group Q of Xcaret. The front of the platform and the stairway, façade, walls, and interior of the structure are stuccoed. It has a recessed lintel but no molding. Inside there are signs of an altar. The walls of the structure meet the low ceiling of the cave, so the height of the vertical walls varies to fit the natural formation.

Approximately 450 m from the Ángeles cave, in another branch of this cave system, there is a second underground temple, called Chicleros. In this case, the building is located a few meters west of the entrance, with the façade facing the cave opening. There are three distinguishable construction stages. The original construction consists of a quadrangular platform on which an altar was placed and covered with a thick layer of stucco. In the second stage, the temple was erected above and surrounding the original altar, with stuccoed vertical walls and without traces of a recessed lintel. It appears to have been roofed with large capstones, of which only one is preserved on the

FIGURE 13.8 Miniature temple in the cave known as Ángeles (photograph courtesy of Dominique Rissolo).

south side. These first two iterations were made with roughly carved stones, while the most recent stage is a rectangular platform that was attached to the front, on the west side. This building was also documented via photogrammetry. Unfortunately, it has been severely looted—penetrated from the front of the stucco platform to the back, under the altar, exposing the different construction episodes. We recovered ceramic remains, including a brazier of the Espita appliqué type of the Late Postclassic (Robles Castellanos 1990). In other parts of the cave, simple walls were observed made with undressed stones. In addition, albarradas were observed outside the cave.

In another system, located between 2 km and 3.5 km southwest of the Río Secreto, subterranean structures have also been reported, such as an altar in the cave of La Rosita, a temple in the Satachanah cave, and another surface temple built over the Kisim cave (Martos López 2002, 212–29). An additional altar was reported in another cave, Balankanche, in Calica, Quintana Roo, that must not be confused with the one located in Yucatán, close to Chichén Itzá (Martos López 2010, 92–96).

Typology of the Underground Architecture

To date, we have been able to collect data from thirty-seven sites in the caves of coastal Quintana Roo with evidence of public religious architecture, although there are likely to be many more. Nevertheless, this large and significant sample allows us to establish a typology based on dimensions, location, orientation, forms, relative construction quality, and ornamentation as well as the identification of architectural details.

Although examples of underground architecture have been recorded for more than a century (Strecker 1981), there has not been a systematic study of architectural modifications in caves. It is surprising how little attention has been paid to architecture in subterranean environments as a unit of analysis, especially when taking into account the work that has been done in Belize, Guatemala, and the interior of Quintana Roo, where a pyramidal structure was reported inside the cave of Actun Toh (Rissolo 2003, 38; see also Moyes 2012, 95).

Albarradas

In comparison with other areas of the peninsula, the frequency of albarradas (dry-stone walls) on the east coast is overwhelming. Previous research at sites such as Mayapán and Chunchucmil suggests that they were built to delimit adjacent property, marking the edges of the property to ensure spaces in which daily activities were carried out (Dahlin 2000; Garza Tarazona and Kurjack Basco 1980, 53–54; Hare, Masson, and Russell 2014; Pollock et al. 1962, 165–320; Vlcek 1978). But the presence of these walls in an area as large as that of the east coast could also be related to agricultural production to retain scarce soils and in certain cases may have also functioned as walkways (Vargas Pacheco, Vilalta, and Santillán 1986, 63–64; see also Batún-Alpuche, this volume; Fedick et al. 2000; Leonard 2013).

Similar systems of rock alignments have been studied in detail in other zones, such as the wetlands in the Yalahau region on the northern coast, where they have been typified according to their shape, size, and probable function (Leonard 2013, 511–30). Also, intensive surveys of the north-central coastal region documented the presence of albarradas, rock alignments, and walkways (Covarrubias Reyna et al. 2011). However, the frequency, density, and extensive nature of these constructions are noticeably more pronounced in the east coast region.

In the caves, we have observed repeated cases of albarradas bordering the depressions or collapses where cave entrances are located. Surface albarradas also act as directional elements toward the caves and water sources, since they start or end right at the edge of these depressions. Inside, the albarradas form enclosed or delimited spaces of varied shapes and dimensions, generally located in the twilight or entrance portions of the caves (Martos López 2002, 200).

Walls in Caves

Walls are perhaps the most common elements that can be found inside the caves of Quintana Roo. They are usually simple and short alignments of undressed and loosely stacked stones. Sometimes these low linear walls are used to cover natural cavities, delimit certain parts of the caves, and even restrict access to sections such as bodies of water (Martos López 2002, 199). In this region, a cave that does not contain at least this type of feature or arrangement can be considered atypical.

Corridors and Traps

Corridors are frequently encountered and are formed when parallel walls of low, simple courses of *lajas* or flat stones are anchored vertically, leaving "walkways" about 30 cm wide (+/- 2–5 cm). Sometimes the corridors are formed by simple, low walls and in other cases by adjacent constructions of quadrangular or rectangular walls. They may have served as traps for small animals, such as agoutis, which are abundant in these forests and often enter caves in search of water and shelter. In one case, ceramic net weights were found associated with this type of structure. But it has also been documented that corridors are often oriented on axes from north to south or east to west, which opens the possibility that their function is perhaps related to the notion of caves as places of origin or regeneration of life (Martos López 2002, 202–3). Certain structures, similar to corridors, can be considered a variant of these because they are constructed in the same way but covered with slabs, forming conduits that typically lead to water sources. They are often associated with walls that block other possible access points to the cave pools, and it is therefore likely that they functioned as traps, which may have also included perishable components (Martos López 2002, 204).

Stairways

As caves and cenotes are the only sources of drinking water in this region, it makes sense that there are steps to facilitate access. These can have different qualities of construction, from simple steps to managed slopes, to complex and elaborate constructions (Martos López 2002, 205–8). Like the corridors, the stairways could also have been associated with the procurement of water for rain rites and rituals. Such could be the case of the "hieroglyphic" stairway of Tancah Cave, carved in the bedrock, which is additionally accompanied by a stela, emphasizing its sacred character (Rissolo 2005a, 2005b). Despite the seemingly utilitarian nature of stairways, examples such as carved steps in Tancah Cave possess symbolic attributes.

Public Architecture

Public buildings are associated with community cohesion. Considerable energy and materials were invested in the construction of structures, grouped into nuclei, whose function was to maintain the power and authority of specific social sectors through politics, religion, and control of the economy (Garza Tarazona and Kurjack Basco 1980). The appropriation of the landscape in the selection of settlement locales went beyond subsistence considerations and was tied to the reproduction of sacred geography, through which the leaders could exercise their control over society.

Maya population centers resorted to this monumentality of the architectural center from the Formative to the Early Postclassic periods. However, with few exceptions (e.g., the coast of Quintana Roo), construction activity decreased significantly in other regions of the peninsula during the Late Postclassic. The East Coast architecture of the Postclassic may not be considered monumental (in comparison to other earlier traditions). However, the social role was essentially analogous to that of the great structures of the Classic period. During this period, builders placed diminutive temples on abandoned buildings, along coastlines, and within caves (E. Andrews and A. Andrews 1975; Lothrop 1924; see also Lorenzen 2003).

Altars

Altars are the simplest forms of public architecture found in caves, but they also appear within temples at surface sites (which may, in turn, be architectonic representations of caves). Cave altars are relatively consistent in form and typically consist of quadrangular stuccoed masonry platforms supporting benches or "thrones" atop stone slabs or speleothems. Many of these thrones or altar surfaces are now vacant—their venerated residents (including sculpted figures) were destroyed a long time ago. This removal is often evidenced by the broken mortar or scar of where the resident was once fastened. Cave altars are typically located at entrances—either outside the dripline or within twilight areas. (In both cases, they typically face the outside.) The simplest form is that of a low stucco bench, like at the Camp Paamul site, set on a basal platform of rough masonry. Similar altars have been reported in two caves at Xelha (González and Rojas 2006; Navarrete 1974) and in La Rosita Cave at Calica (Martos López 2002, 97–101; 2010).

Sometimes altars are simple unstuccoed platforms, such as the construction in Balankanche Cave, Calica, Quintana Roo (Martos López 2002, 92–96), and Nohoch Kan cave near Akumal. Altars can also consist of three walls surrounding a throne and can be constructed on rocks or the surface of the cave, as in Paamul, Cenote Perdido, or Yokdzonot, near Punta Laguna. These forms can also be found on stuccoed basal platforms such as those of Group Q of Xcaret (E. Andrews and A. Andrews 1975, 44–45) or in the cave of Mystic Monkey (Sprouse, personal communication, 2018). These lat-

FIGURE 13.9 Altar in Nohoch Tuyul (photograph courtesy of Miguel Covarrubias Reyna).

ter examples as well as the altars in Nohoch Tuyul (figure 13.9) and Tah Maja (Rojas Sandoval 2015) have attached or recessed staircases.

Another variant of altars in caves involves the incorporation of speleothems into the structure. Although there are fewer known examples of this type—in Mil Columnas, Paamul II (Rojas Sandoval and Covarrubias Reyna 2017c; see figure 13.6), in Olokum cave of the Pacto system (Sprouse, personal communication, 2018), and in the Sistema Pool Tunich (Rissolo 2008)—dripstone columns were incorporated into the basal platforms.

A rather peculiar altar form is characterized by stepped wall-like elements enclosing the offertory space. Actun Merech (figure 13.10), near the main structure of the Punta Piedra site, has erroneously been considered as the northern part of Xcaret (Leira Guillermo and Terrones 1982; Martos López 2010, 102–7; Rissolo 2004). This altar has a stucco wall, in the form of a half circle (with four steps on each end), which encloses a small square altar with a vertical recessed slab. This is all built on a basal platform that is also stuccoed. A second example was found in Gruta de las Caritas, in the Actun Chen area. Unlike the altar in Actun Merech, its masonry walls intersect with the wall of the cave. It has six steps on one side and five on the other, and in the center of the stuccoed quadrangular altar emerges a stalagmite rather than a vertical slab (Rissolo 2004).

Oratories

Oratories or shrines are essentially miniature temples of the East Coast type. These structures often consist of masonry walls and simple stone slab roofs, or sometimes they take advantage of the natural ceiling of the cave. Unlike

FIGURE 13.10 Altar in Actun Merech (also known as Cueva de Hemiciclo) (photograph courtesy of Miguel Covarrubias Reyna).

temples, their architectural complexity, dimensions, and construction quality are of a lower order. The most basic form of oratory is that of an open-fronted "box" made with vertically placed slabs for walls and a slab placed on top as the roof (often without the use of mortar or stucco). Examples of this type of oratory have been reported within Ocho Balas (Germán Yañez, personal communication, 2018) and at the entrance to a small cave in Kantenah (Covarrubias Reyna 2018).

Slightly more sophisticated constructions can be found in sites such as El Horno, near Paamul, where a small masonry enclosure, with a stucco façade and a small altar-shaped bench in the interior, was built directly on the cave floor. Consistent with the East Coast architectural canon, a recessed lintel is visible (figure 13.11). Variations can include the use of small basal platforms and elaborate internal altars, sometimes with vertical recessed slabs. Other examples of this type of structure include the oratories in Group S and Group Y Caves at Xcaret (E. Andrews and A. Andrews 1975, 46–50; Martos López 2010, 108–13), though it should be noted that the latter belongs to the site of Punta Piedra (Terrones and Leira 1984).

FIGURE 13.11 Oratory or shrine known as El Horno, near Paamul (photograph courtesy of Dominique Rissolo).

Oratories have also been reported in the Satachanah cave (Martos López 2010, 114–22), in the Naval System (Mystery Line), in Gruta de las Caritas (Rissolo 2004), and in the Sistema Pool Tunich (Rissolo et al. 2017). The latter cave contained a fragmented but complete Chen Mul effigy censer, the precise provenience of which is unknown. In all these examples, the small dimensions and the simplicity of the design are consistent.

Temples

Unlike altars and oratories, temples are generally larger in scale and more complex in terms of design and architectural detail. They are quite similar to contemporaneous temples at surface sites, some of which are considered markers for coastal navigation or part of the architectural core of the hundreds of settlements on the Quintana Roo coastline. Associated with caves, these temples can be found either inside entrance chambers (facing the entrance) or on the surface at or above the cave entrance. Invariably, they are placed on basal platforms—their façades decorated with recessed lintels, moldings of varied shapes, and sometimes stucco sculptures—with altars inside. Many such temples were painted (with the sheltering environment of the cave preserving traces of pigment and design). The Xcaret Group R cave temple, a small structure, was decorated with stucco sculptures, including that of a feline (E. Andrews and A. Andrews 1975, 45–46). Given the simplicity of its façade and its small size, it could be considered a transition between the oratory and the temple.

Other cave temples—exhibiting moldings on façades, recessed lintels sometimes with traces of paint, remains of stucco sculptures, stairs, foundation platforms, and internal altars, in exceptional cases with preserved wooden beams—include the aforementioned Temple of the Aluxes (see figure 13.3), the Ocho Balas Temple (see figure 13.4), the Ángeles Cave Temple (see figure 13.8), and the Chicleros Temple (Rissolo et al. 2016; Rissolo et al. 2017; Rojas Sandoval 2015).

The walls of the Ángeles Cave Temple, in the Río Secreto system, meet the low cave ceiling directly below a natural skylight, which illuminates the temple interior when the sun is high. Although it is small in size and lacks ornamentation, it can be considered as a transition between oratory and temple, as it has an elaborate stairway and a doorway with a recessed lintel.

In Chicleros Cave, the unfortunate damage to the temple by looters allowed us to observe the process of transformation through successive constructive stages, from a quadrangular altar on a basal platform with a recessed staircase into a temple with stuccoed walls that enclosed the original construction. No evidence of the roof or lintel is preserved.

The largest, most well-constructed, and best-preserved example of a Postclassic cave temple is found in Ocho Balas (also known as Oratorio). It was constructed on a stuccoed *banqueta* atop a basal platform and known cave temple with a three-element molding. Its preservation is so exceptional that it still retains its beam-and-mortar roof (figure 13.12).

Aktun Na Kan, near Xpuha, houses another example of a small temple, with the façade facing the entrance and a stucco molding that ends in the shape of a snake head in the northeast corner. On the ground, in front of its entrance, are the remains of a stucco sculpture depicting a reptile, possibly an iguana, with its gaze directed toward the temple's doorway, where traces of blue paint on the lintel and jambs were observed (Leira Guillermo and Terrones 1986; Martos López 2010, 123–28).

FIGURE 13.12 Stuccoed interior of the cave temple at Ocho Balas; note the state of preservation of the beam and mortar roof (photograph courtesy of Dominique Rissolo).

Regarding surface temples associated with cave entrances, the Paamul II site is a clear example of the cave-pyramid complex. Another exceptional case is the site called El Templo, near Xelha, where a pair of East Coast buildings—one with two adjoining rooms (already collapsed) and a relatively well-preserved temple—was built around a watery cave. The latter is positioned just above the entrance.

This building has its façade, with a recessed lintel, oriented toward the cave. It has a molding of three elements with a central frieze. The looted interior shows the footprint of a quadrangular altar. It is laid on a platform without steps, constructed directly atop the cave entrance, which also has a wall on the north side of the entrance zone (Covarrubias Reyna 2017). A similar case has been recorded in the Kisim cave, in Calica, where another temple, accompanied by an oratory adjacent to its southeast side, is located directly above the entrance to the cave (Martos López 2002, fig. 61). We are aware of other examples, in this area, of temples and oratories inside caves or near cave entrances. Unfortunately, their locations are sometimes kept secret from other researchers and authorities, while photos and the like are shared via popular media.

Rooms

On the Yucatán Peninsula, numerous caves have masonry dividing walls with doorways forming rooms (Covarrubias Reyna and Burgos 2009). In Quintana Roo, to date, only one such cave room, in Taka'an Dzonot (between Tulum and Cobá), has been documented (Rojas Sandoval and Covarrubias Reyna 2017b). The walls—more than 1 m wide and built parallel to one another—create an artificial gallery between two chambers with bodies of water, taking advantage of the morphology of the cave and integrating speleothems. Although no diagnostic pottery was found on the surface, the construction technique (roughly dressed stones and the quality of the mortar and stucco) suggests that the feature corresponds to the Late Postclassic. The openings are low and narrow (figure 13.13), restricting access from the first chamber, which has little ambient light, and the second body of water, which is in the dark. The effect is one of restricted access to a cave pool made dark by the construction of the room.

Conclusion

This study of the architectonic transformation of subterranean space along the central east coast region of Quintana Roo not only resulted in a comprehensive contemporary inventory of constructed features but better enables us to address questions of function and meaning of regional cave use practices. Indeed, it is likely that additional sites with underground structures will be documented in the future, as a number of areas in Quintana Roo are still largely unsurveyed. Settlement pattern surveys suggest that the Maya of the eastern peninsula took full advantage of the landscape in which they chose to live. The presence of numerous caves generated patterns of behavior differentiated from those of other regions (Bonor Villarejo 1989a, 11), at least during the two main occupations from the Late Formative to the Early Classic and during the Late Postclassic.

By constructing a world inside the caves, the Maya re-created cosmic space, reifying cosmogonic principles and improving and embodying the experiences of their ancestors (Moyes 2012, 107). To understand the integral development of the east coast of the peninsula, we must move beyond interpreting its dense Postclassic occupation as a society singularly dedicated to coastal trade. Instead, we need to consider the use of space in relation to the interac-

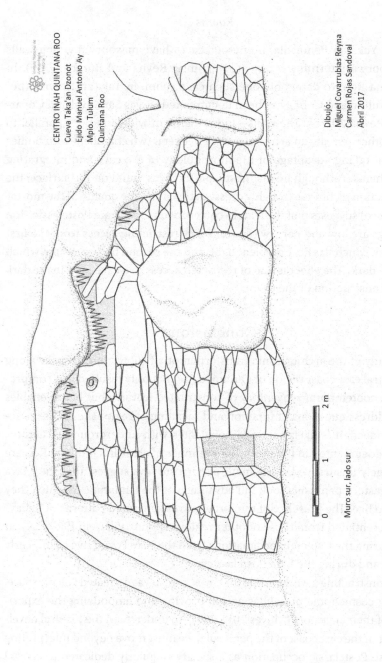

FIGURE 13.13 Masonry wall and doorway in Taka'an Dzonot (illustration by Miguel Covarrubias Reyna and Carmen Rojas Sandoval).

tion between communities and the places where they settled in a diachronic way, including the use of caves, where besides activities for sustenance, they would allow us to enter into the basic essence of the ideology and religion that impelled them (Cornell and Velázquez Morlet 2020; Moyes 2012).

Works Cited

Andrews, Anthony P. 1981. "El 'guerrero' de Loltun: Comentario analítico." *Boletín de la Escuela de Ciencias Antropológicas de la Universidad de Yucatán* 8/9 (48/49): 36–50.

Andrews, Anthony P. 1983. "Reconocimiento arqueológico de Tulum a Punta Allen, Quintana Roo." *Boletín de la Escuela de Ciencias Antropológicas de la Universidad de Yucatán* 11 (61): 15–31.

Andrews, Anthony P. 1986. "Reconocimiento arqueológico de Cancún a Playa del Carmen, Quintana Roo." *Boletín de la Escuela de Ciencias Antropológicas de la Universidad de Yucatán* 13 (78): 3–19.

Andrews, E. Wyllys, IV. 1970. *Balankanche, Throne of the Tiger Priest*. Middle American Research Institute 32. New Orleans: Tulane University.

Andrews, E. Wyllys, IV, and Anthony P. Andrews. 1975. *A Preliminary Study of the Ruins of Xcaret, Quintana Roo, Mexico, With Notes on Other Archaeological Remains on the Central East Coast of the Yucatan Peninsula*. Middle American Research Institute 40. New Orleans: Tulane University.

Arnold, Dean E. 2005. "Maya Blue and Palygorskite: A Second Possible Pre-Columbian Source." *Ancient Mesoamerica* 16 (1): 51–62.

Awe, Jaime J., ed. 1998. "The Western Belize Regional Cave Project: A Report of the 1997 Field Season." Department of Anthropology Occasional Paper no. 1. University of New Hampshire, Durham.

Bonor Villarejo, Juan L. 1989a. "El complejo cueva-pirámide en la cultura maya antigua." *Boletín de la Escuela de Ciencias Antropológicas de la Universidad de Yucatán* 16 (99): 3–16.

Bonor Villarejo, Juan L. 1989b. *Las cuevas mayas: Simbolismo y ritual*. Madrid: Universidad Compultense de Madrid.

Brady, James E. 1989. "An Investigation of Maya Ritual Cave Use with Special Reference to Naj Tunich, Peten, Guatemala." PhD diss., University of California, Los Angeles.

Brady, James E., and Dominique Rissolo. 2006. "A Reappraisal of Ancient Maya Cave Mining." *Journal of Anthropological Research* 62 (4): 471–90.

Brady, James E., Ann Scott, Allan Cobb, Irma Rodas, John Fogarty, and Monica Urquizu Sanchez. 1997. "Glimpses of the Dark Side of the Petexbatun Project." *Ancient Mesoamerica* 8 (2): 353–64.

Chatters, James C., Douglas J. Kennett, Yemane Asmerom, Brian M. Kemp, Victor Polyak, Alberto Nava Blank, Patricia A. Beddows, Eduard Reinhardt, Joaquin

Arroyo-Cabrales, Deborah A. Bolnick, Ripan S. Malhi, Brendan Culleton, Pilar Luna Erreguerena, Dominique Rissolo, Shanti Morell-Hart, and Thomas W. Stafford Jr. 2014. "Late Pleistocene Human Skeleton and mtDNA Link Paleoamericans and Modern Native Americans." *Science* 344 (6185): 750–54.

Cornell, Per, and Adriana Velázquez Morlet. 2020. "Time, Built Space, and the Question of the Household in the Case of Ecab, Quintana Roo, Mexico: Maya Settlement Organisation in the Late Postclassic Period." In *"For My Descendants and Myself, a Nice and Pleasant Abode": Agency, Micro-History and Built Environment*, edited by Göran Tagesson, Per Cornell, Mark Gardiner, Liz Thomas, and Katherine Weikert, 67–84. Buildings in Society International BISI III, Stockholm 2017. Oxford: Archaeopress.

Covarrubias Reyna, Miguel. 2017. "Informe de los recorridos de superficie realizados en el área Tulum-Coba, Quintana Roo." Archivo del Centro INAH Quintana Roo, Chetumal.

Covarrubias Reyna, Miguel. 2018. "Informe de la prospección arqueológica realizada en el predio Kantenah III Lote 009-2, Municipio de Solidaridad, Quintana Roo." Archivo del Centro INAH Quintana Roo, Chetumal.

Covarrubias Reyna, Miguel. 2019a. "Informe de la prospección arqueológica realizada en el predio San José FIV Lote 082, Municipio de Solidaridad, Quintana Roo." Archivo del Centro INAH Quintana Roo, Chetumal.

Covarrubias Reyna, Miguel. 2019b. "Informe de la prospección arqueológica realizada en terrenos del Plan Maestro Amikoo, Punta Maroma, Municipio de Solidaridad, Quintana Roo." Archivo de la Coordinación Nacional de Arqueología del INAH, Mexico City.

Covarrubias Reyna, Miguel. 2020. "Field Surveys South of Coba." *Mexicon* 42 (1): 16–22.

Covarrubias Reyna, Miguel, and Rafael Burgos. 2009. "Las ruinas del Rancho San Andrés, municipio de Dzlam González, Yucatán." *Mexicon* 31 (4): 85–87.

Covarrubias Reyna, Miguel, Rafael Burgos, Yoly Palomo, Sara Dzul, Rodolfo Canto, María Luisa Parra, and Hugo González. 2011. "Proyecto de Investigaciones Arqueológicas en Dzilam González: Informe de la Primera Temporada de Campo (julio–septiembre 2010)." Archivo de la Sección de Arqueología del Centro INAH Yucatán, Mérida.

Dahlin, Bruce. 2000. "The Barricade and Abandonment of Chunchucmil: Implications for Northern Maya Warfare." *Latin American Antiquity* 11 (3): 283–98.

Fedick, Scott L., Bethany A. Morrison, Bente Juhl Andersen, Sylviane Boucher, Jorge Ceja Acosta, and Jennifer P. Mathews. 2000. "Wetland Manipulation in the Yalahau Region of the Northern Maya Lowlands." *Journal of Field Archaeology* 27 (2): 131–52.

Folan, William J., Ellen R. Kintz, and Laraine A. Fletcher. 1983. *Cobá: A Classic Maya Metropolis*. New York: Academic Press.

Garza Tarazona, Silvia, and Edward Barna Kurjack Basco. 1980. *Atlas arqueológico del Estado de Yucatán*. Mexico City: Secretaría de Educación Pública, Instituto Nacional de Antropología e Historia.

Glover, Jeffrey B. 2006. "The Yalahau Regional Settlement Pattern Survey: A Study of Ancient Maya Social Organization in Northern Quintana Roo, Mexico." PhD diss., University of California, Riverside.

González, Arturo, and Carmen Rojas. 2006. "Informe Técnico, Atlas Arqueológico Subacuático para el Registro, Estudio y Protección de los Cenotes en la Península de Yucatán." Archivo del Centro INAH Quintana Roo, Chetumal.

González, Arturo, Carmen Rojas, Alejandro Terrazas, Martha Benavente, and Wolfgang Stinnesbeck. 2006. "Poblamiento temprano en la península de Yucatán: Evidencias localizadas en cuevas sumergidas de Quintana Roo, México." In *II Simposio Internacional del Hombre Temprano en América, 2004*, 73–90. Mexico City: Instituto Nacional de Antropología e Historia.

Hare, Timothy, Marilyn Masson, and Bradley Russell. 2014. "High-Density LiDAR Mapping of the Ancient City of Mayapán." *Remote Sensing* 6 (9): 9064–85.

Leira Guillermo, Luis and Enrique Terrones. 1982. "Plano de la Cueva Actun Merech, Proyecto Punta Piedra." Archivo del Centro INAH Quintana Roo, Chetumal.

Leira Guillermo, Luis, and Enrique Terrones. 1982–86. "Mapas del Proyecto Punta Piedra." Archivo del Centro INAH Quintana Roo, Chetumal.

Leira Guillermo, Luis, and Enrique Terrones. 1986. "Aktun Na Kan, una cueva maya en Quintana Roo." *Boletín de la Escuela de Ciencias Antropológicas de la Universidad de Yucatán* 14 (79): 3–10.

Leonard, Daniel I. 2013. "The Yalahau Regional Wetland Survey: Ancient Maya Land Use in Northern Quintana Roo, Mexico." PhD diss., University of California, Riverside.

López López, Benito, and Miguel Covarrubias. 2018. "Informe del salvamento arqueológico en el predio 'San Vicente' del Proyecto TAEMA." Archivo del Centro INAH Quintana Roo, Chetumal.

Lorenzen, Karl James. 2003. "Miniature Masonry Shrines of the Yucatan Peninsula: Ancestor Deification in the Late Postclassic Maya Ritual and Religion." PhD diss., University of California, Riverside.

Lothrop, Samuel K. 1924. *Tulum, an Archaeological Study of the East Coast of Yucatan*. Publication 335. Washington, D.C.: Carnegie Institution of Washington.

Martos López, Luis Alberto. 2002. *Por las tierras mayas de oriente: Arqueología en el área de CALICA, Quintana Roo*. Mexico City: Instituto Nacional de Antropología e Historia.

Martos López, Luis Alberto. 2010. "Cuevas de la región central-oriental de la península de Yucatán: Un análisis desde la perspectiva simbólica." PhD diss., Escuela Nacional de Antropología e Historia, Mexico City.

Mason, Gregory. 1927. *Silver Cities of Yucatán*. New York: Putnam and Sons.

Mathews, Jennifer P. 1998. "The Ties That Bind: The Ancient Maya Interaction Spheres of the Late Preclassic and Early Classic Periods in the Northern Yucatan Peninsula." PhD diss., University of California, Riverside.

Moyes, Holley. 2006. "The Sacred Landscape as a Political Resource: A Case Study of Ancient Maya Cave Use at Chechem Ha Cave, Belize, Central America." PhD diss., State University of New York at Buffalo.

Moyes, Holley. 2012. "Constructing the Underworld: The Built Environment in Ancient Mesoamerican Caves." In *Heart of Earth: Studies in Maya Ritual Cave Use*, edited by James E. Brady, 95–110. Bulletin 23. Austin, Tex.: Association for Mexican Cave Studies.

Navarrete, Carlos. 1974. "Material cerámico de la cueva de Xelhá, Quintana Roo." *Notas Antropológicas* 1 (8): 53–57.

Peissel, Michel. 1963. *The Lost World of Quintana Roo*. New York: Dutton.

Piña Chan, Román. 1960. "Excavaciones en algunas cuevas de la región texcocana." *Revista Mexicana de Estudios Antropológicos* 14:53–65.

Pollock, Harry E. D., Ralph L. Roys, T. Proskouriakoff, and A. Ledyard Smith. 1962. *Mayapan, Yucatan, Mexico*. Publication 619. Washington, D.C.: Carnegie Institution of Washington.

Rissolo, Dominique. 2003. *Ancient Maya Cave Use in the Yalahau Region, Northern Quintana Roo, Mexico*. Bulletin 12. Austin, Tex.: Association for Mexican Cave Studies.

Rissolo, Dominique. 2004. "Maya Cave Shrines Along the Central Quintana Roo Coast." *Bulletin* 27:57–59.

Rissolo, Dominique. 2005a. "Beneath the Yalahau: Emerging Patterns of Ancient Maya Ritual Cave Use from Northern Quintana Roo, Mexico." In *In the Maw of the Earth Monster: Mesoamerican Ritual Cave Use*, edited by James E. Brady and Keith M. Prufer, 342–72. Austin: University of Texas Press.

Rissolo, Dominique. 2005b. "Tancah Cave Revisited." *Bulletin* 28:78–82.

Rissolo, Dominique. 2008. "Regional Cave Studies Along the Central Coast of Quintana Roo: Constant Challenges and Recent Advances in the Xcaret-Xamanhá Area." Paper presented at the 73rd Annual Meeting of the Society for American Archaeology, Vancouver, B.C., Canada.

Rissolo, Dominique, Michael R. Hess, Aliya R. Hoff, Dominique Meyer, Fabio Esteban Amador, Adriana Velazquez Morlet, Vid Petrovic, and Falko Kuester. 2016. "Imaging and Visualizing Maya Cave Shrines in Northern Quintana Roo, Mexico." In *Proceedings of the 8th International Congress on Archaeology, Computer Graphics, Cultural Heritage, and Innovation*, 382–84. Valencia, Spain: Editorial Universitat Politecnica de Valencia.

Rissolo, Dominique, Eric Lo, Michael R. Hess, Dominique E. Meyer, and Fabio E. Amador. 2017. "Digital Preservation of Ancient Maya Cave Architecture: Recent Field Efforts in Quintana Roo, Mexico." *International Archives of the Photogrammetry, Remote Sensing, and Spatial Information Sciences* 42 (2): 613–16.

Robles Castellanos, Fernando. 1990. *Secuencia Cerámica de la Región de Cobá, Quintana Roo*. Colección Científica no. 184. Mexico City: Instituto Nacional de Antropología e Historia.

Rojas Sandoval, Carmen. 2011. "Los cenotes como cámaras mortuorias entre los mayas prehispánicos." Master's thesis, Escuela Nacional de Antropología e Historia, Mexico City.

Rojas Sandoval, Carmen. 2015. "Informe de las inspecciones realizadas en cuevas y cenotes de Quintana Roo del 2013 al 2015." Archivo del Centro INAH Quintana Roo, Chetumal.

Rojas Sandoval, Carmen, and Miguel Covarrubias Reyna. 2017a. "Informe de la visita de inspección, Cueva Mil Columnas o Balam Ha, Parque Dos Ojos, Ejido Jacinto Pat, Municipio de Tulum, Quintana Roo." Archivo del Centro INAH Quintana Roo, Chetumal.

Rojas Sandoval, Carmen, and Miguel Covarrubias Reyna. 2017b. "Reporte de la visita de inspección, Cueva Taka'an (Escondida), Manuel Antonio Ay, Municipio de Tulum, Quintana Roo." M.S. Archivo del Centro INAH Quintana Roo, Chetumal.

Rojas Sandoval, Carmen, and Miguel Covarrubias Reyna. 2017c. "Reporte de la visita de inspección, Cueva Trono o Niño Perdido, Municipio de Solidaridad, Quintana Roo." Archivo del Centro INAH Quintana Roo, Chetumal.

Strecker, Matthias. 1981. "Exploraciones arqueológicas de Teobert Maler en cuevas yucatecas." *Boletín de la Escuela de Ciencias Antropológicas de la Universidad de Yucatán* 49–49:20–31.

Terrones, Enrique, and Luis Leira. 1984. "Plano de la Cueva Grupo Y de Xcaret, Proyecto Punta Piedra." Archivo del Centro INAH Quintana Roo, Chetumal.

Terrones, Enrique, Luis Leira, and Edwin Campos. 2015. "Mapa del sitio arqueológico Paamul." Archivo del Centro INAH Quintana Roo, Chetumal.

Vargas Pacheco, Ernesto, Marta Vilalta, and Patricia Santillán. 1986. "Apuntes para el análisis del patrón de asentamiento en Tulum." *Estudios de Cultura Maya* 16:55–84.

Vlcek, David T. 1978. "Muros de delimitación residencial de Chunchucmil." *Boletín de la Escuela de Ciencias Antropológicas de la Universidad de Yucatán* 5 (28): 55–64.

CHAPTER 14

Not Seeing Is Believing

The Production of Space in Ancient Maya Cave Sites

HOLLEY MOYES

> All holy or cursed places, places characterized by the presence or absence of gods, associated with the death of gods, or with hidden powers and their exorcism—all such places qualify as special preserves. Hence in absolute space the absolute has no place, for otherwise it would be a "non-place"; and religio-political space has a strange composition, being made up of areas set apart, reserved—and so mysterious.
>
> *Henri LeFebvre,* The Production of Space

Ever since Frederick Catherwood tantalized the public with his nineteenth-century renderings of temples emerging from the jungles of Mesoamerica, architecture has been a focal point in ancient Maya studies. David Webster noted that architecture, while not immune from transformation processes, is typically less affected than portable artifacts or perishable materials in the archaeological record. Structures sit "solidly and reassuringly where we find them," rendering recoverable patterns and indicating the intentionality in structure placement (Webster 1998, 15). Therefore, due to the excellent preservation of architecture, it is not surprising that architectural studies have flourished in Mesoamerican scholarship. From the built environment, archaeologists have inferred patterns of behavior and social organization as well as cultural meanings based on purposeful designs that coded symbolic messages (e.g., Chase and Chase 2001; Christie 2003; Fox 1996; Houston 1998; Kubler 1993; Proskouriakoff 1976; von Schwerin 2011). Yet while a rich literature for understanding temples and structures abounds, there has been little systematic consideration of architectural features found in ritual cave sites (see, for exceptions, Awe and Morton, this volume; Brady 1989; Moyes 2012a, 2020; Rissolo 2005; Rojas Sandoval, Covarrubias Reyna, and Rissolo, this volume). For the ancient Maya, caves were not only natural spaces but also constructed environments. The study of cave architecture provides a framework for understanding the influence and impact that cave rites exercised on the ritual participants. Following Amos Rappaport, environments impart nonverbal communications directly to the receiver via culturally encoded clues. Environmental cues provide information to constrain and guide behavior, influence communication, and create meaning (Rappaport 1982, 57). In the case of caves, as natural settings, they create a backdrop for ritual performance that is inherently sacred, authentic, and imbued with meaning.

In this chapter, I consider Henri LeFebvre's work *The Production of Space* ([1974] 2004) as a tool for analyses of ancient Maya cave space and to consider ways in which cave architecture contributes to spatial production. Fundamental to LeFebvre's thesis is that space is not simply a Euclidian concept that can be measured or described but is socially *produced*. This idea of social production serves to wrest spatial analyses from the natural sciences and place spatial analyses into a humanistic social realm. For LeFebvre, spaces take on a reality of its own, which serves as a tool for thought and action, and thus becomes a means of control and domination ([1974] 2004, 11, 26). Though his agenda is Marxist in nature and primarily concerned with modern societies, his intellectual program may be more broadly applied to societies with political hierarchies and differential power relationships such as the ancient Maya.

LeFebvre's work concerns itself with the physical (nature, the cosmos), the mental (logical and formal abstractions), and the social (who or what occupies space and how). Methodologically, to understand space one must consider three major components: (1) spatial practice (the relations of people to space and how it is used), (2) representations of space (the meaning and order of space by way of architectural constructions and how this is encoded by the users), and (3) representational spaces (how spaces are symbolized and imagined, the way conceptual space overlays physical space) (LeFebvre [1974] 2004, 38–39). Social space may be subjected to formal, structural, or functional analyses, though all three components interrelate and do not exist in isolation (LeFebvre [1974] 2004, 147–48). Form, for instance, may be described as having limits, areas, boundaries, or volumes, but it also encompasses ideologies and functionality. Structurally, space may be thought of in terms of part-whole relationships, between "micro" (e.g., architectural) and "macro" (spatial-strategic) levels. Here, scale and proportion require consideration.

Social space is "encoded" in the context of a specific historic period, in which members of that society would have comprehended and thus acted within that code. LeFebvre ([1974] 1994, 17–18, 40) argues that an already produced space can be "decoded" and "read," partially by considering the interaction of the body in space and with spatial representations. However, he warns that space is produced to be "lived" and points out that if spaces are produced with the intent to be "read" (such as monuments that have a clearly intelligible message), then they likely contain hidden agendas and conceal intentions and actions ([1974] 2004, 143–44).

Architecture cannot be understood on its own but as a production of space that entails local ideologies and power relationships. Architecture has the ability to mediate gestures (behaviors) and create codes that conform to religious and political ideas. Constructions play the potential roles of creating centers, focal points, and peripheries, delineating transportation routes and access points, creating or occluding sightlines, or parsing space as public or private. In Lefebvre's words, "walls, enclosures, and façades serve to define both a *scene* (where something takes place) and an *obscene* area to which everything that cannot or may not happen on the scene is relegated: whatever is inadmissible, be it malefic or forbidden, thus has its own hidden space on the near or far side of the frontier" ([1974] 2004, 36). These formal/functional characteristics of produced space are also laden with meanings encoded by users. For archaeologists to "read" a produced space of a past people requires knowledge of cosmologies, socio/political structures, political economies, histories, and religious belief systems, which articulate their cultural expressions in spatial representations.

In this chapter, I consider how ancient Maya people viewed caves as both representations of space and as representational spaces, discussing the meanings of caves in Maya thought. I then describe the formal characteristics of archaeological cave sites and how architecture structures cave space. To better understand the relationship between form and function, I take a phenomenological approach that incorporates observations of bodily engagements with the cave and its spatial representations (architectural elaborations). I argue that architecture in caves expresses hierarchies and power differentials between humans and nonhuman actors. These crafted spaces whose architectural features framed and organized the rites conducted therein were potent symbols in forging and maintaining power relations. Based on the cosmological associations of caves in Maya thought, architectural elaborations, and the organization of space, I propose that rites in caves exercised power not only by what was seen but by what was unseen.

Caves in Context

Throughout Mesoamerica, caves were considered to be sacred spaces employed in esoteric rites (Bassie-Sweet 1996; Brady 1989, 1997; Brady and Ashmore 1999, 124; Brady and Prufer 2005; Heyden 1975; Moyes and Brady 2012; Stone 1995; Thompson 1975). Both earth and underworld deities were associated with caves, and it was within these venues that they could best be propitiated (Moyes 2018). This helps explain why natural caves continue to be regarded as ritual spaces among modern Maya people (Christenson 2008; Moyes and Brady 2012; Prufer and Brady 2005).

Caves figure prominently in Maya cosmology. Ancient Maya peoples conceived of their world as a three-tiered universe, consisting of the sky creating the dome of the heavens, the four-sided earth that is the abode of humans, and the world beneath the earth—the underworld (Bassie-Sweet 1996; Freidel, Schele, and Parker 1993; Thompson 1970, 195). The earth itself was thought to float on a watery base associated with the underworld. In the Quiché Mayan language, this watery abode was referred to as Xibalba, the "Place of Fear" (Christenson 2007, 114) or "Place of Fright" (Miller and Taube 1997, 177), and Maya peoples in the Yucatán Peninsula refer to the underworld as Metnal, or "Place of the Dead" (MacLeod and Puleston 1978, 1). Based on the ethnohistoric creation myth recounted in the *Popol Vuh* creation story as well as on ethnographic data reported by J. Eric S. Thompson (1970), archaeologists Barbara MacLeod and Dennis E. Puleston (1978) argued that the ancient Maya conceptualized caves as entrances to the underworld, thus home to the evil lords of Xibalba, who presided over death and disease.

According to Mary Ellen Miller and Karl A. Taube (1997, 177), at the time of the conquest, most Central Mexican people conceived of the underworld as consisting of nine levels or layers, which are reminiscent of the torture "houses" that the Hero Twins must endure in the creation story. Ethnographic data suggest that the sky and the underworld are made up of layers, though the number of levels varies between groups. Thompson (1970, 195) reported that the underworld was composed of four steps descending from the western horizon to the nadir of the fifth level, and another four steps ascending to the eastern horizon. The Tzotzil of Larraínzar also conceive of the underworld as having nine levels (Holland 1962, 94–96). Humans live in the bottom two levels of the sky and earth deities are located within the sky's lowest level. The ninth level of the underworld constitutes Olontik, or "Land of the Dead." There are deities associated with each level, and the underworld gods are considered to be malevolent, bringing evil and death to humans. These deities roam the earth at night and at daybreak reenter the underworld through caves, where they are thought to make their homes. Earth deities are more easily controlled than Sky or Underworld denizens, but underworld beings must be constantly solicited for protection against the evil forces they control (Holland 1962, 126–33). In Chamula, Chiapas, the underworld is envisioned as a single layer supported by Miguel, the Earth Bearer. According to Gary H. Gossen (1974, 21), caves are considered part of the earth, though they are associated with water, dampness, darkness, and lowness, suggesting that they are, in fact, transitional zones between the middle world and the underworld. Collectively, ethnographic concepts suggest that the lowest parts of the earth level are transitional and may be thought of as the first level of the underworld, which is encountered in the descent to its nether regions.

Among contemporary Maya people, caves are often considered dangerous places with evil indwelling spirits. Ethnographic analogy suggests that relatively few people have actually entered cave dark zones, although many may have made pilgrimages to cave entrances. It is unlikely that in the past, anyone other than ritual specialists would have ever used caves or conducted rites in rock shelters (Prufer 2002, 2005), and modern accounts attest that cave entrances are guarded by dangerous entities. For example, Allen J. Christenson (2001, 84–85) reported that among the Tz'utujil Maya at Santiago Atitlan, Guatemala, the nearby cave of Paq'alib'al is guarded by pumas, jaguars, and snakes. Similarly, at Santa Eulalia in the Guatemalan highlands, Oliver La Farge (1947, 128–29) recorded a story of a Ladino woman who once went into the dark zone of the cave of Yalan Na' and was kidnapped by a snake. She was not released until the Prayermakers (*h'men*) came for her, and shortly after the incident, the woman went insane. In the village of Socotz in western Belize, a monster known as the *zizimit* carried sinners off to a cave to be eaten (Coe and Coe 1951, 160–61). Evon Z. Vogt (1969, 455) noted that during lineage ceremonies in Zinacantan, Chiapas, at the crosses at Senior and Junior Stomach Cave, "the participants were extraordinarily quiet, and there was an aura of fear as the shamans made their offerings, especially to the Earth

Lord." The Earth Lord was thought to live underground and was envisioned as a fat Ladino who controlled the water holes and would exchange riches for a person's soul (Vogt 1969, 302). Also, among the Tzotzil is the "Blackman," a hyperpotent cave-dwelling demon that impregnates women, causing them to die from overmenstruation or multiple births (Blaffer 1972, 20, 17, 148–49; Holland 1962, 173–80). William R. Holland (1962, 173–80) adds that the Blackman is one of many deities of death thought to reside in caves.

The association of death and infirmity with cave denizens likely contributes to the idea that caves are regarded as toxic to the body. Working in Yucatán, William F. Hanks noted that caves are considered chaotic underworld spaces that pollute the body and are inhabited by harmful witches. Hanks sums up the modern Yucatecan attitude toward caves: "the stagnant, dank atmosphere is itself perceived to be polluting to the body, but beyond this, it is the potential for harboring evil that motivates caution" (1984, 134). Although reports of underworld helper spirits can also be located in the literature (Hanks 1990, 134), most ethnographers emphasize the evil or negative aspects of direct contact with cave dwellers. At Yalcoba in Yucatán, the cave-dwelling *alux* play evil tricks and make people sick (Sosa 1985, 411). Tzeltal people believe that dangerous spirits of the hills and caves have the power to mislead, make slaves of people, or give illness (Nash 1970, 23–24). This agrees with the Ritual of the Bacabs (Roys 1965, 67–68), which describes disease-causing winds as having originated in caves. Though the forms of cave dwellers differ, among modern Maya people the pervasiveness of the beliefs that caves contain evil or harmful entities suggests that this may be an old idea. These types of beliefs no doubt discouraged many nonspecialists from venturing unattended into the interior of caves in both pre- and postcontact Mesoamerica. The esoteric nature of cave rites likely accounts for why ethnographers have noted the difficulty in witnessing cave rituals (La Farge 1947, 127; Petryshyn 1973; Prechtel and Carlsen 1988, 123; Tozzer 1907, 148–49). One of the few ethnographic eyewitness accounts was a cave ceremony recorded by Alfredo Barrera-Vásquez (Andrews 1970, 72–164). E. Wyllys Andrews IV and his crew were working at the Yucatec cave of Balankanche in 1959 when the local *h'men* (priest/shaman) informed the team that because they had violated the sacred precinct, they were in danger and needed a ceremony to protect them (Andrews 1970, 72).

Knowing the inherent dangers, one may wonder why anyone would want to approach a cave. The few surviving modern cave rites are primarily agricultural fertility and rain rituals, which has led a number of archaeologists to argue that related rites occurred in the past (Brady 1989; MacLeod and Puleston 1978; Morehart 2005; Moyes et al. 2009; Nielsen and Brady 2006; Rissolo 2005). The association with caves and fertility is demonstrated in the Formative period San Bartolo murals in Guatemala, which illustrate a woman handing tamales to the Maize god along with a gourd filled with water. This suggests a scene of primordial sustenance (Saturno et al. 2005). The association of caves with the Maize god is established in the *Popol Vuh*, where the Maize God is left by his sons to dwell in the underworld, cyclically emerging to the earth as the maize plant each growing season (Christenson 2007, 190–91).

Rain deities are also thought to dwell in caves. This is well illustrated for the Classic period Maya. Illustrated on a Classic period vase, Chaak, the rain deity, is depicted sitting in his cave/house (Coe 1978, 78, no. 11). Depictions of Chaak seated in his cave are also found in two of the last surviving Maya books: the Dresden Codex, on pages 30a and 67b (Bassie-Sweet 1991, 91–95); and the Madrid Codex, pages 29 and 73 (Bassie-Sweet 1996, 98–103). A reified example of this is found at the cave of La Pailita in Guatemala, where a life-sized sculpture of Chaak sits on his throne in the cave's entrance chamber (Graham 1997). Interestingly, in iconography, earth deities such as Chaak are usually depicted at entrances of caves, suggesting that they live in the more superficial areas, whereas the Lords of the Underworld are found in the lower depths as described in the *Popol Vuh*. I have suggested elsewhere that these different cave denizens may reside in different areas of the cave and thus must be encountered according to where they dwell (Moyes 2012a).

Caves in the Establishment of Community

For the ancient Maya, the natural landscape—mountains, caves, waterholes, ravines, boulders, and trees—was fundamental in grounding supernatural realms in real-world environments, linking mythic space to natural features (Brady and Ashmore 1999; Stone 1992; Taube 1994). In iconographic renderings, mountains are depicted as anthropomorphic entities imbued with life (Saturno et. al 2005; Schávelzon 1980; Stuart 1997). David S. Stuart (1997, 15) notes that anthropomorphic mountains (*witz* or *wits*) are represented as beings with large eyes and a cleft or cracked head. As the homes of earth deities and ancestors, anthropomorphic mountains were replicated in temple architecture. Rooms at their summits represented cave entrances, illustrated as toothy U-shaped mouths, that linked the underworld interior of the mountain to the earth and sky (Gendrop 1980; Schávelzon 1980; Stuart 1997).

Ethnohistorically, we find that caves are salient features in boundary marking that define usufruct rights between communities and indwelling earth deities. According to Nancy M. Farriss (1984, 274), "every small savanna, every rock outcrop, ceiba tree, and cenote (sinkhole) in the district, and each little section of bush had its own name." The earliest land deeds were brief documents that would mention a territory deriving its name from a water hole or cenote with which it was associated (Farriss 1984, 129, 148). This is supported by Angel J. García-Zambrano (1994) in his work on early Spanish land titles that describes how Indigenous boundaries were established and maintained by ritual action or "foundational" rites. In deciding where to settle, immigrants sought ideal locations based on cosmological principles that aligned with the quincuncial model of the earth (see also Stanton et al., this volume). Preferred landscapes consisted of a valley surrounded by four mountains, one for each cardinal direction, irrigated by water holes, rivers, lakes, and/or lagoons. A fifth mountain, ideally containing a cave and springs and representing the center of the model, protruded in the middle of the valley. Once consecrated by the leader, the cave became the cosmogenic heart of the new town, legitimizing the settlers' rights for occupying that space and establishing the ruler's authority over that site. To establish community, leaders conducted foundational rites that circumambulated the boundaries visiting boundary-marking features on the landscape. The circuit symbolically designated property rights and created the community perimeter protected by indwelling deities. These practices continue today. For instance, in the village of Zinacantan, mountains are considered homes of ancestral deities and caves as the place where one communicates with deities of the earth. These features are visited by cargo holders during ritual circuits that circumambulate the community, functioning as boundary maintenance mechanisms within the social system (Vogt 1969, 375–91). The modern Q'eqchi' propitiates the *tzuultaq'a*, the spirit of the mountain and local earth owner. Each mountain has its own spirit for whom sacrifices are made in caves. Richard Wilson ([1964] 1995, 75) explains the relationship between the tzuultaq'as and communities as follows:

> In general, offerings are made to define a deferential relationship with authority. They are the basis of a traditional subsistence-based "moral

economy." Q'eqchi's give food and presents to priests, landowners, government officials, and others who stand in a superior position over them. The giver is in the subordinate role but hopes to negotiate the receiver into an obligation to wield his or her power in a beneficial manner. In eating the offering food, the consumer swallows the hook of responsibility. The offering, then, placates the tzuultaq'as but also contains elements of manipulation and egalitarianism. . . . Sacrifice establishes and maintains a relationship of reciprocity and balances out the inequalities between deities and people to a degree.

The special function of caves in ideal cosmological landscapes and the bonds created between communities and indwelling deities help explain why cave symbols were often incorporated into Classic period toponyms or politically charged emblem glyphs of Maya sites (Stuart 1997; Vogt and Stuart 2005). It is therefore not surprising that from early on in Maya history, caves became political resources for the creation and maintenance of political power (Moyes and Prufer 2013). Evidence suggests that ancient Maya rulers linked themselves to cosmological forces, ideologically or quite literally by co-opting the natural landscape through cave rituals or creating artificial caves in their site constructions as a path to power (Brady and Veni 1992; Moyes 2006; Moyes and Prufer 2013). At the site of Uxbenká in southern Belize, Early Classic leaders established a mountain/cave shrine coeval with the construction of the first monumental construction (Moyes and Prufer 2013). The shrine consisted of a constructed cave located on a high cliff face that could be viewed from the site core and an outdoor performance space directly below. An altar was installed in the rear of the cave and a wooden altarpiece resembling a small canoe sat atop the altar. Below the cave was a small ritual site with an open plaza space and platforms clearly designed for ritual performances. The geographic position of the cave in relation to the site core, the presence of a monumental construction program that required organized labor, and the coeval construction of the cave shrine with the building of the first stone architecture at the site core suggest that the ritual complex served as a venue for foundational rites.

It is not uncommon to discover that cave use predates the construction of surface architecture (Moyes et al. 2017; Rissolo 2005), which supports the foundational role of caves in the establishment of ancient Maya communities. For instance, Actun Chechem Ha (Poisonwood Water Cave) in the Macal Valley in Belize has the earliest securely dated ritual cave use in the Maya lowlands. Early villagers entered deep within the cave in the Early Formative period, but there is no evidence to suggest that the valley was settled until later in the Middle Formative. We suspect that worshippers were making pilgrimages to the cave from the adjacent Belize valley prior to moving into the area.

The importance of caves to community stability may also be the reason that they were likely targeted in acts of warfare. Pierre Robert Colas (1998, 2000) was the first to propose that caves were the settings for political conflicts and mediations between rival polities. Epigraphic texts suggest that caves associated with martial actions were entered and burned, and speleothems were broken in acts of desecration (Helmke and Brady 2014). Though the archaeological evidence for these types of events is somewhat elusive, it is clear from texts at Naj Tunich cave in Guatemala that at least some sites may have been part of these political machinations, particularly those visited by apical elites.

Cave Morphology

What do we mean by "cave"? We may all have an image of what we think a cave is, but in reality caves are somewhat difficult to define scientifically. In the *Encyclopedia of Caves*, they are described as "a natural opening in the Earth, large enough to admit a human being" (Culver and White 2004, 5). As a nonspecific term, "cave" has come to mean any cavity in the earth, though ontologically they are holes. There are three basic types of holes that may be applied to cave morphology (Casati and Varzi 1994): superficial hollows dependent on surfaces (these can include rock shelters and shallow and deep caves with single entrances), perforating tunnels through which a string can pass (caves with multiple entrances), and internal cavities like holes in Swiss cheese, which are dependent on three-dimensional objects and have no contact with the outside environment (these could include caves that are closed off either naturally or anthropogenically). Distinguishing between the cave and rock shelters is critical to cave interpretations because of the sense of enclosure and the quality of light available. The quality of light may be divided into three zones: light, twilight, and dark (Faulkner 1988). Superficial hollows such as open rock shelters include light and twilight zones but not dark zones. They have often been used for habitation, but these same sites may also contain ritual deposits. Though shelters may be used in habitation, the use of cave dark zones as living space is extremely rare (Moyes 2012b, 5–7).

Cave entrances may be horizontally or vertically accessed. The Maya tended to use those with horizontal entrances that could be entered without specialized equipment, although ancient people could and did build ladders or found other means to enter vertical shafts. We classify horizontal entrances as large (>5 m in width and >2 m in height), medium (1–5 m in width and 1–2 m in height), small (<1 m in width and >1 m in height), and fissures (<1 m in height with varying width). Vertical entrances are sinks or shafts that necessitate down climbs or technical drops. They come in a variety of forms (cylindrical, conical, bowl, or pan-shaped), can be quite small or may measure hundreds of meters across and tens of meters in depth, and may contain water or be filled in with sediment. Sinkholes (cenotes) are closed depressions in the earth's surface with internal drainage caused by subsurface dissolution of soluble bedrock (Miao et al. 2013). Sinkholes are sometimes deep and difficult to access; therefore, ancient people rarely used deep sinks. Shafts frequently contain "bad air" (high levels of CO^2), causing difficulty in breathing and rendering them potentially deadly. We classify vertical entrances by the maximum width of the diameter of the opening: small manhole-like entrances (<1–5 m), medium (<5–10 m), and large (<10 m) (Moyes and Montgomery 2019, 6).

Architecture in Ancient Maya Caves

Over the past twenty years, the Belize Cave Research Project and the Minanha Cave Project under the direction of Holley Moyes and Jaime J. Awe, the Uxbenká Cave Project directed by Moyes and Keith M. Prufer, and the Las Cuevas Archaeological Reconnaissance directed by Moyes have systematically recorded architecture in caves. Collectively, of the eighty-four caves visited by these projects throughout Belize, forty contained architectural modifications. Of these, thirty sites have been mapped and photographed, with artifacts inventoried. The focus here is on the use of space and spatial planning. This intensive and extensive research provides a database from which it is possible to draw some generalizations about how cave space is structured, though admittedly, no two caves are exactly alike. The caves in the sample are true caves with dark zones, and though some are shallower than others, none would be classified as rock shelters. Unfortunately, cave archaeologists must assume that most open caves have been looted to some degree. Although this makes our jobs more difficult, spatial analyses of features that are not entirely dependent on artifact assemblages for their interpretation provide a way forward for better understanding ritual practices.

Architectural features in Belizean caves include walls, platforms, floors, stairs, terraces, blockages, constructed rooms and crawl spaces, benches, altars, and niche closures (see Rojas Sandoval, Covarrubias Reyna, and Rissolo, this volume, for additional examples). They are often "suggested" by the cave's natural morphology, serving to enhance, emphasize, or organize the space for human use. Construction is typically informal, consisting of dry-laid cobbles or boulders, though some may be more labor intensive and use chinked masonry. Occasionally, constructions are held together with mud- or limestone-based mortars. Clay is opportunistically collected from the cave floor to be packed into walls, or mud mortars may be mixed with organics such as grasses. Plastered surfaces occur in some areas, and this appears to be primarily a regional variation found in far western Belize in the Chiquibul Forest Reserve or in southern Belize. Rarely do we find cut stone in caves, but materials such as natural limestone cobbles and small (volleyball-sized) to medium-sized (.50–1 m) boulders native to the site are employed opportunistically. Often speleothems such as stalactites, stalagmites, or spalls are incorporated into the constructions.

Architectural features may be divided into two basic categories: Type 1 consists of constructions that facilitate access—such as stairs or terraces—or enhance visibility and focus attention, such as platforms or altars. These may be thought of as "prosocial" in that they facilitate communication. Type 2 are constructions that block access or visibility, such as walls, blockages, partitions, or enclosures. These features may be thought of as "asocial" because they suggest limited access or secretiveness. Features may function as means to direct transit routes—channeling ritual participants through particular pathways (also noted by Awe and Morton, this volume)—or force changes in posture, such as crawling or bending to enter a space when moving from one area to another.

In terms of spatial layout, most Type 1 architectural features are found in light zones, particularly in caves with horizontal entrances. Therefore, platforms, terraces, and stairs primarily contribute to performances in light or twilight areas. Terraces and stairways are almost ubiquitously constructed when caves have sloping entrances descending to a lower cave floor. These constructions are found in small, cramped caves as well as large cathedral-like spaces. From a practical perspective, they facilitate entry into the cave and prevent erosion of the sediments.

Larger cave entrances are elaborated with platforms that create focal areas for performances or orations. The largest entrance areas were designed for audiences of hundreds to a few thousand people, but it is unlikely that they supported the throngs that would have gathered in plazas to witness large spectacles as described by Takeshi Inomata (2006, 816). This suggests that ancient cave rites were somewhat esoteric, catering to a more exclusive community of participants. It is telling that these features are typically absent in dark zones within the cave tunnel system. This suggests that light and dark areas are used for different purposes and different audiences and indicates that participants in cave rites are likely to possess varying degrees of agency and privilege. Smaller caves are more intimate but still include these features. For instance, at K'in Kaba Actun (Birthday Cave) in the Chiquibul Forest Reserve, plastered platforms are located in the light zone of the rather small entrance chamber (measuring 3.5 × 8 m). The largest (Platform 2) measures 5 m in diameter. It sits atop a giant boulder and consists of a layer of cobbles used as a leveling mechanism topped with a thick layer of smooth plaster. What is striking is that the ceiling height does not allow for even a short person to stand on the platform (figure 14.1), so it cannot be assumed that platforms were designed exclusively for dancing or other performances that involved standing. Alternatively, it is possible that some platforms may have served as mesas to hold offerings for deities (Brady 2003).

Cave entrances are often blocked with boulders. This is most common in small, horizontal-restricted entrances that can be easily covered and obscured. It is rare to find intact blocked caves, but blockages may be inferred because looters tend to create toss zones where they have pulled the rock away to allow themselves entry. Nonetheless, there are at least two known intact examples in Belize. Chechem Ha Cave in the Macal River drainage (between the sites of Las Ruinas and Minanha) was discovered by a local farmer on a hunting expedition. He reported that his dog ran into a hole and he followed it into the cave. In this case, limestone boulders were used to conceal the cave mouth. Excavations and sediment analyses demonstrated that the entrance was closed off and reopened on several occasions. Today, the entrance has been gated to protect the site (Moyes 2006; figure 14.2a). Another example in which the blockage was intact comes from nearby Cho'otz

FIGURE 14.1 Nancy Pistole sits on top of Platform 2 in K'in Kaba Actun (photograph by Matt Oliphant, courtesy of Belize Regional Cave Project).

Ch'en (Trumpet Tree Cave). It is currently entered via a 1.85 m drop in the ceiling where a Trumpet tree has grown through the roof, but this was not the original entrance. The entrance was a tight squeeze in the southernmost area of the tunnel, measuring 1 m across and .4 m in height. The entry was blocked in antiquity, and because looters could enter the site through the hole in the ceiling, it was never unblocked. This is an excellent example of a blocked entrance that remains intact (figure 14.2b, 14.2c).

Caves with vertical entrances are more difficult to access, yet these sites may also have entrance blockages. Once the drops are negotiated, Cormorant Cave, Lubuul Actun (Fall Down Cave), and K'aana Actun (Sky Cave) in the Macal drainage and Alvin's Cave in northern Belize are examples of caves that contain constructions at the base of the vertical drop that blocked the entrances to the tunnels. At Luubul, a fissure in the cave wall at the entrance was blocked off but opened by looters. This was likely an informal "doorway" that could be closed off when the cave was not used (figure 14.3a). A more formal approach was employed at Cormorant Cave, where upon reaching

FIGURE 14.2 Blocked cave entrances: (a) entrance to Chechem Ha Cave blocked with boulders; (b) exterior view of intact entrance blockage of Cho'otz Ch'en; (c) interior view of intact entrance blockage of Cho'otz Ch'en (photographs courtesy of Belize Regional Cave Project).

FIGURE 14.3 Vertical cave entrances: (a) Nancy Pistole negotiates coming out of the entrance to Luubul Actun, whose blocked squeeze was opened by looters (photograph by Matt Oliphant); (b) Erin Ray poses in the doorway of the constructed wall leading to the tunnel system of Cormorant Cave; (c) mud-plastered wall with a constructed doorway at the entrance to tunnel system in K'aana Actun (Nancy Pistole pictured, photograph by Matt Oliphant) (all photographs courtesy of Belize Regional Cave Project).

the base of the drop, there is a constructed wall with a doorway leading to the tunnel system that could be "opened" and "closed" with loose rock (figure 14.3b), a common feature in constructed entrances. A vertical drop is required to enter K'aana Actun (Sky Cave), where approximately 50 m from the entrance, there is a natural constriction in the cave that leads to the deeper dark zone areas (figure 14.3c). Similarly, the entrance of Alvin's Cave in northern Belize requires a technical drop. At the base of the descent, a constructed wall spans the width of the cave, forcing one to crawl through a small doorway that abuts the east wall of the cave. Because of its poor condition, it is unclear if the wall rose all the way to the ceiling.

Horizontal caves that sport large entrances often have interior walls or blockages that restrict access to tunnel systems and deeper areas of the cave. Tush Ku Bin K'in (Sunset Cave) at the Macal drainage provides an excellent example. Here, the entrance to the tunnel system is occluded and a small low doorway below forces one to squeeze through the restricted entrance portal (figure 14.4a). A similar configuration is found at the entrance to the tunnels at nearby Sayab Ak (Watervine Cave), where speleothem formations have been filled in with rock and mud plaster to occlude the larger upper entrance. A small crawl space below was opened by knocking off speleothem formations to allow access to the deepest recesses of the cave (figure 14.4b). It appears from these and other examples that the larger access is intentionally blocked, forcing ritual participants to crawl from one area to the next.

Partitions only partially occlude tunnels and rarely go all the way to the ceiling. They are located almost exclusively in light or twilight areas. James E. Brady (1989, 402–6) suggests that partitioning of space in caves may have served to create dark zone spaces or to differentiate public from private rituals. However, these partitions seem to do neither. They are located at entrances, yet they do not create dark zones, and while they do occlude site lines, creating some degree of privacy, anything in front of or behind the wall can be heard on both sides. These features may serve to restrict access, demarcate space, or channel foot traffic. Their function may also be symbolic, demarcating when one is leaving the earthly realm to enter the netherworld (see Moyes 2012a). Partitions are found at Bird Tower Cave, Zuhuy Ch'en (Pure Cave) and Eduardo Quiroz in the Chiquibul Forest Reserve, Actun Am Actun (Cave Spider Cave) in the Mountain Pine Ridge, and U Mehen Tsek' Actun (Son of Skull Cave) in the Macal drainage, among others. Particularly good examples are found at Bird Tower Cave, where a partition separates

FIGURE 14.4 Blocked tunnel entrances: (a) Tush Ku Bin K'in (Sunset Cave) to the tunnel system is occluded and a small, low doorway forces one to squeeze through the restricted portal; Holley Moyes poses in the occluded entrance in a looter's hole in the wall (*top*) and Nancy Pistole (*bottom*) is pictured in the entrance squeeze (photograph by Matt Oliphant); (b) speleothem formations have been filled in with rock and mud plaster, so the tunnel system is entered via the small doorway and crawl space at Sayab Ak, where Don Antonio (*top*) and Cheyenne Mai (*bottom*) are pictured (photographs courtesy of Belize Regional Cave Project).

the entrance chamber from the darker areas of the cave (figure 14.5a), and at Zuhuy Che'n just beyond the twilight areas at the beginning of the tunnel system (figure 14.5b). The wall at Bird Tower Cave spans the width of the tunnel opening and is neatly constructed of dry-laid limestone boulders and speleothems. At Zuhuy Che'n, boulders fill in naturally occurring speleothem formations, leaving a narrow access opening abutting the cave wall.

The most common architectural features located in cave tunnel systems (dark zones) are Type 2 features such as walls and blockages. These completely occlude the tunnels and usually contain constructed "doorways" or entrance gaps. Demarcating a tunnel system with walls and blockages suggests decreased access and hence more exclusivity as participants move into the depths of the cave. For example, at Actun Uo (Uo Frog Cave), a site located in the Chiquibul Forest Reserve, constructed walls are located at junctures in the main passages marking the entrances to side tunnels. The Wall 4 feature, placed within a natural constriction of the cave, is composed of well-sorted limestone boulders with mud plaster on the exterior face and a small doorway abutting the cave wall, forcing one to crawl into the side tunnel (figure 14.6a). Blockages are primarily constructed where tunnels naturally constrict and are found at junctures where passages join or at entrances to alcoves or chambers. They are typically informally constructed using boulders, speleothems, and spalls collected from the cave's interior, and are most abundantly found in caves with long winding tunnel systems such as K'aana, Eduardo Quiroz, K'in Kaba, and Zuhuy Ch'en (figure 14.6b). Small gaps, usually less than a meter wide, create access points that can be "opened" or "closed" with loose rock. In almost every instance, the loose rock from the opening lies in front of the structure where it was pulled away by looters to "open" access, demonstrating that the original users left the blockage "closed." Charcoal from torches or burning events is often located in front of the blockage.

Throughout cave sites, in light, twilight, and dark zones, it is not unusual to find small niches either constructed or opportunistically employed that have been covered by rock. For the purpose of our project, these are defined as small superficial hollows that cannot be entered by a human. Therefore, one must reach inside to place offerings. These sometimes have been blocked with cobbles. What is surprising is that there is often little evidence to suggest that blocked niches contained anything at all, though archaeologists rarely find these intact, so they may have been cleaned out by looters. Al-

FIGURE 14.5 Cave partitions: (a) Holley Moyes stands next to the doorway opening in the partition that separates the entrance chamber from the darker areas of Bird Tower Cave; (b) Don Antonio Mai stands in the narrow opening in the partition at the entrance to the tunnel system in Zuhuy Che'n (photographs courtesy of Belize Regional Cave Project).

FIGURE 14.6 Cave blockages: (a) Holley Moyes sits in the constructed doorway of a tunnel blockage placed within a natural constriction in Actun Uo; (b) Don Antonio Mai negotiates the blockage doorway at Zuhuy Ch'en (photographs by Matt Oliphant, courtesy of Belize Regional Cave Project).

ternatively, it is possible that blocked niches do not function as receptacles for offerings at all and were associated with little-known rites in which evil winds or maleficent spirits were ritually contained.

Enclosures may be present in all areas of the cave and create private spaces blocking visibility but not sound, suggesting that an added level of privacy is desirable for rites conducted within those areas. There is an excellent example of this in Actun Isabella near the Maya site of Minanha. Here, abutting the east wall of the cave is a stalacto-stalagmitic formation with a hollow center that forms a large alcove (Alcove 1) measuring 5.4 × 3 m with a ceiling height of 1.6–2 m. Dry-laid small boulders, cobbles, and broken speleothems blocked holes in "windows" between the natural stalagmitic formations (figure 14.7a). The area is entered on the west side and a stone wall creates a constricted "doorway," which may have been blocked or "closed" at one time, as evidenced by a pile of jumbled rock next to the wall. Another good example is found at Actun Ka'am Be'en (Ofrendas or Offering Cave), located in the Macal River drainage near San Antonio village. Crawl 5 is a constructed crawl space opportunistically built beneath an overhang in the cave wall (figure 14.7b). The area is approximately 3 m in length and 1 m or less in width built by placing flat limestone slabs upright against the top of the overhang held in place by mud mortar. The entrance to the feature was blocked by a large flat stone that could be rolled to one side. Inside, the floor was covered with a thick layer of charcoal. Partially intact vessels, sherds, and other artifacts lined the walls.

The most elaborate example of an enclosure within a cave comes from Actun Uo. Within the cave's second entrance chamber is a formally constructed, semicircular-shaped structure abutting the cave wall. The structure is a single-chambered room with a constructed doorway. It stands 3–4 m high with an interior width of 3 m (figure 14.8). The structure was built with unshaped but well-sorted blocks of limestone, incorporating several larger pieces of flat bedrock. The base of the masonry is dry-laid, with mud plaster incorporated into the upper coursing. There were no artifacts inside the structure but some evidence of burning. The structure is unique to caves in the area and clearly functions as some sort of room. There is a possibility that it may be a sweat bath, though one would expect to see a fire pit or fire-cracked rock inside if this were the case.

All these features would be expected to have coded ideological meanings in addition to their practical functions. Aside from privileges associated

FIGURE 14.7 Cave enclosures: (a) enclosure at Actun Isabella opportunistically using drapery (photograph courtesy of Minanha Cave Project); (b) Actun Ka'am Be'en, Crawl 5, constructed crawl space abutting wall (photograph courtesy of Belize Regional Cave Project).

FIGURE 14.8 Holley Moyes sits in a doorway of a constructed semicircular-shaped structure abutting the cave wall at Actun Uo (photograph courtesy of Las Cuevas Archaeological Reconnaissance).

with entering cave dark zones, given the widespread beliefs that malicious, dangerous, or, at best, capricious powerful entities inhabit these areas, it may also be unwise for the uninitiated or ritually impure to venture into the netherworld. We know that ethnographically, there is much spiritual preparation involved in readying for cave rites that may include fasting, sexual abstinence, and prayer (Adams and Brady 2005, 309; Wilson [1964] 1995, 70–71). Therefore, walls and blockages not only may serve as boundaries but may demarcate levels of the underworld as one travels deeper within the cave. Therefore, these architectural features may also serve to discourage the unprepared participant from advancing into the deeper areas—thus drawing closer to powerful entities. The structures may remind intruders that those who enter the deity's territories or realms must be prepared and fortified for spiritual encounters. The physical demarcation of these spiritual realms also provides a reified place where worthy participants may seek permission to enter a deity's abode. The opening and closure of these access points may also serve to keep others out as well as to keep nonhuman actors from escaping the cave and roaming the earth. Likewise, enclosures in caves may serve similar functions of containing cave spirits or winds either during or after esoteric rites.

Aside from considerations of the function and meaning of individual constructions, to understand or "read" a produced space, the cave itself and its unique morphology must be considered. Architectural features enhance and contribute to the constructed holistic integrated space, creating a time/space journey for ritual participants. Therefore, it is at the scale of the cave itself that the relationship between features becomes apparent, creating a narrative to help us better understand the logic and power relationships inherent in cave use. Toward this end, I offer the following example.

The Cave at Las Cuevas

One of the most architecturally elaborated caves in the Maya lowlands is the cave at Las Cuevas. Located in the Chiquibul Forest Reserve in western Belize, Las Cuevas is a small to midsized surface site that has a cave site running beneath the surface architecture. While it is not unusual for Maya sites to be associated with caves, we rarely see such a direct connection or such an extensive tunnel system beneath a site core (e.g., Moyes and Brady 2012; Rojas Sandoval, Covarrubias Reyna, and Rissolo, this volume). The site has been investigated by the Las Cuevas Archaeological Reconnaissance project under the direction of the author since 2011 (Moyes 2012a, 2020; Moyes et al. 2012a). The cave has been looted and the artifact assemblage is no doubt incomplete, but the analysis of small artifacts and architectural features is informative. Small items that have little appeal to looters remain good indicators of ritual practices and their spatial loci (Moyes, Hernandez, et al. 2015).

The surface site consists of twenty-six structures that include temples, a palace, long linear constructions, and a ballcourt organized on an east–west axis facing two plazas, A and B (figure 14.9). Its layout is somewhat unusual because the structures surround a dry cenote that lies at the center of the site. Elsewhere my colleagues and I suggested, based on the presence of nonlocal ceramic types, the remote location, low-density surrounding populations, opportunistic site placement surrounding, and constructions that instantiate cosmological principles, that Las Cuevas served as a pilgrimage place in the turbulent Late Classic period.

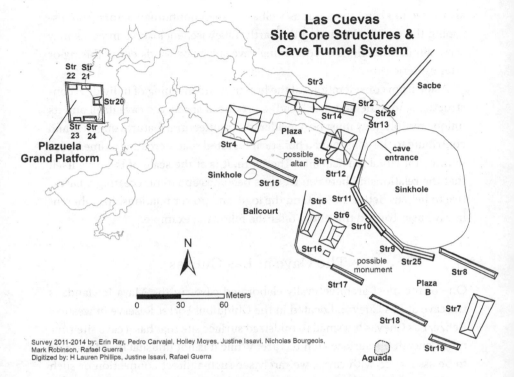

FIGURE 14.9 Plan map of Las Cuevas showing a cave running beneath the plaza (courtesy of Las Cuevas Archaeological Reconnaissance).

The east-facing mouth of the cave sits directly below the eastern structure (Str. 1) in Plaza A, one of the largest structures at the site, standing 11 m high. Our excavations uncovered pieces of molded stucco in the collapsed material in the top levels, indicating that a stucco frieze had adorned the upper doorway in the final building phase. The stucco pieces included round elements, smooth curved elements, and a conical piece that is a giant tooth, suggesting the frieze represented the maw of the witz or "earth" monster. Although we have not been able to reconstruct the entire frieze, the witz motif identifies Str. 1 as a sacred mountain sitting atop the cave entrance.

Based on five field seasons of excavation and test pitting (Kosakowsky et al. 2013; Moyes et al. 2012), both ceramic analyses and three Accelerator Mass Spectrometry (AMS) dates from Temple 1 demonstrate that the surface site was constructed in the late part of the Late Classic period (AD 700–900). Cave use may have slightly predated the surface building program. Both ceramics and a suite of twenty AMS dates demonstrate that cave use began in the Early Late Classic and continued through the latter half of the Late Classic. This suggests that the cave was used before the site was constructed. This bolsters the idea of caves being "foundational"—starting as distant pilgrimage places well before they were surrounded by population centers. However, architectural elaborations in the cave are likely Late Classic coeval with the surface constructions.

Excavations in and around the sinkhole demonstrated that there were clear constructed pathways leading from the surface site to the cave (Arksey 2017, 90–104; Arksey and Moyes 2015). Ritual participants entered the sinkhole from two 50 cm wide gaps between low linear structures (Strs. 10 and 11, Strs. 11 and 12) on the west side of the sinkhole (figure 14.10). Here, remnant terraces descended 15 m to the base landing on a platform adjacent to the stairway leading into the cave. The path was strewn with ceramic sherds and other artifacts, suggesting that scattering may have taken place on the way to the cave entrance.

The cave's massive mouth measures 28 m wide and 9 m high. Upon entry, the cathedral-like entrance chamber is heavily modified with monumental architectural constructions, including terraces, retaining walls, stairs, and platforms covered with layers of thick plaster (Moyes, Robinson, et al. 2015; Ray, Moyes, and Howe 2018; figure 14.11). In the center of the chamber dividing the north and south areas is a sinkhole with an underground river that surfaces at its base. The river has clear running water that rises during heavy rains. A stairway leads from the surface into the sinkhole. Formal plastered platforms fan out in an amphitheater-like configuration, reaching upward toward the outer walls in the southeast area of the chamber. The project has located and identified seventy-five individual platforms, indicating that the cave was used for large, well-organized ceremonies that could support approximately 600–1,300 participants (Moyes 2020).

At the northwest end of the chamber, the light zone fades to twilight and into darkness. Platforms and stairways in the rear of the entrance abut terraces leading to Wall 1, a well-constructed feature that completely occludes the passage placed within a natural cave constriction (figure 14.12a). A formal entrance or "doorway" forces one to bow or duck when entering Chamber 1. Loose limestone boulders strewn on the exterior of the wall suggest that the entrance was blocked or "closed" with loose rock at some point in the past. Beyond Wall 1 is the main tunnel system, measuring 335 m

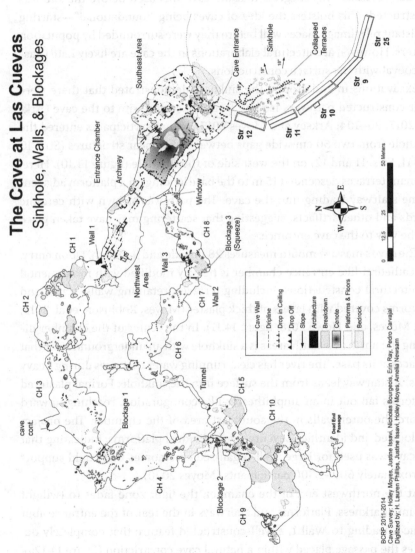

FIGURE 14.10 Base map of the cave at Las Cuevas showing walls and blockages and the sinkhole entrance (courtesy of Las Cuevas Archaeological Reconnaissance).

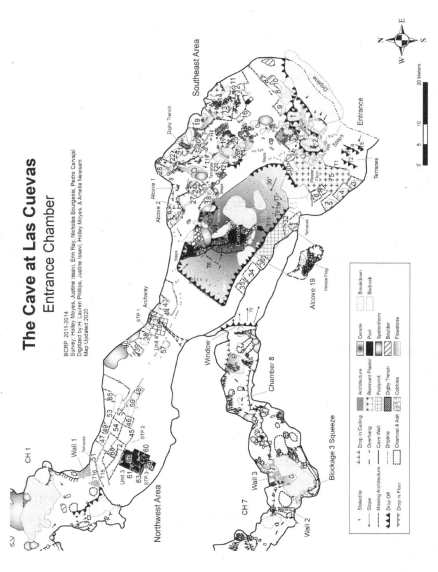

FIGURE 14.11 Map of the entrance chamber of the cave at Las Cuevas (courtesy of Las Cuevas Archaeological Reconnaissance).

in overall length. It comprises ten rooms and passages that circle around themselves and terminate at a window in Chamber 8 located 8 m above the floor of the west wall of the entrance chamber.

As one moves through the system, there are two additional walls and three blockages (see figure 14.10). The highest concentration of artifacts in the cave is found in Chambers 1–3, where more than thirty-seven thousand ceramic sherds have been scattered over the floors, having been trampled into the soft clay matrix (Moyes, Robinson, et al. 2015). Moving from Chamber 3 to Chamber 4, access is impeded by a constructed blockage with a small "doorway" defined by upright flat stones that create a "door jam." This forces one to crawl through a tight squeeze into Chamber 4. A second constructed blockage, placed where the cave naturally constricts, separates Chambers 4 and 5. From Chamber 5 it is possible to detour from the main passage to Chambers 9 and 10. Chamber 10 is a large cavernous area that contained the most variation in the cave's artifact assemblage, including obsidian blades, jewelry, celts, *metate* (grinding stone) fragments, and sherds. Both chambers are dead ends. In the main passage, continuing through Chamber 5, one enters a narrow, tubular passage leading to Chamber 6.

The cave passage naturally constricts between Chambers 6 and 7. Here, a second wall construction (Wall 2) spans the tunnel, reaching from floor to ceiling. The wall is composed of small to medium limestone boulders and speleothems held in place by mud mortar (see figure 14.12b). Like Wall 1, it contains a *constructed* doorway. Charcoal was noted on the floor of the wall's exterior. At the entrance to the next chamber, there is a large area of breakdown (fallen boulders) in the center of the chamber. To the north of the breakdown is a wall (Wall 3) composed of well-laid small- to medium-sized limestone boulders. It has been collapsed by looters but completely occluded the passage, directing ritual participants to enter Chamber 8 via a small constructed 5 m long muddy crawl space (Blockage 3; figure 14.12c) on the south side of the chamber. The tunnel terminates in Chamber 8 with a sheer drop-off from a window overlooking the entrance chamber (figure 14.13a). From the window, one can view the cave mouth and sinkhole as well as the platforms and terraces on the southeast side (figure 14.13b). During the day, light can be seen pouring into the entrance. The acoustics are quite impressive from the window and even a soft voice may be heard on the east platforms. One can imagine a grand oration being presented from this high vantage point.

FIGURE 14.12 Doorways and blockage at Las Cuevas: (a) Wall 1 separates twilight areas in the entrance from dark zone tunnels; note the constructed doorway; (b) Wall 2 in Chamber 7 occludes the passage; (c) Justine Issavi emerges from the constructed blockage linking Chambers 7 and 8 (courtesy of Las Cuevas Archaeological Reconnaissance).

FIGURE 14.13 Entrance chamber at Las Cuevas: (a) view from the window in Chamber 8; (b) view of the lit Chamber 8 window from platforms (photograph by Matt Oliphant, courtesy of Belize Regional Cave Project).

At Las Cuevas, from the very beginning of the ritual journey, access to the cave is controlled. One enters the cave beneath the temple/mountain via the narrow passages between linear structures at the edge of the sinkhole that lead to a pathway descending to the cave entrance. A stairway eases access into the entrance chamber and descends to the interior river that surfaces at the base of the sinkhole located at the center of the cave's entrance chamber. The platforms, stairways, and terraces structuring the chamber are clearly indicative of a more public aspect of ritual performance, though access to the space is restricted. When considering the thousands of people who participated in spectacles in open plazas on the surface (Inomata 2006, 816, table 1), cave rites were designed for fewer participants and so not entirely "public." Wall 1 at the rear of the entrance creates a further restriction via its small, low doorway, which forces participants to stoop in order to enter Chamber 1. The number of potsherds in Chambers 1–3 suggests that this was a focus of ritual activity. However, as one moves through the cave, the density of artifacts drops off continually after Chamber 3, as illustrated by a density analysis (Moyes, Hernandez, et al. 2015; figure 14.14). As artifact density falls (arguably correlating with fewer ritual participants), there is an increase in charcoal density, suggesting an increase in burning activities. Based on this available data, it appears that there is ritual variation within the cave as one moves through the system. Alcoves and niches located along the pathways containing charcoal and artifacts are testaments to small gatherings in these enclosed spaces.

Fewer participants reach Chamber 8, culminating in the privileged oratory position provided by the window overlooking the entrance chamber. Walls and blockages guide the spiritual journey and dissuade or bar those without requisite mental and spiritual preparation or required permissions from human or nonhuman actors from progressing through the cave. Here we see a dialog between the natural and constructed spaces in which constructions enhance the natural features to create a time/space model of sacrality as one progresses through the tunnels, ultimately emerging into the light. It is possible that these were nocturnal ceremonies that ended at dawn as the light was beginning to pour into the cave. This is reminiscent of spiritual journeys undertaken by Day Keeper initiates at Utatlan, where an all-night vigil ends at the cave of the Dawning Place to watch the sunrise, looking out from high up on the mountain referred to as the Window of the World (Earle 2008, 85–88).

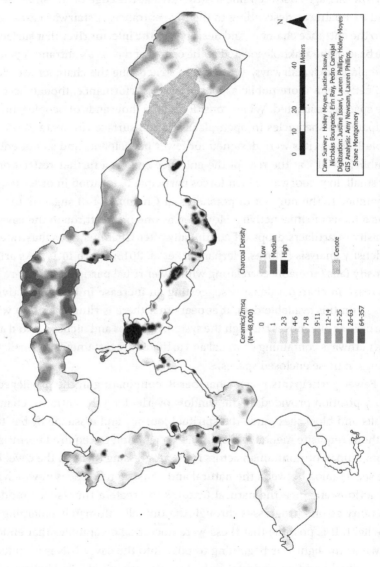

FIGURE 14.14 Map of the cave at Las Cuevas showing data representation of artifact and charcoal density analyses (courtesy of Las Cuevas Archaeological Reconnaissance).

Ritual Circuits

Moving from a surface context into the sinkhole and through the light, twilight, and dark zones of the cave could be considered as a "ritual circuit" or "pathway" followed by ritual specialists during a political or religious ceremony as proposed by Kathryn V. Reese-Taylor (2002). This is most similar to her "Base to Summit" procession undertaken to unite the cosmos and transform the ruler from a mortal to a deity. However, nowhere does she mention caves in her program, nor does she entertain circuits that would include subterranean spaces (Arksey and Moyes 2015, 114). I prefer to think of entering a cave as a "pilgrimage" or "journey" that leads participants from the quotidian world of everyday life into the chaotic netherworld (Moyes 2020). In Maya thought, there is an opposition between "town or inhabited space" (*kaah*), which is structured, ordered, and safe, and "forest" (*kaash*), which, although it is considered to be chaotic, wild, and dangerous, is the seat of supernatural power and the abode of spirits (Hanks 1990, 306–7). Therefore, this journey would not be taken lightly, nor would it have been undertaken by the unprepared.

Natural caves provided a cosmologically salient and symbolically meaningful backdrop to frame such ritual undertakings. These journeys were structured by the organization of space and encoded architectural representations that shaped time/space narratives for the participants. Constructions were in dialogue with the existing space, often taking cues from the morphology of the cave itself. Architecture marked spaces of transition and restricted access to cave interiors and therefore access to indwelling deities. Enclosures created private areas for individual or small-scale esoteric rites.

The question remains, who controls these spaces? Certainly, indwelling deities were believed to have ultimate power over the earthly realm, but they could be placated, controlled, and bargained with. It is unlikely in the Classic period that an average person would possess the stature or knowledge to encounter or propitiate these powerful entities, yet there has been much discussion about elite versus nonelite cave use. Jaime J. Awe, Cameron Griffith, and Sherry Gibbs (2005) argue that the presence of uncarved monuments, including the setting up of large speleothems in caves, suggests that high-status groups or individuals were the ones to control cave sites. There can be little doubt that caves such as Las Cuevas, elaborated with monumental architecture and positioned within a site core, were elite controlled. The architectural modifications at Las Cuevas mirror studies of palace architecture, which demonstrate that over time an ever-increasing number of walls, doors, and passages created progressively restricted access to inner sanctums specifically designed to separate elites from commoners (Awe 1992; Awe, Campbell, and Conlon 1991; Houston 1998, 522–23; Pendergast 1992, 62–63). But conversely, the large semipublic space in the entrance chamber of Las Cuevas may indicate a loosening of prohibitions in elite cave use, allowing participation by the lesser elite, community leaders, or even commoners who stood witness to those making the ritual journey through the underworld. The crowd likely stood vigil awaiting the high-status individual or leader to emerge at the window high above the crowd to deliver a message regarding the encounter. The rites in the cave depths remained partially hidden as mysteries for the uninitiated or those with lesser status. In this sense, what was unseen was as powerful as what was seen.

In this way, cave use in the Late Classic period could be viewed as a revitalization movement in which old ideologies were employed in new ritual practices. While participation by the public or lesser elites appears to be increasingly egalitarian, these ceremonies would have reinforced elite hegemonies and privileges. Here the hidden or not-so-hidden agenda may have been to gather communities to support elites during a time of stress in the Late Classic period. As the world as they knew it crumbled around them, leaders, perhaps even a charismatic leader, organized rites and ceremonies at Las Cuevas that promoted solidarity for a stressed people while maintaining and reinforcing social hierarchies.

We know the end of the story. The Late Classic sociopolitical system crumbled, and Las Cuevas was abandoned. But what comes into focus from the archaeological record through the lens of spatial production is the way that leadership carried on in the face of entropy. Through their constructions, leaders creatively drew on ideologies, tropes, and mysteries that had served them well in the past, inviting more participation from the community in rites and ceremonies yet retaining their secretive and esoteric nature. While some argue that strife and warfare were at the heart of Maya sociopolitical change, efforts by leadership at Las Cuevas suggest that measures to allay fears, reduce stress, and unite communities were undertaken. In the end, it may have been loss of faith, in both leadership and ritual programs, that brought about the resulting sociopolitical transformations.

Conclusion

Considering Maya caves and their architectural elaborations as social productions affords us a better understanding of the role that these venues played in establishing and maintaining stability within ancient Maya communities. By considering the context and meanings of caves as both features of a sacred landscape and loci for ritual practice, we attain a clearer picture of the importance of these sites in power dynamics and are reminded that power, performance, and ideology are inextricably linked (Demarrais, Castillo, and Earle 1996; Kertzer 1988). Studies of cave architecture through the lens of spatial production transport cave research from the dark depths of the underworld into a broader discourse of ancient Maya history, illuminating the importance of religion and ideology in comprehending social processes.

Acknowledgments

I would like to thank the hard-working staff at the Belize Institute of Archaeology, especially Josue Ramos, who assisted us in the field. This work could not have happened without the assistance of the institute's director, Dr. John Morris, who granted the permit to work at Las Cuevas. I would also like to acknowledge my mentor and in-country partner Dr. Jaime J. Awe, to whom I am eternally grateful. Thanks to local partners Israel Canto, Saul Haines, Jaime Iglesias, Don Antonio and Javier Mai, Carlos Mendez, and Gonzalo Pleitez, and to the many crew members who collaborated in this work, including Nicholas Bourgeois, Maureen Carpenter, Shayna Hernandez, Justine Issavi, Shane Montgomery, Lauren Phillips, Laura Kosakowsky, Amy Newsome, Erin Ray, Mark Robinson, Rafael Guerra, and Barbara Voorhies. Our funding for the Las Cuevas project was generously provided by Alphawood Foundation, the Hellman Foundation, National Geographic Foundation, and the University of California, Merced.

Works Cited

Adams, Abigail, and James E. Brady. 2005. "Ethnographic Notes on Maya Q'eqchi' Cave Rites." In *In the Maw of the Earth Monster: Mesoamerican Ritual Cave Use*, edited by James E. Brady and Keith M. Prufer, 301–27. Austin: University of Texas Press.

Andrews, E. Wyllys, I. 1970. *Balankanche, Throne of the Tiger Priest*. Middle American Research Institute Publication 32. New Orleans: Tulane University.

Arksey, Marieka. 2017. "Expanding the Ritual Landscape: Politicized Use of the Spaces Outside of Caves During the Last Classic Maya Collapse." PhD diss., University of California, Merced.

Arksey, Marieka, and Holley Moyes. 2015. "Ancient Maya Ritual Pathways: Performing Power Outside the Cave at Las Cuevas, Belize." In *Papers of the 47th Annual Chacmool Archaeological Conference, Breaking Barriers*, edited by Robyn Crook, Kim Edwards, and Colleen Hughes, 106–17. Alberta, Canada: Chacmool Archaeological Association of the University of Calgary.

Awe, Jaime J. 1992. "Dawn in the Land Between the Rivers: Formative Occupation at Cahal Pech, Belize and Its Implications for Preclassic Development in the Maya Lowlands." PhD diss., University of London.

Awe, Jamie J., Mark D. Campbell, and Jim Conlon. 1991. "Preliminary Analysis of the Spatial Configuration of the Site Core at Cahal Pech, Belize, and Its Implications for Lowland Maya Social Organization." *Mexicon* 13 (2): 25–30.

Awe, Jaime J., Cameron Griffith, and Sherry Gibbs. 2005. "Cave Stelae and Megalithic Monuments in Western Belize." In *In the Maw of the Earth Monster: Mesoamerican Ritual Cave Use*, edited by James E. Brady and Keith M. Prufer, 223–48. Austin: University of Texas Press.

Bassie-Sweet, Karen. 1991 *From the Mouth of the Dark Cave: Commemorative Sculpture of the Late Classic Maya*. Norman: University of Oklahoma Press.

Bassie-Sweet, Karen. 1996. *At the Edge of the World: Caves and Late Classic Maya World View*. Norman: University of Oklahoma Press.

Blaffer, Sarah C. 1972. *The Black-Man of Zinacantan: A Central American Legend*. Austin: University of Texas Press.

Brady, James E. 1989. "Investigation of Maya Ritual Cave Use with Special Reference to Naj Tunich, Peten, Guatemala." PhD diss., University of California, Los Angeles.

Brady, James E. 1997. "Settlement Configuration and Cosmology: The Role of Caves at Dos Pilas." *American Anthropologist* 99 (3): 602–18.

Brady, James E. 2003. "In My Hill, My Valley: The Importance of Place in Ancient Maya Ritual." In *Mesas & Cosmologies in Mesoamerica*, edited by Douglas Sharon, 83–91. San Diego Museum Papers 42. San Diego: San Diego Museum.

Brady, James E., and Wendy Ashmore. 1999. "Mountains, Caves, Water: Ideational Landscapes of the Ancient Maya." In *Archaeologies of Landscapes: Contemporary Perspectives*, edited by Wendy Ashmore and A. Bernard Knapp, 124–45. Oxford: Blackwell.

Brady, James E., and Keith M. Prufer, eds. 2005. *In the Maw of the Earth Monster: Mesoamerican Ritual Cave Use*. Austin: University of Texas Press.

Brady, James E., and George Veni. 1992. "Man-Made and Pseudo-Karst Caves: The Implications of Subsurface Features within Maya Centers." *Geoarchaeology* 7 (2): 149–67.

Casati, Roberto, and Achille C. Varzi. 1994. *Holes and Other Superficialities*. Cambridge, Mass.: MIT Press.

Chase, Arlen F., and Diane Z. Chase. 2001. "The Royal Court of Caracol, Belize: Its Palaces and People." In *Royal Courts of the Ancient Maya*, vol. 2, edited by Takeshi Inomata and Stephane D. Houston, 102–37. Boulder, Colo.: Westview Press.

Christenson, Allen J. 2001. *Art and Society in a Highland Maya Community: The Altarpiece of Santiago Atitlán*. Austin: University of Texas Press.

Christenson, Allen J., trans. 2007. *Popol Vuh: The Sacred Book of the Maya*. Norman: University of Oklahoma Press.

Christenson, Allen J. 2008. "Places of Emergence: Sacred Mountains and Cofradía Ceremonies." In *Pre-Columbian Landscapes of Creation and Origin*, edited by John Edward Staller, 95–121. New York: Springer.

Christie, Jessica Joyce. 2003. *Maya Palaces and Elite Residences: An Interdisciplinary Approach*. Austin: University of Texas Press.

Coe, Michael D. 1978. *Lords of the Underworld*. Princeton, N.J.: Princeton University Press.

Coe, William R., and Michael D. Coe. 1951. *Ethnological Material from British Honduras*. Notes on Middle American Archaeology and Ethnology 104. Washington, D.C.: Carnegie Institution of Washington.

Colas, Pierre Robert. 1998. "Ritual and Politics in the Underworld." *Mexicon* 20 (5): 99–104.

Colas, Pierre Robert. 2000. "Tok' and Tok: Two Examples of Rebus Writing in Maya Script." In *The Sacred and the Profane: Architecture and Identity in the Maya Lowlands*, edited by Pierre Robert Colas, Kai Delvendahl, Marcus Kuhnert, and Annette Schubart, 83–92. Acta Mesoamericana 10. Markt Schwaben: Anton Sauerwein.

Culver, David C., and William B. White. 2004. *Encyclopedia of Caves*. Burlington, Mass.: Academic Press.

Demarrais, Elizabeth, Luis Jaime Castillo, and Timothy Earle. 1996. "Ideology, Materialization and Power Strategies." *Current Anthropology* 37 (1): 15–31.

Earle, Duncan. 2008. "Caves Across Time and Space: Reading-Related Landscapes in K'iche' Maya Text, Ritual, and History." In *Pre-Columbian Landscapes of Creation and Origin*, edited by John Edward Staller, 67–93. New York: Springer.

Farriss, Nancy M. 1984. *Maya Society Under Colonial Rule: The Collective Enterprise of Survival*. Princeton, N.J.: Princeton University Press.

Faulkner, Charles H. 1988. "Painters of the 'Dark Zone.'" *Archaeology* 41 (2): 30–38.

Fox, John Gerard. 1996. "Playing with Power: Ballcourts and Political Ritual in Southern Mesoamerica." *Current Anthropology* 37 (3): 483–509.

Freidel, David, Linda Schele, and Joy Parker. 1993. *Maya Cosmos: Three Thousand Years on the Shaman's Path*. New York: William Morrow.

García-Zambrano, Angel J. 1994. "Early Colonial Evidence of Pre-Columbian Rituals of Foundation." In *Seventh Palenque Round Table*, vol. 11, *1989*, edited by Merle G. Robertson and Virginia Field, 217–27. San Francisco, Calif.: Pre-Columbian Art Research Institute.

Gendrop, Paul. 1980. "Dragon-Mouth Entrances: Zoomorphic Portals in the Architecture of Central Yucatan." In *Third Palenque Round Table, 1978*, pt. 2, edited by Merle Greene Robertson, 138–50. Austin: University of Texas Press.

Gossen, Gary H. 1974. *Chamulas in the World of the Sun: Time and Space in a Maya Oral Tradition.* Cambridge, Mass.: Harvard University Press.

Graham, Ian. 1997. "Discovery of a Maya Ritual Cave in Peten, Guatemala." *Symbols* (Spring): 28–31.

Hanks, William F. 1984. "Sanctification, Structure, and Experience in a Yucatec Ritual Event." *Journal of American Folklore* 97 (384): 131–66.

Hanks, William F. 1990. *Referential Practice: Language and Lived Space Among the Maya*. Chicago: University of Chicago Press.

Helmke, Christophe, and James Brady. 2014. "Epigraphic and Archaeological Evidence for Cave Desecration in Ancient Maya Warfare." In *A Celebration of the Life and Work of Pierre Robert Colas*, edited by Christophe Helmke and Frauke Sachse, 195–227. Munich: Verlag Anton Saurwein.

Heyden, Doris. 1975. "An Interpretation of the Cave Underneath the Pyramid of the Sun in Teotihuacan, Mexico." *American Antiquity* 40 (2): 131–47.

Holland, William R. 1962. *Highland Folk Medicine: A Study of Culture Change*. Tucson: University of Arizona Press.

Houston, Stephen D. 1998. "Finding Function and Meaning in Classic Maya Architecture." In *Function and Meaning in Classic Maya Architecture: A Symposium at Dumbarton Oaks, 7th and 8th October 1994*, edited by Stephen D. Houston, 519–38. Washington, D.C.: Dumbarton Oaks Research Library and Collection.

Inomata, Takeshi. 2006. "Plazas, Performers, and Spectators: Political Theaters of the Classic Maya." *Current Anthropology* 47 (5): 805–42.

Kertzer, David I. 1988. *Rituals, Politics, and Power.* New Haven, Conn.: Yale University Press.

Kosakowsky, Laura, Holley Moyes, Mark Robinson, and Barbara Voorhies. 2013. "Ceramics of Las Cuevas and the Chiquibul: At World's End." *Research Reports in Belizean Archaeology* 10:25–32.

Kubler, George. 1993. *The Art and Architecture of Ancient America: The Mexican, Maya, and Andean Peoples*. New Haven, Conn.: Yale University Press.

La Farge, Oliver. 1947. *Santa Eulalia: The Religion of a Cuchumatán Indian Town*. Chicago: University of Chicago Press.

LeFebvre, Henri. (1974) 2004. *The Production of Space*. Translated by Donald Nicholson-Smith. Malden, Mass.: Blackwell.

MacLeod, Barbara, and Dennis E. Puleston. 1978. "Pathways into Darkness: The Search for the Road to Xibalbá." In *Tercera Mesa Redonda de Palenque*, vol. 4, edited by Merle Greene Robertson and Donnan Call Jeffers, 71–77. Monterey: Herald Printers.

Miao, Xin, Xiaomin Qiu, Shuo-Sheng Wu, Jun Luo, Douglas R. Gouzie, and Hongjie Xie. 2013. "Developing Efficient Procedures for Automated Sinkhole Extraction from Lidar DEMs." *Photogrammetric Engineering Remote Sensing* 79 (6): 545–54.

Miller, Mary Ellen, and Karl A. Taube. 1997. *The Gods and Symbols of Ancient Mexico and the Maya: An Illustrated Dictionary of Mesoamerican Religion.* London: Thames and Hudson.

Morehart, Christopher T. 2005. "Plants and Caves in Ancient Maya Society." In *Stone Houses and Earth Lords: Maya Religion in the Cave Context,* edited by Keith M. Prufer and James E. Brady, 167–86. Boulder: University Press of Colorado.

Moyes, Holley. 2006. "The Sacred Landscape as a Political Resource: A Case Study of Ancient Maya Cave Use at Chechem Ha Cave, Belize, Central America." PhD diss., State University of New York at Buffalo.

Moyes, Holley. 2012a. "Constructing the Underworld: The Built Environment in Ancient Mesoamerican Caves." In *Heart of Earth: Studies in Maya Ritual Cave Use,* edited by James E. Brady, 95–110. Bulletin 23. Austin, Tex.: Association for Mexican Cave Studies.

Moyes, Holley. 2012b. "Introduction." In *Sacred Darkness: A Global Perspective on the Ritual Use of Caves,* edited by Holley Moyes, 1–14. Boulder: University Press of Colorado.

Moyes, Holley. 2018. "Xibalba, the Place of Fear: Caves and the Ancient Maya Underworld." In *Verenda Numina: Temor y experiencia religiosa en el mundo antiguo,* edited by Silvia Alfayé, 171–90. Antigüedad, Religiones y Sociedades 14. Madrid: Universidad Carlos III de Madrid.

Moyes, Holley. 2020. "Capturing the Forest: Ancient Maya Ritual Caves as Built Environments." In *Approaches to Monumental Landscapes of the Ancient Maya,* edited by Brett A. Houk, Barbara Arroyo, and Terry G. Powis, 313–34. Gainesville: University Press of Florida.

Moyes, Holley, Jaime J. Awe, George Brook, and James Webster. 2009. "The Ancient Maya Drought Cult: Late Classic Cave Use in Belize." *Latin American Antiquity* 20 (1): 175–206.

Moyes, Holley, and James E. Brady. 2012. "Caves as Sacred Space in Mesoamerica." In *Sacred Darkness: A Global Perspective on the Ritual Use of Caves,* edited by Holley Moyes, 151–70. Boulder: University Press of Colorado.

Moyes, Holley, Shayna Hernandez, H. Lauren Phillips, and Shane Montgomery. 2015a. "Little Finds Big Results: The Utility of Small Artifacts in the Spatial Analyses of Looted Sites." In *Papers of the 47th Annual Chacmool Archaeological Conference, Breaking Barriers,* edited by Robyn Crook, Kim Edwards, and Colleen Hughes, 87–98. Calgary: Chacmool Archaeological Association of the University of Calgary.

Moyes, Holley, Laura Kosakowski, Erin Ray, and Jaime J. Awe. 2017. "The Chronology of Ancient Maya Cave Use in Belize." *Research Reports in Belizean Archaeology* 14:327–338.

Moyes, Holley, and Shane Montgomery. 2019. "Locating Cave Entrances Using Lidar-Derived Local Relief Modeling." *Geosciences* 9 (98): 1–22.

Moyes, Holley, and Keith M. Prufer. 2013. "The Geopolitics of Emerging Maya Rulers: A Case Study of Kayuko Naj Tunich, a Foundational Shrine at Uxbenká, Southern Belize." *Journal of Anthropological Research* 69 (2): 225–48.

Moyes, Holley, Mark Robinson, Laura Kosakowsky, and Barbara Voorhies. 2012. "Better Late than Never: Preliminary Investigations at Las Cuevas." *Research Reports in Belizean Archaeology* 9:221–31.

Moyes, Holley, Mark Robinson, Barbara Voorhies, Laura Kosakowsky, Marieka Arksey, Erin Ray, and Shayna Hernandez. 2015. "Dreams at Las Cuevas: A Location of High Devotional Expression of the Late Classic Maya." *Research Reports in Belizean Archaeology* 12:239–49.

Nash, June. 1970. *In the Eyes of the Ancestors: Belief and Behavior in a Maya Community*. New Haven, Conn.: Yale University Press.

Nielsen, Jesper, and James E. Brady. 2006. "The Couple in the Cave: Origin Iconography on a Ceramic Vessel from Los Naranjos, Honduras." *Ancient Mesoamerica* 17 (2): 203–17.

Pendergast, David M. 1992. "Noblesse Oblige: The Elites of Altun Ha and Lamanai, Belize." In *Mesoamerican Elites: An Archaeological Assessment*, edited by Diane Z. Chase and Arlen F. Chase, 62–79. Norman: University of Oklahoma Press.

Petryshyn, Jaroslaw Theodore. 1973. *Worship in the Rain Forest: Ritual Sites of the Lacandon Mayas*. Chicago: W.O.P.

Prechtel, Martin, and Robert Carlsen. 1988. "Weaving and Cosmos Amongst the Tzutujil Maya of Guatemala." *RES: Anthropology and Aesthetics* 15 (Spring): 123–32.

Proskouriakoff, Tatiana. 1976. *An Album of Maya Architecture*. Norman: University of Oklahoma Press.

Prufer, Keith M. 2002. "Communities, Caves, and Ritual Specialists: A Study of Sacred Space in the Maya Mountains of Southern Belize." PhD diss., Southern Illinois University, Carbondale.

Prufer, Keith M. 2005. "Shamans, Caves, and the Roles of Ritual Specialists in Maya Society." In *In the Maw of the Earth Monster: Mesoamerican Ritual Cave Use*, edited by James E. Brady and Keith M. Prufer, 186–222. Austin: University of Texas Press.

Prufer, Keith M., and James E. Brady. 2005. "Concluding Comments." In *In the Maw of the Earth Monster: Mesoamerican Ritual Cave Use*, edited by James E. Brady and Keith M. Prufer, 403–11. Austin: University of Texas Press.

Rappaport, Amos. 1982. *The Meaning of the Built Environment: A Nonverbal Communication Approach*. Tucson: University of Arizona Press.

Ray, Erin, Holley Moyes, and Linda Howe. 2018. "Plastered: Cave Constructions at Las Cuevas." *Research Reports in Belizean Archaeology* 15:253–64.

Reese-Taylor, Kathryn V. 2002. "Ritual Circuits as Key Elements in Maya Civic Center Designs." In *Heart of Creation: The Mesoamerican World and the Legacy of Linda Schele*, edited by Andrea J. Stone, 143–65. Tuscaloosa: University of Alabama Press.

Rissolo, Dominique. 2005. "Beneath the Yalahau: Emerging Patterns of Ancient Maya Ritual Cave Use from Northern Quintana Roo, Mexico." In *In the Maw of the Earth Monster: Mesoamerican Ritual Cave Use*, edited by James E. Brady and Keith M. Prufer, 342–72. Austin: University of Texas Press.

Roys, Ralph L. 1965. *Ritual of the Bacabs*. Norman: University of Oklahoma Press.

Saturno, William A., Karl A. Taube, David Stuart, and Heather Hurst. 2005. *The Murals of San Bartolo, El Petén, Guatemala*. Pt. 1, *The North Wall*. Ancient America 7. Barnardsville, N.C.: Center for Ancient American Studies.

Schávelzon, Daniel. 1980. "Temples, Caves, or Monsters? Notes on Zoomorphic Facades in Pre-Hispanic Architecture." In *Third Palenque Round Table, 1978*, pt. 2, edited by Merle Greene Robertson, 151–62. Austin: University of Texas Press.

Sosa, John R. 1985. "The Maya Sky, the Maya World: A Symbolic Analysis of Yucatec Maya Cosmology." PhD diss., State University of New York at Albany.

Stone, Andrea. 1992. "From Ritual in the Landscape to Capture in the Urban Center: The Recreation of Ritual Environments in Mesoamerica." *Journal of Ritual Studies* 6 (1): 109–32.

Stone, Andrea. 1995. *Images from the Underworld: Naj Tunich and the Tradition of Maya Cave Painting*. Austin: University of Texas Press.

Stuart, David S. 1997. "The Hills Are Alive: Sacred Mountains in the Maya Cosmos." *Symbols* (Spring): 13–17.

Taube, Karl A. 1994. "Flower Mountain: Concepts of Life, Beauty, and Paradise among the Classic Maya." *RES: Anthropology and Aesthetics* 45 (Spring): 69–98.

Thompson, J. Eric S. 1970. *Maya History and Religion*. Norman: University of Oklahoma Press.

Thompson, J. Eric S. 1975. "Introduction to the Reprint Edition." In *Hill-Caves of Yucatan*, by Henry C. Mercer, vii–xliv. Norman: University of Oklahoma Press.

Tozzer, Alfred M. 1907. *A Comparative Study of the Mayas and the Lacandones*. New York: Archaeological Institute of America.

Vogt, Evon Z. 1969. *Zinacantan: A Maya Community in the Highlands of Chiapas*. Cambridge, Mass.: Harvard University Press.

Vogt, Evon Z., and David Stuart. 2005. "Some Notes on Ritual Caves Among the Ancient and Modern Maya." In *In the Maw of the Earth Monster: Mesoamerican Ritual Cave Use*, edited by James E. Brady and Keith M. Prufer, 155–85. Austin: University of Texas Press.

von Schwerin, Jennifer. 2011. "The Sacred Mountain in Social Context. Symbolism and History in Maya Architecture: Temple 22 at Copan, Honduras." *Ancient Mesoamerica* 22 (2): 271–300.

Webster, David. 1998. "Classic Maya Architecture: Implications and Comparisons." In *Function and Meaning in Classic Maya Architecture*, edited by Stephan D. Houston, 5–48. Washington, D.C.: Dumbarton Oaks Research Library and Collection.

Wilson, Richard. (1964) 1995. *Maya Resurgence in Guatemala: Q'eqchi' Experiences*. Norman: University of Oklahoma Press.

CONTRIBUTORS

Elias Alcocer Puerto is a human ecologist, having received a master's in science from the Centro de Investigación y de Estudios Avanzados at the Instituto Politécnico Nacional, and his bachelor's degree in anthropology from the Universidad Autónoma de Yucatán. Elías has taught and continues to give courses in environmental and cultural anthropology, Maya history, human ecology, and environmental tourism at the Universidad de Oriente, the Universidad Nacional Autónoma de México, and the Universidad Autónoma de Yucatán. Throughout his career, he has developed and been engaged with many national and international nonprofit organizations that provide opportunities for young people to interact with their environment and further their education.

Alejandra Alonso Olvera is a professor and archaeological conservator appointed to the Conservation Department at the Instituto Nacional de Antropología e Historia (INAH) in Mexico City in 1993. Her undergraduate degree was in conservation and restoration of cultural heritage at the Escuela Nacional de Conservación y Restauración at INAH. She received a master's degree in anthropology from the Universidad Autónoma de México and a PhD in archaeology with a specialization in Maya archaeology from the University of Calgary. She has co-edited a special issue on Maya archaeology in Yucatán Peninsula for the journal *Ancient Mesoamerica*. She also has published books, book chapters, and several articles in different specialized journals, on the conservation of cultural heritage and archaeology. She has participated in different conservation projects, including at Dzibanché, Kohunlich, Naachtun, Tajín, Templo Mayor, Ichmul de Morley, Calakmul, Xuenkal, and Ek Balam. Since 2001, she has directed the conservation and study of architectonic decorations at Ek Balam. Since 2017, she has been responsible for documenting and treating the mural paintings of the Calakmul North Acropolis. Currently, she co-directs the Ichmul de Morley Archaeological Project along with J. Gregory Smith. Alejandra teaches different courses at the Escuela Nacional de Antropología e Historia, and since 2012 she has taught at the University of Calgary.

Traci Ardren is a professor of anthropology at the University of Miami and holds a PhD from Yale University. Her research focuses on issues of identity and other forms of symbolic representation in the archaeological record, especially the ways in which differences are explained through gender. Current preoccupations include the role of cuisine in identity formation in the later periods of Classic Maya culture and prehistoric southern Florida as well as the ways plants agitate humans. Traci directs the Matecumbe Chiefdom Project, which looks at the political organization and environmental adaptation of the Prehispanic occupants of the Florida Keys. She is also co-director of the Proyecto Sakbe Yaxuna-Coba, centered at the Classic Maya site of Yaxuna, in Yucatán, Mexico, where she investigates the ways ancient road systems allowed for the flow of information and ideas as well as how culinary tourism and modern foodways intersect. As Consulting Curator for Mesoamerican Art, she curated a number of exhibits at the Lowe Art Museum at the University of Miami. She grew up in and around the Ringling Museum of Art, and exploring the many ways in which objects are allowed to convey our wants and needs is a lifelong fascination.

Jaime J. Awe is a professor of anthropology at Northern Arizona University, emeritus director of the Belize Institute of Archaeology, and co-director of the Belize Valley Archaeological Reconnaissance Project. He received his MA at Trent University in Ontario, Canada, and his PhD from the Institute of Archaeology at University College London. Between 2003 and 2014, he served as the first director of the Belize Institute of Archaeology with responsibility for managing the archaeological heritage of Belize. During his extensive professional career, he has directed conservation efforts at several major archaeological sites in Belize, and his research has focused on questions that span from the Paleo-Indian period to the time of European conquest in the sixteenth century. More recently, his research has addressed questions related to the rise and decline of Maya cultural complexity, and prehistoric human–environment interaction in western Belize.

Alejandra Badillo Sánchez earned a BA degree in archaeology from the Escuela Nacional de Antropología e Historia in Mexico City in 2005, an MA in anthropology at the Instituto de Investigaciones Antropológicas at the Universidad Autónoma de México in Mexico City in 2013, and a PhD in history from the Centro de Investigaciones y Estudios Superiores en Antropología Social in Mérida, Yucatán, in 2019. She was a master's and doctoral fellow with the Consejo Nacional de Ciencia y Tecnología (CONACYT), and she is a postdoc at the Universidad Autónoma de Yucatán during 2020–21, studying the memory of the Caste War. She has conducted salvage archaeology, the conservation of cultural heritage, and archaeological research on projects in San Luis Potosí, Veracruz, Oaxaca, and Chiapas, and has been a member of the Cochuah Regional Archaeological Survey project in Quintana Roo since 2010. Her doctoral thesis earned an honorable mention for the Atanasio G. Saravia Award for its interdisciplinary history and archaeological research on the landscape and conflict that resulted from the Maya Caste War.

Nicolas C. Barth is an assistant professor of geology in the Department of Earth & Planetary Sciences at the University of California, Riverside. He received his doctorate from the University of Otago, New Zealand, in 2013 and has broad expertise in structural geology and geomorphology. He often uses high-resolution topographic data (LiDAR, structure from motion) to elucidate hidden landscapes. Through collaboration with Travis Stanton, he has carried out fieldwork in central Yucatán and performed LiDAR analyses in support of landscape characterization and Maya land use.

Grace Lloyd Bascopé, PhD, is a medical and environmental anthropologist who has been engaged in both research and development projects in the central part of Yucatán, Mexico, for the past thirty years. She is a resident research associate at the Botanical Research Institute of Texas and is the director of Mexico projects for the Maya Research Program. She formerly taught at Texas Christian University and at the University of North Texas.

Adolfo Iván Batún-Alpuche has a BA in archaeology from the Universidad Autónoma de Yucatán and a master's and PhD from the University of Florida. His studies have focused on Maya economics and agrarian practices during the Prehispanic and Colonial periods, following a community collaborative and decolonizing approach. Currently, he is a professor at the Universidad de Oriente in Valladolid, Yucatán.

Elizabeth Beckner is a graduate student in the Department of Anthropology at the University of California, Riverside. In the 2016 and 2017 summer field seasons, she was a field assistant for the Proyecto de Interacción Política del Centro de Yucatán, and in 2018, she was part of the survey team for the Proyecto Sakbe Yaxuna-Coba. Her research focus shifted after an experience with a group of undergraduate students led her to pursue new research questions in cultural anthropology. Currently, her research interests revolve around diversity in higher education, feminist anthropology, and motherhood.

M. Kathryn Brown is the Lutcher Brown Endowed Professor of Anthropology at the University of Texas at San Antonio. She received her PhD from Southern Methodist University in 2003. Her research examines the rise of complexity in Maya civilization. Her publications include *Ancient Mesoamerican Warfare* (with Travis Stanton), *Pathways to Complexity: A View from the Maya Lowlands* (with George J. Bey III), and *A Forest of History: The Maya After the Emergence of Divine Kingship* (with Travis Stanton).

Bernadette Cap served as an Andrew W. Mellon Postdoctoral Curatorial Fellow at the San Antonio Museum of Art and is a full-time faculty member in anthropology at San Antonio College. She received BAs in anthropology and geology from Cleveland State University and earned her PhD in anthropology, with a focus on the archaeology of Mesoamerica, at the University of Wisconsin–Madison. She has conducted research in Belize since 2003 and is the associate director of the Mopan Valley Archaeology Project. Through her research, she has contributed evidence to settle the debate surrounding the existence of marketplace facilities among the Classic Maya. This resulted in the Best Dissertation Award from the Society of American Archaeology. She continues to examine the ways in which marketplace facilities are placed on the physical and sociopolitical landscape as well as the economic organization that supports a market exchange system. She also specializes in remote sensing, soil studies, microartifact analyses, and collections management.

Miguel Covarrubias Reyna has conducted graduate studies in archaeology at the Escuela Nacional de Antropología e Historia (ENAH) in Mexico City and the Universidad Autónoma de Yucatán. He has been working for the past twenty-five years in the Yucatán Peninsula as a freelance researcher for the Instituto Nacional de Antropología e Historia, specifically at the central northern plains and the east coast, locating several hundreds of undocumented sites. He has published thirty scientific papers in different journals and books and has spoken at twenty international conferences and congresses in Mexico, the United States, and Europe. His interests concern site recording, speleology, GIS development, geophysical techniques, and forensic archaeology. He has been teaching Maya archaeology at private online universities.

Juan Fernandez Diaz received a BSc degree in electrical and industrial engineering from the Universidad Nacional Autónoma de Honduras, Tegucigalpa, Honduras, in 2001, and MSc and PhD degrees from the University of Florida, Gainesville, in 2007 and 2010. His research focuses on the development and applications of active remote sensing technologies. He is currently a research assistant professor at the University of Houston, Texas, and serves as co-principal investigator for the National Center for Airborne Laser Mapping (NCALM) at the National Science Foundation. Since the 2009 LiDAR survey of Caracol in Belize, NCALM has collected more than 13,000 square kilometers of high-density LiDAR (> 15 pulses/m^2) in Mesoamerica for archaeological research.

Alberto G. Flores Colin is an archaeologist who graduated from the Escuela Nacional de Antropología e Historia in Mexico City and has a doctorate in anthropological sciences from the Universidad Autónoma de Yucatán. He has collaborated on various archaeological projects in Campeche, Quintana Roo, and Yucatán. He is the author of several publications in Mexico and other countries. He is currently doing postdoctoral research at the Universidad Autónoma de Campeche and is co-principal investigator in the Cochuah Regional Archaeological Survey project. In 2016, he won the Instituto

Nacional de Antropología e Historia's Alfonso Caso Award for his thesis, "Antiguas calzadas mayas." His research interests are Maya causeways, settlement patterns, mobility, architecture, and geographic information systems.

Thomas H. Guderjan is a professor of anthropology, chair of the Department of Social Sciences, and director of the Center for Social Science Research at the University of Texas at Tyler. He received his PhD from Southern Methodist University and is the author of *The Nature of an Ancient Maya City: Resources, Interaction and Power at Blue Creek, Belize, Ancient Maya Traders of Ambergris Caye* and *The Value of Things: Prehistoric to Contemporary Commodities in the Maya Region* (co-edited with Jennifer P. Mathews), as well as many professional articles and book chapters. His research interests include the structure of Maya cities and landscapes, agricultural production systems, and the events and processes leading to the abandonment of Maya cities.

C. Colleen Hanratty is an anthropologist with the Center for Social Sciences Research at the University of Texas at Tyler and co-director of the Blue Creek Archaeological Project. She has conducted archaeological research in the southeastern and southwestern United States, Mexico, Peru, and Belize. Her research focuses on the built environment and production studies of material culture.

Héctor Hernández Álvarez is an archaeologist with a PhD in Mesoamerican studies (2011) from the Universidad Nacional Autónoma de México, professor and researcher on the Facultad de Ciencias Antropológicas of the Universidad Autónoma de Yucatán, and member of the National Researchers System, Consejo Nacional de Ciencia y Tecnología. He has participated in and directed research projects at Prehispanic, historic, and contemporary sites of Yucatán like Yaxunah, Hacienda San Pedro Cholul, Chacmultún, and Rancho Hobonil. Recent publications include the chapter "The Archaeology of Henequen Haciendas: San Pedro Cholul as a Case Study," with L. Fernández and M. Zimmermann, in *The Maya World*, edited by S. Hutson and T. Ardren (2020), the article "Collaborative Archaeology, Relational Memory, and Stakeholder Action at Three Henequen Haciendas in Yucatan, Mexico," with M. Zimmermann, L. Fernández, J. Venegas, and L. Pantoja, in *Heritage* (2020), the book *La vida cotidiana durante la*

Edad de Oro Yucateca: Arqueología de los trabajadores henequeneros de la hacienda San Pedro Cholul (2020), and the article "Historical and Archaeological Perspectives on Childhood Mortality and Morbidity in a Henequen Hacienda in Yucatán at the Turn of the 20th Century," with A. Cucina, in *Childhood in the Past* (2019).

Scott R. Hutson received his PhD from the University of California at Berkeley and teaches anthropology at the University of Kentucky. He has written *The Ancient Urban Maya* (2016) and *Dwelling, Identity, and the Maya* (2010). He also edited *Ancient Maya Commerce: Multi-Disciplinary Research at Chunchucmil* (2017) and, with Traci Ardren, *The Maya World* (2020) and *The Social Experience of Childhood in Ancient Mesoamerica* (2006).

Joshua J. Kwoka received a PhD in anthropology from the University at Buffalo (2014), where he served as director of the Teotihuacan Archaeology Laboratory until joining the Department of Anthropology at Georgia State University as a lecturer in 2021. He has published numerous peer-reviewed journal articles and book chapters on the Maya, Aztec, Teotihuacan, and Haudenosaunee. His research interests include lithic technology, along with the emergence and institutionalization of inequality.

Whitney Lytle is the director of Curation and Education at the Boothbay Railway Village, a historic museum in Maine. She earned her BA in anthropology from Kent State University, her MA in anthropology from Texas State University, and her PhD in anthropology, with a focus on the archaeology of Mesoamerica, from the University of Texas at San Antonio. Whitney began her research in Belize in 2008 and has been a member of the Mopan Valley Preclassic Project since 2011. Her research focuses on ritual practices and their involvement in the creation, maintenance, and resignification of special places in the built environment. Her recent work has centered on the sociopolitical role of ancestors in the manipulation of sacred spaces over long periods of occupation and reoccupation. She also has extensive experience in public outreach and education.

Aline Magnoni is an anthropological archaeologist who specializes in Maya archaeology. Aline co-directed the Proyecto Sakbe Yaxuna-Coba and the Proyecto de Interacción Política de Yucatán, and she was the assistant director of the Pakbeh Regional Economy Program at the site of Chunchucmil, Yucatán, Mexico. Her research interests include landscape and household archaeology, LiDAR and GIS spatial analysis, identity representations in the context of tourism, ethics in archaeological practice, and community archaeology. Aline is also currently researching topics in international development, focusing on the use of rigorous evidence obtained through inclusive and participatory approaches, which take into account the complexities of operating contexts, to ensure that all people, including marginalized and underrepresented groups, can be engaged stakeholders and active agents in their development process. Aline received a PhD from Tulane University and taught at the same university for a decade.

Jennifer P. Mathews is a professor of anthropology and chair of the Department of Sociology and Anthropology at Trinity University. Her undergraduate degree was in anthropology from San Diego State University, and she received her master's and PhD in anthropology, with a specialization in Maya archaeology, from the University of California at Riverside. She is the co-editor of three volumes: *Quintana Roo Archaeology* (with Justine Shaw), *Lifeways in the Northern Maya Lowlands: New Approaches to Archaeology in the Yucatán Peninsula* (with Bethany Morrison), and *The Value of Things: Prehistoric to Contemporary Commodities in the Maya Region* (with Thomas H. Guderjan). She also published the monographs *Chicle: Chewing Gum of the Americas: From the Ancient Maya to William Wrigley* (with Gillian P. Schultz, 2009) and *Sugarcane and Rum: The Bittersweet History of Labor and Life on the Yucatán Peninsula* (with John Gust, 2020). She was named the 2019 recipient of the Dr. and Mrs. Z. T. Scott Faculty and the Piper Professorship in 2020 in recognition of her outstanding abilities as a teacher and mentor.

Stephanie J. Miller is currently a PhD candidate in the Department of Anthropology at the University of California, Riverside, conducting archaeological research on the Yaxuna–Cobá *sakbe*, the longest road in the ancient Maya world. They graduated from UC Riverside with a master's degree in anthropology in 2016, and from the University of Cincinnati with a BA in art history in 2010. Their primary research interests are Mesoamerican archaeology (Maya focus), ancient road systems, household archaeology, archaeology of community, the historical development of archaeological theory, and land-based pedagogies. They find inspiration and utility in the theories of space and place, theories of gender, and queer theory.

Shawn G. Morton is an anthropological archaeologist with an interest in urban and architectural studies, ritual and religion, survey and visualization, community-engaged approaches, and Mesoamerica and the Caribbean. He earned his MA and PhD from the University of Calgary and has conducted archaeological field research in Canada, Mexico, Guatemala, Belize, and Nicaragua. He is the instructor of anthropology at Grande Prairie Regional College, Alberta, Canada, and co-directs the Stann Creek Regional Archaeology Project in Belize.

Holley Moyes is a professor of archaeology at the University of California, Merced, in the Department of Anthropology and Heritage Studies and an affiliate in the Department of Cognitive and Information Sciences. She specializes in ritual cave use, and her volume *Sacred Darkness: A Global Perspective on the Ritual Use of Caves* (2013) is a testament to the ubiquity of ritual practice in caves over time and space. Her field research over the past twenty years has focused on ancient Maya ritual cave sites and their role in the development, maintenance, and disintegration of the Classic Maya period political system. Her work spans both theory and methods, including the use of photogrammetry, GIS, and LiDAR. She researches the role of caves in myth and cosmologies and has published on multiple aspects of ritual cave use, including changes in practice, environmental relationships, energetics, chronologies, uses of space, architectural elaborations, ritual density, pilgrimage, and foundational rites. She is currently the principal investigator of the Las Cuevas Archaeological Reconnaissance, which conducts research at the Las Cuevas site in Belize and its surrounds, providing an opportunity to examine ritual behavior during the tumultuous Late Classic period when Maya society was undergoing radical socio/political changes due to internal and external stresses.

Dominique Rissolo is an assistant research scientist with the Qualcomm Institute at the University of California, San Diego, where he co-leads the Cultural Heritage Engineering Initiative. As an archaeologist, Dominique's interdisciplinary research focuses on paleocoastal human ecology and the development of ancient maritime trade networks along the Yucatán coast. His work on the Yucatán Peninsula has also focused on ancient Maya and

Paleoamerican cave and cenote use as well as coastal and near-coastal settlement patterns and the rise of social complexity in the region. Dominique co-directs the Costa Escondida and Hoyo Negro projects and is also a member of the NOAA Ocean Exploration Advisory Board.

Patrick Rohrer is a doctoral candidate in the Department of Anthropology at the University of California, Riverside. He has worked on archaeology projects in Belize, Peru, Bolivia, Mexico, and Florida—including underwater projects in rivers, bays, and the Gulf of Mexico. His current research combines his primary interests in cultural water management strategies, environment and climate change, LiDAR and remote sensing, settlement patterns, archaeology, and underwater archaeology. Working in the northern Yucatán Peninsula along the Yaxuna–Cobá corridor, he is also currently studying Yucatec Maya to better understand and collaborate with Indigenous communities facing similar obstacles to those that affected populations in the region more than a millennia ago.

Carmen Rojas Sandoval received a master's in archaeology at the Escuela Nacional de Antropología e Historia in Mexico City. She is a permanent researcher at the Instituto Nacional de Antropología e Historia in the State of Quintana Roo, heading the Underwater Maya Cemeteries Project. She has been responsible for the recovery of six human remains dating from the Pleistocene, between 13,000 and 8,000 B.P., as well as extinct fauna such as *Panthera balamoides*, a previously unknown jaguar-like species, and *Xibalbaonix oviceps*, a new genus of giant sloth. As an advanced diver and speleologist, she has reported more than fifty archaeological and paleontological sites ranging between the late Pleistocene and Prehispanic periods.

Justine M. Shaw is a professor of anthropology at the College of the Redwoods and a research associate at Humboldt State University. She has served as the co-principal investigator of the Cochuah Regional Archaeological Survey (formerly the Proyecto Arqueológico Yo'okop) since 2000. Her research interests include the Terminal Classic transition, regional settlement patterns, climate change and drought, and Maya *sakbe'ob*. She has recently begun investigating a series of small structures built immediately after the collapse of sites in the Cochuah region. Her major publications include *The*

Maya of the Cochuah Region: Archaeological and Ethnographic Perspectives on the Northern Lowlands (editor and contributor), *White Roads of the Yucatán: Changing Social Landscapes of the Yucatec Maya, Quintana Roo Archaeology* (co-edited with Jennifer P. Mathews), "Climate Change and Deforestation: Implications for the Maya Collapse," and "Roads to Ruins: The Role of Maya Sakbe'ob in Ancient Maya Society."

J. Gregory Smith is a professor of anthropology at Northwest College in Powell, Wyoming. He earned a BA in geography and a BS in anthropology from Central Washington University before moving on to the University of Pittsburgh for a PhD in anthropology. Most of his research has been in Mesoamerica (especially the Maya area), but he has also conducted archaeological fieldwork in Mongolia, Ecuador, and across the United States. While he certainly enjoys research, he is first and foremost a teacher of community college students. His greatest professional passion is taking students out of the classroom and off to archaeologically themed destinations such as Peru, England, Mexico, Greece, the American Southwest, Guatemala, and most recently Egypt. When not teaching, he co-directs the Ichmul de Morley Archaeological Project with Alejandra Alonso Olvera in northern Yucatán and is cultivating a research interest in the Indus area as well.

Travis W. Stanton is a professor of anthropology at the University of California, Riverside. He has been conducting field research in the State of Yucatán since 1995 and graduated with his doctorate from Southern Methodist University in 2000. His primary research interests are in Mesoamerican archaeology (with a focus on the Maya area), state formation and collapse, ceramic technology, landscape archaeology, memory, prehistoric violence and warfare, settlement patterns, remote sensing, ethnoarchaeology, and experimental archaeology. He currently works in central Yucatán and northern Quintana Roo, Mexico. He also works with Indigenous Maya potters in the town of Muna in a collaborative project designed to understand ancient Maya pottery technology. His publications include *Ancient Mesoamerican Warfare* and *Forest of History* (both co-edited with M. Kathryn Brown), *Ruins of the Past* (co-edited with Aline Magnoni), and the co-authored books *Before Kukulkán*, *The Initial Series Group at Chichen Itza*, *The Past in the Present*, and *Excavations at Yaxuná, 1986–1996*.

Karl A. Taube is a Distinguished Professor at the University of California, Riverside, and has been a faculty member since 1989. He received his doctoral degree from the Department of Anthropology at Yale in 1988. In 1983 and 1984, he engaged in a year of archaeological, linguistic, and ethnographic research in a rural Yucatec Maya community in northern Quintana Roo close to Cobá. His primary research interests concern ancient Mesoamerican religion and art, although he also studies contemporary Mesoamerican ethnography as well as that of the Greater Southwest, including the Hopi. He has published more than one hundred chapters and articles as well as twelve books and monographs, with another in press with Travis Stanton and other contributors concerning the Initial Series Group at Chichén Itzá that will be published this fall. Among his books are *The Major Gods of Yucatán*, *Olmec Art at Dumbarton Oaks*, *Aztec and Maya Myths*, and *Gods and Symbols of Ancient Mexico and the Maya*, co-authored with Mary Ellen Miller.

Daniel Vallejo-Cáliz is a PhD candidate in the Department of Anthropology at the University of Kentucky. He has worked in the northern Maya lowlands since 2006 and has participated in projects at the sites of Xuenkal, Ek Balam, Yaxuná, Ikil, and the Ucí-Cansahcab region. He has published articles on various themes, including abandonment practices, archaeologist subjectivity, community engagement, complexity, and field archaeology.

INDEX

Abrams, Elliott M., 29
Actun Balam (Belize), 206
Actuncan (Belize), 53
Actun Chechem Ha (Belize), 381
Actun Ibach (Belize), 207
Actun Spukil (Belize), 204
Actun Unich Muknal (Belize), 381
Actun Uo (Belize), 391
aguada, 56, 64, 82, 175, 221, 224
Alvin's Cave (Belize), 386, 389
Ambergris Caye (Belize), 252, 260
ancestors, 52, 57, 64, 99, 108, 227, 253, 339, 365, 379, 423
andadores, 190, 191, 209
Andres, Christopher R., 203, 204
apiary, 280, 282, 285, 345. *See also* beekeeping
Ashmore, Wendy, 4, 52, 54, 55

Baking Pot (Belize), 256
Balankanche' Cave (Yucatán, Mexico), 337, 340, 356, 359, 378
ballcourt: at Blue Creek, 61; at Chichén Itzá, 124, 139, 147, 148; at Chunchucmil, 61; at Ek Balam, 132, 139, 147; at Las Cuevas, 397; at Lower Barton Creek, 197, 199; at Lower Dover, 196; at Tikal, 61; at Tipan, 204; at Xunantunich, 61, 62, 64, 65, 201; at Yaxkukul, 147, 148; at Yo'okop, 220
Barbachano, Miguel, 165, 166
Barrera Rubio, Alfredo, 189, 190, 290
Batabs, 33, 138

Becan (Campeche, Mexico), 11, 186, 252, 256, 267
beekeeping, 283, 309. *See also* apiary
Belize Cave Research Project, 383
Bey, George J., III, 119, 122, 124, 126, 130, 146, 150, 151
Blue Creek (Belize), 11–12, 61, 250, 252, 253, 255–57, 265, 267
borderlands, 5–6, 120–22, 127–31, 135, 139, 141, 143–46, 148–52
Brady, James E., 205, 389
Braswell, Geoffrey, 124, 127, 131, 132
Braswell, Jennifer, 57
Bravo, General Ignacio, 166, 173, 177
Buena Vista (Belize), 265
Buena Vista Archaeological Project (BVAP), 277, 289
Buena Vista Cozumel (Quintana Roo, Mexico), 11, 273–87

Cahal Pech (Belize), 192–96, 199, 204, 256
Calakmul (Campeche, Mexico), 5, 62, 112
Cansahcab (Yucatán, Mexico), 17, 25–41
cardinal directions, 5, 52, 55, 74, 76, 77, 90, 122, 134, 339, 376, 380. *See also* world tree
Carnegie Institution of Washington, 191, 220
Caste War, 12, 104, 165, 166, 220, 221, 237
Castillo Borges, Victor R., 122
Catherwood, Fredrick, 190, 373
Central Belize Archaeological Survey (CBAS), 201
Chaak (rain god), 340, 379

Chakalal (Quintana Roo, Mexico), 343–48, 349
Chan Kom, (Village, Yucatán, Mexico), 261
Chan Santa Cruz (Village, Quintana Roo, Mexico), 12, 104, 166, 168, 169, 171, 175, 177, 178, 181, 189
Chase, Arlen, 192
Chase, Diane, 192
Chen Cedral Cozumel (Quintana Roo, Mexico), 274
chert, 56, 59, 60, 62, 126, 129, 133, 151, 261
Chicanna (Campeche, Mexico), 256
Chichbes, 191, 209
Chichén Itzá (Yucatán, Mexico), 5, 9, 111, 119–63, 217, 232, 305, 310, 319, 322, 340, 356
Chichimila, (Yucatán, Mexico), 165
Chicle, 4, 99, 101, 103, 104, 107, 109, 168, 220
Chunchucmil (Yucatán, Mexico), 61, 189, 190, 191, 252, 268, 269, 357
Chunhuayum (Yucatán, Mexico), 26, 38
Cobá (Quintana Roo, Mexico), 5, 8, 41, 71–96, 120, 126, 127, 190, 217, 218, 224, 231, 256, 261, 277, 339, 340, 341, 365, 418
Cochuah Regional Archaeological Survey (CRAS), 166, 220, 419, 421, 426
Coe, Michael D., 30, 33, 74–75
communal labor, 20, 27, 33, 40, 108, 217, 224, 237–38, 321, 358, 381
Cormorant Cave (Belize), 386, 388
cosmology, 49, 52, 55, 60, 62, 74–76, 375, 376, 380–81, 398
cultural ecology, 7

Dahlin, Bruce, 9, 189, 191
Decauville railroad, 99, 100, 106–7, 108, 109, 110, 177
De Charnay, M. De'sire', 122, 124
Demarest, Arthur, 189
depopulation, 26, 149, 169, 181, 294
Díaz, President Porfirio, 101–2, 105, 106, 168, 169, 170, 180, 181
Dos Pilas, (Guatemala), 189, 337
Dresden Codex, 75, 376

East Coast style architecture, 341, 343, 345, 347–48, 351, 359, 361, 362, 364
Edwardo Quiroz Cave, (Belize), 207
E-Group, 195, 201
Ek Balam, (Yucatán, Mexico), 6, 9, 119–63
Ek Waynal (Belize), 207
El Mirador (Guatemala), 19, 114, 115

El Naranjal, (Quintana Roo, Mexico), 341
El Peru'-Waka' (Guatemala), 260
El Zotz (Guatemala), 260
emblem glyph, 73, 124, 125, 134–35, 381
emic approaches, 8, 9, 72, 73, 74, 78, 88, 89, 134, 137, 251
eminent domain, 218, 239, 240
ethnohistoric model, 137–38, 139, 265–66

feathered serpent. *See* Quetzalcoatl
Fedick, Scott L., 191
field house, 89, 267

Gallareta Negrón, Tomas, 119, 124, 130, 146, 150, 151
García, General Lorenzo, 172
gender, 139–40, 143, 144–45, 241–42, 249, 319, 418, 425
Glover, Jeffrey B., 191
God L, 63, 65
Google, Earth, 88; Maps, 128

haciendas, 100, 105, 106, 107, 108, 109, 116, 166, 169, 181
Halakal (Yucatán, Mexico), 127, 135, 137, 151
Hansen, Richard, 113–16
hardwood industry, 99, 100, 103, 104, 109, 167, 169, 170. *See also* mahogany; *palo de tinte*
Helmke, Christophe, 59
henequen, 4, 99, 101, 105, 106, 107, 108, 167, 422, 423
Hero Twins, 376
Houston, Stephen, 58
Hubichen (Yucatán, Mexico), 38–41
human remains, 12, 30–31, 57, 58–59, 196, 255, 337, 338, 339–41

Ichmul de Morley (Yucatán, Mexico), 129-132, 135, 136, 139, 141–46, 151
incensarios (censers), 12, 61, 146, 148, 349, 351, 352, 354, 362
Indigenous property rights, 11, 104–7
Inhofe, Senator James, 114
Ixil (Yucatán, Mexico), 82, 88
Ixpaatun (Quintana Roo, Mexico), 11
Izamal (Yucatán, Mexico), 26, 52, 111, 167, 231

jade, 11–12, 59, 61, 340

Kancab (Yucatán, Mexico), 19, 22, 33–37
Keller, Angela, 54, 55, 56, 57, 61

Killion, Thomas W., 249
Kinich Na (Quintana Roo, Mexico), 256

Lacandon Maya, 103
Lamanai (Belize), 7
Landa, Bishop Diego de, 29, 33, 35, 38, 74–75, 188
landscape archaeology, 73, 427
Las Cuevas (Belize), 13, 205, 206, 373–415
Las Cuevas Archaeological Reconnaissance Project, 205, 383, 397
Le Febre, Henri, 373, 374, 375
LiDAR: at Cobá, 10, 73–77, 80, 81–86, 88, 90, 120, 218; at Kinich Na, 256; at Mayapán, 209; as tool to see into the jungle landscape, 7–8, 10, 11, 73, 78, 120, 140; at Ucí, 35, 38, 120, 224; at Xnoha, 11, 249, 250, 257, 259, 260, 262, 267
Linear Stone Boundary Markers (LSBMs), 9, 10, 249–77
Loltun Cave (Yucatán, Mexico), 337
Looper, Matthew, 59
Lower Barton Ramie (Belize), 197–99
Lower Dover (Belize), 192, 196–97
Luubul Actun (Belize), 386, 388

MacLeod, Barbara, 207, 376
Madrid Codex, 75
mahogany, 103, 104, 109, 167. *See also* hardwood industry
Maize God, 379
Maler, Teobert, 135, 337
marine shell, artifacts, 133–34; disk, 58, 59, 133
marketplaces, 49, 51, 61, 62–65, 131, 150, 229, 273, 284, 292, 307, 420
Mason, Gregory, 220
Maya Disneyland, 113–16
Mayapán (Yucatán, Mexico), 138, 149, 151, 190, 191, 209, 277, 357
Maya Research Program (MRP), 250, 419
Maya Tren/Train Maya, 2, 110–13
Megalithic architecture, 27, 29, 31–32, 36, 343
memory work, 7–9, 11, 12, 22
Méndez, Santiago, 165, 166
merchant rest houses, 143, 144
metate, 38, 56, 57, 82, 280, 329–30, 349, 402
military, architecture, 165, 170, 178–82; boundaries, 134, 170–78; campaign, 99, 102, 165–67, 172–82; defenses, 11, 12, 166; occupation, 168, 179, 181; population, 165; post, 178, 179; technology, 209

Miller, Mary Ellen, 188, 376, 428
Minanha (Belize), 383, 385, 394, 395
Minanha Cave Project, 383
moat, 174, 175, 176, 180, 188, 256
Mopan Valley Preclassic Project (MVPP), 50, 53, 54, 55, 57, 420, 423
Morley, Sylvanus G., 135, 187, 189
murals, at Bonampak, 188, 379; at Calakmul, 62, 63, 418; at Chakalal, 343; at Chichén Itzá, 151; at San Bartolo, 75
Muyil (Quintana Roo, Mexico), 232

Naj Tunich (Guatemala), 337, 382
Nakbe (Guatemala), 114
New Archaeology School, 5

obsidian, as raw material, 62, 150; blades, 56, 58–59, 402; bloodletting implements, 59; at Chichén Itza, 128, 129, 131–33, 147, 148, 150; debris, 62; eccentrics, 60, 62; at Ek Balam, 150; at Tikal, 129

Paamul (Quintana Roo, Mexico), 348–51
palo de tinte, 167, 169. *See also* hardwood industry
Panama Canal, 102
Pendergast, David M., 206, 207
Petroglyph Cave (Belize), 207
pilgrimage, 36, 40; to caves, 73, 382, 397, 399, 407, 425; to Cozumel, 274, 284; at Izamal, 52; at Las Cuevas, 397; networks, 40; route, 49
placemaking, 7–9, 11
Playa del Carmen (Quintana Roo, Mexico), 252, 260
Pollock, Harry E.D., 88, 220
Popola de Dzitas (Yucatán, Mexico), 129–32, 149
Popol Vuh, 376, 379
portals, 56, 204, 225, 389, 390
processions, 21–22, 29–30, 36, 42, 51–52, 65, 74–76, 241, 407–15
Puleston, Dennis, 5, 140, 376
Punta Piedra (Quintana Roo, Mexico), 352–56

quadripartite. *See* cardinal directions
Quen Santo (Guatemala), 205
Quetzalcoatl *(feathered serpent)*, 58, 124, 125, 126, 130, 146, 148, 151, 343

Rara'muri people, Chihuahua, 102
Reents-Budet, Dorie, 207

Reese-Taylor, Kathryn V., 407
rejolladas, 128, 273, 278, 280, 282, 283, 284
reptile eye glyph, 151
Ringle, William, 119, 122, 124, 126, 127, 130, 135, 146
Rio Secreto Park (Quintana Roo, Mexico), 352–55, 356, 363
Roys, Ralph, 137–38, 143, 149

sacrifice, 63, 75, 188, 340–41, 381
saltworks, 139, 150
Sampeck, Kathryn, 41
San Bartolo (Guatemala), 75, 379
San Gervasio Cozumel (Quintana Roo, Mexico), 274, 280
San Lorenzo (Belize), 40
Santa Cruz (Yucatán, Mexico), 129, 134, 143, 144, 145, 146, 149, 150, 151
sascabera, 221, 222, 280, 348
Sayab Ak (Belize), 380, 390
Sayil (Yucatán, Mexico), 146, 224
scribe, 55, 255
settlement pattern survey, 5, 274, 341, 365
Shook, Edwin M., 191
solar/solares, 10, 252, 261–66, 273, 283, 289–315, 323, 325
Spinden, Herbert, 220, 343, 348
spindle whorl, 62
Stephens, John Lloyd, 190
Stone, Andrea, 57
Stuart, David S., 58, 379
sugarcane, 4, 99, 107, 108

Talking Cross Cult, 166, 237
Taylor, Walter W., 3–5, 14
telegraph, 104, 173, 179, 181
Templo de la Cueva de los Aluxes (Quintana Roo, Mexico), 345, 347, 363
Thompson, J. Eric S., 88, 187, 189, 205, 206, 337, 376
Tikal (Guatemala), 5, 61, 129, 140, 151, 188, 210, 252, 260
Tintal (Guatemala), 114, 260
Tipan Chen Uitz (Belize), 201–4
tobacco, 30
Tozzer, Alfred M., 188
Trombold, Charles, 6
Trump, President Donald, 209, 251
Tulum (Quintana Roo, Mexico), 11, 111, 191, 348, 365
Tush Ku Bin K'in (Belize), 389, 390

Tzonotchel (Village, Quintana Roo, Mexico), 171

Uaxactun (Guatemala), 140, 260
Ucanha (Yucatán, Mexico), 17, 26, 33–37, 42, 217, 224, 232
Uci' (Yucatán, Mexico), 6, 25–41
Uxbenka (Belize), 381, 383
Uxbenká Cave Project, 383
Uxmal (Yucatán, Mexico), 9, 252

vision serpent, 58

Wakna (Guatemala), 114
Wallerstein, Immanuel, 254–55
Webster, David, 9, 188, 189, 210, 373
Western Development Theory, 103, 104, 109
wilderness (in opposition to domesticated spaces), 76–77, 89–90, 99, 100–5, 109, 168
World Systems Theory, 250, 254, 255, 267
world tree, 52, 75. *See also*, cardinal directions

Xamanha (Quintana Roo, Mexico), 227, 277, 352
Xcaret (Quintana Roo, Mexico), 277, 337, 352, 354, 355, 359, 360, 361–63
Xelha' (Quintana Roo, Mexico), 82, 337, 359, 364
Xibalba (underworld), 12, 52, 55–57, 60, 61, 63, 65, 73, 339, 376–80, 396, 408, 409
Xnoha (Belize), 10, 250–72
Xulnal (Guatemala), 114
Xultun (Guatemala), 260
Xunantunich Archaeological Project (XAP), 54, 199
Xunantunich (Belize), 6, 40, 49–69, 77, 299–301

Yaeger, Jason, 40, 53, 265
Yalahau region (Quintana Roo, Mexico), 191, 357
Yaxuna (archaeological site, Yucatán, Mexico), 25, 38, 41, 75, 77, 81, 82, 83, 87, 88, 89, 90, 260
Yaxunah, (Village, Yucatán, Mexico), 11, 251, 252, 261, 262, 289–315, 317–36
Yo'okop (Quintana Roo, Mexico), 6, 24–41, 217–47

Zapatistas, 112